From the front cover: This photograph (underlying the title) shows US military police confront striking Okinawan base workers on 5 June 1969. Courtesy of Okinawa Times

WHY ARE WE IN OKINAWA?

WHY ARE WE IN OKINAWA?

A History of Violence

JON MITCHELL

BLOOMSBURY ACADEMIC
NEW YORK • LONDON • OXFORD • NEW DELHI • SYDNEY

BLOOMSBURY ACADEMIC
Bloomsbury Publishing Inc
1359 Broadway, New York, NY 10018, USA
50 Bedford Square, London, WC1B 3DP, UK
29 Earlsfort Terrace, Dublin 2, Ireland

BLOOMSBURY, BLOOMSBURY ACADEMIC and the Diana logo are trademarks of
Bloomsbury Publishing Plc

First published in the United States of America 2026

Copyright © Bloomsbury Publishing 2026

Cover design: Chloe Batch

Cover photograph © *Okinawa Times* / Cover art © *The Ryukyu Beltway* by Yuken Teruya

All rights reserved. No part of this publication may be reproduced or transmitted in any form or by any means, electronic or mechanical, including photocopying, recording, or any information storage or retrieval system, without prior permission in writing from the publishers.

Bloomsbury Publishing Inc does not have any control over, or responsibility for, any third-party websites referred to or in this book. All internet addresses given in this book were correct at the time of going to press. The author and publisher regret any inconvenience caused if addresses have changed or sites have ceased to exist but can accept no responsibility for any such changes.

Library of Congress Cataloguing-in-Publication Data Available

HB: 978-1-5381-8839-2
ePub: 979-8-7651-5994-1
ePDF: 979-8-7651-6502-7

Typeset by Deanta Global Publishing Services, Chennai, India
Printed and bound in the United States of America

To find out more about our authors and books visit www.bloomsbury.com and sign up for our newsletters.

CONTENTS

Foreword: Challenging the Projects of Empires viii

An Introduction 1

1 The Ryukyu Kingdom: A Bridge of Nations 7

2 Disposal, Discrimination, and Diaspora 27

3 The Storm of Iron 45

4 Forgotten Island 69

5 Showcases of Democracy 89

6 The Vietnam War in Okinawa 107

7 Reversion 125

8 Broken Promises 139

9 Relieving the Burden 157

10 All Okinawa vs. Japan and the United States 173

11 Islands of Peace? 189

Coda: So Why Are We Really in Okinawa? 203

Notes 221
Bibliography 257
Acknowledgments 261
Index 264

FOREWORD
CHALLENGING THE PROJECTS OF EMPIRES

Hideki Yoshikawa

Director, Okinawa Environmental Justice Project

When I think of Jon Mitchell and his work for Okinawa and beyond, a particular Japanese expression comes to mind: "To bring a change to society, we need *wakamono* (the young), *bakamono* (the fool), or *yosomono* (the outsider)." The saying captures the difficulty of social change in Japan, where conformity prevails and hinders efforts for reform from within. It emphasizes that only those who are unconstrained by conventional norms and dare to challenge them can engender real transformation.

I relate this expression to Mitchell and his work because they belong to a social movement that challenges Japanese and US injustices against Okinawans, today most visible in the overwhelming presence of military bases in our islands. As a Welshman residing on mainland Japan, he embodies the category of outsider who enables people in Okinawa to better understand what is left unspoken. Those who challenge the status quo and bring about change must have a strong commitment to the cause, possess the necessary skills and methods to effect change, and be willing to be part of the community despite their nonconformist stance. Mitchell's work reminds us that because the issues we face are linked to external factors, there are always broader implications for our efforts to address them at a local level.

Mitchell was born and grew up in Wales, a country with a history of discrimination and poverty that parallels Okinawa's—combined with an equally proud pacifist tradition. These similarities laid the groundwork for his understanding of Okinawa when he first traveled to the islands as a journalist in the late 2000s. At the time of his initial visits, Japanese and international perceptions of Okinawa were in flux. Throughout the 1990s, the Japanese government and mass media had perpetuated stereotypes of Okinawa as a subtropical tourist destination inhabited by happy-go-lucky, laidback locals—images that concealed the everyday realities for many Okinawans living in communities still heavily militarized decades after World War II. Many base-related issues remained unresolved—the thunderous noise from US military aircraft overflying communities, environmental pollution, and crimes committed by service members. The Japanese government refused to address these issues, preferring to dismiss them as just "Okinawa problems."

The abduction and rape of a twelve-year-old Okinawan girl by three US troops in 1995 was a painful manifestation of both the dangers of militarization and US-Japan indifference. Faced with Okinawans' furious demands to close the bases, Washington and Tokyo opted for a policy of deceit and preservation. On one hand, they promised to return some US facilities to civilian use, but on the other hand, they proposed the construction of replacement bases in environmentally precious areas of northern Okinawa. These new bases would solidify the US position as the sole global superpower and ensure Japan remained a client state under Washington's hegemony.

During US administration of the islands (1945–1972), Okinawans participated in mass civil disobedience against US colonial rule. Now, in reaction to these new injustices, protests against the US military had regained traction under the rallying cries of "Protect Henoko and Oura Bay" and "No helipads in Takae." Local efforts to examine—or reexamine—the impacts of war and militarization of their islands were reenergized, and Okinawans expressed their resistance to militarism via elections and referendums. However, attempts to oppose the US and Japanese governments faced many barriers. There were structural obstacles, such as the US-Japan Security Treaty and the Status of Forces Agreement, which exempted the US military from Japanese laws. Also, like many other militarized islands in the Pacific, Okinawa's economy was closely linked to the bases, along with complex kinship and local ties that made it hard for those whose family members worked on the bases to openly oppose militarization. Moreover, most Okinawan peace activists lacked the ability to speak the lingua franca of the US empire, English. Thus, awareness of Okinawans' courageous struggle was mostly limited to Japanese linguistic borders, with little information reaching the wider world (a problem that undoubtedly pleased the Japanese and US governments).

Against this background, Mitchell began his work in Okinawa. At first, he focused on investigating the devastating legacy of Agent Orange, a problem also explored by Welsh photojournalist Philip Jones Griffiths. Although many Okinawans had suspected the storage and use of the toxic defoliant in Okinawa during the Vietnam War era, the US and Japanese governments had always denied its presence, and Japanese journalists had failed to investigate the problem. Mitchell employed groundbreaking methods to challenge the situation. He tracked down US veterans suffering from exposure to Agent Orange while stationed in Okinawa and corroborated their accounts with Okinawans who had encountered the poisons; he also traveled to Vietnam to interview people whose lives had been ruined by the defoliant. Throughout this process, Mitchell relentlessly pursued US government documents that revealed traces of Agent Orange in Okinawa and Guam. This research laid the foundation for dozens of newspaper stories;

an award-winning documentary produced with an Okinawan TV company; and Mitchell's first book, *Tsuiseki: Okinawa no Karehazai* (2014).

Skillfully translated by University of the Ryukyus professor Abe Kosuzu, the book enables Okinawan and Japanese readers to grasp the details of Agent Orange's impact and the severity of an issue many had heard of—or experienced—but knew little about. The book has become an important part of a social movement that confronts the tragic legacy of Agent Orange and the Vietnam War in Okinawa. I have heard Okinawan peace activists quote from the book in their talks at rallies and workshops. They speak to Mitchell's dedication to the cause and his willingness to join the local struggle. His writing also shows how US service members fell victim to militarism: Countless troops were exposed to Agent Orange while stationed in Okinawa but suffered in silence due to their government's efforts to hide the tragedy and evade responsibility. Thanks to Mitchell's diligence, today many of these sick service members are receiving support from the Department of Veterans Affairs.

After unearthing the impacts of Agent Orange, Mitchell turned his attention to the broader range of US military contamination in Okinawa. He adopted an approach never before used by journalists in Japan to investigate environmental damage: the US Freedom of Information Act (FOIA). The thousands of pages of documents he obtained in this way are the basis of his second Japanese book, *Tsuiseki: Nichibei Chii Kyōtei to Kichi Kōgai* (2018), again skillfully translated by Professor Abe. It reveals how the US military—the world's worst polluter—contaminated Okinawa with such toxins as nerve agents, depleted uranium, and per- and polyfluoroalkyl substances (PFAS) "forever chemicals." Mitchell also explores the ways in which the US military, the US government, and the Japanese government manipulated the Status of Forces Agreement and its related systems to hide and distort the reality of contamination in Okinawa.

The lopsided power relationship between the two governments and the people of Okinawa is so formidable that challenging the status quo often feels futile. But Mitchell's work offers hope for those who confront these iniquities. He shares stories of how US service members, who were victims of contamination on the other side of the fence, spoke up for the truth. He also recounts how he faced obstruction and intimidation from the US government while pursuing his investigations into environmental damage. These personal stories, juxtaposed with descriptions of toxic chemicals, reaffirms the power of individual effort and the transformative nature of storytelling.

In 2020, Mitchell's two Japanese books evolved into *Poisoning the Pacific: The US Military's Secret Dumping of Plutonium, Chemical Weapons, and Agent Orange.* As well as describing the calamitous impact of militarization on Okinawa's environment, the book expands the chronological and thematic frameworks of his previous work to encompass the wider Pacific region from the early twentieth century to the present. The result is a compelling exploration of the relationship between war, militarization, and environmental degradation, which have been largely hidden by the United States and Japan. Starting with the Japanese army's deployment of biological and chemical munitions against Chinese troops and civilians during the Second Sino-Japanese War (1937–1945), Mitchell then describes how, after the war, Japanese scientists collaborated with US occupation forces to transfer details of their nation's weapons of mass destruction programs to the US military. He also discusses the atomic bombings of Hiroshima and Nagasaki and the testing of nuclear bombs in the Marshall Islands to show how the United States repeatedly attempted to conceal the dangers posed by radioactive fallout. Similarly, he details how the US government and Japanese far-right politicians foisted nuclear power onto Japan—the dangers of which can be seen in the ongoing disaster at the Fukushima Daiichi Nuclear Power Plant. Using documents obtained through FOIA, Mitchell extends his investigations to the US territories of Guam, the Commonwealth of the Northern Mariana Islands, and Johnston Atoll to elucidate the inextricable links between colonialism and environmental contamination.

The analytical power and practical implications of *Poisoning the Pacific* should be noted. Mitchell shows that although militarization and war occur in the name of nation-states jostling for geopolitical dominance, ultimately, all countries involved absorb each other's toxic technologies, destroying their citizens' lives and polluting the environment for generations to come. To counter this violent trajectory, Mitchell advocates for alternative approaches anchored in the principles of environmental justice; his discussions on specific tactics, such as the use of FOIA and international human rights mechanisms, are especially pragmatic.

In 2020, alongside the publication of *Poisoning the Pacific*, Mitchell coauthored a booklet for publisher Iwanami Shoten, which, for the first time in Japanese, reveals the risks of PFAS "forever chemicals" that have seeped from US bases in Okinawa and contaminated the drinking water for one-third of the population. Three years later, he wrote a hands-on guide for Okinawans and Japanese on how to use the FOIA to obtain information about military, State Department, and CIA operations in Japan. Mitchell has also donated the documents he obtained via FOIA to the libraries of George Washington University, Okinawa International University and the University of Hawai'i at Mānoa. In many respects, these are part of his efforts to empower local communities to challenge more effectively the problems caused by the US empire of bases.

Mitchell's latest book is what we have expected from him when we review the trajectory of his work over the last sixteen years. *Why Are We in Okinawa? A History of Violence* has been a highly anticipated book because it traces the roots of US and Japanese colonization of Okinawa from the late nineteenth century to the current era, unearthing previously unknown outrages along the way. Among other topics, he discusses the construction of new US bases in Henoko and Takae. He diligently gathered information, interviewed participants, and observed what was happening in Okinawa as he embarked on the challenging task of exposing what the United States has dubbed its "Pivot to Asia" (a misnomer because since World War II, the US military has never really left the region).

Construction of new US bases in Okinawa shares many similarities with the injustices Mitchell has examined in his previous work: the US and Japanese governments' indifference to Okinawan voices, Tokyo's manipulation of the judicial system, and its interference in local politics. As for Henoko and Takae, the issues surrounding the bases' construction have unfolded before him, sometimes with Mitchell as part of the process. He has witnessed protests on the ground and on the sea, he has accompanied Okinawan delegations to the National Diet in Tokyo to make their cases, and he has observed environmental NGOs' attempts to internationalize the Henoko issues in the US courts and at the United Nations. In this way, Mitchell captures Okinawans' genuine voices—angry, frustrated, or joyous when celebrating (rare) victories—while connecting them to the geopolitical context of East Asia and the world. With the recent narratives of the "Chinese threat" and "Taiwan contingency" constantly propagated by the Japanese and US governments and mass media, it is vital that the voices of Okinawans, who would be on the frontlines of a future China-US war, are not drowned out.

As an Okinawan involved with issues surrounding the US military in Okinawa, particularly opposition to the Henoko base construction, and as an Asian increasingly concerned about the volatile situation in the region, I have high hopes that Mitchell's close-up discussion of Okinawa's struggles will reach a broader international audience and contribute to larger efforts for peace in the Pacific and further afield. Our local stories become more impactful when they are woven into the global narratives of peace and demilitarization. I hope that Mitchell's *yosomono* (outsider) analysis of local movements will encourage us insiders to critically assess our efforts and develop more effective tactics to confront the formidable challenges of militarization and potential war. I am convinced that the thoroughness of Mitchell's investigation, his determination for justice and the cause, and his writing will contribute to realizing these hopes.

An Introduction

In the United States, 1955 was the year that galvanized the civil rights movement. That summer, the lynching of teenager Emmett Till and the subsequent acquittal of his White killers exposed the brutal injustices faced by African Americans. Then in the winter, Rosa Parks's refusal to surrender her bus seat prompted the Montgomery bus boycott that thrust young Martin Luther King Jr. to the forefront of the struggle for racial equality, reshaping the history of the nation. In the same year, a parallel movement emerged in reaction to American violence and discrimination, and it adopted the same tactics of peaceful civil disobedience; this struggle was fought some 12,000 kilometers from the Jim Crow South (see map 0.1), and today, it remains largely unknown in the United States and the rest of the world.

In the final months of World War II, the Japanese-run islands of Okinawa had been invaded then occupied by the US military and subsequently administered as a colony overseen by a succession of army generals. The 800,000 inhabitants were denied the freedoms of speech, the press, and unionization; they lacked the right to elect their chief executive; and those employed by the military were relegated to the bottom of a racially tiered wage scale. In 1955, the accumulation of abuses pushed Okinawans to the breaking point. In March, the military embarked on land grabs to expand its already-gigantic bases, deploying armed troops who forced families from their ancestral properties, beat resisters, and then bulldozed their homes. Six months later, an army sergeant raped and murdered a six-year-old girl, the latest in a series of heinous crimes by military personnel, who enjoyed immunity from civilian courts. Then, in October, more Okinawan children were injured when the army test-fired an atomic cannon near their primary school, shattering its windows. Ten years had passed since the end of World War II, but for residents, no peace had arrived. Responding to these injustices, in the coming months, hundreds of thousands of Okinawans rose up in outrage, staging mass demonstrations to demand an end to US occupation. Known as the All-Island Struggle (Shimagurumi Tōsō), this was the start of one of the world's most tenacious civil rights movements—grassroots, absolutely pacifist, and often led by women. Since 1955, Okinawans have never stopped protesting.

* * *

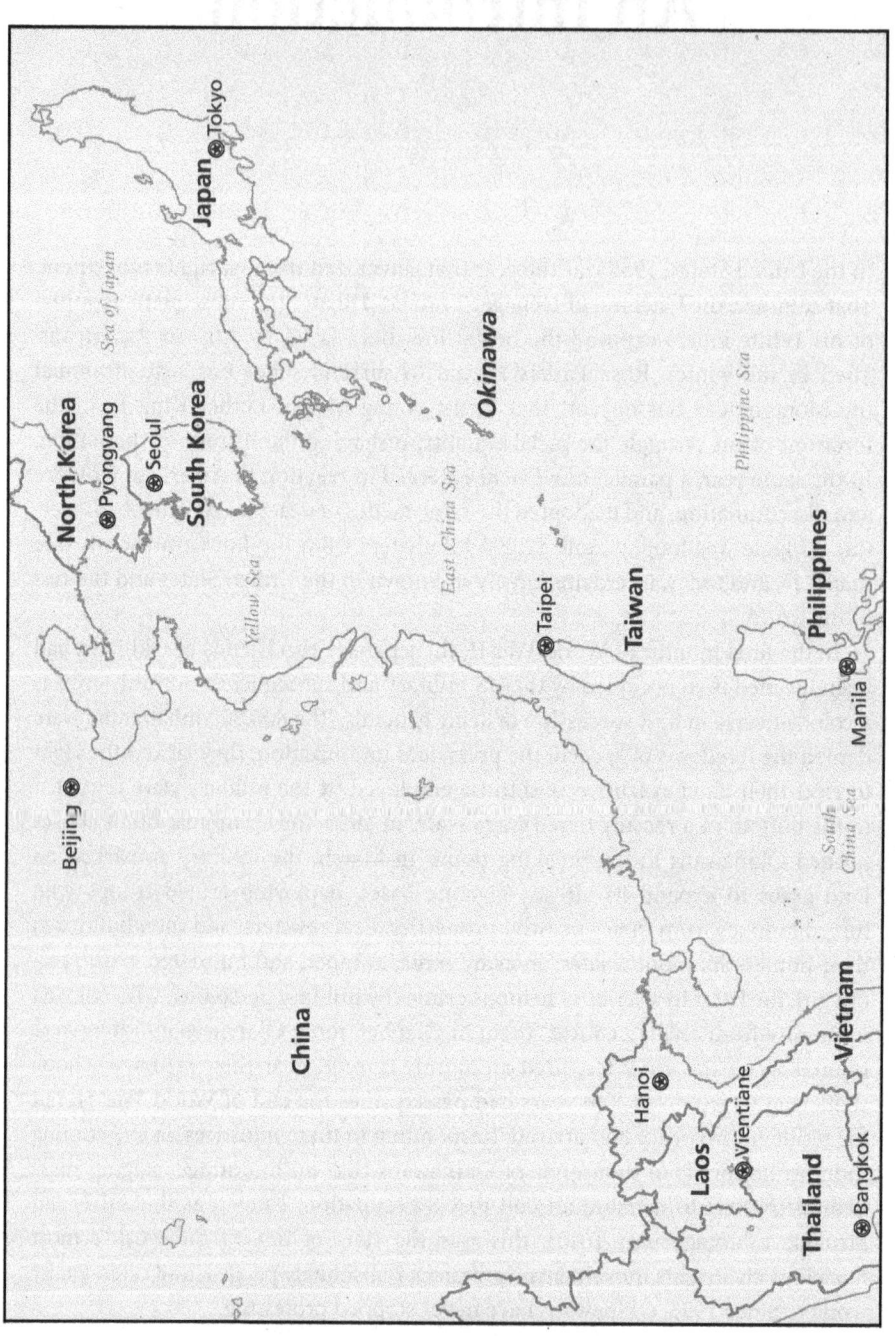

MAP 0.1 *A regional map which shows Okinawa in relation to China, Taiwan, the Korean Peninsula and Japan.*

Okinawa is unlike anywhere else in Japan. During the Middle Ages, it was home to the Ryukyu Kingdom, a multiethnic hub of maritime commerce that prospered thanks to Chinese sponsorship. Then, in the nineteenth century, the islands were annexed by Japan, who tried to assimilate them into the homeland by eradicating their culture and languages; discrimination, combined with exploitative taxes, triggered a widespread diaspora (today, some 420,000 Okinawan descendants live overseas.) In World War II, Japan's leaders—at the behest of Emperor Hirohito—sacrificed the islands to delay the American assault of the mainland. Okinawa was the only prefecture to experience invasion, and 122,000 Okinawans died, many executed by imperial troops for speaking their own languages. After the war, the Japanese government—again following a suggestion by the emperor—granted the United States administrative control of the islands in exchange for the return of its own sovereignty. Okinawa, along with the Philippines and Micronesia, became key components in a US strategy that, in the words of General Douglas MacArthur, envisaged the Pacific Ocean as the "Anglo-Saxon lake."[1]

In Okinawa, the military displaced one-third of the main island's residents to build bases where it stockpiled nuclear and chemical weapons and launched wars in Korea and Southeast Asia; in 1965, the commander of US Pacific forces pronounced, "Without Okinawa, we couldn't continue fighting the Vietnam war." Military needs took priority over those of civilians, who lacked labor protections, access to welfare support, and reliable health care. Inside the bases, Okinawans were assigned the most dangerous jobs, and outside, the military ensured prostitution remained legal (by 1970, it was the islands' top money maker). Throughout the 1960s and '70s, troops also smuggled heroin via the bases, in what US lawmakers dubbed the "Okinawa system." Against this backdrop of oppression and poverty, Okinawans organized a mass resistance movement as creative as it was popular. They marched, they struck, and they petitioned until their opposition became so intense that, in 1972, the United States was forced to relinquish administrative control back to Japan. The transition brought little relief for Okinawans, though, because Japan's leaders encouraged the United States to retain its bases. At the same time, Tokyo worked to transform the islands into a cut-rate tourist destination for mainlanders, who, unlike Okinawans, had prospered in the postwar decades.[2]

Today, many Okinawans' anger focuses on the thirty-one US bases crammed into their prefecture, which is smaller than the size of Rhode Island. Not only do service personnel continue to break the law—and evade punishment due to bilateral agreements—but also the heavy military footprint hobbles economic and infrastructural development. The bases occupy 15 percent of the main island but contribute only 5 percent to the prefecture's overall economy. Okinawans are the poorest people in Japan, and their land and water has been severely contaminated by the military, which is not required to pay for cleanup.

Islanders' opposition also targets the Japanese government, which has colluded to keep the bases away from mainland constituencies while simultaneously launching attacks on Okinawans' history and identity. Japanese leaders have sought to erase from school textbooks mention of their soldiers' wartime atrocities against islanders, and they ignore United Nations' recommendations to recognize residents as indigenous, denying them the legal protections such status would grant. Anti-Okinawan prejudice is common in Japanese books, magazines, and social media; such discrimination dates back more than a century, when mainland businesses displayed signs prohibiting entry to Okinawans (and Koreans, Japan's other long-oppressed minority). Prejudice, too, continues to permeate the ranks of US leadership—from the top diplomat who in 2011 called islanders "lazy" and "masters in extorting" to Marine Corps training lectures that inform troops how Okinawans had "double standards" and their grievances were "more emotional than logical."[3]

Despite this, there is little sustained discussion about such inequities in mainland Japanese or overseas media. Although the silence is sometimes punctuated by coverage of particularly cold-blooded military crimes (such as the 1995 gang rape of a primary schoolgirl), this sporadic reporting makes these occurrences seem exceptions rather than the continuation of a violent trend against Okinawan women that began, quite literally, when US troops landed in the islands in spring 1945.

This lack of discussion can be attributed to geopolitics and secrecy. Since the start of the Cold War, the US and Japanese governments have insisted the islands need to be militarized to provide a bulwark against the communist threat from the Soviet Union, North Korea, North Vietnam, and China. In 1969, one US Army press release, "Why We Are Here," encapsulated the logic: "On mainland China, a mere 400 miles [644 km] from Okinawa, 735 million people are dedicated to the ultimate enslavement of the people of Asia. These forces have been arrested by the superior military power of the United States and her allies." The bases are needed, proponents argue, because they deter enemies, Okinawan wishes be damned. The logic is familiar for other Pacific peoples opposing military occupation in Guam, the Marshall Islands, Hawai'i, and elsewhere. Another reason for lack of widespread awareness can be traced to the twenty-seven-year period of American administration when the military controlled media access to the islands, ensuring news of its abuses could not reach Congress or the US public. Nowadays, such overt restrictions have been replaced by opaque bilateral agreements that keep US-Japan decision-making processes—and many abuses—out of the public eye. (One of the few ways to uncover what the two governments would rather remain unknown is the US Freedom of Information Act; documents I obtained through this route inform the latter half of this book.)[4]

* * *

Against this backdrop of violence, discrimination, and ignorance, this book aims to fulfill three main purposes. First, it intends to provide readers with some answers to the question its title poses: How did the US bases become concentrated in Okinawa, and why are they still there? To understand this, it is important to know how the once-independent Ryukyu Kingdom was transformed into a Japanese prefecture (the focus of the first two chapters). In answering these questions, this book distills the work of Okinawan, Japanese, and international researchers with sixteen years of my own investigations for the *Japan Times*, the country's largest English-language newspaper, and *Okinawa Times*, one of the prefecture's Japanese-language newspapers.

The second purpose of this book is to provide an accurate understanding of Okinawa's history as a counterpoint to recent Chinese government attempts to assert territorial claims over the islands. Historically, China was instrumental in the development of Okinawa's culture (but it never ruled there), and today, its influence is widely visible in the islands' food and architecture; until recently, many residents viewed China favorably. In the 2010s, though, this began to change when one senior People's Liberation Army officer announced, "The Ryukyus do not belong to Japan," and Beijing declared how delegitimizing Japan's sovereignty of Okinawa was a "fair game" "to be played as a powerful card when necessary." As China grows more militarily assertive, such calls have been escalating, particularly online. Ironically, this disinformation is lubricated by the failure of the United States and Japan to rectify or acknowledge their own troubling treatment of Okinawa, giving Chinese nationalists room to exploit the gaps in knowledge. Now more than ever, it is important to have a clear-eyed comprehension of Okinawa's history and why many residents are tired of being pawns in the play of greater powers—whether they be Japan, the United States, or China.[5]

Finally, this book explains how Okinawans have developed one of the most remarkable civil rights movements in modern history. Rooted in the trauma of World War II, islanders from all walks of life have embraced nonviolence and succeeded in winning very real improvements. In the twenty-first century, vibrant resistance continues to permeate Okinawan society—its art, music, and comedy—shattering stereotypical views of a staid political culture in Japan and offering a potential model for the nation that embraces diversity, political and historical awareness, and democratic participation. The Okinawan peace movement—and the figures who shaped it—are a source of profound inspiration. I hope this book helps them to receive the long-overdue recognition they deserve so it can, even in a small way, contribute to the struggle for justice they have fought so hard to acquire and inspire other communities to sustain hope during these dark, troubled times.

A Note on Name Order and Spellings

In this book, Okinawan and Japanese names generally appear in the traditional order of surname first and given name second (e.g., Onaga Takeshi, Tamaki Denny). However, when individuals have adopted the reverse order in English-language contexts, that preference is respected (e.g., Yuken Teruya, Miyume Tanji).

Macrons are used to indicate long vowels in Japanese (e.g., Shimagurumi Tōsō, Zengunrō), but they are omitted when a term has entered common English usage (e.g., Tokyo, Ryukyu) or when the individual customarily removes them (e.g., Ota Masahide).

All translations are my own; I take full responsibility for any errors or inconsistencies.

1

The Ryukyu Kingdom
A Bridge of Nations

*"The country of Ryukyu is a magnificent land in the southern sea. . . .
With its ships, it bridges many nations and abounds with the products and
precious treasures of foreign lands."*
—THE BRIDGE OF NATIONS BELL, SHURI CASTLE[1]

The Ryukyu Archipelago is a string of approximately two hundred islands stretching 1,200 kilometers from Kyushu to within a glimpse of Taiwan. Lacking fresh water and fertile soil, most of these islands are too inhospitable to sustain human life, and even on the more habitable ones, the environment can be harsh. Warm seas spawn powerful typhoons, and plate tectonics trigger earthquakes, sometimes generating tsunami that inundate low-lying lands. Yet despite these geographical drawbacks, the archipelago produced one of the most important states in the region: the Ryukyu Kingdom.

From the fifteenth century, an ethnically diverse population transformed Okinawa, the archipelago's largest island, into a hub of international commerce. Its merchants navigated vast distances to trade the most valuable products the region could offer, and the island melded cultures from neighboring countries into its own unique forms of architecture, music, and martial arts. During the 450 years of the kingdom's existence, its citizens became world renowned for their bravery, fairness, and courtesy. One British visitor in the 1800s called them the "most pacific people upon earth." In the words of modern-day Okinawan historian Akamine Mamoru, the Ryukyu Kingdom was the "Cornerstone of East Asia."[2]

The key to the kingdom's success lay in its close relationship with the region's preeminent superpower, China. For most of the Middle Ages, China's economic and technological development surpassed other nations in East Asia—if not

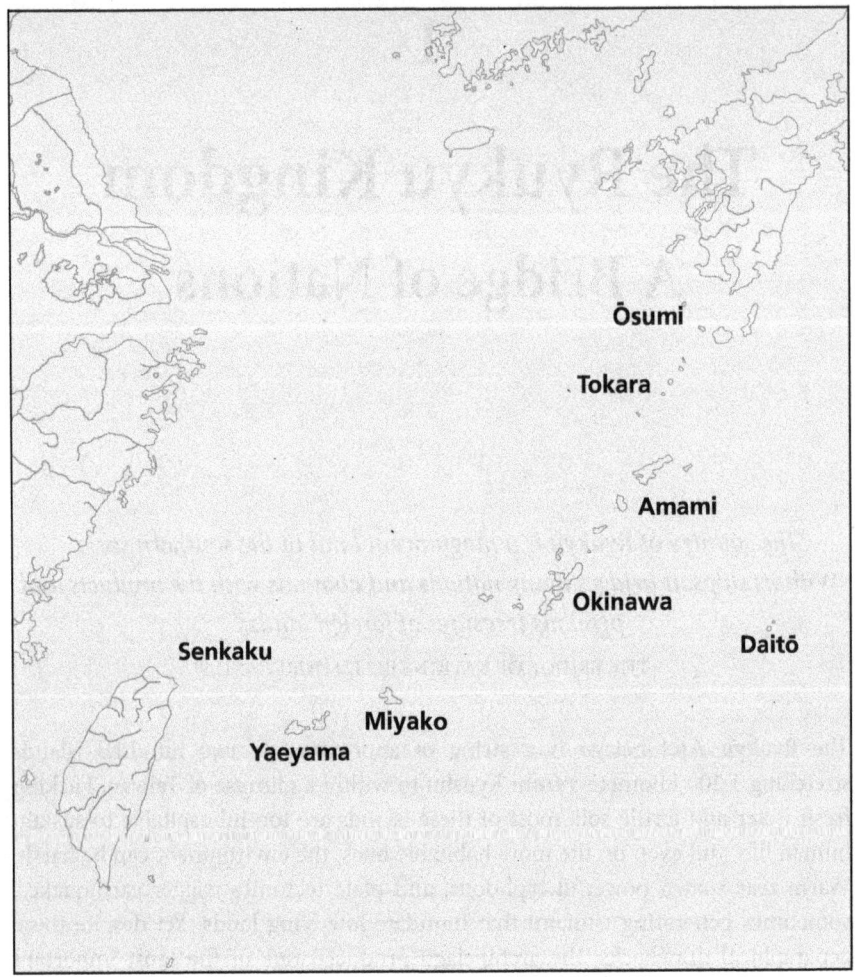

MAP 1.1 *Map of the Ryukyu Archipelago*

the world. The country extolled a Confucian system that envisaged itself as the center of civilization, surrounded by unenlightened barbarian states. At the head of this system was the emperor—the son of heaven—who was ordained to rule all mankind with benevolent authority. To maintain harmony with its neighbors, China developed a system whereby foreign rulers could visit Beijing and formally recognize the emperor's supremacy by becoming his vassal and bringing tribute. Such states included current-day Korea, Vietnam, and Thailand. These leaders usually benefited from the relationship: Imperial recognition provided their own rule with legitimacy, and China rarely interfered in domestic affairs. Moreover, the emperor responded with gifts that outvalued those given in tribute.

For centuries, China had promulgated a vigorous trade network on land and sea, where communities of Chinese merchants organized commerce in foreign ports. But in the 1370s, the China-led maritime trading network faltered when Emperor Hongwu declared a ban on sea voyages. The prohibition was an attempt to eliminate bands of pirates who had been terrorizing coastal communities and to gain government control of unregulated commerce. Under the ban, the only foreigners permitted to enter China were official envoys from vassal states carrying tribute to the emperor. In addition, they were also allowed to import their own wares for trade.[3]

The maritime ban created a lucrative opportunity for states prepared to become vassals—and Okinawa was keen to cash in. At the time, the main island was controlled by three rival kings governing its northern, central, and southern provinces. In 1372, a Chinese envoy visited Okinawa and invited the king of the central region to provide tribute to the emperor; he promptly dispatched his brother to Beijing to be recognized. In the coming years, the kings of the other two districts also became tribute states, and all three rulers of the small island began conducting trade with the most powerful state in East Asia.[4]

China enthusiastically promoted the ambitions of Okinawa's fledgling merchants. Whereas it limited the frequency of visits from other vassal states, it granted Okinawa special treatment, allowing it to send unlimited tribute missions to Beijing. To facilitate trade, China even provided more than thirty ships and supplied navigators and translators. Such magnanimity was largely based on military considerations. Okinawa supplied Beijing with horses and the sulfur from which it manufactured gunpowder. Also, China hoped that by enriching the island's coffers, it might become a tempting target for pirates, thus deflecting attention from its own coastal communities.[5]

By 1429, King Shō Hashi of Okinawa's central region had defeated his two rivals, and the island was unified as the Ryukyu Kingdom. Taking full advantage as China's favored trading partner, the new state became a powerhouse of regional commerce. Ships departed from Naha harbor, carrying crews of more than two hundred men, heavily armed to combat pirates. The voyage to the ports of Southeast Asia—today's Vietnam, Thailand, and Indonesia—took several weeks. After arriving, the Chinese translators accompanying the Ryukyuan vessels negotiated with local Chinese merchants to purchase luxury wares, such as ivory, pepper, and precious woods valued for producing dyes and incense. The northern route took Ryukyuan ships to Japan—a supplier of folding fans, copper, and swords—and Korea, where in addition to trading, they repatriated Koreans who had been rescued from wrecks or pirate enslavement.[6]

Ryukyuan sailors earned a reputation for honesty and bravery. In the early 1500s, one Portuguese administrator in Malacca noted, "They are very truthful men. They do not buy slaves, nor would they sell one of their own men for the whole world, and they would die over this.... The Lequios (Ryukyuans) are men who sell their merchandise freely for credit, and if they are lied to when they collect payment, they collect it sword in hand."[7]

After packing their ships with the most desirable goods of the era, Ryukyuan traders sailed to China to deliver their tribute. With each vassal state designated a specific port of entry, Ryukyuan ships docked at Fuzhou, Fujian Province. In the city, the Chinese government provided diplomatic quarters where the visitors could recover from the voyage and conduct trade with their Chinese counterparts, particularly for the regional specialty, ceramics. For the Ryukyuan merchants, their arrival in Fuzhou heralded the start of another perilous journey to transport their wares three thousand kilometers to the capital, Beijing. The months-long trip took them via roads and canals; today, the tombs of Ryukyuans still attest to the dangers they faced. Upon their arrival at the capital, the merchants proffered their hard-earned tribute and conducted private transactions with the goods picked up in ports along the way.[8]

Having completed their business in Beijing, the Ryukyu crews made the long journey back to Fuzhou; then, after stocking up on Chinese wares, they sailed homeward. In addition to carrying material goods, Ryukyuans also brought back practical skills, particularly related to Chinese agriculture. In the years to come, among the most significant was the cultivation of sugarcane and sweet potato, the latter of which became a staple crop in the kingdom, nourishing communities dependent on unproductive land.

Thanks to China's patronage and the endeavors of the islands' merchants, the Ryukyu Kingdom experienced an unprecedented golden age of prosperity in the fifteenth and sixteenth centuries. Visitors to Naha were impressed with its storehouses of exotic wares from around the region. The city teemed with Southeast Asian merchants; Japanese monks who established Buddhist temples in the kingdom; and, in later years, Koreans invited to build pottery kilns. Near Naha Port, the Kume District was home to a long-established Chinese community, some of whom had close ties to Ryukyuan royalty, signifying their high social status. The kingdom's records were written in Chinese, while residents spoke the islands' languages, which resembled—but were distinct from—Japanese.[9]

East of Naha lay Shuri City, the capital of the kingdom. Resplendent on a tall hill stood the home of the royal family: Shuri Castle. Its Chinese-style gateway was often adorned with a lacquer plaque reading *Shurei no Kuni* (Nation of Propriety), based on a compliment bestowed by the Chinese emperor in 1579. The castle embodied the royal family's political and spiritual power. Within its grounds, there were sacred springs, a large pond in the shape of a dragon's head (the *Ryūtan*), and quarters for female priests. Officially appointed by the king, women held high positions in the indigenous religion, conducting ceremonies to ensure abundant harvests and the safe sailings of the tribute missions. At the investitures of Ryukyuan kings, Chinese delegations were invited to Shuri Castle, where they were treated to lavish banquets and celebrations lasting many months. In the castle's main hall hung a seven-hundred-kilogram bronze bell, cast in 1458. Its inscription lauded the magnificence of the kingdom, its precious treasures, and its ships that served to bridge the nations of the region.[10]

The Golden Days Decline

As the sixteenth century progressed, the Ryukyu Kingdom's status as one of the region's busiest commercial hubs began to slip. Portugal and Spain muscled into Asia, establishing colonies and cornering trade. Meanwhile, China loosened its maritime bans, permitting some private international commerce, which undercut the need for Ryukyuan merchants. Exacerbating the kingdom's problems were pressures from its northern neighbor, Japan.[11]

At this time, Japan lacked a centralized government; instead it was fragmented into hundreds of domains, each headed by a feudal lord (daimyo) who competed with other feudal lords for influence. Conflict was so common that the fifteenth and sixteenth centuries became known as the Sengoku Jidai (Warring-States Period). One of the most powerful samurai clans were the Shimazu of Satsuma (modern-day Kyushu), who were hungry to extend their influence throughout western Japan and further. For decades, the Shimazu had sought control over the Ryukyu Kingdom and its trading privileges with China, but Shuri officials had managed to curb their encroachment.

In the late 1500s, though, the Shimazu clan conducted a series of power plays to assert its dominance over the Ryukyu Kingdom. Among these attempts were accusations that the island had breached the samurai's all-important code of honor by failing to send sufficient congratulations on the succession of the clan's new lord. The most serious situation occurred in 1592, when mainland samurai, led by the powerful daimyo Toyotomi Hideyoshi, launched an invasion of Korea, a Chinese vassal. The Satsuma ordered the kingdom to provide rations for the occupying troops. Not only did the Ryukyuan authorities delay sending the food, but they also tipped off Beijing about the upcoming invasion plans. (The Japanese assault ultimately ended in failure.)[12]

In the early seventeenth century, the Sengoku Jidai came to an end following the largest battle of the era at Sekigahara (modern-day Gifu Prefecture). The victorious Tokugawa Ieyasu was proclaimed shogun (military commander), and he consolidated control over the nation by constructing a massive castle in Edo (modern-day Tokyo). To ensure the loyalty of the other daimyo, he forced them to dispatch their families to live in Edo. The system ushered in a long period of relative stability in Japan overseen by hereditary shoguns.

Hoping to establish trade with China, the Tokugawa shogunate asked the Shuri government to liaise with Beijing, but the Ryukyuans demurred. At the same time, the Shimazu clan was experiencing financial problems, so it looked south to solve them. The clan drew up plans to seize Amami-Ōshima, the large island in the north of the Ryukyu Kingdom. To secure the support of the Tokugawa shogunate for the invasion, the Satsuma expanded their preparations to encompass the entire kingdom, arguing this would pressure the Ryukyuans to liaise with China to open to Japanese trade. For the clan, the invasion provided an additional bonus: It would punish the Shuri government for its failure to supply food for the earlier invasion of Korea, during which many Satsuma troops had starved.[13]

Samurai Invade the Ryukyu Kingdom

For its assault on the Ryukyu Kingdom, the Shimazu clan gathered one hundred ships and approximately three thousand troops, including many veterans of the wars the clan had waged in the preceding years. On 7 March 1609, this flotilla arrived at Amami-Ōshima and seized the island after encountering little resistance; primary goal accomplished, the samurai headed south. Prior to the capture of its northernmost island, King Shō Nei's government had not taken seriously the likelihood of a Satsuma invasion—some believed their state was too secluded to be attacked, while others anticipated rescue by the Chinese military—but now they rushed to muster defending forces. On Tokunoshima, south of Amami-Ōshima, one thousand Ryukyuans were waiting for the samurai, however they proved no match for the heavily armed invaders, and they were soon overcome. Samurai killed some three hundred Ryukyuans, taking dozens of heads as trophies.[14]

On 26 March, the Shimazu clan landed on the northern coast of Okinawa Island itself. They razed properties, then ensnared the local forces in an ambush, slaughtering approximately five hundred troops. After reboarding their ships, the Satsuma sailed along the western coast and landed at Yomitan, central Okinawa. Some of the troops split away from the main force and, traveling by sea, launched an assault on Naha Port. Here, the Ryukyuans fared better due to their past experiences fending off attacks from pirates. This time, too, they blocked the entrance to the harbor with a massive chain and fired on the invaders' vessels with cannons; the tactics forced the samurai to retreat.

With their assault by sea thwarted, the Satsuma launched a land attack on the capital. Adopting a scorched-earth strategy, they set alight large parts of the area around Shuri, and at the Chinese community Kume, they clashed with Ryukyuan defenders, killing hundreds. The samurai surrounded Shuri Castle, where the king and his officials were ensconced. The invaders relayed assurances that they intended to seize only the northern islands but allow the bulk of the kingdom to continue to exist; as a result, on 3 April, the king surrendered.

For the kingdom, the human and economic cost of the month-long war was devastating. At least one thousand Ryukyuans had been killed, large areas of the capital lay in ruins, and properties had been looted; on the invaders' side, approximately two hundred had died. The political ramifications for the kingdom were even more serious. The samurai transported King Shō Nei and his top officials to Japan, where they were detained for two and a half years. Although the samurai kept their promise to allow the kingdom's ongoing existence, they imposed controls that had grave consequences for its future. First, the detainees had to sign and seal a surrender agreement that stated that their kingdom had historically been under the dominion of the Satsuma. When one of the Ryukyuans refused, he was promptly executed. Second, the Satsuma retained their control of the kingdom's northern islands, including Amami-Ōshima and Tokunoshima, where, in the following years, the samurai transformed the large island into a virtual colony cultivating sugarcane for Japanese consumption. Likewise, in the rest of the kingdom, the Satsuma overseers imposed taxation amounting to approximately one-quarter of its annual gross domestic product and demanded additional payment of other goods. Worst of all, the samurai declared that henceforth they would manage the kingdom's overseas trade.[15]

The invasion had dealt a serious blow to Ryukyuan sovereignty, stripping away a large chunk of its territory and placing under Shimazu control its finances and commerce with China. Moreover, by forcing the kingdom to declare that it had belonged to the samurai for a long time, it imposed a fiction that rewrote the reality of the islands' past. The arbitrary division of the kingdom and the manipulation of historical fact to justify their exploitation foreshadowed Ryukyuans' mistreatment by other powerful aggressors in the centuries to come.

Fortunately for the Satsuma, soon after their invasion, unexpected developments in Japan made their conquest even more lucrative. Japan's rulers were becoming concerned by the arrival of European visitors. The spread of Christianity heightened fears among daimyo that their samurai might grow more loyal to a foreign pope than their own local lords, and the importation of weapons threatened the newly established status quo. To offset these risks, Japan took a leaf out of China's book and imposed a series of increasingly strict isolationist policies. First, it prohibited Christianity; then it forbade visits by European ships. By 1641, the only ports open for international trade were Nagasaki, for Dutch and Chinese merchants, and two other smaller harbors. The isolationist policies—known as *sakoku*—remained in place for more than two centuries.

With most of Japan sealed off from the world, Ryukyu's importance as an international trading hub rose once more—and the Satsuma were sure to make the most of the situation. The kingdom's trade was under their control, so they used its tribute missions to China to obtain the in-demand goods made scarce by Japan's maritime bans, particularly silks and medicines. Not only did the Satsuma pocket the kingdom's earnings, but they also hid many of the profits from the central government.[16]

For residents of the Ryukyu Kingdom, which had once prided itself as the "Bridge of Nations," these were painful times. Their islands had been divided, and their finances were drained by Satsuma taxation and trade controls. To guarantee compliance, the samurai prohibited Ryukyuans from carrying weapons and forced the government to install a network of *metsuke* spies to monitor the populace. The kingdom possessed a strict caste system: Beneath the royalty, there was a class of aristocrats (*yukatchu*) and then commoners, most of whom lived in poverty. Conditions in the outer Miyako and Yaeyama Islands were even harsher. Here the Shuri government imposed a per-capita tax on every resident, which, combined with *yukatchu* corruption, forced most of the population into destitution. In 1771, a gigantic tsunami swamped the islands, killing 12,000 people, rendering much of the land impossible to farm, and triggering an eight-decades-long famine—but even then, the Shuri authorities did not slacken their tax demands.

Meanwhile, the kingdom attempted to resist Satsuma rule by aligning itself more closely with its superpower sponsor, China. Guided by the expat Chinese community at Kume, the island underwent an extensive process of Sinification. The Ryukyu royalty adopted the clothes and ceremonies of the imperial household in Beijing, and in 1768, it rebuilt the main hall at Shuri Castle to incorporate features resembling the Forbidden City. The Chinese geomantic practice feng shui permeated the castle via sculptures of propitious dragons and the prominence of natural springs, essential resources on water-short Okinawa. Feng shui spread through the islands, influencing many of the distinctive features still visible today: the placement of *shīsā* lion-dogs on rooftops and, most prominently, the large yonic tombs modeled on those in Fuzhou, where generations of bones are interred and families gather to feast in honor of their ancestors. Relations between China and Ryukyu were consolidated by the dispatch of island students to the prestigious National Academy in Beijing for education in Confucianism and to Fuzhou, where they learned medicine, law, and music. From these interactions emerged *ti*—the forerunner of karate—and *kobudo* (martial arts using weapons); at the king's investiture ceremony in 1866, high-ranking Ryukyuans staged a display of karate for their visitors.[17]

The kingdom envisaged its increased orientation toward China as a method to resist further Japanese interference—but conversely, the Satsuma encouraged the shift. Being the only fiefdom with ersatz dominion over a foreign state enhanced its domestic prestige; especially during annual visits to Edo, the Satsuma basked in the glory of parading their exotically dressed Ryukyuan subjects along the roads to the capital. Within the kingdom itself, the samurai hid obvious displays of the

Japanese presence due to fears that, if discovered, Beijing might halt its commerce. When Chinese delegations came to the kingdom, for example, the authorities provided scripts to anyone who might interact with the visitors and even issued Ryukyuan sailors with burn orders to destroy Japanese documents if their vessels ran aground.[18]

Such precautions were unwarranted. China, which was undergoing its own dynastic upheavals, was aware of the 1609 invasion and subsequent Japanese meddling in the kingdom's administration, but it did not care. Provided the Shuri government continued to send tribute and display the necessary protocol regarding royal investitures, the domestic wranglings of its vassal states lay outside its purview, and despite what some Ryukyuans hoped, military support was out of the question.

For the two centuries following the samurai invasion, the tiny kingdom survived by threading a path between its two powerful neighbors. In the words of historian Akamine, it turned itself into a "buffer zone" to ensure its continued existence. But, by the 1800s, the world had changed, and geopolitical forces were converging which would upset the kingdom's precarious position.[19]

Western Incursions

By the late eighteenth century, more and more European voyagers were venturing into the seas around the Ryukyu Kingdom, hoping to use the islands as stepping stones to the still-sealed Japan. Many of these visitors left with positive impressions. In 1816, Dr. John M'Leod, a surgeon aboard a British navy ship, marveled at the beauty of the sea and the landscape. He was even more amazed by the character of the Ryukyuans, describing them as the "most pacific people upon earth." He wrote, "They all seemed to be gifted with a sort of politeness which had the fairest claim to be termed natural; for there was nothing constrained, nothing stiff or studied in it."[20]

Other European visitors wrote similarly effusive reports, emphasizing Ryukyuans' honesty, kindness, and lack of aggression.[21] They provided food for foreign crews, treated the sick, and repaired damaged vessels before sending them on their way. As word spread of Ryukyuans' congeniality, Western nations began to regard the kingdom as a safe place to dock. For the Shuri government, each visiting ship provoked a dilemma, necessitating an ever-more difficult balancing act. If the kingdom opened fully to Western trade, then there would be repercussions from China and Japan. As a result, Ryukyuans were forced to provide supplies for free, straining the already-weak economy. However, if the kingdom tried to repel foreign vessels, then European powers might seize the islands in the same way they were colonizing swathes of Asia.

One case best highlights the Ryukyuans' quandary: the presence of Hungarian British missionary Dr. Bernard Jean Bettelheim. In 1846, Bettelheim had smuggled himself and his family into Naha, then proceeded to establish a one-man mission by occupying a Buddhist temple, driving away the resident priests, and throwing out their artifacts. Whereas most countries might have forcibly evicted such an intruder, the Ryukyuan authorities—fearful of foreign repercussions—could only implore him to leave. For the next seven years, Bettelheim ran amuck. Armed with a riding crop and accompanied by two vicious dogs, he preached in the streets and yelled sermons over the walls of Shuri Castle. In one letter, Bettelheim described breaking into a family's house: "I was little moved with the cries of the women or the frightened screams of the children, but seated myself in the first room I could get access to and began to preach."[22]

The Ryukyu government attempted to control Bettelheim by assigning dozens of guards to monitor his activities, but the costs merely added to the country's financial woes. Despite the authorities' remarkably restrained response, Bettelheim dispatched reports to the British government and the press alleging inhumane treatment. In 1848, when the *USS Preble* docked at Naha, the missionary decried the dishonesty of the Ryukyuan people to the ship's commander. Upon his return to the United States, the commander relayed Bettelheim's assessment to the Department of the Navy. In the coming years, the rogue missionary's falsehoods played a pivotal role in shaping US policy toward the kingdom.[23]

"Mars, Mammon, and God": US Manifest Destiny in Asia

Bettelheim's rampages in Ryukyu reflected Western behavior throughout the region. In the first half of the 1800s, European nations consolidated their colonization of Asia; the Netherlands controlled the Dutch East Indies (modern-day Indonesia); the French were pushing into Indochina (today's Cambodia, Laos, and Vietnam); and the British dominated India. After centuries of prominence as the regional superpower, China's influence was collapsing, wracked by internal uprisings and external pressures. For decades, British and American merchants had flooded the country with opium, causing widespread economic and social deprivation. When Beijing attempted to eradicate the trade, Britain dispatched a large naval fleet to punish the Chinese. During this First Opium War (1839–1842), British forces committed widespread rape and looting—and China was defeated. Under the terms of the Treaty of Nanking, Britain received access to Chinese ports plus control of Hong Kong. The treaty also inaugurated a system of extraterritoriality that granted Britons impunity from Chinese law. In the coming years, other Western nations imposed similarly unequal treaties, heralding what became known in China as the Century of Humiliation.

In *sakoku* Japan, the Tokugawa shogunate kept track of international affairs via reports from Dutch merchants at Nagasaki and shipwrecked Japanese sailors returned from overseas. The British defeat of China and rapid spread of European colonialism frightened Japan's government and spurred debate about how best to protect their own nation from foreign occupation. But in mid-nineteenth-century Japan, decision making was slow. Two centuries of peace had stultified the once-warlike samurai into sluggish bureaucrats who lacked assertive leadership. Although few wanted to open Japan's doors to overseas trade, they realized their lack of a modern military rendered it almost defenseless against potential aggressors. And such threats were now encroaching from all sides. From the south came pressure from France, the Netherlands, and Britain; from the north, Russia; and now from the east, there emerged a new menace: the United States.

For decades, whaling had been a mainstay of the US economy. In these days before the discovery of petrochemicals, the mammals were an indispensable natural resource, with their blubber boiled down to oil to light homes and streets and create candles and soaps. But whalers had depleted the Atlantic Ocean stocks, so in the early nineteenth century, American ships were venturing near Hokkaido and northern Japan. Although the seas were bountiful, crews were frustrated by the shogunate's closed-port policy, which prevented them from buying supplies or sheltering in storms. US ships made forays into Japanese waters to pick up stranded sailors and prod the samurai into opening to commerce. Despite the Americans adopting a relatively amicable approach during these incursions, none of the visits went well. Samurai cannon fired warning shots at their vessels, and in 1846, a minor scuffle occurred when a US commander attempted to step onto a Japanese barge. Americans were further angered by Japan's treatment of shipwrecked US sailors, whereby they were incarcerated in harsh conditions before repatriation. As these tensions unfurled, Bettelheim's reports lambasting the Ryukyuans for their purported ill treatment filtered through to the United States, convincing leaders they might need to adopt an aggressive stance with not only Japan but its southern neighbor, too.[24]

American hopes to open Japan to trade were a component of wider ambitions to transform itself into a Pacific power. In 1844, the United States had signed its own unequal treaty with China—the Treaty of Wangxia—that granted Americans trading rights and extraterritoriality. Two years later, the United States took control of Oregon; then in 1848, it defeated Mexico, gaining ports in California from which to venture into the Pacific Ocean. Numerous interest groups were pushing for expansion beyond its geographical boundaries. As well as whalers, merchants wanted access to China to obtain the tea and porcelain demanded by US consumers; missionaries saw Asia as a vast expanse of unconverted peoples;

and most influentially, the military wanted access to the region's ports—especially their coal reserves for future trans-Pacific steamship lines. As historian John W. Dower notes, "The markets and heathen souls of near-mythic 'Asia' now beckoned more enticingly than ever before. Mars, Mammon, and God traveled hand-in-hand in this dawning age of technological and commercial revolution." Many US leaders were convinced that expansion into the Pacific was their nation's ongoing Manifest Destiny—and soon they decided on the man they wanted to spearhead this push.[25]

Commodore Matthew Calbraith Perry

Matthew Calbraith Perry was born into a famous naval family in Newport, Rhode Island, in 1794. At the age of fifteen, he entered service, and during the 1812 war with the British, he was injured when a cannon exploded. In the following years, he rose through the ranks to command his own ship, earning a reputation as a dour disciplinarian who, at times, was also capable of compassion. In the war with Mexico, Perry blockaded ports and marched at the head of his invading forces, actions that made him a national hero and convinced him that the United States ought to spread its influence in the Americas and beyond.

To realize this expansion, Perry instituted reforms within the US Navy, notably the promotion of steam-powered ships. Such vessels could cross the Pacific Ocean in less than three weeks, but they had one major drawback: They burned through coal at the rate of one ton an hour, necessitating access to ports to refuel. Many Americans believed Japan possessed large reserves of coal, making the closed country a tempting target.

In late 1852, Perry received orders to lead the US expedition to open the samurai nation. Despite some reservations—he was suffering from chronic rheumatism and worried that the navy's recent abolition of flogging might render discipline at sea difficult—he accepted the mission. The acting secretary of state tasked Perry to obtain three concessions from Japan: (1) shipwrecked sailors be guaranteed protection, and (2) US ships be allowed to buy supplies and (3) sell—or barter—their own cargoes. Perry was to make two expeditions to Japan. In the first, he would deliver the list of US demands, and in the second, he would return to sign the agreement.[26]

As Perry scrambled to gather information to prepare for his expedition, he read about the Ryukyu Kingdom, drawing on Bettelheim's distorted accounts about the hostility of the islanders. Convinced a tough approach was needed, Perry wrote to the secretary of the navy proposing a takeover of the kingdom. He argued such an occupation could be "justified by the strictest rules of moral law" because

American—and other nations' ships—would be able to safely harbor there. He also suggested it might improve conditions for residents. The secretary of state replied to Perry, approving his plan but cautioning the commander to act "with the consent of the natives," to ensure his men commit no violence, and to "make no use of force" except if attacked. By the end of his voyage, all three directives had been broken.[27]

Gunboat Diplomacy

On 26 May 1853, Commodore Perry and some one thousand men arrived at Naha Port aboard two steamers and two heavily armed sailing ships. From the outset, he established a belligerent tone. When Ryukyuan officials rowed out to greet the Americans, he refused to meet them, citing their lowly ranks. After the Ryukyuans returned to shore, another boat approached, this one carrying Bettelheim. Perry afforded the missionary a warmer welcome, inviting him onboard and listening intently to his complaints about his Ryukyuan hosts.[28]

The arrival of Perry's gunboats came at a difficult time for the kingdom. Extreme weather conditions had caused crop failures, followed by starvation and epidemics. The suffering was worsened by visits from European ships and their demands for supplies for which the authorities were unable to accept payment. As a result, the Shimazu overlords had contemplated throwing open the island to appease these visitors in the hope it might forestall incursions north into the islands of Japan itself. The Tokugawa shogunate approved of such delaying tactics.[29]

At Shuri Castle, the royal court was in shambles. In 1847, the king had died, and now the throne was occupied by his nine-year-old son, Shō Tai. In the year before Perry's arrival, British troops had landed on the island and marched on Shuri, traumatizing the late king's widow, the queen dowager, so severely that she had fallen ill. Left in charge of the kingdom as its de facto head of state was an elderly regent who was frail and ill prepared to conduct international negotiations.[30]

After Perry refused to meet with lower-level officials, the regent sailed out to meet him. The commodore permitted him to board. Then he spelled out his demand: He wanted to visit Shuri Castle. The regent objected. In response, Perry ordered his troops ashore to scout the island and find a building to occupy. With Bettelheim as their guide, the sailors marched to Tomari, a neighborhood near the port, where the missionary helped them to break into what he described as a town hall. When Ryukyuan officials arrived and informed the intruders that the building was a school, the sailors ignored their pleas to leave. The expedition's chief interpreter Samuel Wells Williams condemned the action: "It was a struggle between weakness and right and power and wrong. . . . I was ashamed at having been a party to such a procedure, and pitied these poor, defenseless islanders who could only say no."[31]

Back in Naha, Perry continued to pressure the regent for an audience at Shuri Castle. The elderly official insisted the queen dowager was too sick, and the boy, too young—and besides, neither was residing in the castle—but Perry refused to take no for an answer. On 6 June, the commodore marched on Shuri accompanied by cannons and two hundred men. With no other option, the regent admitted Perry to the castle, which, as he'd explained, housed neither prince nor queen dowager. The Ryukyuans served tea and biscuits to Perry and the Americans as an awkward silence prevailed.[32]

In the following days, the commodore continued to intimidate the residents of Ryukyu, parading cannons along the shoreline, commandeering more buildings, and forcing the regent to provide supplies. Having bullied the Ryukyuans into compliance, Perry then turned his attention to the main objective of his voyage: Japan. Before departing, though, he warned the regent he would soon return.

Six days after leaving Naha, Perry's gunboats neared the mouth of Edo Bay. The Tokugawa authorities had been forewarned of the Americans' impending arrival by their spies in the Ryukyu Kingdom and the Dutch at Nagasaki—but the

FIGURE 1.1 *In 1853, Commodore Matthew Perry visited the Ryukyu Kingdom, where he seized property and demanded access to Shuri Castle. Courtesy of US Navy*

appearance of the Black Ships belching smoke caused panic among the general population. The commander adopted the same arrogant attitude he had upon arrival in the Ryukyu Kingdom. When low-ranking samurai sailed out to his ships, he refused to allow them onboard, only permitting high-level officials. When they prevaricated over his request to visit the capital, he ordered ships to sail toward Edo and take surveys. Japanese officials eventually relented to Perry's demands to come ashore—but south of the capital at Kurihama. Perry landed with hundreds of troops and a marching band—to be met by a Japanese reception committee of more than five thousand heavily armed samurai. The show of force deterred Perry from attempting any of the blatant aggressions he had committed down south.[33]

Perry handed Japanese officials a letter spelling out the US government's three demands—and he told them he would be back the next year to sign the agreement. To emphasize his friendly intentions, Perry gave Japanese officials some gifts, including engravings and history books. Upon his departure, the samurai promptly built a bonfire and burned them.[34]

On 25 July, Perry arrived back in Naha, his mood unmollified by his visit north. After lambasting Ryukyuan officials for their "inhospitable discourtesy," he lectured them on how Americans "are always regardful of, and obedient to, the laws of [other] countries." Perry presented the Ryukyuans with a list of orders. He wanted to be able to directly purchase supplies (a breach of the kingdom's no-trade policy) and the right to lease properties and construct a storehouse for coal. With these latter two demands amounting to an occupation of the kingdom's territory, the Ryukyu authorities refused. Perry's reaction was predictable: He threatened to storm Shuri Castle. The regent acceded to all four demands. The Ryukyuans, wrote clerk J. Willett Spalding, were like a "mouse in the talons of the eagle, they promised everything." On 1 August, Perry departed Naha, leaving behind a ship with sailors to build the coaling station in readiness for his return the following year.[35]

During the winter, Perry and his men stayed in the European colonies of Hong Kong and Macao to repair their ships and stock up on supplies. For some of this time, the commodore was bedbound by arthritic attacks. On Christmas Eve, Perry wrote a letter to the secretary of the navy in which he outlined a proposal to annex the Ryukyu Kingdom. He suggested that he seize the islands to liberate them from Japanese control: "It would be a merit to extend over it the vivifying influence and protection of a government like our own." Preempting any accusations of aggression, Perry assured the secretary he had been behaving in the kingdom, "without the commission of a single wrong upon the people." Wrapping his proposal in the language of Manifest Destiny, Perry explained that it was "necessary for the United States to extend its territorial jurisdiction beyond the limits of the western continent."[36]

In January 1854, the commodore again wrote to the secretary of the navy with a plan to hold hostage the Ryukyu Islands to force Japan to open to trade. Perry justified the grounds for such an occupation as "reclamation for insults and injuries committed upon American citizens." As for accountability, he assured the secretary, "The responsibility will rest solely upon me, and I shall assume it as a measure of political precaution."[37]

The commodore had gone rogue. Here he was proposing unilaterally to annex the Ryukyu Kingdom and establish America's first Asian colony. He rationalized his suggestion with the twin pretexts of humanitarianism and American national interests while hiding his own abuses of the Ryukyuans and falsely accusing them of committing "insults and injuries." It was a carefully constructed argument—but in Washington, saner heads prevailed. Via the secretary of the navy, President Franklin Pierce advised Perry that he appreciated his patriotism, but there was no congressional authority for an occupation of the kingdom, and such a move was unnecessary. By the time the president's reply reached the commander, though, it was already too late.[38]

The Return of Perry

In early 1854, Perry departed China in a fleet that, after merging with other vessels along the way, totaled nine ships and 1,800 men. Far larger than the previous year's expedition, it was designed to prove the Americans meant business. Arriving in Naha on 21 January 1854, US troops marched on Shuri Castle, where Perry announced to the regent that, until the Japanese government accepted his demands to open to trade, the Ryukyu Kingdom was under his control. To facilitate this hostage diplomacy, Perry ordered some sailors to stay on the island while he sailed north.[39]

On 13 February, the flotilla arrived in Japan. After some debate over where to meet—again Perry wanted the capital, Edo, but the samurai refused—the two sides finally agreed on the small village of Kanagawa. For the next weeks, Perry and Japanese officials negotiated the terms of the US-Japan deal. Although armed samurai and marines hovered behind the meetings, the discussions were generally calm. On 31 March, Perry and the daimyo's representative completed the Japan-US Treaty of Peace and Amity. Fundamentally, it complied with the three demands the secretary of state had tasked the commodore to fulfill: Shipwrecked American sailors were guaranteed protection, and ships were permitted to purchase supplies, including coal, at two ports (Shimoda, current Shizuoka Prefecture, and Hakodate, today's Hokkaido). The two nations also agreed that in the near future, Japan would accept a US consul, setting the stage for bilateral trade. The treaty was unprecedented—the first signed by Japan in modern times—and it was a major step in providing the United States with a foothold to extend its Manifest Destiny into Asia.

Overall, the negotiations had been amicable, accompanied by lavish parties and gift giving. Among the Japanese presents were sacks of rice delivered by sumo wrestlers and erotic *shunga* woodblock prints. American gifts included technological marvels never before seen by most Japanese, including a telegraph set and a miniature steam locomotive. (This time the samurai kept the presents instead of burning them.)[40]

After signing the treaty, the Americans sailed to Shimoda and Hakodate to inspect the newly accessible ports. During these visits, some sailors committed petty crimes, such as gambling in temples and stealing from shops. But upon their departure from Japan, translator Williams wrote, "Not a shot has been fired, not a man wounded . . . nor a Japanese to be found who is the worse, so far as we know, for the visit of the American Expedition."[41]

During Perry's absence, things had not gone so cordially in the Ryukyu Kingdom. At Naha market, one American had attempted to steal meat from a butcher. When the store owner tried to stop him, the sailor pulled out a knife, and in the ensuing struggle, the butcher clubbed him to the ground. More seriously, a sailor named William Board had been found dead in the harbor. The Ryukyuans alleged he had been drunk, fell into the water, and drowned. However, Bettelheim and one of the ship's doctors conducted a postmortem and concluded the sailor's skull had been fractured.[42]

Returning to Naha on 1 July, Perry learned of Board's death, and he ordered the Ryukyuan authorities to investigate. If the culprits were not handed over, he threatened, then his troops would occupy the kingdom's forts and blockade Naha Port. Conceding to US demands, the local officials turned to torture. "Many poor fellows have been pinioned and pounded already in their inquiries, and the chains lying around might tell more fearful stories if they could speak," noted Williams.[43]

After the authorities had completed their investigation, they presented Perry with the results: American sailors had embarked on a crime spree, and one of them had raped a woman. According to witnesses' statements, three of Perry's men had broken into a civilian's house, stolen liquor, and gotten drunk. Two of the sailors passed out in the street, while the third, Board, climbed over a wall into a woman's home and threatened her with his knife. "She cried out with a loud voice, but he held on to her; she was too weak to resist, and suffered his ravishment, losing all consciousness of herself," explained investigators. The woman's screams attracted the attention of a relative, who ran into the house and dragged Board away. A crowd of Ryukyuans chased the sailor through the streets, pelting him with stones, one of which struck Board's head, causing him to fall into the sea.[44]

The regent explained to Perry that the local authorities had concealed the circumstances of Board's death because "this rape not only was a great shame to the woman, but was also a mortifying disgrace to the country." The perpetrators would be banished to the impoverished outlying islands, and the local officials who had covered up the crime would be fired, the regent assured. On the American side, the sailors who broke into the house and stole the liquor were tried by court-martial—but Perry's notification to the secretary of the navy does not detail their punishments (if any). The official account of the expedition was careful to record that the commodore did send a "handsome present" to the victim, which turned out to be fifteen pieces of cloth.[45]

With the incident resolved to Perry's satisfaction (if not the Ryukyuans), the commander now turned his attention to the task of prizing open the kingdom to trade. Two years previously, upon his dispatch from the United States, the secretary of state had instructed him to act with the "consent of the natives" and "make no use of force." Now, Perry attempted to conceal his transgressions. In his official account of the treaty negotiations, he repeatedly emphasized that the Ryukyuan authorities willingly agreed to the terms, and the "business was thus happily completed." On the ground, though, members of Perry's party described a different story. The Ryukyuans wanted the text of the treaty to state that it had been signed under duress, but Perry refused.[46]

To ensure the Ryukyuans would not try to back out, on the day the compact was signed, Perry went ashore with a retinue, resembling an invasion force. The display revolted clerk Spalding, who the year before had compared US treatment of Ryukyuans as an eagle and a mouse. Now he again condemned Perry's actions: "Our government should pay a little attention to the fantastic tricks, which its commodorial gentry cut up in such countries, as Loo-Choo: 'fixed ammunition,' 'cutlasses,' and 'ball-cartridges,' taken ashore among a people whose forts are disarmed; among whom not one offensive weapon was noticed after months of intercourse."[47]

On 11 July 1854, Perry and Ryukyuan officials concluded the "Compact between the United States and the Kingdom of Lew-Chew." Although some of its clauses resembled those contained in the Japan-US treaty, such as support for shipwrecked sailors and the right to purchase supplies, Perry's coercion permeates this text. The compact's preamble orders Ryukyuans to treat all US visitors "with great courtesy and friendship." Then it grants Americans free rein of the kingdom—they "shall be at liberty to ramble where they please, without hindrance, or having officials sent to follow them, or to spy what they do." Unlike the treaty with Japan, the Ryukyu compact enshrined Americans' right to extraterritoriality: "If they violently go into houses, or trifle with women, . . . or do other such like illegal acts, they shall be arrested by the local officers, but not maltreated, and shall be reported to the captain of the ship to which they belong, for punishment by him." Adding insult to injury, Perry demanded that the kingdom maintain a cemetery for dead Americans, which included a grave for accused rapist Board.[48]

Both the Japan and the Ryukyu treaties were milestones in American efforts to exert mercantile and military influence in the Western Pacific. They proved that gunboat diplomacy was able to open long-closed nations, setting a pattern to build imperial outposts in the region from Hawai'i to the Philippines. Perry's civil approach in negotiations with Japan contrasted with his bullying behavior toward the Shuri authorities. By extracting humiliating concessions from the small kingdom, he dropped the guise of peaceable diplomacy, applying brute force against a population powerless to resist. At home, the United States embraced such violence against Native Americans, and now in Asia, Perry followed a pattern set by European nations to exert domination and establish the embryo of the US empire for the years to come.

Before leaving, Perry had one final goal: He wanted his accomplishments in the Ryukyu Kingdom to be immortalized at home. What better way than to embed his conquests into the world's tallest building then under construction, the Washington Monument? Perry ordered Ryukyuan officials to bring him stone blocks and a bell to top the structure; they summarily complied. The fate of these gifts provides a fitting postscript for Perry's visit to the islands: One of the stones was deemed inferior and was broken up to scrub a ship's decks; the second was lost and never arrived at the monument. As for the bell, the commander dismissed the first one proffered—so the Ryukyuans brought him the bell from the temple Bettelheim had occupied; this one met Perry's approval. Upon his return to the States, however, architects rejected the bell, and it ended up at the US Naval Academy at Annapolis, where it was rung to celebrate Navy wins in the annual Army vs. Navy football game. On VJ Day, 1945, it was hit so hard it cracked.[49]

Today, Perry's 1853–1854 expedition is celebrated in the United States and Japan. Both his home state of Rhode Island and Shimoda hold annual "Black Ships" commemorations, attended by embassy officials who praise the commodore for inaugurating Japan-US relations. Perry's arrival in the Ryukyu Kingdom is often left unmentioned—but it deserves examination because it presaged American treatment of the islands in the following century and today. Perry's proposal to annex the kingdom to advance American interests mirrored twentieth-century Cold War policy. Likewise, his claim that occupation would improve residents' lives became a common justification for American expansionism not only in Okinawa but also in Hawai'i, Puerto Rico, and elsewhere, as the United States veiled its colonial ambitions behind the guise of humanitarianism.

Although the US government ultimately rejected Perry's proposal to annex the kingdom, the commander's seizure of private property and abuse of the Ryukyuans set an example for his subordinates; they trespassed, robbed, and raped. For the islanders, these crimes were a taste of what would follow in the twentieth and twenty-first centuries—both the violence (which predominantly targeted women) and the military's response, whereby suspects were judged behind closed doors, punishments hidden, and token compensation doled out in lieu of open justice. Perhaps, then, it is unsurprising that modern Black Ships commemorations tend to leave unspoken Perry's visit to the Ryukyu Kingdom because this would necessitate an acknowledgment that, from the outset, US-Okinawa relations were born from intimidation, subjugation, and crime. Future impacts notwithstanding, equally calamitous were the shorter-term consequences of Perry's visit: Within twenty-five years of the commodore's departure, the Ryukyu Kingdom ceased to exist.

2

Disposal, Discrimination, and Diaspora

Four years after Commodore Matthew Perry and the Tokugawa shogunate completed the Japan-US Treaty of Peace and Amity, the United States foisted a trade agreement on Japan that was far from amicable. Under the terms of the 1858 Harris Treaty (named after the first US consul general to Japan, Townsend Harris), American merchants could sell their goods in Japan at ultralow tariffs, and US citizens were granted extraterritoriality, rendering them immune from Japanese law. On the heels of the Americans, European nations pressured the shogunate into signing similarly unequal agreements. Many in Japan feared they would soon be subjugated in the same way as other Asian states, and they doubted that their current leaders were capable enough to avert such a fate.

In 1868, a group of samurai staged an uprising that overthrew more than two and a half centuries of Tokugawa rule. Coming from domains in western Japan—including Satsuma—the rebels were young and low-ranking, but what they lacked in experience and resources, they made up for in political stratagem. They legitimized their revolution by co-opting the oldest and most respected symbol in the nation, the emperor. As head of the Shinto religion, according to Japanese myth, the emperor was descended from the founding gods and was himself a demigod—but at this time, his role was largely ceremonial, and he was housed in a palace in Kyoto. Now, the young samurai put the emperor front and center of their movement by bringing him to Edo—which they renamed Tokyo (the eastern capital)—and embarking on a series of revolutionary changes that overturned the centuries-old status quo.[1]

Under the auspices of Emperor Meiji—whose name meant "enlightened rule"—the new government launched the rapid modernization of almost all aspects of Japan to transform it from a loose affiliation of feudal domains into a unified nation capable of staving off foreign encroachment and proving to the world that Japan was an advanced sovereign state. In one of the earliest reforms, the Meiji leaders abolished the samurai class and replaced the daimyo-run domains with prefectures headed by governors. They adopted the slogan "Enrich the country and strengthen the military" (*Fukoku kyōhei*), which they hoped to achieve via an extraordinary U-turn: The shogunate had excluded foreigners, but now, the Meiji government tapped them for their expertise. Japanese leaders toured the United States and Europe to study their political, economic, and industrial systems, while Japan also imported thousands of foreign experts to oversee the nation's modernization.

Among the Meiji government's top priorities was the creation of a powerful military to suppress domestic backlash against its reforms and counter foreign threats. Under the guidance of Western experts, Japan constructed munition factories, military academies, and docks for warships. To replace the previous system of local armies, in 1872, the government introduced nationwide conscription for every male, training them in modern weaponry and tactics. In 1877, this new army defeated a large uprising of Satsuma warriors who had become discontented with government reforms; the victory ended the samurai era in mainland Japan. The danger from overseas, though, could not be as quickly vanquished. Japan believed it was vulnerable to foreign incursions at its peripheries—notably Ezo (current-day Hokkaido) in the north and the Ryukyu Kingdom in the south—where its borders were ill-defined and poorly defended. Now the Meiji government set out to assert its control.

Ezo was inhabited by the indigenous Ainu, and although the island had some small Japanese settlements, the Tokugawa shogunate had not officially staked any territorial claims there. To the north, Russians had begun to move into the nearby Sakhalin Islands, worrying the Meiji government that Ezo would be targeted next. To counter this threat, in 1869, Tokyo annexed Ezo, renaming it Hokkaido. The Meiji government's colonization was guided by US advisors, based on the same model by which Native American lands had been stolen: Japan declared Hokkaido terra nullius, seized all Ainu territory, and flooded it with settlers. The Meiji authorities successfully secured the northern border from Russian encroachment, but the costs for the indigenous population were catastrophic. They suffered from famine, epidemics, and the eradication of their traditional cultural practices; widespread resistance was ruthlessly suppressed.[2]

To settle the problem of its exposed southern border, Japan dispatched its new military on the nation's first overseas campaign of the modern era.

The Invasion of Taiwan

In December 1871, a ship from the Ryukyu Kingdom was caught in a storm and wrecked off the southern coast of Taiwan. Although the island nominally belonged to China, much of its territory was outside Beijing's governance and controlled by indigenous tribespeople. Survivors from the ship washed ashore at an area that was home to one of these tribes, the Paiwan. Accounts differ about what happened next. Some testimonies state that the Ryukyuans took food and drink from the tribe without displaying the appropriate etiquette, while others say the Paiwan tried—but failed—to obtain a ransom for the return of the castaways. Contradictory accounts aside, the results were indisputable: The tribespeople killed fifty-four Ryukyuans. Twelve other shipwreck survivors were able to escape the attack, and with the help of the Chinese authorities, they returned to the Ryukyu Kingdom. The Shuri government sent money to Beijing in thanks for its assistance.[3]

For Japan, the incident provided the perfect opportunity to advance its claims over the Ryukyu Kingdom. In 1872, Tokyo lodged a complaint with China over the killing of the Ryukyuans, whom it called "Japanese subjects," but Beijing denied its responsibility, asserting Taiwan's territory was not entirely under its control. Within Japan, the military was spoiling for a fight to test the mettle of its new troops and provide former samurai with an outlet to vent anger over their own abolition, especially after the government had shelved plans to invade Korea in 1873, so Meiji leaders gave the army the green light to launch a punitive expedition.[4]

Japan assembled 3,500 troops accompanied by a handful of American Civil War veterans hired as advisors. The incursion into southern Taiwan lasted from May to December 1874, resulting in the deaths of an unknown number of indigenous Taiwanese and more than 550 Japanese troops, most of whom died from malaria. Emperor Meiji awarded one of the American soldiers the Order of the Rising Sun in recognition of his support for the Japanese military.[5]

Despite the high fatalities, Japan claimed the expedition was a success, and it forced China into talks where Beijing agreed to pay compensation for the dead Ryukyuans (only a small portion of the moneys ended up in the kingdom). And Japan received something far more valuable: China recognized that the Ryukyuans were Japanese subjects, substantiating the Meiji government's claims of ownership over the southern territory. The expedition also taught Japan that China was no longer the invincible superpower that had dominated the region for millennia; now it was militarily weak and reluctant to respond to threats to its vassal states. It was a lesson Japan would fully exploit in the years to come.[6]

Ryukyu Shobun: The Disposal of a Kingdom

Following Commodore Perry's departure from the Ryukyu Kingdom in 1854, European powers had arrived to strike similar agreements with the Shuri government. In 1855, France signed the Convention entre la France et les Iles

Liou-Tchou, and four years later, the Netherlands signed the Traktaat tusschen Nederlanden en Lioe-Kioe. Meanwhile, the Ryukyu Kingdom continued to send tribute missions to China. Despite such overseas relations, the kingdom suffered from dire economic problems. The Satsuma were still appropriating the proceeds of the kingdom's trade, plus they had upped taxes on the islands. Ordinary Ryukyuans suffered from extreme poverty; conditions were especially atrocious on the outlying islands of Miyako and Yaeyama, where residents were forced to pay the Shuri government's extortionate poll tax while still recovering from the catastrophic 1771 tsunami. In Tokyo, the new Meiji leaders believed that the kingdom was becoming ever more vulnerable to foreign occupation, and they needed to take control of the islands before another nation acted.[7]

Japan orchestrated its annexation of the Ryukyu Kingdom in incremental steps, initially veiling the takeover behind an illusion of largesse. In 1872, the foreign minister summoned Shuri officials to Tokyo to thank the king for his loyalty to Japan and announce he had been awarded a mansion in the capital and a generous grant. At the same time, Tokyo declared that it had decided to transform the kingdom into a *han* (feudal territory), so henceforth Japan would manage its foreign affairs to better negotiate with China over reparations for the Ryukyuans killed in Taiwan. At this time, Tokyo confiscated the international trade agreements the kingdom had signed with the United States, France, and the Netherlands. (Today, Japan's Ministry of Foreign Affairs still retains these documents, but it claims not to know how it originally obtained them.)[8]

In 1875, the Meiji government accelerated its attempts to annex the Ryukyu Kingdom. The maneuvers were headed by a bureaucrat from the Ministry of Home Affairs, Matsuda Michiyuki, whose name still ignites enmity among Okinawans due to his arrogance toward the islands. Matsuda demanded that the Shuri government halt its relations with China and close its diplomatic quarters at Fuzhou, Fujian Province. He lectured Ryukyuan officials that the ongoing existence of their kingdom was an affront to the Japanese government and complained they were more loyal to their king than the emperor. He delivered a list of demands to reorganize the civil service to conform with nationwide norms, thereby dismantling much of the prevailing aristocratic system, and to introduce national holidays in honor of the Meiji emperor. Matsuda announced a plan to dispatch a garrison of Japanese troops to the kingdom. Although he framed the deployment as necessary to protect the island, Ryukyuans perceived it as a threat to force them into compliance.[9]

Shuri officials rebuffed Matsuda's demands and secretly sent a team of diplomats to China to appeal for its intervention. Beijing hesitated On one hand, now that the tribute system was all but obsolete, the kingdom's economic value was insignificant, but on the other hand, the islands might serve as useful pawns in the power games wracking the region. While China sat on the sidelines, some

Ryukyuan leaders held out hopes that Beijing would dispatch warships to protect the islands from Japan.[10]

In 1875, Japan began to implement the reforms demanded by Matsuda, establishing a military garrison in Naha by seizing large areas of farmland and announcing the restructuring of the feudal ranks. The presence of the Japanese officials sparked demonstrations, especially in the Chinese enclave of Kume, and some residents fled to Fuzhou to petition the Beijing government for support. The Ryukyu officials also dispatched appeals for diplomatic intervention to the signatories of its international treaties: the United States, France, and the Netherlands.[11]

For a time, the kingdom's fate hung in limbo as the Japanese government was preoccupied with the suppression of the 1877 Satsuma uprising. But in late 1878, the Meiji leaders received some information that forced them to refocus: China was planning to request mediation in the Ryukyu issue from Ulysses S. Grant. The former Civil War commander had just completed a two-term presidency, and he was internationally renowned as the man who had saved the Union. After leaving the White House, Grant was now traveling on a global tour scheduled to visit Asia the following year. Japan feared that intercession by the ex-president might complicate—or even scotch—its claims on the kingdom, so it decided to accelerate its annexation.[12]

On 25 March 1879, Matsuda arrived in Naha accompanied by more than 160 police and some 400 soldiers. Two days later, he headed to Shuri Castle and announced that henceforth the kingdom was abolished and the territory was a prefecture of Japan. King Shō Tai was permitted four days to vacate the castle, after which he was to move to Tokyo. Matsuda justified these actions as punishment for ignoring Japan's previous orders to restructure. Japanese officials seized the royal records and transported them to Tokyo.[13]

As Shō Tai prepared to depart Shuri Castle, his retainers packed up vast amounts of gold, silver, and other treasures and relocated them to other royal residences. Then, on 30 March, the king was carried out of the castle in a palanquin accompanied by his two wives, sons, and servants; aristocrats lined the paths and sobbed. Following his departure, Japanese troops occupied Shuri Castle, allowing it in the coming years to fall into disrepair. Two months later, Shō Tai left the islands for Tokyo, where in 1884 he was awarded the title of marquis and lived in luxury until his death in 1902.[14]

The occupation of Shuri Castle and exile of its king brought an end to the 450-year Ryukyu Kingdom. The Meiji government was eager to depict the annexation as a domestic administrative issue. It asserted that the kingdom had been a Japanese vassal since the Satsuma invasion of 1609, and its assimilation aligned with the same processes conducted with the other former domains. Such an argument was disputed then—as today—by critics who stress the kingdom was an independent state that had signed international treaties with three foreign nations. They also emphasize the forcefulness of the annexation, which was conducted by four-hundred-plus armed Japanese, resembling an invasion more than a bureaucratic reshuffling.[15]

English-language descriptions of the annexation reflect these competing visions. The modern Japanese government and many history books refer to the Ryukyu *Disposition*, a word suggesting a rearrangement of the existing order. The term used in Japanese—*shobun*—better reflects the reality of the Meiji government's actions. As well as *disposition*, the word carries two further meanings: The first is *to dispose* [such as in the common expression *gomi o shobun* (to get rid of the trash)], and the second is *to punish*, which is perhaps most appropriate given Matsuda's justification for abolishing the kingdom after it dared to refuse Japanese demands. The appropriate terminology is not a lexical quibble; in the following decades (as later chapters explain), the Japanese and American governments have continued to manipulate semantics to sweeten unjust policies and conceal abuses against the islands' residents.[16]

A Proposal to Divide the Islands

The Meiji government hoped its annexation of the Ryukyu Kingdom would signal to the international community that the islands were Japan's indisputable territory. Beijing, though, after years of prevarication, decided to assert its influence over the tiny kingdom it had hitherto abandoned to its fate. Within the Chinese government, there had been disagreement over how to react to the disposal. Some advocated war—on the grounds that Tokyo's takeover might set a precedent for a seizure of China's vassal, Korea, which Japan had eyed for centuries. The 1874 invasion of Taiwan, though, had shown Beijing that Japan had become militarily powerful, so instead of direct conflict, it sought the mediation of someone who might oppose Tokyo's claims over the kingdom.[17]

Despite no longer being in the US government, ex-President Grant still possessed political sway on the global stage. By the early summer of 1879, his round-the-world tour had brought him to China. In June, government officials met Grant and spelled out their country's close relationship with the Ryukyu Kingdom. They explained that although China had never governed the islands, it had received tribute payments and helped to educate Ryukyuans in Beijing. They also asserted that the islanders would prefer to continue relations with China instead of Japan. The Beijing officials entreated Grant to request that Japan rescind its assertion of sovereignty over the kingdom and allow King Shō Tai to return to his throne. Although the former president did not explicitly express support for the Chinese position, he sympathized with their argument that Japanese control of the islands would severely curtail China's access to the Pacific Ocean.[18]

In July, Grant arrived in Tokyo, where, between tours designed by his Japanese hosts to display their nation's modernization, he discussed the Ryukyu disposal with officials and Emperor Meiji. Japanese leaders politely explained that it was a domestic matter, and no dispute over sovereignty of the islands existed; his official help would not be necessary. The assertion ran counter to what Grant had learned in China, so during talks with the emperor, the ex-president explained Beijing's side of the argument. He suggested a compromise between the two nations: a "boundary running between the Ryukyu Islands so as to give China a wide channel to the Pacific." The idea—which involved partitioning the territory between Japan and China—became known as *bunto kaiyaku*, the divided-islands proposal.[19]

Originally, Japan's leaders had not considered splicing the former kingdom, but wishing to respect Grant's counsel, they decided to adopt his proposal to cede the Miyako and Yaeyama Islands. There was one significant addition: Japan would also ask Beijing for most-favored-nation status in trade. The Chinese government agreed to the proposal—and they planned to return the islands to the control of the exiled king.[20]

The *bunto kaiyaku* appalled some Ryukyuan aristocrats, whose centuries of exploitation of these outlying islands had rendered them impoverished. Chinese officials, too, voiced dissatisfaction over the plan to give Tokyo such generous trading privileges. As a result, in the days before the signing of the deal in late October, the Chinese government backtracked on the agreement. In the following weeks, Japan continued to urge Beijing to sign—but it disregarded the offers. Finally, in January 1881, Tokyo revoked the proposal, informing the Chinese government that the issue was no longer negotiable and the former Ryukyu Kingdom belonged to Japan.[21]

Both the *shobun* and the *bunto kaiyaku* set a precedent for Japan's subsequent treatment of Okinawa. First, the disposal highlighted the fact that the islands could be arbitrarily annexed; then the proposal to divide showed how they could be carved up to satisfy Tokyo's economic and geopolitical whims—with zero consultation or consideration for the people who lived there. The Shimazu samurai had displayed similar behavior in 1609, when they cleaved Amami-Ōshima and Tokunoshima from the kingdom. Likewise, in the early 1850s, the Tokugawa shogunate had approved plans to open the islands to trade in the hope the concession might yield to foreign nations' demands for access while keeping them safely distant from the mainland. The *bunto kaiyaku* was the latest signal that the islands could be sacrificed to serve Japanese needs, presaging Tokyo's twentieth-century policies, when it repeated a similar tactic not once or twice but three times—in 1945, 1951, and 1972—with devastating consequences for the islands' residents.

Preserving the Old Customs

Following its annexation of the Ryukyu Kingdom, Tokyo dispatched a governor and bureaucrats from the mainland to administer the new prefecture. Meanwhile, many ex-samurai from Satsuma, having been defeated in their 1877 rebellion, moved to Okinawa to join the ranks of the new civil service and police force. The moves sparked resistance from former Shuri government officials, some of whom refused to obey their new overseers, while others fled to Fuzhou, where they appealed for Chinese intervention to restore the kingdom to royal rule.[22]

Without the cooperation of the Ryukyu ruling class, Japanese officials realized it would be impossible to administer the new prefecture. They did not even speak the same language as the people they were trying to control. So the Japanese government implemented a policy, later known as *kyūkan onzon*—the preservation of the old customs. Unlike in mainland Japan, where it had abolished the feudal system, including samurai class, during the 1870s, in Okinawa, it allowed the aristocracy (*yukatchu*) to retain their status. It paid stipends to the highest-ranking and offered economic support for the lower ranks. At the same time, the Meiji government retained the Ryukyu Kingdom's system of taxation and land ownership. Such measures won over the support of many of the elite, who were happy to keep their privileges—and Japan was able to reap high revenues in taxes.[23]

For most Okinawans, though, *kyūkan onzon* doomed them to ongoing destitution. Prefectural officials referred to them as "tax-paying machines" whose sole purpose was to provide income to their landlords and the government. In 1882, one survey described the harsh conditions of farmers who dwelled in low hovels built from thatch and bamboo: "They lived with pigs and sheep, were bitten by mosquitoes and flies, ate potatoes, wore poor kimono, were exposed to the elements, had no shoes, and shut themselves up at home, drinking only the occasional awamori." Conditions in Miyako Island, where the poll tax on all residents continued, were even bleaker, and the *yukatchu* refused to allow the children of commoners to attend school. Moreover, local officials' rule was riddled with bribery and corruption.[24]

Economic conditions were so dire that many lower-class aristocrats slipped into poverty. To help them, the governor announced that he would open common land (*somayama*) to development—but the policy ended up benefiting only the wealthy and denied commoners access to much-needed supplies of lumber and water. Ordinary Okinawans rebelled against these injustices, rioting in Aguni Island (1881) and Yabu Village (1883). The governor responded by prohibiting protests. On Miyako Island, a movement developed to demand the abolition of the poll tax—but the *yukatchu* resisted its appeals. In an unprecedented move, the farmers traveled to Tokyo to present a petition to the national government. The poll tax, though, remained in place until 1903.[25]

For two decades following the Ryukyu Disposal, the policy of *kyūkan onzon* ensured that the new prefecture remained undeveloped, locked in the past socially and economically. All of this was in stark contrast to mainland Japan, where modernization was proceeding at breakneck speed.

The Ongoing Meiji Revolution

Between the late nineteenth and early twentieth centuries, mainland Japan underwent one of the most rapid transformations in human history. The Meiji government built extensive rail and telegraph networks and invested in modern mines, shipyards, and factories. To overhaul the nation's finances, it introduced a new currency (the yen), banks, and the country's first stock exchange. In 1889, the government proclaimed a constitution to consolidate domestic power and demonstrate to the international community that Japan was a modern state. Modeled on the constitution of the German Empire, Japan's document recognized the emperor as "sacred and inviolable," with the power to command the military and declare war, but it also established a two-house parliament (the Diet), including an elected lower house. Although suffrage was initially limited to only the highest taxpayers, this was extended in the following years until 1925, when all adult males were granted the right to vote.

On the surface, the reforms influenced almost every aspect of the nation, transforming the lives of ordinary Japanese, some of whom adopted Western clothing and foods like bread, milk, and beer. But in many ways, life was grim; farmers were burdened with the high taxes the government had introduced to finance its reforms, and the new industrial working class—especially women— faced dangerous conditions in the recently built factories. At the same time, there remained large variations throughout the country in customs and dialects. For centuries, people had identified with their local domains, so now Japan's leaders sought to eliminate these parochial loyalties to create a unified national consciousness. They centered this process around the young demigod Emperor Meiji. As the head of the Shinto religion, he represented the spiritual origins of Japan, and now the government employed the symbol of the emperor to inculcate a Japanese identity in two main ways: militarism and education.

Having introduced conscription in 1872, one decade later, the government published the Imperial Precepts to Soldiers and Sailors, which declared that military personnel ought to display unquestionable loyalty to the emperor. Its most famous phrase extoled the credo: "Duty is weightier than a mountain, while death is lighter than a feather." These virtues were embodied at a shrine in Tokyo that in 1879 the emperor named Yasukuni (Peaceful Country). Fusing Shintoism, the sanctity of the emperor, and glorification of the military, it became a site where all those who died for their country were enshrined and worshipped as divinities. Militarism also permeated schools. In 1890, the government issued the Imperial Rescript on Education, which urged students to revere the emperor and "should emergency arise, offer yourselves courageously to the state." The rescript presaged the educational principles in the following years, which indoctrinated young Japanese in their duty to sacrifice themselves for the glory of the emperor.[26]

Japan's rapid social, technological, and political progress enabled it to fend off the colonialism suffered by other Asian states. And slowly, by proving itself a modern nation in the eyes of the West, Japan managed to rectify some of the injustices foisted by the unfair treaties in the early days of its opening. By 1899, Japan was able to end extraterritoriality, now allowing it to judge foreign nationals in its own courts. In the same year, it began to chip away at the low tariffs, finally winning the right to set its own rates in 1911.

Empire Japan

At the same time as Japan managed to resist Western colonization, it set about establishing an empire of its own. Guided by a Japanese brand of Manifest Destiny that envisioned an enlightened, racially superior Japan spreading civilization to its backward neighbors, more pragmatically, imperialism also provided the Meiji government with natural resources and land for its growing population. Japan's colonialism came at the expense of a crumbling China, whose previous mightiness had been hobbled by corruption, uprisings, and foreign incursions.

First, Japan set its sights on the Chinese vassal Korea. Throughout the 1870s and 1880s, Tokyo and Beijing jostled for influence over the peninsula; in 1894, this erupted into the First Sino-Japan War. In the nine-month conflict, Japan's navy and army won overwhelming successes against the Chinese military, extending the combat far beyond Korea, deep into Manchuria. It ended in a humiliating defeat for China; the Treaty of Shimonoseki (1895) forced China to relinquish Korea as a vassal and admit its independence, and it granted Japanese traders access to Chinese ports. The treaty also ceded Taiwan to Japan, where in the coming years, Japan developed its infrastructure and industries while spreading Japanese language and customs at the expense of local culture.

As well as Taiwan, the Treaty of Shimonoseki granted Japan its first foothold on the Chinese mainland, the Liaodong Peninsula, including the strategically important Port Arthur naval base. But now, Japan experienced its own humiliation when it was ordered by Russia, France, and Germany to relinquish control of the peninsula to China. Under the threat of foreign military action, Tokyo reluctantly conceded to the demand. Following Japan's withdrawal, Russia moved into the peninsula for itself, while France and Germany snatched up other Chinese territories. It was a clear signal to the Meiji government that Western nations wanted to derail their colonial ambitions, and they deemed Japan unworthy of respect. The experience rankled with many Japanese leaders.

For the next decade, Russia and Japan competed for control over Manchuria and Korea. Then on 8 February 1904, Japan avenged its earlier humiliation by launching a surprise attack on Russian forces at Port Arthur. In the following year-and-a-half war, a series of large-scale land battles took place in Korea and Manchuria, resulting in the deaths of some 70,000 Russian and 86,000 Japanese troops. Russia dispatched its Baltic fleet, but at the Battle of Tsushima in May 1905, the Japanese navy sank two-thirds of the ships.

With both sides exhausted by the war, Japan and Russia agreed to peace talks overseen by President Theodore Roosevelt. The resulting Treaty of Portsmouth (1905) quashed Russia's colonial ambitions in East Asia, ceding to Japan control of the Liaodong Peninsula and the South Manchuria Railway. This was the first time in modern history that an Asian nation had defeated a European one. The victory cemented Japan's status as the region's preeminent power. In the same year, Japan and the United States also struck a colonialists' secret quid pro quo—the Taft-Katsura Agreement—whereby Washington accepted Tokyo's rule over Korea in return for recognition of its own control over the Philippines.

With this green light from the United States, Japan moved to occupy Korea. First, Tokyo announced the peninsula as its protectorate; then it dissolved the military. Koreans rebelled—but they were viciously suppressed; those who were not killed fled into exile. In August 1910, Tokyo officially annexed Korea, enforcing rule with Japanese military-police brutality and controls of the press. The colonial authorities ordered surveys that stripped property from many Korean farmers. The land was subsequently bought by Japanese corporations and settled by Japanese migrants. In the coming years, Tokyo initiated discriminatory policies that sought to eradicate Korean culture and exploit its people militarily and economically, via conscription and forced labor, and sexually, via comfort stations.

When World War I broke out in 1914, Japan declared itself on the side of the Allies, ostensibly to fulfill an alliance signed with Great Britain a dozen years earlier, but a stronger motivation was the opportunity to expand its territory. Soon after entering the conflict, Japan occupied German possessions in Asia—Tsingtao, China—and in the Pacific—the Marshall Islands, the Carolinas, and the Marianas, including Saipan and neighboring Tinian.

In 1919, Japan's leaders joined the Versailles Peace Conference as victors, and they felt it was finally time to be recognized as equals to their Western allies.

The peace treaty granted Japan possession of Germany's former colonies, but it prohibited any military build-up in the Pacific islands. Japan was appointed a permanent member of the new League of Nations, and Tokyo proposed a clause for its covenant guaranteeing racial equality. Japan hoped this would secure respect from Western nations and recognition as a colonial power, but the motion was blocked by the United States, Great Britain, and Australia. Empire building, the rejection signaled, was a prerogative allowed only for White nations. The snub engendered Japanese bitterness for many years.

Nevertheless, Japan's territorial gains in World War I capped a series of stunning military successes via which, in a little more than two decades, it had staved off the threat of foreign encroachment and built a sprawling empire. Whether Western nations officially recognized Japan as an equal or not, the redrawn map of Asia proved it had become the strongest nation in the region and a colonial power in its own right. For those whose territories had been seized, though, their new Japanese colonizers proved as oppressive as their predecessors.

Okinawa: A Quasi-Colony

As Japan expanded its empire, Okinawa remained a quasi-colony, existing in a limbo in which it was neither an integral part of Japan nor a foreign territory. Unlike in mainland Japan, Okinawans did not possess the right to vote in national elections, nor was there a prefectural assembly. The islands were administered by mainland-born governors, and most administrative positions were held by Japanese bureaucrats. Because Okinawa lacked natural resources, the Meiji government made few investments in the islands' infrastructure and failed to build up industry. Japanese merchants dominated commerce, controlling the import and export of goods to the prefecture, with the cooperation of the former king and aristocratic class. Under the ongoing promotion of the old customs, the *yukatchu* continued to receive stipends, and the lack of land redistribution kept most Okinawans struggling to survive on tiny farms.

Exacerbating the poverty of ordinary Okinawans was the continuing burden of taxes. Japan continued to earn much more money from the prefecture than it invested. For many farmers, the only way to meet these demands was to cultivate sugarcane, which the government allowed to be submitted in lieu of cash tax payments. Encouraged by the national and prefectural governments, more and more farmers transformed their rice paddies into fields of sugarcane. The crops were shipped by the national government to Osaka, where they were sold at fluctuating prices. This dependence on sugar worsened the living conditions of Okinawa's farmers. They became less self-sufficient for food and increasingly reliant on imported rice. At the turn of the century, Okinawa was a backward, sugar-producing territory run for the benefit of Japan—it was trapped in the past by the policy of *kyūkan onzon* and denied the progress of Meiji modernization.

Japanese journalists visiting the islands were struck by the persistence of the feudal system, the disdain that *yukatchu* held toward commoners, and the poverty of farmers. But the journalists expressed little sympathy for Okinawans, instead focusing on how they seemed to subsist on strange foods—sweet potatoes and pork—and wore unusual kimono. They appeared more interested in spending money on their family tombs than their family homes, and they practiced the vulgar pursuit of karate. Combined, these depictions represented Okinawans as *dojin*—literally "dirt people"—primitive aboriginals who were less civilized than "real" Japanese. Buttressing such racist arguments, in the early twentieth century, Japanese university professors traveled to the islands and looted dozens of skeletons from tombs with the purpose of applying eugenics to prove that Okinawans were racially inferior to mainlanders.[27]

Discrimination toward Okinawans was exemplified in 1903 at the Fifth National Industrial Exhibition, Osaka. Promoted as a showcase for Japanese technological development, event organizers further saw it as an opportunity to display the nation's colonial possessions. They built a Human Pavilion (Jinruikan) that exhibited Ainu from Hokkaido and indigenous people from Taiwan. Alongside them, in a thatched hut, were two Okinawan women dressed in traditional Ryukyuan royal robes overseen by a Japanese man holding a whip. When news of the display reached Okinawa, many people were furious. It was an explicit sign of how mainland Japanese regarded them as inferior. A quarter-century after their islands had been made a prefecture, they were still regarded as exotic specimens who were not fully Japanese.[28] The islands' first newspaper, the *Ryukyu Shimpo*, published an editorial decrying the organizers of the Human Pavilion: "They specifically chose [to display] the people of our prefecture together with the aborigines of Taiwan and North Sea Ainu. This makes us seem as primitive as the Ainu. What greater insult could there be to us?"[29]

The comment captured the contradictory feelings of many Okinawans. Although they resented being the butt of discrimination from mainland Japanese, at the same time, rather than empathizing with other colonial subjects, they adopted the same prejudicial attitudes as their oppressors toward the Ainu. The Human Pavilion episode was an eye-opener for Okinawans, and for many, the takeaway was simple: To avoid being perceived as uncivilized *dojin*, they would need to suppress the aspects of their identity that differentiated them from mainland Japanese; assimilation (*dōka*) was the pathway to achieve acceptance.

Assimilation

The First Sino-Japan War (1894–1895) was a turning point. During the conflict, some Okinawans still loyal to the former Ryukyu Kingdom visited temples to pray that China would win in the hope that Chinese forces would then liberate their islands. But Japan's overwhelming victory convinced many Okinawans that China's days of power were now past, and their futures lay with Japan. In the coming years, the push for assimilation was external, imposed by the national government, and internal, embraced by local leaders.[30]

Since annexing the kingdom, Japanese authorities had initiated policies to prohibit some indigenous customs, including bans on bone-washing rituals and the traditional men's hairstyle, *katakashira*. Many of these measures undermined the important roles women played in the islands' religions, such as scrapping official recognition (and salaries) of *noro* priestesses because Shinto shrines only permitted male priests. Another noticeable prohibition was related to female tattooing (*hajichi*). Since the days of the Ryukyu Kingdom, Okinawan women's hands had been inked with geometric designs to denote marriage; ward off ill fortune; and deter abductions to Japan, where such tattoos were seen as unattractive. In 1899, the Meiji government outlawed tattooing throughout the nation, hoping to show the international community that Japan was an advanced nation. Some Okinawans welcomed the ban as a means to assimilate. There were even cases where teachers attempted to burn off students' tattoos with hydrochloric acid.[31]

Some members of the islands' elite were the most ardent supporters of assimilation. Iha Fuyu, the pioneering scholar of Okinawan studies, promoted the historical similarities between Okinawa and Japan, and he equated the Ryukyu Disposal as a "liberation of slaves" that freed Okinawans from the constraints of feudalism. The newspaper *Ryukyu Shimpo* was very influential in promoting assimilation. Led by its editor-in-chief Ōta Chōfu, who had penned the essay denouncing the Human Pavilion, he urged Okinawans to embrace assimilation so closely that they should learn to sneeze like Japanese.[32]

As on mainland Japan, the Meiji government attempted to impose a sense of national identity on Okinawans via militarism and education. In the former, the authorities encountered resistance. Whereas Tokyo had introduced conscription in the mainland in 1872, it waited until 1898 to implement it in Okinawa. In contrast to Japan, where centuries of samurai rule had glorified warrior ethics, the Ryukyu Kingdom did not possess such an ingrained culture of militarism. Indeed, some Okinawans sought to dodge the draft by fleeing overseas or making themselves ineligible for conscription by lopping off a finger. Between 1898 and 1915, there were 774 reported cases of draft evasion. In 1910, opposition to military service triggered a full-scale riot in Motobu Village when a conscription officer harassed a resident claiming a medical exemption. More than twenty residents were arrested, and the authorities dispatched an armed officer to the local school to discourage further draft evasion. In response to this resistance, some elite Okinawans railed against conscription dodgers by claiming they made islanders appear unpatriotic.[33]

Major attempts to assimilate centered on language. The Ryukyu Archipelago possesses six distinct language varieties—including those in Amami, Okinawa Island, and Yaeyama. Although these languages share some similarities with Japanese, they are mutually incomprehensible—akin to the differences between English and German. Despite these variations, when Matsuda and Japanese bureaucrats annexed Okinawa in the 1870s, they defined the Ryukyuan languages as *dialects* of Japanese. Not only did this categorization devalue the importance of Okinawan languages and, by association, Okinawan culture, but it also contributed to imposing a facade of homogeneity on the country. The "Japanese as one race who share a single language" remains a powerful concept among many conservatives to this day.[34]

In 1907, the prefectural government introduced the Ordinance to Regulate Dialects, which prohibited the use of Okinawan languages in the classroom. Students who broke the rule were forced to wear a *hogen fuda* (dialect plaque), a badge of shame, around their necks—the only way to remove it was to identify another classmate who spoke the language and pass it on to them. It was a self-policing system, similar to the "Welsh Not" in Great Britain that encouraged children to regard their own languages as a source of shame. At the same time, many Okinawans began to adopt Japanese-sounding surnames; for example, changing *Tamagushiku* to *Tamaki* and *Nakandakari* to *Nakamura*.[35]

As some Okinawans began to show a willingness to abandon their Ryukyuan identities, the central government belatedly introduced policies that brought the islands up to date with the rest of the nation. In 1899, it initiated reforms on land ownership. Then in 1909, it abolished the feudal system, ending stipends for the *yukatchu* more than three decades after the abolition of such payments to samurai in mainland Japan. Finally, Tokyo bestowed the political rights long held by other prefectures. In 1909, it permitted the creation of a prefectural assembly, and in 1912, it granted Okinawa's main island the right to vote in national elections—but it did not allow the long-abused residents of Miyako and Yaeyama to vote until seven years later.[36]

On paper, Okinawa Prefecture now appeared to have been integrated into Japan—but in practice, it was still ruled from afar as a quasi-colony run by mediocre bureaucrats who resented being sent to work there. In 1916, Tokyo appointed a new governor, Odagiri Iwatarō, a native of Nagano Prefecture. He quit the position after only a week without even setting foot on the island, likening the posting to a punishment. Newspaper editor Ōta summed up the national government's treatment of Okinawa as a "dumping ground" for inferior public officials.[37]

The Okinawan Diaspora

Following World War I, the Japanese economy fell into depression, and Okinawa was particularly hard hit. In 1921, the prefecture received a further blow when global sugar prices plummeted, but the Japanese government refused to intervene to help. On the contrary, in the 1920s, Okinawa shouldered a disproportionate tax burden, paying triple what the government invested in the prefecture. The impact on Okinawa was devastating: Farmers, companies, and the prefectural government went bankrupt, and unemployment rose to 40 percent. The period became known as *sotetsu jigoku* (cycad hell), as residents were forced to subsist on palm ferns, which, unless carefully prepared, can be poisonous.[38]

With no other means to support themselves, tens of thousands of Okinawans migrated to the mainland or overseas. In Japan, many settled in the industrial belts of Osaka and Yokohama, where they discovered the futility of their attempts to assimilate. Employment offices and boardinghouses displayed signs warning, "No Koreans, no Okinawans." Some mainlanders saw them as backward *dojin* who still worshipped their ancestors and spoke foreign languages. Bosses paid Okinawans lower wages, assigned them to worse dormitories, and even refused to pay compensation after accidents.

On 1 September 1923, a 7.9 magnitude earthquake struck the Tokyo area, killing some 140,000 and sparking catastrophic fires. In the aftermath, Japanese police and vigilantes massacred Koreans and political dissidents, whom they claimed had been committing crimes. Mobs also targeted Okinawan immigrants, who, because of their accents, were suspected of being Koreans. The same earthquake destroyed the records of the Ryukyu Kingdom that had been confiscated by the Japanese government following the disposal and brought for storage in Tokyo. The loss contributed to the erasure of the kingdom's history.[39]

The diaspora overseas began with the efforts of the Kin-born social activist Toyama Kyuzo, known today as the father of migration. In 1899, he organized the first relocation of thirty Okinawans to Hawai'i and, five years later, more than one hundred migrants to the Philippines. Toyama penned a tanka poem, expressing his hopes for Okinawan migration, including the phrase, "Off we go! The world's five continents are our home."[40] In the early years of the twentieth century, Okinawans took Toyama's words to heart, spreading to countries around the globe, particularly Peru, Brazil, and Argentina. Toyama envisaged migration as a means for Okinawans to overcome poverty and discrimination—and in many cases, they succeeded in creating better living conditions. But even overseas, some experienced prejudice not only from the local population but also from Japanese migrants. In Hawai'i, for example, some Japanese avoided marriage to Okinawans and derided them for raising pigs.[41]

In 1924, the United States implemented the Immigration Act, which prohibited Asians from moving there. The Japanese government lodged complaints with Washington, but they were ignored. With America now off-limits, Okinawans headed to the Japanese colonies of Taiwan and the southern mandate islands seized from Germany, especially Saipan and Tinian, where they labored in the sugarcane and fishing industries. Between 1899 and 1938, some 12 percent of Okinawa's population migrated overseas. Their remittances contributed approximately 60 percent of the prefecture's income. Without the toil of these migrants, the situation in the home islands would have been even more dire than it already was.[42]

Living away from home was a lonely and stressful experience for Okinawan migrants, so they created community organizations, the most famous of which are *kenjin kai* (prefectural associations). These groups helped new arrivals to find work and housing, and they organized Okinawan festivals for homesick expats and provided funds for coming-of-age ceremonies and weddings. Some communities also adopted the traditional practice of *moai*, a mutual-aid system whereby members contributed money on a regular basis and could draw upon the pooled funds at times of need.

Although differing in their degrees of political activism, some Okinawan groups fought hard to tackle discrimination and organize better working conditions. The islands' languages, which their bosses could not understand, became tools of resistance, enabling workers openly to discuss strikes and other actions. The Kansai Okinawa Kenjin Kai, created in 1924, was founded by socialists and became very active in organizing for better working conditions in the Osaka region. It provided legal assistance and successfully negotiated compensation for injured workers and those who had been unfairly dismissed, and it initiated collective bargaining with employers to secure better wages.[43]

Overseas, too, *kenjin kai* and similar organizations provided support for Okinawan migrants and helped them to survive life in their new homes. Thanks to the sustained endeavors of overseas Okinawans, those left behind were able to survive the starvation of the *sotetsu* hell. Migrants also gained an awareness of international issues, giving some the ability to see through Japanese government propaganda. As the next chapter shows, this skill helped to save lives during World War II. But migration brought its own risks, particularly for the tens of thousands of Okinawans who joined the grand Japanese imperial venture and moved to the colonies of Saipan and Tinian, places that soon became synonymous with the carnage of the Pacific War.

3

The Storm of Iron

In 1929, the Wall Street crash plunged the global economy into depression, causing turmoil in Japan. Exports plummeted, incomes tumbled, and rural communities starved. As the nation's leaders struggled to relieve the crisis, ultraright organizations asserted the solution lay in increased militarism—at home and overseas. In the 1930s, rogue members of the Japanese army and navy staged a slew of assassinations of cabinet members and attempted coup d'etats aimed at overthrowing the civilian government system. Although these putsches failed, they established the power of militarists in Japanese politics.

Simultaneously, in China, the local garrison of the Japanese army had been urging Tokyo to take control of Manchuria but to no avail. So on 18 September 1931, Japanese soldiers forced their government's hand by staging a false flag attack. They detonated a small explosion near the tracks of the Japanese-run South Manchurian Railway and blamed it on Chinese nationalists. Using the incident as a pretext, in the following weeks, Japanese troops fanned out across Manchuria, forcing the Chinese government into quick capitulation. The army announced the establishment of a puppet state called Manchukuo, but Japan's leaders refused to formally recognize it. After military officers assassinated the prime minister in Tokyo on 15 May 1932, though, the government relented. The occupation was a significant political win for Japanese militarists and a money maker for the army and industrialists. They exploited Manchuria's agriculture and reserves of coal and iron, attracting impoverished Japanese to migrate with promises of jobs and farmland. In the coming years, 1.5 million Japanese flooded into the colony. To fund its occupation, the Japanese army borrowed a lesson from Victorian-era British colonialists and transformed Manchukuo into a narco-state; 20 percent of its revenues were derived from the sale of opium.[1]

Organized Chinese resistance to Japanese rule had been undermined by hostilities between communist and nationalist forces—but the two sides came together in a United Front to expel the occupiers. In 1937, a small-scale skirmish between Chinese and Japanese troops occurred near Beijing—the so-called Marco

Polo Bridge Incident—which spiraled into full-scale conflict. This was the starting point of World War II in Asia. In the coming years, Japanese forces occupied large areas of China, particularly along the coast and railway lines, but their control was often tenuous. Vastly outnumbered by the local population, the Japanese army adopted terror tactics. Assisted by scientists from Japan's top universities, it manufactured biological weapons on an industrial scale and deployed cholera, typhoid, and bubonic plague against Chinese communities; it also made extensive use of chemical munitions. (Japan was the only country to use such weapons in combat during World War II.)[2]

The occupation of Nanking City (then the nation's capital) exemplified Japanese atrocities when, between December 1937 and January 1938, Japanese troops massacred 200,000 to 300,000 civilians and captured soldiers and raped tens of thousands of women. Army officers who participated in the slaughter at Nanking later led Japanese forces in Okinawa, where they and their men displayed similar disdain for civilian life. Likewise, Okinawan conscripts in China experienced firsthand how occupying forces treated the occupied, tragically shaping their responses to the American invasion of their own islands when war arrived in the spring of 1945.[3]

The Homefront

Following the 1937 outbreak of hostilities in China, the Japanese government passed the National Mobilization Law, which placed the country on a war footing. The state took charge of the economy, enabling the conscription of workers into war-related industries; exercised control over the media; and later dissolved political parties. The cabinet launched the "General Mobilization of the National Spirit," which exhorted the public to sacrifice themselves for the nation and display unquestioning loyalty to Emperor Hirohito, who had ascended to the throne in 1926. The Meiji Era rescript for the military was expanded with a Field Service Code (*senjinkun*), ordering soldiers not to "suffer the disgrace of becoming a prisoner." This directive spurred Japanese troops to fight to the death to avoid the shame of returning home alive while also cultivating contempt for enemy soldiers and civilians who surrendered. School curricula were dominated by propaganda extolling the evils of the ABCD powers—the Americans, British, Chinese, and Dutch—and the virtues of the Japanese empire, which it titled the "Greater East Asia Co-Prosperity Sphere."[4]

In Okinawa, six decades had passed since the disposal of the Ryukyu Kingdom, and the islands had nominally been integrated as a prefecture into Japan's political system. Many residents continued to speak their own languages and practice indigenous religious customs, but now, during this era of ultranationalism, behavior that strayed from Japanese norms would be stamped out for the sake of national unity. Once again, assimilation was driven by both the central government and members of the Okinawan elite. Tokyo ordered the establishment of Shinto shrines at the islands' sacred sites to assert the divinity of the emperor and Japanese gods. In schools, teachers increasingly used the "dialect plaques" to denigrate Okinawan languages, and now, the ban was extended into adult society by local authorities, who prohibited the languages in public facilities, even denying service to customers speaking Okinawan in post offices.[5]

In September 1939, the European theater of World War II started when Germany invaded Poland—followed by attacks on the Netherlands, France, and elsewhere. In 1940, Tokyo signed the Tripartite Pact with Germany and Italy; war against the ABCD nations now seemed inevitable. Throughout Japan, the state-run media ratcheted up their propaganda efforts, including in Okinawa, where the police ordered the prefecture's three newspapers to merge into one, the *Okinawa Shimpo*. In the following years, the media promulgated the myth that Japan was invincible, its victories were inevitable, and sacrifice for the emperor was the duty of every subject. In 1940, Okinawan historian Asato Nobu urged residents to embrace Japanese colonialism: "Our empire pushes forward to establish the Greater East Asia Co-Prosperity Sphere as the basis of a new world order.... The duty of the people of our prefecture, galvanized by the spirits of our august ancestors, is to contribute to this national policy."[6]

Formerly, some Okinawans had been reluctant to serve in the military, but this had largely faded. Many islanders were proud of Japan's accomplishments, and they were keen to enter the armed forces. Military service was a means to prove their patriotism and obtain some of the glory of the growing Co-Prosperity Sphere. And that empire was about to expand to a scale few had ever anticipated.

Days of Infamy

Japan had long looked toward the European territories in Southeast Asia as sources of raw materials, such as rubber, tin, and especially oil. Now, with their colonizers' militaries caught up in the war in Europe, Japan saw an opportunity to take control of their Asian possessions. In 1940, Japan struck a deal with Nazi-backed Vichy France to enter the north of French Indochina; then, in July 1941, Japanese troops advanced into its south. The US government reacted by freezing Tokyo's assets in the United States and implementing an embargo of petroleum and other oil products. The ban convinced Japan that it needed to control the oil fields of the Dutch East Indies—but it realized such a move would trigger a military response by the United States. To preempt the risk, Japan decided to eliminate the US Pacific fleet at Pearl Harbor in the American territory of Hawai'i.

On 7 December 1941, Japan struck the US base, destroying 188 aircraft; sinking or damaging more than 20 ships; and killing some 2,400 service members and civilians. (Nonetheless, the raid failed to damage the tactically more significant aircraft carriers or oil depots.) Japan accompanied the attack on Pearl Harbor with a series of near-simultaneous strikes on American and European territories in the Pacific: Guam, the Philippines, Hong Kong, and Malaya. The speed of the assaults and the subsequent occupations were unprecedented. This was colonialism on a hyperaccelerated timeline that by mid-1942 had enlarged the Great Eastern Co-Prosperity Sphere into a vast empire encompassing 7.3 million square kilometers.

The Japanese occupiers promised local populations liberation from their White colonizers, and indeed, some residents welcomed the arrival of Imperial Army troops. But soon the new rulers proved to be as oppressive as their predecessors, seizing property and resources, imposing Japanese culture and emperor worship, and murdering those who opposed the occupation. Encouraged by the Field Service Code, which emphasized the shame of surrender, Japanese soldiers treated captured enemy forces with brutality: slave labor, starvation, and experiments with biological weapons. Approximately one in four Allied POWs in Japanese captivity died; in comparison, the death rate for such prisoners in German captivity was one in twenty-five.[7]

After the attack on Pearl Harbor, too, the United States orchestrated its own mass civil rights violations. Under Executive Order 9066, some 122,000 Japanese Americans were forcibly removed from the West Coast and incarcerated in internment camps. German and Italian Americans were largely spared such treatment. The targeting of Japanese was the latest manifestation of decades of racist US policy, notably the 1924 Immigration Act, which banned Japanese immigration to the States. Throughout the war, the US media and government reports routinely used racial slurs—like "Jap" and "Nip"—to dehumanize Japanese people on a scale far larger than its other, White enemies.[8]

The peak of Japan's new empire was fleeting. In June 1942, the US Navy halted Japanese advances in the Pacific at the Battle of Midway. Two months later, American troops stormed Guadalcanal in their first major land assault of their Pacific campaign. The six-month battle proved Japan had spread itself too thin, and overextended supply lines left its forces without food, ammunition, and medical supplies. As with many of its military defeats, the government hid the truth from the public, instead relaying a continuous stream of propaganda back home. One of the soldiers who died at Guadalcanal was an Okinawan, Ōmasu Matsuichi, from Yonaguni Island. His death was reported to Emperor Hirohito, and Ōmasu was elevated to the status of Okinawa's first *gunshin*, War Deity; the slogan "Follow in

Captain Ōmasu's footsteps!" was coined to encourage other Okinawans to sacrifice themselves for the nation.⁹

Following victory in Guadalcanal, for the next two years, US troops conducted an island-hopping campaign that pushed back Japanese troops from the territories they had seized. The Pacific colonies to which many impoverished Okinawans had migrated in the prewar period became sites of intense combat from which civilians were unable to escape due to US attacks on shipping lanes. When American forces invaded Saipan in June 1944, the Japanese army resorted to desperate tactics: an attempt to spread plague-infested fleas and large-scale suicide attacks that Americans dubbed "Banzai charges." With the island on the verge of capture, Hirohito dispatched a message to the army's commander, instructing him to encourage civilians to kill themselves with the pledge they would receive identical glory as those in the military. At the end of the Battle of Saipan, hundreds of civilians—many clasping their children—jumped from clifftops to their deaths. During these 1944 US assaults of the Pacific islands, Okinawans accounted for 13,000 of the 15,000 Japanese civilians who died. Prior to the war, Japanese economic neglect had forced Okinawans to migrate; then militarism turned their new homes into targets; finally Japanese indoctrination on the shame of capture drove them to their deaths.¹⁰

The Build-Up

In Okinawa Prefecture, Tokyo had neglected to develop defensive fortifications, but now, as US troops drew nearer, Japan rushed to prepare for possible invasion. In March 1944, the Thirty-Second Army was created in Okinawa, soon consisting of 150,000 troops. At the time, Okinawa had a population of some 590,000, so the burden on civilians was immense; the military commandeered public buildings and private homes for barracks and supplies of food.

In the summer of 1944, the two commanders of the Thirty-Second Army who would lead their forces in battle took up their positions. General Ushijima Mitsuru came from a Satsuma samurai family, and he was known for his calm demeanor; in contrast, his second-in-command, Lieutenant General Chō Isamu, had participated in a failed 1931 coup d'etat to install the military in power and possessed a reputation as a thug. Both men had served in Manchukuo and were involved in the Nanking massacre. Infantry regiments under Ushijima's command had slaughtered large numbers of Chinese, while Chō had ordered the mass execution of captured soldiers and demonstrated with his own sword how to kill civilians. Many of the troops now in the Thirty-Second Army had also committed atrocities during service in China.¹¹

In Okinawa, as with other occupied areas, the Japanese military established comfort stations where women—most of them duped or brought unwillingly from Korea—were forced to sexually serve troops. At least one thousand female Koreans were confined in some 146 comfort stations throughout the islands. Conditions were atrocious, and the women were often beaten. Testimony to Japan's colonial treatment of Okinawa, it was the only prefecture where comfort stations were built. The islands' governor—a mainlander—lodged a complaint with the military, decrying the establishment of such facilities on "imperial soil" but to no avail. For many Okinawans, the presence of the stations and their captive women were terrifying signs of how they, too, might be treated if their islands were invaded.[12]

Despite the arrival of enormous numbers of Japanese troops, government censorship kept many Okinawans unaware of how near the war was—but it was far closer than they suspected. US submarines encircled the islands, targeting Japanese vessels. In December 1943, 577 Okinawans died when the *Konan Maru* was torpedoed—but the loss was hidden for almost four decades. In June 1944, the *Toyama Maru* was sunk while transporting troops to Okinawa, killing more than five thousand men. The most infamous sinking occurred in August 1944, when the USS *Bowfin* torpedoed the *Tsushima Maru*, which was carrying Okinawan evacuees to the mainland; 1,375 people were killed, 777 of them children.[13] Although the government hid the scale of such attacks, rumors reached the families of the deceased, convincing many Okinawans that it was too dangerous to attempt to flee the islands.

10/10: The War Arrives in Okinawa

On 10 October 1944, the US military launched its first attack on Okinawa. Consisting of some 1,350 strikes on the main and outlying islands, the all-day air raids reduced 80 percent of Naha to rubble and wrecked airfields, harbors, and ships. More than 1,400 troops and civilians were killed or wounded, and vital reserves of rice and ammunition were destroyed. The Japanese army's attempts to defend the islands were utterly ineffective.

In the days after the raid, the governor took shelter in a cave in Futenma, then later fled to mainland Japan, where he was appointed head of a different prefecture. At a symbolic level, his actions personified Japanese abandonment of Okinawa, while at a practical level, his dereliction of duty hindered attempts to create plans to stock food and evacuate residents. (His replacement, Shimada Akira, proved more conscientious, staying for the battle and ultimately losing his life.) At this time, many other public officials and company owners escaped the island—the newspaper shamed them by publishing their names as "Honorable Deserters."[14]

Following the 10/10 raid, the Japanese army ratcheted up its plans for Okinawa. Along with approximately 20,000–30,000 Korean laborers brought to the islands, it mobilized 50,000 Okinawan adults and children a day to build military infrastructure. From dawn to dusk, they constructed airstrips, dug trenches, and fortified natural *gama* caves; ancestral tombs were transformed into shelters. Deep beneath the ancient home of Ryukyuan royalty, Shuri Castle, Okinawans were ordered to excavate a sprawling headquarters for the Thirty-Second Army Headquarters, from which Ushijima and Chō could command their forces. Only piecemeal attempts were made to evacuate civilians. Some 80,000 were sent to the mainland or Taiwan; for those left in the islands, life with the Japanese military was terrifying. "The troops were totally undisciplined and had confiscated a few houses still standing, behaving as if Okinawa were their occupied land," wrote, Hosokawa Morisada, secretary to the prime minister, in December 1944. "They had no discipline—forcing the residents to live under the same roof with the troops, making use of civilians' possessions as they liked, and raping women."[15]

In late 1944, the army withdrew its elite Ninth Division troops from Okinawa to Taiwan to defend the colony and the Philippines, reducing the strength of the Thirty-Second Army's infantry by one-third. It promised to replace them but did not. By early 1945, the United States had occupied much of Japan's Pacific empire, and its remaining territories—notably the Philippines—were under attack. To many members of the Japanese government, it was clear that the war was lost. In February 1945, former Prime Minister Konoe Fumimaro advised Emperor Hirohito that Japan's defeat was inevitable, so he ought to seek peace. The emperor rejected his advice and called for one more decisive victory to enable better terms at the peace table, ensuring the survival of the imperial system. The only place such a battle could be staged was Okinawa. The ways in which Hirohito orchestrated Japanese policy during World War II were kept secret for many years. His request for one final victory, too, did not become widely known until the mid-1980s. Today, Okinawans see it as one of the ways their islands were sacrificed by the emperor: Hirohito's instruction to prolong the war sealed the fate for their islands and the civilian population.[16]

Few members of the Japanese military or the government believed they could repel a US invasion of Okinawa, particularly after the removal of the elite troops to Taiwan. In the terminology of the board game *Go*, Okinawa was to be a *sute ishi*, a stone to be sacrificed for the greater good. Defenses on the mainland were only 60 percent finished, so the army decided to buy time for their completion by drawing out the fighting in Okinawa for as long as possible. It planned a battle of attrition in which the civilian population and the military would fight together against the Americans. Around 110,000 Okinawans were mobilized into the military, and Lieutenant General Chō outlined their responsibility: "Each civilian ought to have a fighting spirit to kill ten soldiers and destroy our enemy." Since the Meiji Period, the duty to sacrifice themselves in defense of the emperor had been inculcated into all Japanese via education and propaganda. Now it was time for Okinawans to prove their worth as imperial subjects. Elucidating the role of the army in the upcoming battle, Chō explained, "The military's important mission is to win the war. We are not allowed to lose the war in order to save civilians." Okinawans now understood why the army had been deployed to their islands: It was not there to protect them; it was there to protect the mainland. The civilian population was disposable.[17]

Why Okinawa?

During most of 1944, the United States had contemplated invading Taiwan, but military leaders concluded the costs in men and supplies might be too high, so on 3 October 1944, Commander in Chief of the Pacific Fleet Admiral Chester W. Nimitz received orders to seize Okinawa. Whereas Japan perceived the islands as a sacrificial stone, the United States saw them as a stepping stone that would put its military within reach of the ultimate target: Japan. The seizure of Okinawa would provide airstrips to launch bombers, harbors to anchor ships, and bases to stockpile munitions and other supplies.

Because Okinawa would be the first time for US forces to encounter such large numbers of Japanese civilians, the military drew up plans to relocate them from the front lines to elsewhere in the islands so they would not interfere with their operations while also providing humanitarian aid. It distributed handbooks to its troops explaining the habits and history of Okinawans, and it readied tons of rice, soybeans, and canned fish in anticipation of the refugees it would encounter.[18]

To prepare for the invasion, codenamed Operation Iceberg, the US military tapped the knowledge of Ivy League experts in Japanese culture to produce manuals about Okinawa. The *Civil Affairs Handbook: Ryukyu (Loochoo) Islands* emphasized how the "people of the archipelago are not regarded by the Japanese as their racial equals. They are looked upon, as it were, as poor cousins from the country, with peculiar rustic ways of their own, and are consequently discriminated against in various ways." The authors of the handbook concluded, "Inherent in the relations between the Ryukyu people and the Japanese, therefore, are potential seeds of dissension out of which political capital might be made."[19]

The ultimate goal of the psychological warfare teams, stated the Army, was "to promote the idea that Okinawans were ethnically and culturally different from the home-island." To divide and rule was at the core of US strategy for Okinawa from the very start of its planning—and it became a tactic that it pursued long after the battle itself.[20]

Operation Iceberg

The invasion of Okinawa brought together the largest concentration of Allied forces ever used in the Pacific war. More than 1,300 US ships sailed to battle, accompanied for the first time by vessels from the British Royal Navy. US assault troops alone totaled some 180,000 men, while support personnel brought the number to more than a half-million. The commander of the invasion was Army Lieutenant General Simon Bolivar Buckner Jr., the son of a celebrated Confederate Civil War officer.

On 26 March 1945, US forces landed on the Kerama Islands, lying west of Naha. Immediately they issued the Nimitz Proclamation, which suspended Japanese rule of Okinawa and placed "all powers of government and jurisdiction" of the islands, waters, and inhabitants under the control of a US military governor. The proclamation instigated twenty-seven years of de facto martial law over Okinawa and an American presence that continues today.

The Japanese Army had envisioned the Kerama Islands as a base from which to launch suicide boat attacks on US ships, but the 26 March landings took them by surprise, and they abandoned the plan. As the Americans spread across the small islands, Japanese troops only offered light resistance. Soon, any lingering hopes Okinawans had maintained that the Japanese military might protect them were shattered. On Tokashiki Island, the army ordered the civilian population to assemble, then the Home Guard distributed hand grenades and gave the order for mass suicide, but there were not enough to go around and many of the grenades were defective, so the villagers turned to other means.[21]

"I don't remember exactly how we killed our mother, maybe we tried to use rope at first, but in the end we hit her over the head with stones. I was crying as I did it and she was crying too," recalled Kinjo Shigeaki, a sixteen-year-old villager. "I don't remember exactly how we killed our little brother and sister, but it wasn't difficult because they were so small—I think we used a kind of spear. There was wailing and screaming on all sides as people were killing and being killed."[22] In the Kerama Islands, more than six hundred civilians killed themselves. As for the Japanese military officers who had instigated the Okinawan suicides, they surrendered and survived.[23]

Similar tragedies soon unfolded after US forces landed on the western coast of Okinawa Island on 1 April. Near the shore in Yomitan Village, 139 civilians were hiding in a cave called Chibichiri Gama. When American troops arrived outside at 10:00 a.m., villagers confronted them with bamboo spears—only to be shot and wounded. As soldiers surrounded the cave's entrance, the terrified civilians argued about what to do. Among the evacuees were Okinawans who had served in the Japanese military, and they urged group suicide. Some men began to set alight to futons so that they could suffocate, but mothers with babies extinguished the fires and demanded to be allowed to live. The men denounced them as traitors: "If we are Japanese, we should die shouting, 'Long live the Emperor!'"[24]

The following day, American soldiers tried to convince the villagers to surrender with assurances of safety, but those inside the *gama* did not believe them. Frightened of capture, one young woman begged her mother to kill her; eventually her mother agreed and cut her throat, and then she stabbed her own son. So began a cycle of murders and suicides. One villager who had served as a Japanese army nurse in China, where she had witnessed atrocities, gathered family members and injected them with poison. Other villagers set alight to the futons, filling the cave with smoke. In Chibichiri Gama, eighty-four Okinawans died, including forty-seven children under the age of twelve.[25]

During the Battle of Okinawa, there were at least thirty such group suicides, the result of orders that civilians and soldiers must live and die as one, combined with propaganda extolling the disgrace of falling prisoner and the atrocities they would face if captured. The presence of Japanese soldiers—or veterans—sparked mass suicides. On islands where no troops were stationed, such slaughters did not take place. In some cases, Okinawans who had experienced life overseas succeeded in preventing mass suicides. At another cave in Yomitan, Shimuku Gama, a former migrant to Hawai'i, Higa Heizo, successfully persuaded some one thousand of his fellow villagers that the Americans were not as barbaric as propaganda depicted so they ought to surrender instead of committing suicide. They followed his advice and survived.[26]

Suicide Tactics

Historically, Japan has extolled suicide as a glorious virtue, and due to a combination of this culture and sheer desperation, it became a cornerstone of its military strategy in the Battle of Okinawa via two main tactics: the use of *tokkōtai* special-attack air units (a.k.a. kamikaze) and the doomed dispatch of the world's largest-ever battleship, the *Yamato*.

The Japanese military had first experimented with kamikaze tactics in October 1944 during the Battle of the Leyte Gulf, but in April 1945, they were adopted as official policy by Imperial Headquarters. Throughout the Battle of Okinawa, wave after wave of kamikaze raids were launched from airfields in Kyushu (and some from Taiwan) against the US ships off the coast of Okinawa, hoping they would be able to halt the invasion.

At the time, Japanese propaganda framed these suicide missions in images of purity, likening the young pilots to ephemeral cherry blossoms, and today, the kamikaze are widely fetishized in Japanese popular culture. But the reality was often very different. Many of the pilots had received scant training before assignment to near-derelict aircraft, and prior to takeoff, they were fed chocolates laced with methamphetamine to keep them furiously alert for the flight to Okinawa. In the early days of the battle, the men departed with at least some sense of hope that their deaths might strike a decisive blow against the enemy, but as the fighting continued with no sign the kamikaze were denting the US invasion, morale diminished. "When it came time for their take off, the pilots' attitudes ranged from the despair of sheep headed for slaughter to open expressions of contempt for their superior officers," recalled one Imperial Japanese Navy rear admiral. "There were frequent and obvious cases of pilots returning from sorties claiming that they could not locate any enemy ships, and one pilot even strafed his commanding officer's quarters as he took off."[27]

Between 6 April and 22 June, the Japanese army and navy launched 1,900 kamikaze attacks, but the majority were shot down by US forces. By luck and sheer numbers, some pilots were able to strike their targets, sinking 26 ships and damaging 164; approximately five thousand American personnel died. It was the heaviest death toll of sailors in the history of the US Navy. Because the kamikaze failed to destroy any aircraft carriers, though, their impact on the overall outcome of the battle was negligible.[28]

On 26 March, at the imperial bunker in Tokyo, Emperor Hirohito convened with the chief of the navy general staff to discuss tactics for the Battle of Okinawa. Already in February, he had requested one final decisive victory; now, his comments hinted at his dissatisfaction with the strategy, and the navy ought to do more to help. After the meeting, the navy decided to dispatch its showpiece—the 70,000-ton *Yamato*—to Okinawa on a one-way mission, whereby it would run aground on Okinawa's shoreline to serve as a steel fortress to repel US forces. The mission was doomed from the outset. US cryptanalysts had long before cracked Japanese military codes, and when *Yamato* set sail from Yamaguchi Prefecture without air support on 6 April, she was soon spotted by US submarines. The following day, the battleship was sunk in a skirmish that lasted less than two hours, with the loss of more than three thousand Japanese sailors. Once again, the debacle illustrated the emperor's power to influence military tactics, particularly related to the war in Okinawa.[29]

The Land Battle

Back on land, American forces were moving quickly across central Okinawa. By 2 April, advanced troops had already reached the east coast, cutting the island in half. As they headed north, though, they encountered heavy fighting with dug-in Japanese forces on the Motobu Peninsula and the nearby island of Iejima, where the entire civilian population had been mobilized to fight. Villagers armed with spears and women with babies strapped to their backs were ordered into suicide raids against the Americans. In six days of fighting, more than 2,000 Japanese soldiers and 1,500 civilians died; 172 US troops lost their lives.[30]

On the main island, US forces headed south toward the Japanese army's defensive lines near Shuri Castle. The more land American troops seized, the more civilians they encountered sheltering in caves and family tombs. US personnel—including some of Japanese or Okinawan ancestry—often tried to persuade residents to surrender, promising they would not be harmed. Many American troops kept their assurances, treating prisoners of war and civilians with compassion; providing them with first aid, water, and food; and transporting them to internment camps. Surrendered soldiers were sent to Honouliuli Internment Camp, Hawai'i, but civilians were mainly held in northern Okinawa and the Kerama Islands. There, the military tried to implement their carefully planned humanitarian operations, but they were overwhelmed with the actual scale; 6,400 Okinawans died from hunger and lack of medical treatment, and malaria was rife.[31]

American conduct toward surrendering soldiers and civilians was frequently humane—but there were exceptions. Some troops shot those who tried to give themselves up, while others looted corpses, collecting scalps and ears. Sexual violence against women was endemic. Almost as soon as American forces arrived on mainland Okinawa, some started raping civilians. US troops assaulted women on the beaches and in fields. They broke into houses and attacked women in front of their families. On the Motobu Peninsula, marines raped almost the entire female population of one village. The internment camps afforded little protection. In field hospitals, Americans assaulted patients and those tending to them. They also raped the Korean comfort women who had already suffered months of sexual abuse from Japanese troops. One marine recalled walking past some ten soldiers standing along the roadside: "I could see they were taking turns raping an oriental woman. I was furious, but our outfit kept marching by as though nothing unusual was going on."[32]

On the Japanese side, soldiers committed war crimes against captured Americans. Shot-down pilots were beaten to death or tied up and left outdoors to be killed by their own shells. The most infamous incident occurred on Ishigaki Island on 15 April, when three American airmen were captured and interrogated; two were beheaded, one was stabbed, and their corpses were then used for bayonet practice.[33]

Both sides' atrocities were fueled by years of propaganda that had inculcated the belief that the enemy was subhuman. The Japanese were "monkeys," "rats," and "cockroaches" whose treachery was embodied by the surprise attack on Pearl

Harbor. Americans were *oni* demons whose sense of White supremacy stoked their lynching of African Americans at home and the killing of Japanese prisoners in the Pacific. "Race hate fed atrocities, and atrocities in turn fanned the fires of race hate," writes historian John W. Dower. "The dehumanization of the Other contributed immeasurably to the psychological distancing that facilitates killing, not only on the battlefield but also in the plans adopted by strategists far removed from the actual scene of combat."[34]

Embroiled within this US-Japan mutual racial hatred were the Okinawans. Despite attempts by the military to educate service members that the islanders were ethnically and culturally distinct from Japanese, many Americans saw them simply as the same Asian enemy. Likewise, many Japanese soldiers regarded Okinawans as inferior to pure-blooded members of the Yamato race. Before the battle, Japanese troops had treated Okinawa as occupied territory; now, with combat intensifying, the Japanese military codified its prejudice into something far more murderous. On 9 April, the Thirty-Second Army issued a proclamation stating, "From now on, soldiers as well as civilians are all required to use nothing but standard Japanese. Those who speak Okinawan will be regarded as spies and receive appropriate punishment."[35]

The order brought decades of policies punishing Okinawans for speaking their own languages to a terrifying crescendo. Here was the *hogen fuda* system brought to its lethal conclusion. During the battle, the Japanese military used accusations of spying to brutalize civilians and force them to submit to their demands. Despite no evidence of actual spying, more than one thousand Okinawan civilians were executed. Paranoia drove some of the abuses. The military had mobilized Okinawans to build its defenses, so now, it worried that captured civilians might reveal their locations. Japanese soldiers shot Okinawans attempting to give themselves up, and they shot Okinawans in possession of American-dropped surrender leaflets. In mid-May, Japanese troops embarked on a killing spree in northern Okinawa; "local headmen beheaded and about 50 women and children murdered," noted Lieutenant General Buckner in his diary.[36]

As well as these direct executions, Japanese troops killed civilians by requisitioning their caves, thus forcing them into the ongoing bombardments, and stealing their food. In the Yaeyama Islands, in order to seize livestock, soldiers forced residents to relocate to areas they knew were rife with malaria. Such experiences led Okinawans to equate the battle with the image of tigers at the front gate and wolves at the back. They were slaughtered by not only US forces but also the very Japanese soldiers who were supposed to be protecting them. Likewise, the Japanese military was responsible for the deaths of the other group long discriminated in Japan: Koreans. Males who had been brought to Okinawa as laborers were assigned dangerous tasks, such as transporting ammunition, and they were often prohibited from entering military shelters. Japanese soldiers executed Korean laborers on accusations of stealing food or attempting to escape. On Aka Island, thirteen Koreans were killed "as an example to others."[37]

Children in the Military

Japanese military disdain for civilians was exemplified by the mobilization of children. Without any legal basis, the army pressed boys from the age of fourteen into the Emperor's Blood and Iron Corps (Tekketsu Kinnotai), or signal corps, and girls as young as fifteen into nursing brigades. Okinawan boys were ordered to run messages and supplies between military bunkers and repair communication lines. Later in the battle, they were given improvised explosives and directed to throw themselves beneath American tanks. The largest of the female nursing units was the Himeyuri Student Corps, which consisted of 240 pupils and teachers from two prestigious schools in Naha. Starting in January 1945, the girls received rudimentary medical training. Then, on the eve of the US invasion, they were assigned to the army's network of hospital caves in Haebaru Town, southeast of Naha. Assured of Japanese victory and expecting their deployment to be short, many of the girls brought along their schoolbooks so they wouldn't fall behind in their studies.[38]

Soon the horrific reality of their duties became apparent. Wounded Japanese soldiers were brought into the caves with missing limbs or full-body burns from US flamethrowers. The girls were tasked with restraining the soldiers during surgery. They also had to venture outside the caves to dispose of amputated body parts and collect water. The shelters became packed, and conditions deteriorated. The soldiers' wounds became so infected that the nurses had to carry away bucketloads of maggots. Meanwhile, patients crazed by pain and trauma lashed out at their caregivers. Testimony to the power of the propaganda they'd been fed, one student, Miyara Ruri, recalled her shock when dying soldiers called out for their mothers instead of shouting, "Long live the emperor!"

From late April to mid-May, US and Japanese forces fought for the hills north of Shuri. Here, the Thirty-Second Army had ordered the construction of complex defensive positions to ensnare the enemy. The tactic succeeded in slowing US advances. Further delaying the Americans was the arrival of the rainy season on 21 May, which brought weeks of torrential downpours. "The scene was nothing but mud; shell fire; flooded craters with their silent, pathetic, rotting occupants; knocked-out tanks and amtracs; and discarded equipment—utter desolation," recalled marine Eugene Sledge. As troops fought in the mud, US ships, aircraft, and artillery subjected the island to unrelenting barrages of rockets, napalm, and other explosives. By the end of the battle, approximately one bomb had fallen for each square meter of the island, leading Okinawans to refer to the battle as the Tetsu no Bōfū—the Storm of Iron.[39]

Toward the end of May, Shuri Castle and its environs had been transformed into a moonscape. For Ushijima and his senior officers sheltering underground, it was clear that there was no prospect of reinforcements from the Imperial Headquarters. The *Yamato* had been sunk, and requests for air support were ignored. Soon the Thirty-Second Army Headquarters would be overrun by Americans. Ushijima had to decide whether to make his brief final stand at Shuri or prolong the battle by relocating his forces south into the midst of tens of thousands of civilians.[40]

On 27 May, General Ushijima, Lieutenant General Chō, and their remaining soldiers began to abandon Shuri and head to the southern coast. The only Okinawan officer at the headquarters deplored the decision: "If we'd held Shuri as our last line of defense right to the end, far fewer civilians would have died," said Adaniya Ken.[41] The governor of the island confronted Ushijima, calling the decision foolhardy and questioning the need to embroil civilians in the combat to come. Ushijima replied that the mission of the Thirty-Second Army was to drag out the fighting—even for one more day—to slow the US invasion of mainland Japan.[42]

For the Japanese military, this had always been the purpose of the battle. They were not in Okinawa to defend the population or even defeat the US military. They were there to inflict as much bloodshed as possible on American forces to enable a stronger negotiating position at the postwar peace table. And they planned the battle to buy time for the mainland to prepare its defenses, which at this point were still incomplete. Ushijima's decision to retreat south was the ultimate manifestation of the *sute ishi* tactic: The army and Okinawans would be sacrificed to encourage the Americans to accept a negotiated surrender that would protect the imperial household.[43]

In June, 100,000 Okinawans were thrust into an ever-shrinking space toward the southernmost tip of the island. Here, in the final weeks of the battle, more than 80 percent of civilian deaths occurred, slaughtered by both sides' militaries. Japanese soldiers forced families from their shelters and stole their food and sometimes their clothes to masquerade as noncombatants.[44] "About half the [Japanese] troops were fighting in a daze, and rape was common," wrote US Army historians.[45] At the same time, US forces went from cave to cave, employing flamethrowers, gasoline, and explosives to clear their occupants. One common weapon was white phosphorous, which produced toxic smoke, and its fragments were virtually impossible to extinguish. "You can't use water on it, just Vaseline, but the Okinawans didn't have any—or anything else. So, lots of them just burned and burned," recalled one US medic.[46]

As fighting forced civilians to the southern cliffs, US patrol boats circled offshore and made announcements urging them to surrender. Just like in Saipan, though,

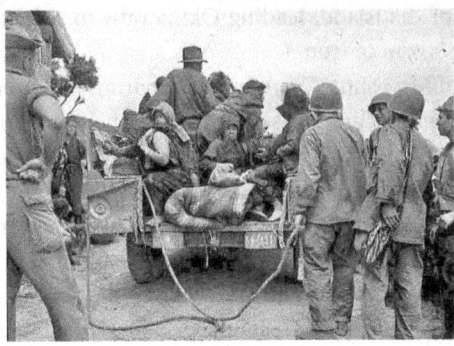

FIGURE 3.1 *A US military jeep carries Okinawans who had been hiding in a cave on 10 April 1945. Courtesy of US Navy/Okinawa Prefectural Archives*

many Okinawans ignored the calls and jumped to their deaths. Some civilians were massacred by US forces. On 18 June, American troops killed a group of more than fifty who had surrendered from their *gama*.[47]

Among those forced into this maelstrom were the young nurses of the Himeyuri Student Corps. After the army retreated from Shuri, it ordered the abandonment of the Haebaru caves, and patients too injured to walk were poisoned with cyanide. The young women marched south to Itoman, where the army had established aid shelters in caves from which their civilian occupants had been evicted. There, in atrocious conditions, the nurses resumed their work of trying to care for wounded troops. On 18 June, the army issued a deactivation order to the corps, evicting many students from their shelters into the Storm of Iron outside. Some girls were killed by bombs, and others committed suicide with grenades or by jumping into the sea. American troops surrounded the Ihara Third Surgical Cave, where some nurses were hiding. The soldiers called for them to surrender, but when nobody came out, they tossed in white phosphorous grenades, killing forty-two nurses and teachers. Of the 240 original members of the Himeyuri Student Corps, 136 lost their lives; the vast majority—117—died after the army order to deactivate.[48]

Neither of the two militaries' commanders survived the battle. On 18 June, Lieutenant General Buckner was visiting near the front lines. Despite previous protestations from his men that the three silver stars on his helmet made him a tempting target, this time, too, he wore it for his visit. Japanese artillery struck his position, and he was killed by shrapnel. Buckner was the highest-ranking US military officer to die in combat during World War II. Three days later, at their command post near Mabuni, General Ushijima and Lieutenant General Chō enjoyed a sumptuous final dinner accompanied by Scotch whisky brought with them from Shuri. Early the next morning, they walked out of their shelter overlooking the sea and committed suicide by hara-kiri. Ushijima's final

FIGURE 3.2 *An elderly Okinawan survivor walks through the ruined center of Naha City on 30 May 1945. Courtesy of US Marine Corps/Okinawa Prefectural Archives*

orders instructed the remaining soldiers to "fight to the end for the sake of the motherland." Chō added the directive, "Do not suffer the shame of being taken prisoner."[49]

On 22 June, US forces declared an end to organized resistance, but Japanese troops continued to fight, and nine thousand of them died in the following week. The Japanese slaughter of Okinawans continued unabated, notably on Kume Island. When US forces sent civilians there to inform the enemy commander that the battle was over, Japanese troops embarked on a torture and killing spree. They murdered the messenger, a village chief, and a family, and they executed Koreans for consuming food dropped by US planes. The Japanese commander later admitted that he had ordered the killings to deter the civilians from rebelling against his troops.[50]

Toward the Homeland

Even while the fighting raged in the south, with the civilian population interned in camps, US forces constructed bases in the center of the island. Sometimes, they

FIGURE 3.3 *Taken on 14 June 1945, the original caption for this US Marine Corps photograph explains how a US service member "ponders over the 'pin up' fashion on Okinawa." Courtesy of US Marine Corps/Okinawa Prefectural Archives*

expanded the facilities formerly occupied by the Japanese military; other times, they leveled villages to build new bases. What had not been destroyed by combat was now flattened by bulldozers. The village of Kadena was turned into a massive roundabout for military traffic, and the nearby village of Hija was buried beneath a runway, today's Kadena Air Base. Further south, Ginowan Village and its environs used to be the administrative and transport hub of central Okinawa—replete with government offices, schools, and a renowned pine tree boulevard. After interning the residents, army engineers bulldozed the communities to build the base now known as Futenma Air Station. Both the Kadena and Futenma bases are still occupied by the United States, but many Americans are unaware of their histories, sited atop bustling municipalities, with runways built from the rubble of houses demolished by army engineers.[51]

For the US military, the seizure of Okinawa was a stepping stone toward the ultimate goal of invading mainland Japan. By May, it was using its airstrips in Okinawa to launch raids on the main Japanese islands. From Saipan, too, US aircraft had been conducting large-scale attacks on urban areas. On the night of 10 March 1945, the bombing of Tokyo had killed some 100,000 people, and by the summer, more than sixty other cities had been firebombed, killing many of the Okinawans who had migrated to industrial areas before the war.

The Japanese government had sacrificed Okinawa to buy time to construct its mainland defenses, so what had it been doing in this period? The military planned guerrilla warfare, so it stockpiled chemical weapons disguised as bottles of beer, while children were drilled to fight with bamboo spears. In Osaka, the commander of the army proposed killing the very young, the elderly, and the weak to allay food shortages for the rest of the population. The preservation of the imperial household was afforded the highest priority. Beneath the mountains of Matsushiro, Nagano Prefecture, the government constructed massive shelters to house Hirohito and his retinue; official agencies; and the public propaganda service, Nippon Hōsō Kyōkai (NHK). Most of the construction work was conducted by some six thousand Korean laborers. Toiling in brutal conditions, they died from cave-ins, starvation, and execution by guards. The military destroyed its records related to the project, but as many as one thousand Koreans are believed to have died.[52]

At the same time as the Japanese government was preparing for a US invasion of the mainland, behind the scenes via diplomatic back channels, it was signaling a desire to surrender. "The poor damn Japanese were putting feelers out by the ton," recalled one senior War Department official. But attached to any offer to capitulate, Tokyo had one condition: It must be allowed to keep the emperor system. This was a compromise many Allied leaders were unwilling to make. On 26 July, the leaders of the United States, Great Britain, and China issued the Potsdam Declaration, which spelled out their terms for Japanese surrender. They demanded that it be unconditional, and they warned, "The alternative for Japan is prompt and utter destruction." The Japanese government refused.[53]

Even before Tokyo's rejection of the Potsdam Declaration, President Harry S. Truman had approved the use of a new weapon that many in the military believed would force Japan to its knees. On 6 August, a B-29 bomber took off from Tinian Island near Saipan, carrying a bomb with a core of enriched uranium. Its target was Hiroshima City, which the US military had left largely intact to assess the effects of the new weapon. "Little Boy" split the atom six hundred meters above downtown, instantaneously releasing the force of 15,000 tons of TNT. The flash vaporized thousands near the hypocenter and burned those more than two kilometers away. The subsequent blast flattened buildings with such force that it bent their steel frames. Following the initial explosion, radioactive fallout spread over a wide area. Because the bomb destroyed public records, estimating an accurate death toll is difficult. By the end of 1945, approximately 140,000 had died (98 percent of them civilians). In the following months, many more fell sick with cancers, and leukemia rates for children reached eighteen times the national average.[54]

Three days later, another B-29 took off from Tinian, this time carrying a plutonium-packed device nicknamed "Fat Man." Cloud cover at its primary target, Kokura City, forced a diversion to Nagasaki City, where the bomb detonated three kilometers off its mark, exploding over Japan's largest Catholic community. In the short term, fatalities were an estimated 80,000, less than 0.5 percent of whom were military. The B-29's diversion made it low on fuel, so on the return to Tinian, it was forced to conduct an emergency landing—in Okinawa, at a US airfield in Yomitan.[55]

The extent to which the atomic bombs influenced Japan's decision to surrender is the focus of intense debate. US Secretary of War Henry Stimson manufactured the argument that the attacks had ended the war and avoided an invasion that he claimed would have led to one million US casualties. However, after the surrender, top military commanders stated the bombs had been unnecessary, and the war had already been won by the time they were dropped. One of the primary reasons for their use was to prevent the Soviet Union from laying territorial claims over Japan and its former colonies after the war. In the words of Secretary of State James F. Byrnes, the bombs should be dropped to stop the Soviets "get so much in on the kill." On 8 August, the Soviet Union had broken a longstanding Neutrality Pact with Japan, and Red Army troops swept through Manchuria and Korea. Japan's leaders feared the Soviet Union would push into Hokkaido, and the invasion might even trigger a domestic communist uprising. They figured they stood a better chance retaining the emperor system if they negotiated with the United States.[56]

At noon on 15 August, NHK broadcasted a radio message recorded by Emperor Hirohito, the first time for him to address the public. In a reedy voice that many Japanese people could not understand due to its royal syntax and poor sound quality, he thanked his subjects and those in Japan's colonies "who have consistently co-operated with the empire towards the emancipation of East Asia." He explained that the "war situation has developed not necessarily to Japan's advantage," so he had ordered the acceptance of the Potsdam Declaration. Not once did he use the word *surrender* or hint at any regret or responsibility for the suffering of the millions Japan had caused. Instead, placing the blame on a "new and most cruel bomb," Hirohito framed his decision as humanitarian—it was the only way to protect Japanese people and "human civilization" from obliteration. His message was riddled with praise for the divinity of the empire, ending with a call for Japanese people to continue to "enhance the innate glory of the imperial state."[57]

The message was so incomprehensible to most listeners that after the recording ended, the NHK announcer had to clarify what it meant: Their nation had surrendered. In response, on mainland Japan, some people, notably military officers, committed suicide, but the overwhelming reaction was relief. The war, which had killed some three million Japanese and devastated their cities, was finally over. In the internment camps in Okinawa, there were no radios or newspapers, so the US military printed the surrender speech onto flyers to distribute to detainees, as well as dropping them by airplane in the mountainous areas where civilians and soldiers were still hiding. Throughout the United States, people reacted with jubilation. At the US Naval Academy at Annapolis, exuberant cadets surrounded the Gokokuji bell that Commodore Matthew Perry had brought back from the Ryukyu Kingdom in 1854. They battered the bell with anything they could find—"garden rakes, dumbbells, and tenpins"—striking until it split.[58]

On 2 September, officials from Japan, the United States, and Allied nations convened to sign the official surrender proclamation. The ceremony took place in Tokyo Bay aboard the USS *Missouri*, one of the ships damaged by kamikaze strikes during the Battle of Okinawa. Here, too, the specter of Perry loomed over the proceedings. Displayed on the ship's deck was a thirty-one-star American flag that the commodore had flown on his first visit to Japan in 1853. In his radio address, General Douglas MacArthur, supreme commander for the Allied Powers, also invoked the memory of the captain of the Black Ships:

> We stand in Tokyo today reminiscent of our countryman, Commodore Perry, ninety-two years ago. His purpose was to bring to Japan an era of enlightenment and progress, by lifting the veil of isolation to the friendship, trade, and commerce of the world. But alas the knowledge thereby gained of western science was forged into an instrument of oppression and human enslavement.[59]

MacArthur's take on Perry's visit to Japan co-opted the commodore's visit for the current moment, rewriting the lessons for victor and vanquished. Framing gunboat diplomacy as an expression of US friendship buried Perry's intention to establish colonial outposts and open Asian markets to US merchants via unequal treaties. Similarly, MacArthur's assertion that the knowledge of Western science was to blame for Japan's aggression was disingenuous. The more important lesson Japan's leaders learned from the arrival of Perry (and then other European powers) was that the only way to survive was imperialism and the need to seize foreign territory of their own. Ultimately, the application of this knowledge led to the outbreak of the Pacific War, a conflict fought over the control of colonial possessions in which millions of civilians lost their lives.

Although Japan's surrender spelled the end of the Greater East Asia Co-Prosperity Sphere, the speed with which its military had initially overrun the former European and US overseers—and then its own swift collapse—highlighted the vulnerability of colonial rule. Following World War II, independence struggles spread throughout East Asia and more widely, posing the question of how the United States, now the strongest Pacific power, would respond. Would it side with the anticolonial movements? Would it buttress the rule of the former regimes and its own control over the Philippines, Guam, and elsewhere? Or would it decide to remain neutral? American responses gouged the geopolitics of East Asia for decades to come and, ultimately, determined the postwar fate of Okinawa.

The Final Toll

Five days after Japan's official surrender in Tokyo Bay, a smaller ceremony was held at the Tenth Army Headquarters at Kadena, where the Japanese Ryukyu Islands garrison officially capitulated. The procedures, which only lasted ten minutes, brought the Battle of Okinawa to its official end. It had been the largest land battle in the Pacific region and the final major battle of World War II. Among those killed were 12,520 American and some 66,000 mainland Japanese troops. For Okinawans, the battle was catastrophic: 122,000 Okinawans, including 28,000 conscripted to fight for the Japanese army. Among the fatalities were 10,101 children under the age of fourteen who died after being forced from their shelters so soldiers could hide and another 945 who died after being forced to help the military, including 76 who starved after their food was stolen; 313 children died from suicide. Of the Emperor's Blood and Iron Corps and Himeyuri nurses, almost half had lost their lives—some 1,105 out of 2,312 children. In the Yaeyama Islands, where the Japanese army had evicted residents to malaria-infested areas, more than 3,600 people died from the disease.[60]

The precise number of Koreans killed in Okinawa is not known. At least 1,000 comfort women and as many as 30,000 men had been brought to the islands but fewer than 3,000 survivors were recorded by the Americans. Uncertain, too, is the number of Okinawan women raped by American troops. Most of those attacked were too malnourished to conceive or they managed to terminate their pregnancies, but nine months after the landings, Okinawan women began to give birth to biracial babies. Some they smothered; others they raised.[61]

The combat had been so intense that 26,200 US troops were evacuated due to combat fatigue, the highest in World War II, and many more suffered from post-traumatic stress disorder (PTSD). Today, 40 percent of Okinawan survivors, too, have been categorized as high risk of PTSD, with potential triggers including the noise from American military aircraft and fireworks, a common attraction at the islands' tourist resorts.[62]

During the battle, the volume of explosives used was staggering. On the US side alone, the army and navy fired some 2.4 million shells. Approximately one in twenty of these munitions failed to detonate. This unexploded ordnance has continued to kill and maim Okinawans, and cleanup is estimated to continue for another one hundred years.[63]

The 10/10 air raids and the actual battle destroyed two-thirds of Okinawa's buildings and devastated its infrastructure, including the railway, electric power, and water supplies. Public records were incinerated, making it difficult for survivors to prove ownership of their property. The battle also obliterated some of the last vestiges of the Ryukyu Kingdom: its diplomatic records and eleven properties designated as national treasures, such as temples and Shuri Castle. In a futile attempt to protect the Bridge of Nations Bell, Okinawans hid it in the castle's moat, but it was damaged by fire and bullets. US troops looted personal items—photographs, flags, and swords—and significant cultural artifacts, such as religious statues and paintings of Ryukyu royalty. Then there were the human treasures swept away by the Storm of Iron: a generation of elders who survived the postdisposal chaos, the diaspora, and famine—only to be massacred by Japanese and American troops. Lost alongside them was much of their irreplaceable knowledge and many of the practices of traditional Ryukyuan culture—music, dance, and martial arts.[64]

4

Forgotten Island

The United States had envisaged the capture of Okinawa as preparation for an assault on the Japanese home islands, but Emperor Hirohito's surrender on 15 August 1945 rendered moot the plan to invade Japan. Now US leaders needed to decide what to do with the islands that had cost so much blood and money to capture.

They faced a dilemma.

Before and during World War II, the US government had repeatedly promised it would not pursue any overseas expansion. In August 1941, President Franklin Roosevelt signed the Atlantic Charter, in which he pledged to refrain from territorial aggrandizement. Then two years later, he repeated the promise in the Cairo Declaration, which outlined the goal of removing Japanese forces from China, Taiwan, and the Pacific Islands seized in World War I and creating a "free and independent" Korea. Although the declaration contained a commitment to expel Japan "from all other territories which she has taken by violence and greed," it did not specify the postwar fate of Okinawa.[1] Nevertheless, at a dinner in the Egyptian capital in December 1943, Roosevelt met China's leader, Generalissimo Chiang Kai-shek, and offered to cede Okinawa to his control. The following month, at a meeting of the Pacific War Council in Washington, DC, Roosevelt again voiced his opinion that China ought to administer Okinawa. The president imagined the offer as a restoration of Chinese rights based on his shaky understanding that Beijing had appointed a "king of Loo Choo" in the past (his proposal had not been endorsed by the State Department).[2]

At this time, China's attitude toward taking control of Okinawa was mixed. Some officials had a better grasp of modern history than the US president. They understood that China's tributary relationship with the Ryukyu Kingdom had ended almost seven decades previously, and they believed most Okinawans identified as Japanese. But other members of the government expressed a desire to possess the islands, notably Chiang himself, who referred to them as Chinese territory that was essential for national defense.[3]

Within the US government, too, there was disagreement. State Department officials generally believed that Okinawa ought to remain under Japanese control, but the military perceived the islands as part of a new network of bases projecting power across the western Pacific. One outspoken advocate of American control of Okinawa was the man in charge of the invasion, Lieutenant General Simon Bolivar Buckner Jr. Before the assault, he had argued that the islands should be occupied "for preventing trouble from any Asiatic power"; then the actual battle had cemented his position. On 23 April, he wrote, "We should control this island as a protectorate, mandate, or some other name that would have the Okinawans as aliens not permitted to enter our country as citizens and add to our already complex race problems."[4]

Buckner's comment highlights two significant issues that bedeviled US advocates of occupation in the years to come. First, how should they counter accusations of colonialism, a word that, given America's own history of revolution, was anathema to public opinion? Buckner's dithering over whether to administer Okinawa as a "protectorate, mandate, or some other name" foreshadows the lexical play of other American officials as they attempted to avoid the word *colony* in their occupation of the islands. Not only a matter of vocabulary, how Okinawa was categorized would affect whether residents would be able to migrate to the United States. US officials wanted to seize islanders' land without granting them the reciprocal right to move to America. The debate mirrored US dealings with its other de facto colonies—the Philippines, Puerto Rico, and Guam—where, in the early twentieth century, Supreme Court judges labeled residents "savage tribes" and ruled "Anglo-Saxon" administration "impossible." Under these insular case decisions, inhabitants were denied the full rights of the US constitution.

Meanwhile, as American casualties rose during the Battle of Okinawa, military leaders grew more convinced that relinquishing control of the islands would betray the sacrifice of those who had lost their lives. On 9 August, the day that the United States dropped the atomic bomb on Nagasaki City, President Harry S. Truman backtracked on his predecessor's pledge not to seek overseas expansion: "Though the United States wants no territory or profit or selfish advantage out of this war, we are going to maintain the military bases necessary for the complete protection of our interests and world peace." On the day prior to his announcement, the Soviet Union had entered the war against Japan, and the president's comments signaled the United States was girding itself for the postwar carve-up.[5]

On 15 August, Hirohito announced that Japan would accept the demands made by the Allies' Potsdam Declaration, but that proclamation, too, provided no clarification of Okinawa's postwar fate. Although it stated Japanese territories were to be limited to the four main islands and "minor islands" determined by the Allies, whether Okinawa was included was unclear.

Following the emperor's surrender, as the United States turned its attention to the occupation of mainland Japan, American officials continued to debate Okinawa's future. The State Department argued against ongoing occupation due to the administrative costs and the "thankless task of governing three-quarters of a million people of totally alien culture and outlook." However, the Joint Chiefs of Staff argued Okinawa was "vital to our future security interests," so the United States ought to retain control "for the next twenty-five, fifty, one hundred years and beyond." As US officials vacillated, on the ground, the impact on Okinawans' lives was calamitous.[6]

The Junk Heap of the Pacific

For the civilian population, having survived the Storm of Iron that had killed 122,000 of their fellow Okinawans was only the start of the life-and-death struggle they now faced under American occupation. By the end of the battle, 330,000 refugees were interned in sixteen camps, where conditions were appalling. They were exposed to storms and sun and dependent on military rations so inadequate that some refugees resorted to eating vermin cooked in motor oil. Almost 6,500 civilians died during US internment from malnutrition, malaria and other diseases. In early 1946, the situation worsened when the camps were inundated by Okinawans repatriated from mainland Japan; Taiwan; and the Pacific islands, such as Saipan. Totaling more than 173,000, these returnees raised the population by almost one-third, straining already-precarious food supplies and shelter. During these bleak times, the global diaspora rallied to support its homeland. In 1948, Okinawan Americans from Hawai'i braved storms and sea mines to ship 550 pigs to restock those killed in the battle; they also sent goats, clothes, and medical supplies. Help arrived, too, from Okinawan communities as far away as Canada and Brazil. Once again, migrants' ties to their home islands helped those left behind to survive.[7]

While the US military struggled to provide sufficient food and shelter, it did attempt to instill a semblance of civil society to replace what the battle had obliterated. It established schools for children and some vocational training centers for adults. It allowed Okinawans to form working parties to travel outside the camps to gather food, and it also permitted the creation of a police force—albeit one that had no jurisdiction over US military personnel. Such measures were borne from sheer necessity—the military lacked the manpower to manage such a large population—and a genuine desire to encourage local governance, particularly during the first year of the occupation, when US Navy personnel administered the islands. In September 1945, the navy organized elections in which all Okinawans over the age of twenty-five were allowed to vote for mayors and local assembly members. An unprecedented step, this was the first time Okinawan women were allowed to vote, predating female suffrage on mainland Japan by more than a half-year. Okinawans were eager to exercise their new democratic rights: 88 percent of eligible men and 81 percent of women cast their votes in 1948.[8]

In 1946, representatives from local councils selected Shikiya Kōshin as the islands' governor, the first-ever Okinawan to hold the position. Although military officials lauded the selection of a governor as a "capstone . . . for progressive self-government," in reality, US policy provided only the illusion of democracy. One political affairs officer made it clear who was in charge when he compared the US military to the cat and the Okinawans to the mouse. Moreover, Governor Shikiya confided to the visiting US consul that the true extent of his authority was confined to nodding and smiling at the Americans.[9]

By the summer of 1946, many of the navy officers who had instigated civil reforms had been replaced by members of the army, and perfunctory efforts to promote democracy faded. In December 1947, the army activated its 526th Counter Intelligence Corps Detachment in Okinawa to monitor subversive behavior, and it became notorious for intimidating political activists and journalists. When Okinawan voters elected progressive candidates, the army was quick to conclude they had been manipulated by communist agitators. Partly to blame for the military's misconception was the stereotype among many Americans, propagated by such publications as the pre-invasion civil affairs handbook, that Okinawans were too docile to demand reforms themselves; outsiders must be to blame. The military failed to understand how its own treatment of Okinawans was fomenting widespread discontent.[10]

The 1907 Hague Convention set out the laws and customs by which wars should be fought, including Article 46, which states, "Private property cannot be confiscated." But the US military flouted the prohibition, justifying land seizures because Okinawans were the enemy, and victory had come at the expense of more than 12,500 American lives.[11]

When Okinawans were permitted to trickle back to their communities, they discovered the realities of living under military occupation. Their homes had been leveled, and their tombs and farmland were buried beneath rubble and crushed coral runways. Approximately one-fifth of arable land had been confiscated, forcing displaced Okinawans to set up hovels around the perimeters of the new bases. Left to fend for themselves, they scavenged for food and housing supplies in military garbage dumps and the unexploded-ordnance-ridden battlefields, all the while retrieving the bones of those who'd lost their lives. With many Okinawan men killed or disabled by combat, it was often women who bore the responsibility of providing for their families.[12] One US army documentary describes the grim conditions: "Okinawa after the war was a forlorn place. Equipment shot up during the war and equipment piled up for the invasion of Japan lay around to rot and rust away. The rock was forgotten—now it was called the junk heap of the Pacific."[13]

It wasn't only the equipment that was rotten. When *Time* magazine correspondent Frank Gibney visited in 1949, he wrote an article—"Okinawa: Forgotten Island"—in which he describes a "dumping ground for Army misfits and rejects from more comfortable posts," where "morale and discipline have probably been worse than that of any U.S. force in the world." During a six-month period, soldiers committed twenty-nine murders, eighteen rapes, sixteen robberies, and thirty-three assaults, wrote Gibney.[14]

Numbers alone cannot capture the brutality of US treatment toward Okinawans. Witness testimonies compiled by the Okinawa Human Rights Association detail how service members shot civilians as they fished or scavenged for food, ran them down in jeeps and trucks, and robbed them in the streets. At times, the nonchalance of the violence bordered on the sociopathic[15]:

- In 1946, two soldiers entered the yard of a home in Gushikawa, where a family was preparing dinner. They handed a young boy a grenade and ran away. The explosion killed two people and injured another six. Relatives had to sell their land to pay for the resulting medical costs.
- In 1948, a military truck drove up behind a twenty-three-year-old woman walking along the road in Onna. One of the passengers tried to grab the towel wrapped around her head, causing her to fall beneath the vehicle's wheels. She was crushed to death.
- In 1950, a hard-of-hearing carpenter employed by Kadena Air Base was taking a nap after lunch. As a prank, a US service member scooped him into the blade of a bulldozer then shook him out. The carpenter struck his head and died.

Female Okinawans continued to bear the brunt of military violence. According to police records, between 1946 and 1948, nine hundred women were victims of such serious crimes as rape or murder. Local police were powerless; they had no jurisdiction over military personnel, and if they tried to intervene in assaults, they were often attacked. To protect themselves, Okinawans hung empty artillery shells outside their villages to ring as warning bells when US troops approached. Male relatives hid women's shoes, while their wives and daughters sheltered inside closets and beneath the floorboards.[16]

Among this unrelenting violence against Okinawans, one act of resistance stands out. In August 1945, residents of Katsuyama Village, northern Okinawa, ambushed three marines who had repeatedly visited their community to rape women. With the help of two Japanese army holdouts, villagers shot and beat the Americans to death and dumped their corpses in a cave. When the marines did not return to their base, they were listed as missing. Not until 1998 was the Americans' fate revealed, after one villager's guilty conscience persuaded him to reveal what had happened. Okinawan police went to the cave, where they recovered three skeletons. Subsequent checks of their dental records confirmed they belonged to the missing personnel. Ultimately, nobody was charged with any wrongdoing over the incident. What makes the Katsuyama case so exceptional is that despite pervasive American violence against islanders during this period, it is the only known episode of Okinawans taking up arms and killing US service members.[17]

As well as deliberate acts of violence, Okinawans were exposed to an equally lethal trend: military negligence. Between 1950 and 1951, seven Okinawans died after being struck by fuel tanks dropped by fighter jets. Meanwhile, on Iheya Island, northern Okinawa, US forces abandoned drums of arsenic near a village well, fatally poisoning eight residents. The incident foreshadowed wider contamination of Okinawa's drinking water in the decades to come.[18]

During this period, military negligence culminated on the small island that had suffered so badly in the war: Iejima. After the brutal combat in which the Japanese army had forced the entire population to fight, including women with babies strapped to their backs, the survivors were interned outside the island for almost two years. When they were finally allowed to return home, Iejima was unrecognizable. Every tree and building had been flattened by combat or US bulldozers, and skeletons still lay unburied. The islanders collected the bones into empty fuel drums and scavenged wood to build makeshift huts. For food, they were forced to eat the leaves of the sweet potatoes that had grown abundantly from soil nourished by the war dead.[19]

Still scattered across Iejima were piles of US munitions abandoned by the military and left to rust. After villagers complained about the risks, the army eventually agreed to dispose of one of the largest stockpiles by its standard operating procedure: dumping at sea. On 6 August 1948, the military moored a flat-bottomed boat known as an LCT—a landing craft tank—next to the civilian ferry berth. Soldiers trucked munitions to the ship, where they tasked Iejima villagers with loading them. By the afternoon, there were 125 tons of rockets stacked on the LCT's deck, alongside ten drums of gasoline, with bungs left open to allow for expansion in the hot weather. It was a tinderbox waiting for a spark, and when it came, the timing couldn't have been worse.[20]

At 5:00 p.m., a ferry from the main island pulled alongside the LCT, and its passengers disembarked to meet awaiting family and friends. At the same time, an army truck arrived and dropped off two soldiers carrying kitchen supplies they'd borrowed earlier from the LCT's crew. The service members clambered aboard the ship and ran across the piles of stacked rockets, dislodging some onto the steel deck.

One of the passengers who had just disembarked from the ferry, eleven-year-old Shimabukuro Seitoku, recalled what happened next: "There was a tremendous explosion, one that seemed like it would burst my ears. My surroundings turned pitch black. After a while, things brightened up again and when I looked around me, I saw people racing in all directions and I heard people screaming." The white beach had turned black; chunks of the LCT, munitions, and bodies were scattered far and wide. "Everyone was in a state of panic. It was a living hell. You could tell that there were human corpses, but you couldn't tell whose they were or anything else," recalled Shimabukuro.[21]

The explosion killed 107 people, injured 73, and flattened eight homes. Army investigators identified numerous safety violations and ruled "that discipline was lax, and that proper command supervision was not being exercised." They also concluded that some blame should rest with the US civilian who had overseen the loading operations, but before he could be interviewed, the morning after the accident, he lay down in his bunk and shot himself in the head. The Iejima LCT explosion was the largest loss of life in the postwar period. In its aftermath, the military only provided token compensation to the surviving families of those it had employed loading the rockets onto the boat, but it refused to pay anything for the other civilians who had lost their lives or been injured. Not until 1965 were the wounded and bereaved finally able to receive payments when, after a long campaign for justice, Okinawans persuaded the US government to offer reparations to residents whose lives or property had been damaged in the period between the end of the war and the peace treaty of 1952.[22]

The Emperor's Message

While the US authorities treated Okinawa as a dumping ground for undisciplined troops, in mainland Japan, they were instigating ambitious changes that rivaled those of the Meiji Revolution in scope. During the early stages of its occupation, American officials—led by Supreme Commander of the Allied Powers General Douglas MacArthur—combined a punitive approach toward the Japanese leaders who had led their country into war with progressive policies for the rest of the population. The United States disbanded the Japanese armed forces and scrapped its remaining weaponry and equipment. It arrested top Japanese military and government leaders, ultimately leading to the execution of seven following the Tokyo War Crime Trials in 1948. It also purged some 200,000 wartime officials from holding public posts. At the same time, in mainland Japan, the occupiers redistributed land to tenant farmers, allowed workers to unionize, and reformed the education system.

In 1947, US authorities introduced a new constitution to replace the one written during the Meiji Period six decades previously. The document was extraordinarily progressive, guaranteeing equal rights to all, regardless of "race, creed, sex, social status, or family origin." It provided universal suffrage and freedoms of speech and the press and declared the right to own or hold property was "inviolable." The constitution's most radical aspect was Article 9, under which the "Japanese people forever renounce war as a sovereign right of the nation"; it promised "land, sea, and air forces, as well as other war potential, will never be maintained." For centuries, Japan had glorified militarism—from the samurai, through the Meiji Era *Imperial Precepts* to World War II—but now the constitution sought to transform Japan into a pacifist nation. It was a revolutionary shift—and one that was overwhelmingly supported by a Japanese public exhausted by a war that had flattened their cities and killed millions.

During these early stages of the US occupation, one important issue remained unresolved: how to deal with the emperor. Many Americans advocated abolishing the imperial system and putting Hirohito on trial for war crimes. World War II had been fought in his name, and he had guided military strategy. But MacArthur and other members of the occupying forces argued Hirohito ought to be allowed to stay. In a January 1946 cable to the army chief of staff, MacArthur claimed to have conducted an investigation into Hirohito and uncovered no evidence of wartime responsibility. He warned the president that if America pursued war crime charges, there would be large-scale unrest, possibly triggering a communist takeover. And so the rehabilitation of the emperor's image began. As historian John W. Dower explains, the US occupiers whitewashed Hirohito's past sins: "He was turned into an almost saintly figure who did not even bear moral responsibility for the war."[23]

Under the new constitution, the emperor was reduced from his position as a divinity and military commander to the "symbol of the State and unity of the people." The document guaranteed "he shall not have powers related to government." But old habits die hard, and soon after the constitution came into effect, Hirohito decided to weigh into the debate about the future of the prefecture where his wartime policies had caused untold devastation: Okinawa. In September 1947, via his liaison, the emperor told State Department representative William Sebald that he hoped America would keep control of the islands. He suggested that "United States military occupation of Okinawa . . . should be based upon the fiction of a long-term lease—25 to 50 years or more—with sovereignty retained in Japan." The public, he contended, would support such a plan because they feared the "menace of Russia," and it would prevent the Soviet Union or China from "demanding similar rights" over Okinawa.[24]

Sebald evaluated Hirohito's offer as "largely based upon self-interest." Gifting Okinawa to the Americans would put him in the good graces of the occupiers, who were still under pressure from some of the Allied nations—and Japanese citizens—to prosecute Hirohito for war crimes. But despite Sebald's suspicions of an ulterior motive, the emperor's message made its way to US policymakers, where it provided justification for them to retain control of Okinawa. The United States had transformed Hirohito's new role into a symbolic position to absolve him of responsibility for the war, yet it was still willing to take advantage of his political intervention because it benefited US interests.[25]

For Okinawans, Hirohito's offer was reminiscent of the *bunto kaiyaku* proposal suggested by the government of his grandfather Emperor Meiji to divide their islands between China and Japan. But this time, the imperial betrayal was all the more reprehensible, given Hirohito's wartime encouragement to sacrifice Okinawa as a *sute ishi* to delay the US invasion of Japan. Now, in 1947, with tens of thousands of Okinawans dead, the emperor was offering to abandon their islands to preserve the imperial household again. Okinawa was disposable—to be spliced on the emperor's whim, with no thoughts to the residents who lived there. (When Hirohito's message was eventually revealed in 1979, it triggered fury in Okinawa, but it was largely ignored by mainland Japanese media.)

One year later, US government officials were still mulling Okinawa's fate. In August 1948, the new Central Intelligence Agency released its own assessment outlining the merits and demerits of three scenarios: handing the territory to China, returning it to Japan, or maintaining US control. With the likelihood of a communist takeover of China now imminent, the agency calculated, "Recognition of China's claims would involve a tremendous risk," and Okinawans would resent Chinese control over their islands. The CIA was more inclined toward reversion to Japan—"political, historical, and ethnical claims of the Japanese . . . are substantial"—but the agency was concerned that another nation might attempt to seize the islands from a disarmed Japan. As for US retention, the CIA weighed the possibility within its ambivalent attitude toward Japan: On one hand, US occupation of Okinawa would enable it to discourage resurgent Japanese militarism, but on the other hand, US forces in the islands would also allow it to defend Japan from foreign attack. Moreover, the CIA argued that controlling Okinawa would allow the United States to strike Soviet forces in Asia.[26]

Finally, in May 1949, the US government came to a decision on the future of not only Okinawa but also Japan. In a top-secret memo—NSC 13/3—the National Security Council recommended a halt to the purge of Japanese militarists, the swift conclusion of remaining war crime trials, and the release of those it did not intend to prosecute. As a result, some high-profile suspected war criminals, including the ultranationalist Kodama Yoshio and future Prime Minister Nobusuke Kishi, were released without charge. The army also granted amnesty to the architects of Japan's biological weapons program in return for US access to their human research. The National Security Council recommended the downsizing of US occupation forces in mainland Japan "to reduce to a minimum the psychological impact" on the

Japanese public, concerted efforts to support economic recovery, and a propaganda campaign to create favorable attitudes toward the United States. These measures set in motion a rollback of liberal policies (known as the Reverse Course). In the coming months, there were crackdowns on union members and other left-wing workers, whereby more than 20,000 people were dismissed by the end of 1950.[27]

As for Okinawa, NSC 13/3 declared, "The United States intends to retain on a long-term basis the facilities at Okinawa and such other facilities as are deemed by the Joint Chiefs of Staff to be necessary.... The military bases at or near Okinawa should be developed accordingly." Until now, the bases had been temporary, but henceforth, the United States was committed to a lengthy presence in Okinawa. The costs would be borne by the US government (unlike in the mainland, where the Japanese government financed the occupation), and the NSC also recommended the military ought to support the "economic and social well-being" of Okinawans. As a result, Congress approved almost $100 million for military construction projects in Okinawa, providing a windfall for the mainland Japanese companies that were awarded the building contracts.[28]

In the long-running debate between the Department of Defense and the Department of State over Okinawa's future, the military had won. Now it was left to the State Department to find a way to justify American occupation that would sidestep accusations of colonialism while simultaneously denying Okinawans the right to migrate to the United States. The State Department turned to a ruse the government had adopted elsewhere in the Pacific: administration under a "strategic area trustee agreement." After liberating Japan's former Micronesian colonies, the United States had devised a way to maintain its occupation via the new United Nations, over which it wielded strong control. In 1947, the UN-sanctioned strategic trust system granted the United States control over the Micronesian islands, which permitted the right to militarize them and control access for security reasons. In return, the United States agreed to "promote the economic advancement and self-sufficiency of the inhabitants."[29]

This arrangement deflected complaints of colonialism while giving the United States unlimited control over large expanses of the region via the so-called Trust Territory of the Pacific Islands. Soon, it made the most of its power to do what it could not do elsewhere: namely test its new nuclear stockpile and run covert operations. In the Marshall Islands, the military tricked residents into consenting to atomic detonations, relocated them to barren islands, then conducted sixty-seven tests, the equivalent of one and a half Hiroshima-scale blasts a day between 1946 and 1958. (US policy was characterized best by Henry Kissinger, who said, "There are only ninety thousand people out there. Who gives a damn?")[30] Meanwhile, on Saipan, the CIA declared the island off-limits to construct a vast facility to train Chinese anticommunist guerrillas. When the agency abandoned the island in 1962, it left behind large areas of polluted land. Such treatment did not bode well for Okinawa.[31]

The Treaty of San Francisco

During World War II, the Soviet Union and the United States had been able to maintain an uneasy alliance focused on defeating the Axis nations, predicated on massive Soviet casualties, as they bore the brunt of defeating Germany on the ground, but by the time of Japan's surrender in 1945, this cooperation had unraveled into rivalry, which deepened into the Cold War. In 1949, the United States was stunned by a series of Communist advances. In August, the Soviet Union successfully tested its own atomic bomb, shattering the US monopoly on the apocalypse. Two months later, Mao Zedong established the People's Republic of China, forcing Chiang and the nationalists to retreat to Taiwan. In June 1950, the Cold War turned hot in Korea, when northern troops invaded the south. In the following months, Chinese and Soviet troops entered the conflict, fighting against forces from the United States and some twenty other nations under the banner of the United Nations but with American command. The Korean Peninsula had largely been spared conflict during World War II, but now it was decimated by a back-and-forth war that saw its capital, Seoul, change hands four times and ultimately cost the lives of more than 1.5 million Korean civilians. For Japan, though, the war on the peninsula was, in the words of Prime Minister Yoshida Shigeru, a "gift of the gods." Under US policies to promote Japan's industry, companies were tasked with providing "special procurements" for the war, including machinery production, building supplies, vehicle repairs, and even weapons manufacturing. Between the start of the conflict and the end of 1953, Japan received approximately $2.3 billion in contracts, a major factor in the nation's recovery from its wartime devastation.[32]

Against this tumultuous backdrop, in September 1951, the United States convened a conference in San Francisco to officially end the war with Japan. Under the terms of the peace treaty, Japan renounced its claims to the southern Pacific islands, Taiwan, and its colonies in mainland Asia (notably in China and Korea); it accepted the rulings of the Tokyo War Crime Trials; and it agreed to enter into future negotiations for reparations with countries it had occupied during the war. The conference reflected the new rivalries of the postwar era. The United States did not invite the governments of China or Taiwan to the meeting, and although, the Soviet Union attended, it refused to sign the treaty. The conference signaled to the international community that Japan was now firmly embedded in the Pax Americana.[33]

The United States heralded the treaty as a restoration of Japan's sovereignty—but in fact it was as unequal as the ones foisted on the nation a century before. Washington forced Tokyo to submit to two conditions. First, it had to sign the Security Treaty between the United States and Japan, guaranteeing America the right to retain its bases on mainland Japan and prohibiting Japan from permitting other countries the same right. At this time, there were some 2,800 US facilities in Japan, some of which were used to launch air raids in the Korean War. The second condition was the separation of Okinawa from Japan under the guise of a UN agreement. Article 3 of the peace treaty stated, "Japan will concur in any proposal of the United States to the United Nations to place [Okinawa] under its trusteeship system, with the United States as the sole administering authority." The treaty granted the United States the "right to exercise all and any powers of administration, legislation and jurisdiction over the territory and inhabitants of these islands, including their territorial waters." Abandoning Okinawa to US administration was the price for Japan regaining its sovereignty over its main islands.

Among the countries that argued for Okinawa's return to Japan were the Soviet Union, China, and India; an aide to the Japanese Prime Minister, too, voiced his desire for the reversion of the islands, albeit in muted terms, cautioning that US control "would be a continual source of bitterness."[34] To placate the objections of Japan and other nations, the State Department invented yet another new phrase: Although the United States administered Okinawa, Japan possessed "residual sovereignty." With its suggestion that US rule of the islands was only temporary, it was another word game to muddy the reality that Okinawa was now an American military colony—while also denying Okinawans the right of US citizenship and the ability to migrate there.[35]

A Day of Disgrace

For Okinawans, the Treaty of San Francisco was a second Ryukyu Disposal. Once again, their sovereignty had been ridden roughshod—this time by both Japan and the United States, who had determined their futures with zero concern or input from residents themselves and placed them at the mercy of the US military for an indefinite period. In Okinawa, opposition to the treaty was prodigious; 277,000 residents–almost three-quarters of the adult population—signed a petition demanding their islands' return to Japan. Given the Imperial Army's wartime brutalities, the call might seem incongruous, but memories of the battle were outweighed by desires for the protection of Japan's new constitution, which they believed would protect them from the quotidian violence of the US bases. The day that the treaty took effect—28 April 1952—became known as the Day of Disgrace (*Kutsujoku no Hi*) to many Okinawans lamenting their place as an American military colony.[36]

Even before the treaty formally placed Okinawa under US control, NSC 13/3 had set in motion the expansion of military facilities in the island. Between 1950 and 1954, the area of Okinawan land occupied by bases rose from 17 percent to 26 percent. The expansion was accelerated by the Korean War. Some of the first US air raids of the conflict were carried out by bombers launched from Kadena Air Base, and throughout the conflict, Okinawa was a key staging post as well as the major site for rest and recreation for US forces in Korea.[37]

Driven off their farmland and with the economy still devastated by war and lack of US investment, many Okinawans had no option but to work for the military. Conditions were dangerous and exploitative. Okinawans received the lowest wages on a discriminatory scale tiered by race: Americans were the highest paid, followed by Filipinos, then Japanese, and finally Okinawans. Local workers employed directly by the military were banned from joining unions. In Japan, workers' rights were protected under the constitution, but in Okinawa, where the military ruled, no such freedoms existed.[38]

Prior to the Treaty of San Francisco, many US officers argued Okinawa was enemy territory, and the Hague Convention notwithstanding, the land they occupied was theirs by right of conquest. But the Joint Chiefs of Staff slowly came to the realization that to avoid international condemnation, it would be necessary to provide Okinawans with payment for the land the military was using. In mid-1952, US authorities announced the amount they were prepared to pay: For a thirty-square-meter plot, landowners would receive around twenty yen per year, roughly the equivalent of a couple of bottles of soda and woefully inadequate to support a family. Unsurprisingly, 98 percent of landowners refused to sign the proffered leases.

In response, in 1953, the US military issued Ordinance 109, under which it asserted the right to seize land without the consent of its owners. According to the constitutions of Japan and the United States, such seizures would have been illegal, but because Okinawa existed in a gray zone, unprotected by either country's laws, the military felt empowered to issue such decrees. After announcing Ordinance 109, US troops moved into the village of Mawashi, bulldozing homes and evicting landowners. Then soldiers entered Oroku Village, where they were met by 1,500 protesting residents. Here, too, the military seized the area with tanks, bayonets, and tear gas. The army blamed Okinawans' resistance on communist agitators.[39]

Against the backdrop of this brutality, the US authorities in Okinawa held celebrations to mark the centenary of Commodore Matthew Perry's arrival in the Ryukyu Kingdom. They organized parades, issued commemorative stamps, and sponsored an essay-writing contest on the topic "How Can We Best Cultivate

Ryukyuan-American Friendship?" No doubt, the commodore, who had proposed the annexation of Okinawa, would have been proud to see his grand scheme now so thoroughly and ruthlessly realized.[40]

The seizures of land at Mawashi and Oroku were only the start. In the coming months, the military turned its attention to two communities that would be remembered as the birthplaces of the Okinawan peace movement: Iejima and Isahama.

Iejima and the Gandhi of Okinawa

On Iejima, the island still traumatized by the LCT explosion, the army now planned to impose a new outrage: the construction of an air-to-surface bombing range, primarily for dropping dummy nuclear weapons. First, US authorities dispatched soldiers there on the pretext of surveying the island. After finishing the work, they asked the landowners to sign some documents written in English. Unbeknownst to the farmers, they were voluntary evacuation papers. After seizing the land, the military began its bombing runs.[41]

Soon, the army decided to expand the range, but this time landowners had cottoned on to their tricks, and they began to organize. They were led by Ahagon Shōkō, who came to be known as the "Gandhi of Okinawa." Born in 1901, he had migrated to Cuba and Peru as a young man to earn money to become a teacher. Then, in his early thirties, he returned to Okinawa, where he bought land on Iejima to build an agricultural school. During the battle, his only son died in fighting on the main island, while Ahagon and his wife fell captive on Iejima. Following internment, the two returned home to discover that the US military was occupying two-thirds of the island. Ahagon, a firm believer in nonviolent resistance, created guidelines with his neighbors for their negotiations with the military. They should hold nothing in their hands and not lose their tempers. When talking to soldiers, they ought to do so "with love in your heart and doing your best to be reasonable." They should adopt the "attitude of teaching and leading young children." The US military, though, was not interested in listening.[42]

On 11 March 1955, an army landing craft deployed three hundred troops onto Iejima's shore. Confronted by villagers, the lead officer announced the island had been captured during World War II by the blood of American soldiers, that the farmers had no authority over the land—and now they had to evacuate. One resident who resisted was beaten and arrested. As soldiers proceeded to clear the village at bayonet-point, they dragged a sick six-year-old child from her bed, then bulldozed the residence. Troops marched into the home of a war widow, shouting "Mama-san, give us a match!" and stood around to watch the building burn. Families begged the soldiers to cease their destruction, but officers thrust money into their hands, forced them to stamp their family seals onto receipts, then took photographs to fake their acquiescence of receiving compensation. In the coming days, soldiers stole vegetables and bartered them for alcohol. Then they got drunk and used the villagers' goats for target practice. They also shot and seriously wounded a young girl.[43]

To draw attention to US abuses, Iejima's farmers traveled to the main island, where they held what they called a March of Beggars (*Kojiki Kōshin*), based on the principle that "To beg is shameful but stealing land is more shameful." Between July 1955 and February 1956, they walked the length of Okinawa, explaining about the injustices occurring on Iejima. At each village they stopped, they were welcomed with sympathy and donations of food.[44]

Upon their return to Iejima, the farmers found their land off-limits, forcing them to live in hovels hammered together by scraps of wood provided by the military. The islanders grew sick from malnutrition and skin diseases. Determined to assert ownership of their stolen land, they ventured into the bombing range, hoisting flags to alert the pilots to their presence. Soldiers arrested eighty farmers and razed their crops with gasoline to deter them from returning. With no alternative to survive, they turned to a lethal new harvest: collecting the scrap metal from the bombs dropped by the military. Between 1959 and 1961, three farmers were killed and eleven were injured when they were struck by shells or bullets or the ordnance they were attempting to disarm exploded.[45]

Isahama: "I Saw a Village Die"

Before the Battle of Okinawa, the central district of Isahama (in present-day Ginowan City), had been renowned for its paddy fields of rice fed by bountiful spring water. But when landowners returned from internment, they found much of the area occupied by a military base, Camp Zukeran (the current Camp Foster). Residents moved onto the areas still available where they set about building homes and replanting their fields, and by 1955, their hard work had started to pay off. Then, the military announced it needed their land to expand the base. In return, it offered to provide financial support for two hundred days. Female villagers, many of whom had lost their husbands in the war, refused to surrender their homes, so they organized a sit-in (*suwarikomi*).[46]

On 11 March 1955, the same day that the army moved against Iejima's farmers, soldiers entered Isahama and dragged away villagers attempting to block their heavy equipment. The US authorities branded the resisters outside agitators. During the struggles, villagers hoisted a flag bearing a slogan that captured

FIGURE 4.1 *In 1955, young villagers on Iejima stand next to a cross appealing to US soldiers' Christian consciences to return their stolen land. Courtesy of Wabiai no Sato*

Okinawans' relationship to their property: "Money is for one year. Land is for ten thousand years." Then as now, land holds a special, spiritual importance for Okinawans; it is where generations are born, raise families and crops, and finally are interred in large family tombs. "For Okinawans, land is the resting place of the soul and reflects a man's character," one farmer told US officials.[47]

In July, US troops returned to Isahama to seize more farms. This time they attacked from both land and sea. Arriving before dawn, soldiers blocked the main road and encircled the village in barbed wire to keep out the press and supporters. After allowing residents a moment to gather a few possessions, troops tore down their houses with bulldozers. Simultaneously, soldiers launched an assault from the sea, where they had anchored a dredger from which they ran a large pipe to

FIGURE 4.2 *In July 1955, a woman with a baby stands beside a banner in Isahama proclaiming the slogan that became a rallying cry for the dispossessed: "Money is for one year. Land is for ten thousand years." Courtesy of Government of Ryukyu Islands/Okinawa Prefectural Archives*

inundate the farmers' fields with sand and seawater. Among the crowds bearing witness to the destruction was Harold Rickard, an American missionary and outspoken critic of the US occupation who had spent time with Ahagon on Iejima. Describing Isahama, he wrote, "On July 19, 1955, I saw a village die. With it died the hopes of the people who had lived there." The military relocated Isahama's residents to hilly land that was impossible to farm. After the displaced families' temporary financial support expired, they were left to fend for themselves.[48]

The Murder of Nagayama Yumiko

At the same time as Okinawans were experiencing the theft of their ancestral land, military crimes continued unabated. In the first half of 1955, US service members committed actual or attempted assaults of at least eleven Okinawan women; only some of the suspects were court-martialed, but any punishments they received were not made public.[49]

On the evening of 3 September 1955, six-year-old Nagayama Yumiko went missing in Ishikawa City. The next morning, military police discovered her body at a garbage dump near Kadena Air Base. She was partially clothed, and she had been sexually assaulted.[50] In the following days, US authorities announced they had charged thirty-one-year-old army Sergeant Isaac Jackson Hurt with rape and murder. Before entering the military, he had served eleven months in a stateside prison for assault and attempted rape, but he had hidden the crimes on his enlistment papers. Upon his arrest in the Nagayama case, he told investigators, "I read the newspaper about the girl's killing. I feel I might have been the one."[51]

To quell Okinawans' outrage, US authorities dispatched its top officer, Major General James E. Moore, to a town meeting, but after expressing his sympathy, he rebuked Okinawans for their mistrust in the military justice system, calling it an "insult to the American people." Even as Hurt awaited judgment, soldiers continued their sexual assaults elsewhere on the island.[52]

At his court-martial in November 1955, Hurt proclaimed his innocence, but the ten members of the trial board found him guilty and sentenced him to death. The severity of the punishment—combined with the fact that the military had publicized the verdict—sated many Okinawans' anger, and they assumed the sentence would be speedily administered. As with so many matters related to military misconduct in Okinawa, though, the true details only emerged many years later. After his court-martial, Hurt was sent to a military prison at Fort Leavenworth, Kansas, where US senators pressured the government to study the matter, expressing concern about the anti-American sentiments it had triggered. In 1960, President Dwight Eisenhower commuted Hurt's death sentence to forty five years with no possibility of parole.[53] Subsequently, following Hurt's complaints that he had been "sacrificed to appease the dissident political elements who were demanding an end to American mil. Occupation," he was released on parole in 1977.[54] Hurt found a job as a night watchman and got married. When he died in 1984, he received an official veterans' grave marker provided by the Department of Veterans' Affairs, despite having been found guilty of the rape and murder of a minor. Service to your nation, it seems, outweighs even the most heinous of crimes.[55]

***

The Battle of Okinawa ended in 1945, but a decade later, residents were still denied the peace it promised. Unfathomable trauma for Okinawans happened in 1955. As official policy, American forces initiated land seizures, illegal under international law and the constitutions of the United States and Japan. At the same time, troops carried out horrific attacks against Okinawan civilians but often escaped justice due to impunity from local laws. Even when they were punished, their sentences were hidden or, as in the case of Isaac Hurt, commuted by US authorities. This combination of abuses committed at a structural and individual level mirrored those faced by African Americans in the US South, which in 1955 sparked large-scale, organized opposition. In the same year, Okinawans, too, built grassroots, nonviolent resistance with widespread participation led by charismatic leaders. This was America's unknown civil rights movement.

The strategies deployed by the residents of Iejima and Isahama became staples of opposition in the coming years, and they are still employed today. Such peaceful tactics were born of necessity—unarmed farmers stood no chance of defeating soldiers from the most powerful military on the planet—but also, they stemmed from absolute pacifism, a rejection of the violence they had experienced during the Battle of Okinawa. The resistance of Ahagon Shōkō and his fellow islanders on the March of Beggars and the pride of Isahama's women and their slogan "Money is for one year. Land is for ten thousand years" still remind Okinawans of what their predecessors endured, how they resisted, and why they continue to struggle for justice.

5

Showcases of Democracy

In January 1954, the top US official in Okinawa, Major General David Ogden, compared his administration to the islands' founding gods. He lauded the army for teaching residents "new skills and new ways of life" and proclaimed a "modern-day parallel to the ancient story of creation as told in Luchuan (Ryukyuan) mythology"—the introduction of a "new democratic form of government." It was a lofty boast—so what was this fantastical democracy bestowed on the islands' islands' populace?[1]

Shortly after the Battle of Okinawa, the military had divided the islands into four districts and permitted residents to elect officials, but when they voted for candidates advocating reversion to Japan, the military scrapped the experiment. In its place, the United States created a centralized two-tier system. At the top was the US Civil Administration of the Ryukyu Islands (USCAR), but the word *civil* was a misnomer; it was dominated by the military and headed by a high-ranking officer. Below was the Government of the Ryukyu Islands (GRI) that while including an elected legislature, was headed by a chief executive appointed by the military. Although Ogden had heralded the USCAR-GRI system as a mythical advance, for all intents and purposes, it perpetuated the martial law imposed under the Nimitz Proclamation of March 1945. Because the islands were legally part of neither the United States nor Japan, residents were denied the constitutional guarantees of either nation, notably the freedoms of speech, the press, labor organization, and the inviolability of property. Nor could Okinawans freely travel to and from the islands. Residents wishing to go to mainland Japan needed a USCAR-issued passport, a request that was frequently denied. Likewise, Japanese people deemed undesirable by the military were barred entry to Okinawa.

In 1955, the American Civil Liberties Union (ACLU) outlined the key abuses of USCAR rule. It described Okinawan officials as "puppets" and detailed how the military used economic coercion to enforce its rule by withholding funds from proreversion mayors and smearing those who advocated for return to Japan as communists. It also criticized the racist wage scale that relegated Okinawan base workers' salaries to below those of Filipinos and Japanese. In reply, the military accused the ACLU of failing to understand the international status of Okinawa.[2]

Following Okinawan complaints over the land seizures at Isahama, the US House of Representatives Armed Services Committee dispatched Senator Melvin Price and a team of subcommittee members to investigate. From 24 to 26 October 1955, the Americans held hearings in Naha and visited some of the communities affected by the confiscations. Residents explained how they had been forced from their farms and were unable to support their families and how lump-sum offers had been inaccurately assessed. They complained that even after the military took land, it lay unused. Some of those who gave testimony were particularly galled by the building of golf courses on their ancestral properties. Okinawans described how military training in forests prevented them from collecting firewood and made women too afraid to enter them for fear of rape.[3]

Military representatives refuted Okinawans' complaints with accusations of sabotage and theft, while blaming the protests at Isahama on "representatives of Japan's Communistic Party" and Ahagon Shōkō, "who had no legitimate interest in the problem." During the hearings, one of the subcommittee members suggested that Okinawans were seeking higher payments so the "dispossessed landowner could stop working forever," but Higa Shūhei, the chief executive of the GRI, explained that even if they received higher rents, it would only provide for a subsistence level of living, and they would still have to work as day laborers.[4]

Upon their return to the States, the subcommittee published their findings. The Price Report acknowledged military bases had "displaced some 50,000 families, or approximately 250,000 people" (more than one-third of the population of the main island), resulting in a population density of 1,270 persons per square mile (2.6 square kilometers)—seven times higher than in the Philippines—as islanders were crammed into the remaining available land. But the report omitted Okinawans' grievances about the seizure of their property, their lack of democratic rights, or their desires for reversion to Japan.[5]

For the authors, military requirements trumped any humanitarian concerns. The report expressed support for the much-resented one-off payments and further land seizures, but the latter should "be kept to an absolute minimum." The subcommittee fully endorsed continuing occupation: "The highest policy statement which can be quoted in support of this is that of President Eisenhower who, in his State of the Union address on January 7, 1954, said 'We shall maintain indefinitely our bases in Okinawa.'"[6]

One section—titled "Why We Are in Okinawa"—called the islands an "essential part of our worldwide defenses," invaluable because the military was allowed to operate there without any interference by foreign governments. As for the rights of islanders, the senators wrote, "Okinawa has become, in its most precise sense, a 'showcase of democracy.' The eyes of the world, and particularly the hooded eye of the Communist world, are fixed attentively on our actions in Okinawa, the latter in concentrated study to discover what can be used as propaganda against us."[7]

The phrase *showcase of democracy* became infamous in Okinawa, given the irony of how US rule violated all democratic norms. It resembled the authoritarianism of the communist regimes from which USCAR was purportedly protecting islanders. Throughout its rule, the military gave precedence to how the world perceived its administration over how it actually treated Okinawans—the optics of its occupation always overrode the rights of residents.

The Price Report was a crushing disappointment to islanders, who had hoped the visit by American officials would highlight their desperate conditions and bring about improvements. In response, legislature officials and mayors threatened to resign en masse, and more than 100,000 residents gathered to demand a halt to new land seizures and push for the payment of appropriate compensation for property already occupied. The protests became known as the Shimagurumi Tōsō—the All-Island Struggle—bringing together people from all walks of life. Combined with demonstrations triggered by the 1955 murder of Nagayama Yumiko, they formed what historian Arasaki Moriteru called the first mass wave of protest against American occupation, setting a pattern for similar united resistance in the years to come.[8]

Alarmed at the scale of the anger, USCAR adopted increasingly insidious countermeasures. To undermine the support of the urban working class for the All-Island Struggle, the military issued off-limits orders, prohibiting troops from entering entertainment districts. The bans financially crippled communities, especially Koza City near Kadena Air Base, which deterred many workers from openly supporting the demonstrators. Meanwhile, to stifle student sympathies, USCAR compelled the University of the Ryukyus to expel six students for shouting anti-American slogans during a protest rally. USCAR had touted the university, which it built on the hill where Shuri Castle had stood as a symbol of its development of the islands, but the expulsions, leveraged by the threat of withdrawing USCAR funding for the institute, belied such benevolence.[9]

The most nefarious way in which US authorities tried to break Okinawan resistance was its hijacking of existing migration schemes to eliminate troublemakers from the islands. USCAR appointed James L. Tigner from the Hoover Institution, Stanford University, to investigate the possibility of shipping dispossessed Okinawans overseas. Tigner described the plans as a way to "preserve the political stability" of Okinawa: "The prospects of obtaining large tracts of free land in a distant community . . . will give fresh hope to the youth and in this way serve to cope with their discontent and susceptibility to the Communists' false promises of reward."[10] Among those who emigrated at this time were villagers from Isahama, who moved to Brazil. First, the military stole their land, next it abandoned them, and finally it cast them into exile. Other Okinawans displaced during this period went to Uruma Colony, Bolivia. Promised fertile farmland and sound infrastructure, when migrants arrived, to their horror they discovered a remote jungle lacking freshwater supplies. In the first half-year, seventeen migrants died, and many more fell ill.[11]

Senaga Kamejiro

Undaunted by this oppression, Okinawans resisted occupation by throwing their support behind a man who became a persistent thorn in the Americans' side. Senaga Kamejiro was born in 1907 in Tomigusuku Village and moved to mainland Japan to study in the 1920s, when he became involved in left-wing social movements. Arrested under the Peace Preservation Law for organizing a strike, he was sentenced to three years in prison. Upon his release, Senaga became a journalist, and following the Battle of Okinawa, he stood for election as a local mayor. US brutalities against Okinawans convinced him to create the Okinawa People's Party in 1947. An animated public speaker, in 1950, he told one crowd, "If I, Senaga, shout alone, my voice can be heard 50 meters away. If the people gathered here shout together, our voices can be heard by all the citizens of Naha. If the 700,000 people of Okinawa shout in unison, our voices can cross the raging waves of the Pacific Ocean and move the government in Washington."[12]

Senaga's popularity scared the Americans, so they decided he had to go. They rejected his requests for a passport to travel to Japan sixteen times and wiretapped his offices. USCAR suspended the party's magazine, *Jinmin*, for publishing articles revealing US corruption, and it arrested members of the party, including Senaga, on charges of harboring communists from Amami-Ōshima whom the Americans had ordered to leave Okinawa. For the second time in his life, Senaga became a political prisoner—first under the prewar Japanese regime and now an equally oppressive American administration. After serving a one-and-a-half-year prison term, Senaga was released in 1956 and stood for election to become mayor of Naha City. Despite a US-orchestrated slander campaign and Central Intelligence Agency (CIA) funding for his rivals, he won.[13]

The US government reacted by further throttling the few political rights Okinawans possessed. In June 1957, President Eisenhower signed Executive Order 10713 to create the position of high commissioner in Okinawa. Appointed by the secretary of defense, the role had the power to veto or annul acts passed by the Okinawa legislature and rule by ordinance. He also controlled the strings of a large slush fund to sway elections. In total, there would be six high commissioners during US colonial rule—all army generals—and their authoritarianism led residents to dub them the "Emperors of Okinawa."[14]

The first high commissioner, Major General James E. Moore, used his powers to change the law to enable the removal of Senaga from office and prevent him from standing for reelection with an ordinance banning candidates who had criminal records. USCAR had hoped the ouster would break Okinawan resistance, but in the next election, Naha residents voted in a socialist mayor to run their city.[15]

The resolve of Senaga's supporters and the scale of the Shimagurumi Tōsō protests made USCAR realize that antimilitary sentiment was not confined to a handful of agitators—it was widespread. So begrudgingly, US authorities granted Okinawans one important compromise: It discontinued its lump-sum payments for land and instead offered annual payments for their occupied property at a rate six times its initial proposition. This was a sign that, when united, it was possible for Okinawans to win concessions from US authorities.[16]

Soft Power: Semantics and Psychological Operations

To maintain control over Okinawa, US authorities paired brute force with a multifaceted soft-power strategy to conceal the realities of martial rule. Semantics played an important role. USCAR was a *civil* administration, despite being under military control, and the islands' top official was named the high commissioner to avoid using a military title. The grandest trick was designed to hide the fact that Okinawa was a colony. Under the 1952 Treaty of San Francisco, the United States proposed to administer the islands as a United Nations trusteeship. By mid-1953, it had quietly dropped the idea, but it failed to inform Okinawans of its decision. The ploy had served its temporary purpose of deflecting accusations of imperialism.[17]

One of America's most flagrant semantic sleights of hand was its refusal to refer to the islands as *Okinawa*; instead it resurrected the term *Ryukyu*. In a strategy known as *rinichi* (separation from Japan), US authorities tried to dissuade Okinawans from identifying as Japanese by promoting the uniqueness of Ryukyuan culture. In the early days of its occupation, it went so far as to ban Japanese textbooks and attempt to produce school materials in the Okinawan language—but the plan was scrapped as unworkable. US encouragement to promote the Ryukyuan languages backfired. Okinawans understood the policy was designed to break their affinity with Japan, so increasingly, they abandoned their indigenous languages. Some teachers even reintroduced *hogen fuda* (dialect plaques) to punish students. Tragically, *rinichi* policies sped the Ryukyuan languages to the brink of extinction.[18]

USCAR paired such anti-Japanese psychological operations with ones to promote positive attitudes toward the United States. This propaganda was extensive, produced by overlapping agencies, and targeted all social classes. For the intelligentsia, USCAR published a monthly magazine called *Today's Ryukyus* and sent Okinawan students to the United States to nurture future leaders who they hoped would be sympathetic to the occupiers. For agricultural and fishing communities, USCAR distributed almanacs containing greetings from the high commissioner. The mainstay of US propaganda was a magazine published by the army's Seventh Psychological Operations Group called *Shurei no Hikari* (*The Light of Courtesy*), a title that elicited connections to the *Shurei no Kuni* plaque that had adorned the gateway to Shuri Castle. Containing articles emphasizing Ryukyuan culture, approximately 90,000 copies of the magazine were distributed for free every month.[19]

Simultaneously, the military kept tight controls on the islands' media. Unlike in Japan, where the United States had ended censorship in 1949 and the constitution guaranteed freedom of the press, in Okinawa, publishers were required to apply for permission to produce newspapers, magazines, and books. Those who violated the system had their materials confiscated, and their editors were issued warnings by USCAR. Such intimidation encouraged newspapers to adopt self-censorship.[20]

Many Americans living in Okinawa were unaware of the rampant abuses their presence engendered. Most received news from the islands' only English-language newspaper, *Okinawa Morning Star*, which provided a promilitary perspective on local matters. Its coverage of Isahama, for example, described how the seizure "clicked like the well-planned manoeuvre it was" and succeeded "without meeting resistance from either villagers or imported political groups."[21] Such slanted coverage should not come as a surprise: The newspaper was funded by the CIA and included a journalist on the agency's payroll.[22]

Meanwhile, in the United States, relatively few critical stories were published because the military controlled all access to the islands, and when it did allow press visits, it took journalists on carefully scripted tours. USCAR understood that if the US public were to discover the truth about its actions, it might demand change, particularly at a time when military oppression in Okinawa—and residents' nonviolent resistance—paralleled the burgeoning civil rights movement at home. What USCAR feared most was word of its abuses reaching Congress. The Melvin Price visit had been a close call, but it was an exception. The army largely kept the issue of Okinawa out of congressional debates.[23]

Without any civilian oversight from the US public or politicians, USCAR could maintain absolute control over Okinawa, enabling the military and the CIA to run some of America's most secretive projects of the Cold War era. In 1965, one report by the Joint Chiefs of Staff hinted at the scope of the work there: "highly classified intelligence and counterintelligence operations, psychological warfare and propaganda activities, movements of special weapons and ammunition." As in the other US colonies of the Trust Territory of the Pacific Islands, Okinawa was a place where the United States could do things not permitted elsewhere, particularly in the fields of covert operations and deployment of weapons of mass destruction.[24]

The CIA in Okinawa

Okinawa hosted the CIA's main logistical hub for East Asia: Camp Chinen, current-day Nanjo City. Operating under the guise of a large army support base, it contained warehouses for weapons and communication equipment and workshops to forge passports and other documents. In one large building, Okinawan workers packed parachutes for aerial drops, and few suspected the true identity of their employer. Also, safe houses in a remote part of the base housed foreign nationals for specialized training.[25]

From Camp Chinen, the CIA ran covert operations throughout Asia, supporting the French military at Dien Bien Phu at the end of the first Indochina War in 1954, airlifting men and supplies to help Tibetan rebels in the late 1950s, and delivering tons of untraceable weapons to anticommunist forces in Southeast Asia throughout this period. Much information about these operations remains classified, but one account describes how Chinese guerrillas in Okinawa persuaded the CIA to hand over $50 million to fund the overthrow of Mao's government in what turned out to be a "scam."[26]

Facilitating these operations, the CIA flew aircraft under the Civil Air Transport and later Air America, Inc., from US Air Force bases at Kadena and Naha. It also ran a civilian commercial airline, Scheduled Air Services Ryukyus, between Naha and Okinawa's outlying islands, which the US government used to consolidate its influence toward the edges of the territory. In Tainan City, Taiwan, too, Air America, Inc., performed maintenance work for the US Air Force, which the CIA boasted was a "money-maker."[27]

Many of the CIA operations in Okinawa revolved around the collection of intelligence. In Yomitan Village, the CIA ran the Foreign Broadcast Information Service, where large antennas intercepted radio and TV signals from the Koreas, China, and the Soviet Union. Agency employees translated the materials onsite and sent them to other US government departments and embassies around the world. Other towering antennas stood in Kunigami Village, belonging to Voice of America, which transmitted US propaganda into mainland Asia. Such broadcasts required high-powered signals, and Okinawans living near the antennas experienced freakish phenomena: electric burns from the wire fences on their farms; unplugged lightbulbs that glowed; and Chinese voices emanating from tin sidings, which acted like the diaphragms of loudspeakers.[28]

In addition to publishing propaganda for Americans via the *Okinawa Morning Star*, the CIA also worked to subvert Okinawans' support for left-wing politicians by channeling money into members of the conservative Okinawa Liberal Democratic Party (LDP). The support helped to ensure victory for candidates whose policies were more aligned with those of the United States.[29]

US Weapons of Mass Destruction in Okinawa

During World War II, Japan and the United States had manufactured chemical weapons, but only Japan had used them—extensively in China. After the war, the United States increased production of such munitions, and starting in 1953, it deployed them to Chibana Army Ammunition Depot, a sprawling facility attached to Kadena Air Base. The arsenal stored the nerve agents sarin and VX, which, even in tiny volumes, can cause convulsions and death. By 1965, the military was storing more than 13,000 tons of chemical weapons in Okinawa. Near the bunkers, the army kept caged white rabbits, hoping their deaths might provide warning of any spills.[30]

Using the research obtained from wartime Japanese scientists in exchange for their amnesty, the US Army also expanded its biological weapons program. Between 1961 and 1962, America tested the fungus rice blast at three sites in Okinawa to assess whether it could be used to kill crops and force enemies into starvation. At the same time, in the northern Yanbaru forests, the military experimented with potent herbicides, the forerunners to the Vietnam War defoliant Agent Orange. According to one high-ranking officer, the Department of Defense had chosen Okinawa because its vegetation resembled Southeast Asia's, and the military's control over the islands enabled it to run experiments without restrictions.[31]

The third component of the US military's arsenal of weapons of mass destruction was nuclear. The deployment was the most controversial due to the Japanese public's opposition to the weapons. First, the bombings of Hiroshima and Nagasaki had killed hundreds of thousands. Then in March 1954, Japanese fishing crews were exposed to radioactive fallout following a US hydrogen bomb test in the Marshall Islands that was one thousand times more powerful than the Hiroshima blast. In response, 32 million Japanese—one-third of the population—signed petitions to demand the halt to nuclear tests. Mainland anger convinced the US military that stockpiling nuclear weapons there would be politically unfeasible, so it turned to Okinawa, where, in the words of the 1956 Price Report, "there are no restrictions imposed by a foreign government on our rights to store or to employ atomic weapons." Exploiting this freedom to the fullest, the military brought approximately 1,200 nuclear bombs, rockets, and missiles to Okinawa, keeping the majority alongside the chemical munitions at Chibana depot.[32]

Among the first weapons to be brought were atomic cannons, which fired small, 280 mm shells with the same strength as the bomb that had leveled Hiroshima. Reporting on the deployment, the US media belittled residents' concerns: "Japs aroused as atomic guns reach Okinawa," wrote the *Chicago Tribune* in July 1955. Three months later, when the army test-fired one of the cannons—presumably with a nonnuclear shell—the shockwave shattered fifty windows at a nearby elementary school, injuring pupils with flying glass. In 1959, another nuclear accident nearly obliterated Okinawa's capital. Naha Air Base possessed a battery of surface-to-air Nike Hercules missiles tipped with nuclear warheads to destroy incoming enemy aircraft. On 19 June, army technicians were testing one of the missile's electrical systems when a short circuit triggered its engines. Two soldiers were killed by the backwash, and the missile flew into the sea. If the rocket had been pointing inland, Naha residents would have suffered the worst loss of life since the Battle of Okinawa.[33]

Miyamori Elementary School

Eleven days after the misfire at Naha Air Base, tragedy struck thirty kilometers north in Ishikawa City. At 10:40 a.m. on 30 June, pupils at Miyamori Elementary School were sitting down for their morning milk break. In charge of one class of sixth graders was Higa Shizu, who recalled, "Suddenly, there was a roar, violent shaking, and torrents of fire and dust. For a moment, I thought it was the end of the world. I shouted at my students to duck for shelter."[34]

When Higa came to her senses, there was a hole in the ceiling, and the walls had been torn apart. Desks and chairs were burning, some of her pupils lay dead. "As I walked out of the room in search of help, a girl emerged from the burning second-grade classroom. Her entire body was in flames, so I tried to put them out, but the skin on her back peeled off and stuck to my hands," Higa said.[35]

Outside, school buildings were ablaze, and the ground was covered with broken glass. Dazed pupils walked through the debris, bleeding from multiple lacerations and crying out, "*Sensō ga kita!*" ("It's a war!") Some of the teachers, too, believed Okinawa was under attack. They only realized what had happened when neighbors and police arrived on the scene: A fighter jet had crashed into the school.[36]

The F-100D aircraft from Kadena Air Base had first struck a residential area then cartwheeled into the school grounds, destroying the outer tin-walled classrooms before careening into the main building. The pilot had ejected safely and was rescued by military police, who drove him back to the base. Eighteen Okinawans

FIGURE 5.1 *During US occupation, there were 1,200 nuclear weapons in Okinawa. In this 1970 photograph, residents turn their heads as a Mace missile passes through Gushikawa Village. Courtesy of US Air Force*

died in the accident—12 pupils and 6 residents—and 210 other children and adults were injured, some with extensive burns. The crash also damaged or destroyed thirty-five nearby homes.[37]

Immediately after the accident, the US military announced the jet had exploded during a test flight—a force majeure accident beyond anyone's control. But the truth was very different. One month prior to the crash, the US Air Force had sent the jet for modifications at the CIA's "money maker"—the Air America, Inc., maintenance facility in Taiwan. Before returning the aircraft, the technicians had failed to properly secure one of the ducts and clamps in its engine. When the jet arrived back at Kadena Air Base, US Air Force inspectors overlooked the problem. As a result, on 30 June, when it was flying over Okinawa, a fuel leak triggered a midair explosion.[38]

According to accident investigators, at least five service members at Kadena Air Base ought to have spotted the problem before approving the jet to fly. There was a "lack of adequate training, supervision, and procedural discipline," concluded the report. Ultimately, though, the Air Force decided not to punish anyone responsible. Investigators also singled out for blame the negligence of the CIA facility: "The stage for the Ishikawa Tragedy had been set by poor maintenance and quality control procedures at the Air America, Inc., modification center at Tainan."[39]

In its official history, the US Air Force likened the "cumulative series of oversights" to those that had caused the United States to miss the signs leading to the Japanese attack at Pearl Harbor. It is a bizarre allusion that can only be interpreted as a gratuitous attempt at equivalence in the deaths of eighteen Okinawans. The same report also decried "free loaders" who had received excess food from the emergency field kitchens and accused Okinawans of tricking the military into providing too much land for residents made homeless by the crash: "More than one official declared that the Okinawans 'had killed the goose that laid the golden eggs.'"[40]

Despite the tragedy arising as a result of negligence, US authorities dragged their feet on compensating victims. It took almost one year for the military to pay reparations to the families of the dead and seriously injured—and only after persistent campaigns by residents and local leaders. Survivors, whose injuries the military deemed minor, had to wait another year.[41]

The US Military in Japan

On mainland Japan, between 1950 and 1960, public support for the US-Japan military alliance plummeted from 55 percent to 14 percent. During the 1950s, crime and environmental contamination convinced many communities that US forces had outstayed their welcome, and Japan ought to seek neutrality similar to Switzerland. Antibase movements sprung up throughout the nation, most significantly in western Tokyo, where the US military was planning to expand Tachikawa Air Base by taking farmland in the adjacent Sunagawa District. From 1955 to 1957, thousands of demonstrators staged sit-ins to prevent Japanese officials from conducting survey work. Police attacked the peaceful protestors with batons, injuring many. Despite the crackdown, the demonstrators persisted, support spread, and they succeeded. Realizing the risk of provoking wider antimilitary sentiment, US and Japanese authorities shelved—then abandoned—plans to expand the base.[42]

Elsewhere in mainland Japan, including Gifu and Yamanashi Prefectures, local protests forced the military to rethink stationing troops there. During the mid-1950s, it withdrew the bulk of the marine corps and relocated them to Okinawa. As a result, in Japan, the size of the US military presence shrunk by almost three-quarters, from 130,000 to 30,000 hectares; in contrast, it doubled in Okinawa. The shift proved the military was susceptible to public opinion in mainland Japan, but it could ignore Okinawans, who lacked political representation. Moreover, the removals signaled that decisions on where to station bases were more guided by politics than proximity to potential trouble spots: The Korean Peninsula is far closer to mainland Japan than Okinawa.[43]

For Okinawans, there was one more lesson from this restructuring: Although many mainland Japanese had expressed support for Okinawans during the bayonet and bulldozer land seizures, when the marines were moved from their bases in Japan, they stayed silent. The Japanese government also did not protest the relocations. Sympathy for Okinawans' military burden was outweighed by the relief among Japanese that they would no longer need to host the bases themselves. In these 1950s relocations lies the root of the current concentration of US bases in Okinawa, and although many Japanese people and their elected officials still voice opposition to this unfair distribution, they do not volunteer to host the facilities themselves.[44]

As for the US government, the rebalancing of military forces was a relatively minor concession to Japanese public opinion. But in 1959, there was one episode that showed its determination to block any erosion of its fundamental right to keep bases in Japan, and the incident sent shockwaves through US-Japan relations that continue to reverberate today. During the protests at Sunagawa in July 1957, seven demonstrators had been arrested for trespassing onto Tachikawa Air Base. At their trial two years later, Tokyo district court judge Date Akio delivered a "not guilty" verdict on the grounds that the presence of US troops in Japan violated Article 9 of Japan's constitution, which prohibited "war potential." The ruling challenged the very foundation of the Security Treaty, a move the US government refused to countenance. On the day after the judge delivered his verdict, US ambassador to Japan Douglas MacArthur II (nephew of the former occupation commander) met with Japan's foreign minister and told him the ruling "may create confusion in minds of public," and he instructed the Japanese government to appeal Date's decision to the supreme court. The following month, MacArthur met the chief justice of the supreme court who would preside over the case. The judge called the previous ruling "inappropriate" and said he expected it to be overturned. True to his word, the supreme court annulled the verdict that US bases violated the Japanese constitution (and ruled the trespassers guilty). At the time, American interference in the case was widely suspected, but only in 2008 did Japanese researcher Niihara Shoji uncover documentary proof at the US National Archives.[45]

The intervention underscored American power over Japan, showing how the US-Japan alliance trumped the Japanese constitution, elevating the rights of the US military over those of Japanese citizens. Moreover, it belied the myth of the pacifism at the core of postwar Japan. It might "forever renounce war as a sovereign right of the nation," but it had merely outsourced such potential to the United States and with it much of its control over foreign policy. The ability of the United States to overrule Japan's judiciary suggested, seven years after the Treaty of San Francisco had ended US occupation, Japan was not a sovereign nation; instead, it resembled a client state (*jūzoku koku*). But it would be a mistake to oversimplify the relationship as US coercion over a submissive vassal. Japanese leaders were willing partners in their own subordination, more than happy to sacrifice their citizens' rights in return for the power bestowed by US patronage.

Okinawa, you shall see, was not the only place where the showcase of democracy was a sham.

"Neither Liberal nor Democratic": The CIA and the Birth of the LDP

In 1957, Prime Minister Kishi Nobusuke visited the United States, where he pitched the opening ball at a New York Yankees game and golfed with President Dwight D. Eisenhower. It was a remarkable turnaround for a man who, a decade previously, had been sitting in an Allied prison awaiting trial on war crimes charges.[46]

In the late 1930s, Kishi had served in Japan's puppet regime of Manchukuo. Then during World War II, he was vice minister of munitions in the cabinet of Tōjō Hideki. Postsurrender, this work led to his arrest and detention by the Allies, but in 1948, he was set free. Kishi's subsequent return to power was traced by US journalist Tim Weiner in his groundbreaking book *Legacy of Ashes: The History of the CIA*. During a series of meetings in the early 1950s, Kishi met with members of the CIA and State Department in Tokyo and made a proposal: If the United States provided the finances, he would ensure that Japan would back the US fight against communism by supporting the presence of military bases in Japan and ensuring a pro-American foreign policy. Central to Kishi's plans was the establishment of a new political party. "The new Liberal Democratic party under his command would be neither liberal nor democratic, but a right-wing club of feudal leaders rising from the ashes of imperial Japan," wrote Weiner.[47]

In August 1955, Secretary of State John Foster Dulles pledged US support for Kishi's new party. Then President Eisenhower green-lit CIA payments to top LDP officials, which continued for some two decades. Since 1955, the LDP has governed Japan in a virtually uninterrupted run more reminiscent of a one-party state than a healthy, functioning democracy.[48]

In 1957, Kishi became prime minister and traveled to the United States to meet the president who had helped him to establish his party. Between his appearances at the Yankee Stadium and on the golf links with Eisenhower, Kishi only briefly discussed the future of Okinawa. In a meeting with Secretary of State Dulles, the Japanese prime minister asked whether the United States could help some Okinawans to migrate overseas, in effect offering Japan's stamp of approval on the US scheme to banish potential troublemakers.[49]

Upon his return to Japan, Kishi's pledge to support the US-Japan alliance faced a key test. The original US-Japan Security Treaty, which had been foisted on Japan in 1951, was due to be renewed in 1960, but the overwhelming majority of the Japanese public opposed the pact. Some 30 million people—one-third of the population—took to the streets in protest. Given LDP loyalty to the United States, though, there was little risk that Japanese popular will would be allowed to interfere with the US-Japan alliance. On 19 May, the government steamrolled the renewal of the treaty through the Diet. First they ordered five hundred police officers into the parliament building to clear out recalcitrant opposition members. Then at midnight, the house speaker called a sudden vote on the treaty's renewal, which—with the dissenters removed—was summarily approved.[50]

Renamed the Treaty of Mutual Cooperation and Security Between the United States and Japan (a.k.a. Anpo), it was fundamentally the same as the previous agreement, allowing the United States to station military forces in Japan for the "security of Japan and the maintenance of international peace and security in the Far East." The notable amendments from the previous agreement were a vague suggestion that the United States would consult with Japan on how it used its forces and an assurance that the United States would actually defend Japan if under attack.

Accompanying the deal, the two nations signed a Status of Forces Agreement (SOFA), which confirmed the legal immunity of the US military. Article 16 stated that American service members were required "to respect the law of Japan"—not "obey" it—and in the majority of criminal cases, suspects would be tried by the military. Japanese officials were not granted the right to access to bases, which were under the sole management of their commanders, and the military was not responsible for the cleanup of land returned to civilian use. To deal with issues arising from US operations in Japan, SOFA established the US-Japan Joint Committee to hold in camera meetings, the decisions of which were not made public. Since its inception in 1960, the text of SOFA has not been updated.[51]

As for Prime Minister Kishi, after steamrolling the Anpo agreement through parliament, he promptly resigned to avoid dealing with the fallout, but he remained an influential figure in the LDP. Although Washington and Tokyo had succeeded in securing the military alliance for the next decade, they experienced an embarrassing setback. Because Japanese public anger was so intense, President Eisenhower was forced to cancel a trip to Tokyo planned to celebrate the renewal. Instead, he headed to the one place where US authorities hoped they would better be able to orchestrate a friendly reception.

The President Arrives in Okinawa

On 19 June 1960, Eisenhower arrived at Kadena Air Base, the first—and last—US president to visit Okinawa during its period of military administration. Upon landing, the president gave a speech proclaiming, "The Ryukyuan people have a vital role for the free world in the circumstances of this era," and he had come "to learn at first hand more about the region," but his entire stay lasted less than three hours. At Kadena Air Base, he boarded an open-top car for the twenty-four-kilometer drive south to Naha. USCAR had put the newly arrived marines to good use, arming 15,000 with rifles and positioning them along the roadside. It also organized crowds of Okinawans with US flags and signs welcoming the president. But the route was too long to maintain the pretense, and as the motorcade neared Naha, the crowds grew hostile. Some Okinawans carried signs demanding immediate reversion to Japan and the removal of nuclear weapons. Others hurled abuse at Eisenhower and yelled, "Yankee go home!"[52]

When the president's car arrived at the legislature, Okinawan police scuffled with demonstrators, and marines had to restrain the crowd to allow access to the building. Once inside, Eisenhower gave a two-minute speech to an incomplete gathering of elected officials (some had boycotted the talk), followed by a short meeting with the chief executive, during which the US-appointed representative dutifully refrained from raising the issue of reversion but instead asked for more economic support and an annual quota of one hundred Okinawans to emigrate to the United States. Outside, angry crowds forced USCAR to abandon plans to drive Eisenhower back to Kadena Air Base. Rather, they opted for the shorter route to Naha Air Base, from where the president was whisked by helicopter back to Kadena for departure from the island. No tangible improvements arose from Eisenhower's visit.[53]

The Organization of Resistance

In 1960, Okinawan resistance to US occupation became organized. At the forefront stood the Okinawa Prefecture Council for Reversion to the Home Country, also known as the Reversion Council (Fukkikyō). Founded on 28 April—the anniversary of the Day of Disgrace—it comprised a cluster of labor unions, the Okinawa Teachers' Association, and left-wing political parties. Many members had been banned by USCAR from traveling to the mainland. The council advocated for the immediate return of Okinawa to Japan, a call that in hindsight might seem puzzling, given Japanese military atrocities during the Battle of Okinawa. To understand the fervency for reversion, it is important to understand several factors. First, at this time, the extent to which Hirohito and Japanese leaders had sacrificed Okinawa was still hidden. Second, civilians' accounts of Japanese military atrocities had not yet been widely published. Only in the 1980s, for example, did the traumatized survivors of the Chibichiri Gama suicides go public with their experiences. Most importantly, many Okinawans saw reversion as the only way to escape the current abuses of the US military. If their islands were protected by the Japanese constitution, then it would provide them with the freedoms denied by USCAR, especially the pacifist clause, Article 9, which they hoped would remove the bases from their land. The Hinomaru Japanese flag, paraded at meetings and marches, became a symbol of Okinawans' desires for reversion. US authorities tried to dissuade such displays by only permitting it to be flown on certain national holidays.[54]

Working alongside the Reversion Council, the Okinawa Human Rights Association was inspired by the ACLU, and it aimed to hold US occupiers accountable for their abuse of residents. One of its early goals was to fight for compensation for Okinawans who had suffered from military crimes and accidents in the years prior to the Treaty of San Francisco. The association's director was Fukuchi Hiroaki, whose outspoken championing of human rights made him a target of both USCAR and right-wingers. He experienced interrogation by the army's Counter Intelligence Corps and bans to travel to mainland Japan. Then in 1967, he was almost killed when a far-rightist stabbed him over his support for teachers' freedom to participate in political activities.[55]

At this time, another important way in which Okinawans organized against US injustices was via unionizing. Base workers continued to endure dangerous, discriminatory conditions and suffered unfair dismissals, so in 1960, Uehara Kōsuke and his colleagues at Camp Zukeran created a 1,600-member union that in the following years, expanded into the All-Okinawan Military Workers' Union (a.k.a. Zengunrō). As well as pushing for better treatment by their military bosses, the union threw its support behind the Reversion Council and campaigns to remove nuclear weapons from their islands. Although their position as military employees made them vulnerable to dismissal, they also exercised a measure of power because the bases could not operate without their labor. Throughout the 1960s, Zengunrō was a leading force in the push for reversion.[56]

To hide its abuses in Okinawa, USCAR deployed semantics, censorship, and the CIA, ensuring the American public and Congress remained in the dark. Realizing this, Okinawan leaders decided to go over the military's heads to appeal to the international community. In December 1960, the United Nations General Assembly had adopted the Declaration on the Granting of Independence to Colonial Countries and Peoples, under which it pledged to eliminate colonialism and support the right to self-determination. If ever there was a place that needed decolonization, Okinawa was it.

On 1 February 1962, the GRI adopted a resolution drawing on the UN declaration. The Okinawans denounced US rule as "incompatible with the principle of . . . self-determination," and they demanded "all UN member states to pay attention to the unjust rule conducted within Japanese territories against the will of the inhabitants and to take actions to realize the complete and prompt restoration of Japanese sovereignty over Okinawa." The GRI addressed its resolution to the 104 member states of the United Nations. This was the first time for Okinawan leaders to adopt such an organized approach to make the international community aware of their suffering—and it would be a tactic they repeated in the coming years.[57]

Okinawans were determined to return to Japanese administration, but Tokyo rebuffed the GRI's overture: "It is not appropriate to consider Okinawa as a territory suffering from exploitation by the US. It cannot be recognized as a territory described in the [UN] Declaration," responded the government officials.[58] The statement highlighted Japan's subservience to the United States. It prioritized US desires over the needs of Okinawans. Despite this, in the next decade, the islanders redoubled their efforts to secure the protections of the constitution of Japan.

6

The Vietnam War in Okinawa

In 1964, the summer Olympics were held in Tokyo, the first time the games were hosted by an Asian nation. They signaled Japan's return to the world stage and an opportunity to showcase its advanced infrastructure: a new expressway; the Shinkansen, linking Tokyo and Osaka; and, in the heart of the capital, the spectacular National Gymnasium and Olympic Village built on land just returned by the US military. The irony was not lost on Okinawans, whose prospects of shuttering the bases in their own communities seemed further off than ever. The Olympics brought home just how far Okinawa was lagging behind Japan. The military prioritized infrastructure that served its mission, so the islands lacked paved roads, schools, hospitals, and reliable supplies of electricity and water. There was no railway, let alone a superfast bullet train. Most seriously, Okinawans were *poor*. In 1960, the Japanese government had pledged to double the nation's gross national product, and salaries were soaring so families could own the three C status symbols—cars, coolers, and color TVs. But in 1964, Okinawans made two-thirds the amount of Japanese, and they could only dream of possessing such luxuries. Moreover, they lacked Japan's welfare services, state pensions, and universal health care, including access to legal abortions.[1]

Much of Japan's postwar economic growth was thanks to Okinawa. The closure of mainland military bases in the mid-1950s allowed communities to repurpose the land for industrial development. At the same time, Japanese construction companies reaped large profits from building new military facilities in the islands. Moreover, Okinawa was a key market for Japanese exports. Due to America's seizure of agricultural land and failure to develop the manufacturing sector, Okinawans were heavily reliant on imported goods, 70 percent of which came from Japan. This provided Japan with a steady flow of dollars in what economists called the *zaru keizai*—the sieve economy. In 1958, approximately $400 million of Japan's dollar reserve of $1.3 billion originated in Okinawa. Without Okinawa, mainland Japan could not have enjoyed such a sustained economic boom in the postwar era. Sacrificing the islands to militarization enabled Japanese people to live free from the dangers of the bases, while the labors of ordinary Okinawans financed their rising standard of living.[2]

As the gap between Japan and Okinawa widened, islanders' desires for reversion grew ever stronger. The Japanese dream represented a safer, wealthier, and more egalitarian ideal compared to life in an impoverished colony where the most promising employment options were limited to bar staff, golf caddies, and maids.

JFK and Okinawa

John Fitzgerald Kennedy provided Okinawans with some optimism that their hopes of reversion would come true. In March 1962, he became the first American president to explicitly state that Okinawa belonged to Japan, and the islands would ultimately be returned: "I recognize the Ryukyus to be a part of the Japanese homeland and look forward to the day when the security interests of the free world will permit their restoration to full Japanese sovereignty."[3]

The previous October, JFK had dispatched a task force to Okinawa to investigate conditions, the first such high-level visit since Melvin Price and company's three-day visit in 1955. Led by Deputy National Security Advisor Carl Kaysen, the team stayed for three weeks and produced a final report that pulled few punches. Okinawans were "under the administration of an alien military government" that restricted their civil rights via controls of the press, unions, and the right to travel off the island. Because American bases occupied farming land, Okinawans faced economic hardships. Even when the military paid rents, these were a "remarkably small sum" compared to what it paid in Spain and elsewhere. Most Okinawans wanted to return to Japanese administration, reported the task force. Among the only ones who supported US rule were a "small group of businessmen who benefit substantially from our presence" and some conservative leaders "who have in effect quietly told their Ryukyuan counterparts to work with the United States." The Kaysen team offered an astute assessment of the contradictory attitudes between Okinawans and the Japanese government vis-à-vis the military presence. Whereas Okinawans understood the bases made them a "prime target in the event of war," Tokyo's mindset was pure NIMBY-ism: It supported stationing the US military there because it protected Japan "without at the same time posing the political problems for it, which would be created by having the base [sic] in Japan." Concentrating the bases in Okinawa kept the crimes, noise, and contamination there, but for Tokyo, this was acceptable because such problems were out of sight and out of mind of mainland voters.[4]

The Kaysen Report spotlit the military's abuses in Okinawa, and it recommended wide-ranging reforms: more cooperation between the Japanese and US governments for economic and social development, more autonomy for the Government of the Ryukyu Islands (GRI), and fewer restrictions on civil rights. Unsurprisingly, the military rankled at such interference, and before the JFK administration could initiate reforms, it deployed one weapon it had been keeping in reserve: the latest emperor of Okinawa.[5]

Today in Okinawa, the name *Lieutenant General Paul Caraway* still conjures up all that was wrong with US rule. Upon his arrival in the islands in February 1961, the high commissioner had unilaterally added an extra star to his uniform, and his language aide recalled how Caraway saw himself as a god who possessed the unbridled right to exercise control over his subjects. Like his forerunners, Caraway promoted a policy of *rinichi*—separation from Japan—to suppress support for reversion. Under his watch, the military rejected mainland economic support for the islands, further impoverishing residents and even opposing Japanese plans to build medical facilities. Not surprisingly, the Kaysen Report's recommendation for increased cooperation with Tokyo angered Caraway and the military, who demanded that the high commissioner be granted the final say over any reforms. As a result, the Kaysen Report failed to initiate major improvements in Okinawans' lives. So fervent was Caraway's separatism that bans on islanders' travel to Japan rose; even patients seeking medical attention were denied permission to leave.[6]

On 5 March 1963, Caraway cemented his notorious legacy when he took to the stage of the Harborview Club, Naha, to address an audience of Okinawans whom USCAR had been grooming via study-abroad programs into the next generation of pro-US leaders. In his speech, Caraway catalogued the failures of the GRI and proclaimed that "autonomy for the Ryukyus" was "impossible." Then, in a now infamous phrase, he urged his audience to "recognize this myth for the rabble-rousing, excusing, alibi for failures." Hitting his stride, Caraway warned listeners that "men must earn the right to wield power," and it would not "be bestowed carelessly upon the adolescent, the weakling, or the incompetent, no matter how loudly he may shout for it."[7]

So flagrantly insulting was the speech that it upset the few elements of Okinawan society who tolerated US occupation, such as members of the Okinawa Liberal Democratic Party (LDP), and the backlash made it into the pages of the *Washington Post*, which reported residents' sentiments that "democracy in the Ryukyus was a sham." USCAR always strove to control information about its abuses from reaching the American public, but now Caraway's treatment of Okinawans, topped by his Harborview speech, placed the arrogance of US colonialism on a pedestal for the world to see. Not only did it cement Okinawans' commitment to rid themselves of military rule, but it also convinced many Japanese conservatives that the way to assert their national pride to their own electorate was to reunite with Japan the islands it had surrendered in exchange for its own sovereignty in 1951.[8]

Prime Minister Sato to DC

In November 1964, Sato Eisaku, the man who navigated Okinawa's ultimate reversion to Japan, became prime minister. His older brother was ex–Prime Minister Kishi Nobusuke, who, upon his release from prison in 1948, had joked with Sato, "Strange, isn't it? We're all democrats now."[9] Sato had been deeply involved in the LDP since its establishment, serving in several cabinet positions. During his time as minister of finance, he had been pivotal in securing funds from the Central Intelligence Agency (CIA). American government officials liked him. In a secret memo, the State Department described Sato as "strongly and outspokenly pro-American and anti-Communist," adding he was "easy and congenial with foreigners." Opposing Article 9, Sato promoted a nuclear-armed Japan. In conversation with the US ambassador to Tokyo, the prime minister explained that although the public opposed such a policy, they "can be 'educated.'"[10]

Okinawa was one potential source of friction between Sato and US leaders. Like many Japanese people, left wing and right wing alike, he firmly believed the islands were his nation's sovereign territory, and they ought to be returned to Japanese administration. Sixty-six thousand mainland Japanese soldiers had died there in World War II, and their sacrifice mandated Okinawa's return—a similar view to the US military, who believed their own losses justified the islands' retention. For Sato, the reversion of Okinawa became a core tenet of his eight-year premiership. In January 1965, he took his first tentative step toward achieving this goal, when, as custom demands for new Japanese prime ministers, he traveled to Washington, DC. In a secret discussion with the State Department, he floated the proposal that the United States might split its administration of the Ryukyu Islands by keeping the main island, where most military bases were located, but returning the other islands, such as Miyako and the Yaeyamas. The State Department was noncommittal. Meeting President Lyndon B. Johnson, Sato brought up the Kaysen Report and its recommendations that Okinawa be given more autonomy, expressing concerns that the guidance was not being followed. LBJ ensured that his visitor knew he was in charge. Throughout the meeting, the president balanced his feet atop the table, while Sato was left sitting awkwardly on a nearby sofa.[11]

On 13 January, LBJ and Sato issued a joint statement that included a discussion of Okinawa. Section 11 opened with an explicit acknowledgment by both leaders of the importance of US military bases in Okinawa "for the security of the far East." It then recognized Sato's "desire that, as soon as feasible, the administrative control over these islands will be restored to Japan and also a deep interest in the expansion of the autonomy of the inhabitants of the Ryukyus and in further promoting their welfare." The statement continued by stating that LBJ "looks forward to the day when the security interests of the free world in the Far East will permit the realization of this desire." By bookending the issue of reversion with emphasis on US military priorities, the statement made it clear that Okinawa would remain an American colony for as long as the military wished. The United States might be willing to allow Japan to expand autonomy and promote welfare, but for now, any talk of giving up the islands was premature.[12]

Prime Minister Sato to Okinawa

In August 1965, Sato headed to Okinawa, the first Japanese prime minister to visit since the end of World War II. Whereas during Eisenhower's visit in 1960, USCAR propaganda teams had ensured cheering crowds lined the roadside, now for Sato, it stage-managed scenes of apathetic onlookers tepidly waving Japanese flags. Unfazed, the prime minister headed to southern Okinawa, where he shed tears at the entrance of the cave where many Himeyuri Student Corps nurses had lost their lives, and he laid flowers at the memorials to the Japanese army commanders General Ushijima Mitsuru and Lieutenant General Chō Isamu. The Reversion Council organized a mass rally to ensure that Sato heard Okinawans' demands for immediate reversion, the removal of nuclear weapons, and their anger at his support for the military bases in their communities. Bolstering their message, some five thousand demonstrators surrounded Sato's hotel in Naha, compelling him to stay the night in American military housing. While he slept, Okinawan police fought running street battles to disperse the protestors.[13]

Sato's visit is best remembered for the speech he gave on 19 August, in which he declared, "Twenty years have passed since Okinawa was separated from the mainland. Not even for a moment have we forgotten the 900,000 people of Okinawa. Until Okinawa is returned to the homeland, the postwar period will not be over for our country."[14]

It was a powerful statement that convinced many Okinawans that Sato had a genuine desire to achieve the reversion of their islands. Accompanying these words, the prime minister also promised concrete improvements in the lives of Okinawans via increased economic aid and investment in education, which was

FIGURE 6.1 *In August 1965, Sato Eisaku became the first Japanese prime minister to visit US-administered Okinawa, where he famously declared, "Until Okinawa is returned to the homeland, the postwar period will not be over for our country." Courtesy of Government of Ryukyu Islands/Okinawa Prefectural Archives*

still woefully underfunded by the American military. This time, USCAR allowed the support. Caraway had been replaced by the less autocratic Lieutenant Albert Watson II, so in the coming years, Japanese aid to Okinawa rose, and Tokyo moved to align the islands' legal and social systems with those of the mainland. Despite these concessions, though, the US military still refused to broach the broader issue of Okinawa's return to Japanese administration, insisting that reversion, if it occurred, would be contingent on regional peace. But in 1965, that was looking more unattainable than ever.[15]

The US War in Vietnam

During the 1930s and '40s, Japan had dreamed of dismantling Western imperialism in Asia and establishing its own Greater East Asia Co-Prosperity Sphere. Although Japan's surrender brought the plan to an end, the temporary overthrow of colonial governance had proven that centuries of White rule in the region was vulnerable. After the war, in quick succession, anticolonial movements won independence in India; the Dutch East Indies; Malay; and French Indochina (modern-day Vietnam, Laos and Cambodia), and the United States relinquished control of the

Philippines. Meanwhile, in China, after a protracted civil war between Chiang Kai-shek's Nationalists and communist forces, Mao Zedong declared victory in 1949. The human costs of these struggles were atrocious: 500,000 died in Indochina between 1945 and 1955; some 1 million in the partition of India and Pakistan (1946–1948); and more than 2 million soldiers in China, plus approximately 5 million more civilians. While many of these independence movements sought liberation from their former colonial rulers, they were frequently the subject of involvement by the United States and the Soviet Union, who attempted to align the emerging governments to their own ideologies.

In Indochina, since the end of World War II, France had been attempting to retain its rule against independence fighters, led by communist Ho Chi Minh, who was widely supported by the general population. By 1954, the United States was funding 80 percent of France's costs and considering the use of nuclear weapons to ensure victory. The justification for US intervention was articulated by President Eisenhower in April 1954, when he espoused his now famous "falling-domino principle." If Indochina toppled to communism, then next the neighboring countries, with their reserves of natural resources and populations, would also turn red. Eventually, according to Eisenhower, Japan, too, "will have only one place in the world to go—that is, toward the Communist areas in order to live."[16]

For the United States, Okinawa played an essential role in preventing this spread of communism. It was located near enough to Indochina, Taiwan, and China to dispatch troops and bombers but far enough to be out of reach of possible attack. The US Army on the Ryukyu Islands published a press kit, *Why We Are Here* (1969), that encapsulated Okinawa's significance: "A glance at the map of the Far East clearly shows why the location of Okinawa is of great military importance to the Free World nations of the Pacific. In addition, Okinawa and the other Ryukyu Islands constitute the only area in this defensive zone under United States administrative control." This combination of geography plus lack of restrictions on covert operations and storage of nuclear weapons convinced the United States that its forces in Okinawa would effectively counter the seemingly unstoppable spread of communism. But in 1954, despite considerable CIA support (much of it orchestrated from Okinawa's Camp Chinen), the French were defeated by communist forces at the Battle of Dien Bien Phu, effectively ending their colonial rule. In the following years, the United States backed a series of unpopular, corrupt, and brutal leaders in South Vietnam to thwart a communist takeover, and it used Okinawa to deploy Green Berets and fly Air America missions. In March 1965, US covert involvement became overt when it deployed its first combat forces to Da Nang. These, too, came from Okinawa. The dispatch of these troops was a major escalation in the conflict, which kept American combat forces in Vietnam for the next eight years.[17]

In mainland Japan, the majority of people opposed the US war in Vietnam. Opinion polls in 1966 indicated 82 percent of respondents were critical of US policies, millions participated in demonstrations, and Beheiren (Japan Peace for Vietnam Committee) helped deserters from US bases in Japan to escape to Sweden. However, just as during the Korean War, Japanese businesses raked in huge earnings from the conflict in Vietnam—approximately $1 billion a year—providing supplies for the US war effort. Japanese government members voiced approval for the conflict, including Prime Minister Sato, who became the only foreign leader without troops there to visit South Vietnam during the war. The prime minister was aware that displaying such open support for America would make the Japanese public worried that their nation might become embroiled in the conflict, so in June 1965, he tried to allay their concerns by announcing that the "war was far away and that there was no danger that Japan would get involved." For Sato, speaking from the safety of mainland Japan, the conflict in Vietnam might well have seemed very distant. But for Okinawans, it felt like the war was on their doorsteps and their roads, in their seas and in their skies. They were living on the front lines.[18]

"Without Okinawa..."

In the mid-1960s, there were 140 military facilities in Okinawa, leading ex–High Commissioner Caraway to pronounce, "The United States does not have bases on Okinawa. Okinawa is the base. It is not possible to sieve out the military areas of functions ... and separate them from the civilian areas or functions." A brief tour of the main bases illustrates the inextricable relationship between Okinawa and the war in Vietnam.[19]

In the south, Naha Military Port was the Pentagon's main supply artery, handling roughly three-quarters of the supplies used by US forces in Vietnam, from ammunition and barrels of oil to rations, beer, and coffins. Much of this materiel was stockpiled in warehouses at nearby Makiminato Service Area, which also had outdoor storage areas for chemicals and damaged vehicles brought back from the war for repairs. The same base housed the headquarters of the army's Seventh Psychological Operations Group, which, in addition to producing *Shurei no Hikari* and materials targeting Okinawans, printed propaganda leaflets for dropping into Vietnam. In the Yanbaru forests, where the terrain resembled mountainous Southeast Asia, the military constructed mock villages to train US troops and those from its allies, Thailand and South Korea. To increase the realism, residents were recruited at a dollar a day to play the roles of the Asian enemy.[20]

The Vietnam War transformed Kadena Air Base into one of the busiest airports on the planet, racking up some one million flights—one every three minutes—during the conflict. Transport aircraft shuttled troops and supplies to the warzone, B-52s used Kadena's runways to launch carpet-bombing raids, and supersonic SR-71 and A-12 spy planes departed on surveillance missions for the air force and the CIA. The base also housed a large mortuary, where American fatalities were preserved for their final trip home.[21] These functions made the islands so important for the military that Admiral Ulysses S. Grant Sharp, commander of US Pacific forces, declared, "Without Okinawa, we couldn't continue fighting the Vietnam war."[22]

During the war, the military directly employed more than 60,000 Okinawans. Thanks to the organizing efforts of the Zengunrō union, conditions had improved since the worst abuses of the 1950s, but the work remained dangerous. At the Chibana Army Ammunition Depot, for example, Okinawan women packed bombs and repaired faulty munitions, suffering injuries when they accidentally detonated. Many of those working on the bases had experienced the Battle of Okinawa, and now they felt profound guilt that they were contributing to civilian suffering in Southeast Asia. "No matter how much we opposed the Vietnam War, B-52s took off from here to bomb local people and the propaganda leaflets we printed sowed confusion. In the eyes of the Vietnamese, Americans and Okinawans were both aggressors. I'll never forget my feelings of regret," recalled one ex–base worker. Unfortunately, though, for many Okinawans, there were few other means to make a living. In 1967, the islands' per-capita income averaged $588, roughly 60 percent of Japan's. Such cheap pay enabled even low-ranking US military personnel to hire maids (approximately 10,000 worked these jobs), while other Okinawans found employment in the entertainment or service industries catering to Americans.[23]

Unlike in Japan, prostitution was legal in Okinawa. During the 1950s, local businessmen—with the endorsement of the US military—established the Yaejima Approved Prostitution Zone. Impoverished young women were recruited by brokers, who burdened them with debts and forced them to work in brothels, where many experienced violence from their customers. USCAR required hotels, clubs, and restaurants catering to military personnel to display an *A* sign ("Approved for US forces"), whereby every female employee—cooks, waitresses, dancers—was subjected to weekly tests for venereal diseases. During the Vietnam War, there were some 1,200 establishments bearing *A* signs. By 1970, prostitution had become Okinawa's largest industry, overtaking the cultivation of sugarcane. As with much of Okinawa's economy, this money enriched mainland Japan via the sieve-economy effect. Community leader Takazato Suzuyo has argued that the combination of the Treaty of San Francisco and legalized prostitution entailed a double sacrifice of the islands for the benefit of the mainland: "Japan came to the

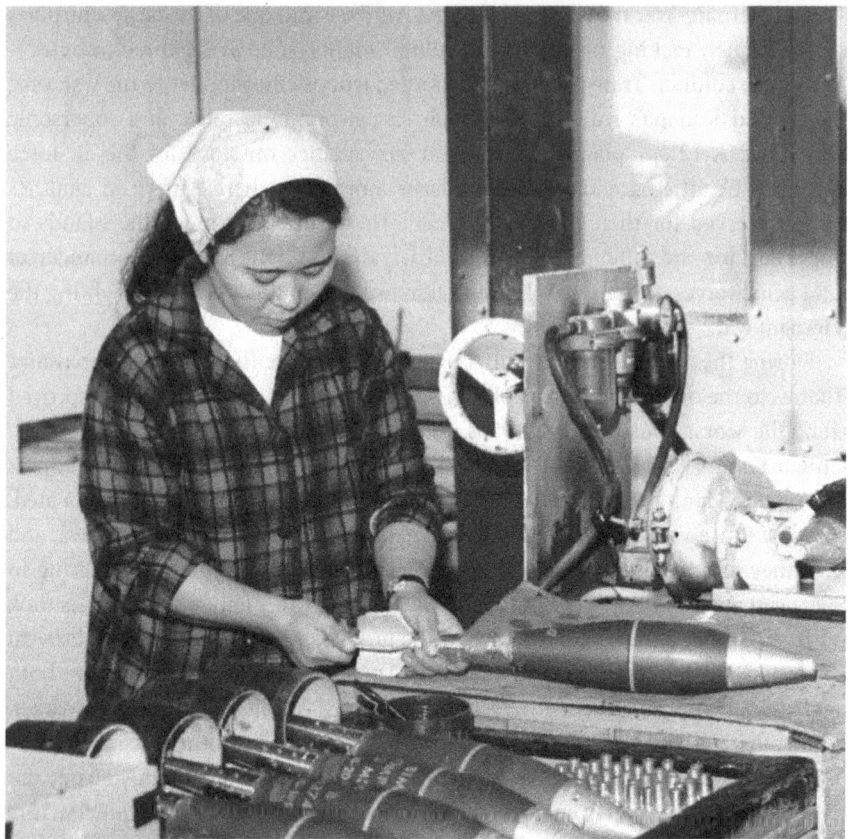

FIGURE 6.2 *During the Vietnam War, more than 60,000 Okinawans were employed by the US military, including women who worked at Chibana Army Ammunition Depot, processing munitions (February 1969). Courtesy of Okinawa Prefectural Archives*

end of the war by using its 'Okinawan' daughter as a breakwater of flesh and then subsequently sold her body to gain economic prosperity."[24]

"We Bring Our Violence into Towns with Us"

During the Vietnam War, the military's intensive use of Okinawa harmed residents in three main ways: accidents, crime, and environmental damage. From 1965, young Okinawans were among those who suffered the most. In March, middle school pupils in Ginoza Village were injured when tear gas seeped into their classrooms from nearby training exercises. The following month, in the same village, a five-year-old girl was struck and killed by a military vehicle. Then in June, an eleven-year old girl was crushed by a trailer dropped by a transport aircraft over Yomitan Village. Ten thousand Okinawans gathered in a mass demonstration—*kenmin taikai*—to protest her death.[25]

During the eight-year period that US combat troops were deployed to Vietnam (March 1965–March 1973), approximately forty-five Okinawans died in military traffic accidents. The worst year was 1971, when American drivers killed fourteen civilians, including a six-year-old girl and a nine-year-old girl in two separate incidents in October. Some perpetrators were found not guilty at courts-martial, and the punishments of others were not disclosed to the public.[26]

As well as negligence, there was the ongoing brutality against civilians. "When we are coming to town, we don't leave our violence on military bases. We bring our violence into towns with us," recalled one marine, Allen Nelson.[27] During the day, troops trained, and at night, they headed off-base, where they got drunk, and some beat to a pulp taxi drivers and bar workers. (Decades later, Nelson became a peace activist and returned to Okinawa to speak about his experiences of the island and the Vietnam War.) Troops fresh from combat would head into Okinawa's streets still dressed in jungle fatigues and exact their trauma on civilians. Others due to be sent to Vietnam assaulted Okinawans in the hope that detention by military police (MPs) might delay their deployment to the war. During the eight years, at least twenty-five Okinawans were murdered by Americans. Military dependents enjoyed the same extraterritoriality as actual service members. In March 1968, after one military daughter strangled a maid, she was found guilty of homicide at a USCAR court, but the presiding judge handed down a suspended sentence, allowing her to be released into the custody of her mother; they left the island.[28]

For centuries, foreigners had been profiting from the opium trade in East Asia, and during the Vietnam War, Americans became the latest profiteers. At the center of their smuggling network was Okinawa. In 1970, the House of Representatives' Committee on Foreign Affairs embarked on a global fact-finding tour to investigate the spread of heroin use. They discovered that "U.S. military and ex-military personnel allied with a few Okinawans" were smuggling heroin from Thailand to the United States via the islands.[29] The lawmakers dubbed the network the "Okinawa System," and they called it the "most despicable crime of modern times."[30] In the summer of 1971, members of the General Accounting Office (the forerunner of the current Government Accountability Office) visited Okinawa to investigate addiction among military personnel. In the air force, 23 percent of personnel had used drugs, including one airman who checked himself into a narcotics amnesty program because "he was working with nuclear material and felt that he should not be working at his assigned position."[31]

MP officers were among the islands' users. "One MP used to snatch purses from Okinawans and use the money to buy heroin," recalled a former member of the Ryukyu Armed Forces Police. "Another went further—he would come on duty, get his gun, and then change into civilian clothes to rob mom-and-pop stores. One owner finally recognized him and filed a complaint. What did the military do? The same as always. They stalled and slowed down the investigation. Then they shipped him off the island."[32]

Ecocide in Okinawa

During the Vietnam War, the term *ecocide* was coined to describe US destruction of Southeast Asia's environment. Military operations devastated Okinawa's ecosystem, too. Spills of sewage, oil, and pesticides flowed from bases into rivers and shorelines, and hazardous chemicals were dumped in civilian landfills. Okinawans' already-fragile drinking-water sources were particularly hard hit. In the late-1960s, USCAR had attempted to solve the island's perennial shortages by tapping into a large aquifer that lay beneath Kadena Air Base, but so much fuel seeped into the ground that the water drawn from wells became flammable.[33]

In 1968, three incidents occurred that terrified Okinawans. During a school excursion in July, more than 230 children suffered chemical burns while swimming in the sea near Gushikawa Village. Some injuries required hospitalization. Prior to the incident, US service members had been spraying herbicides along the shoreline, but the military refused to admit responsibility for the children's injuries. The following month, at Naha Port, three divers were reportedly exposed to radioactive cobalt-60, which had leaked from a US nuclear-powered submarine. The same substance was later detected in shellfish.[34] The CIA dismissed residents' concerns in a top-secret memo stating, "With their well-known 'nuclear allergy' as a basis, the Japanese are easily aroused by scare reports of radioactive pollution of their waters, and of other 'evils' associated with US bases in Japan and Okinawa. . . . These fears and irritants are always present among the Japanese, and are readily susceptible to exploitation by anti-US elements on the slightest pretext."[35] (Predictably it was easier for the US authorities to blame agitators rather than examine how the negligence of its own military contributed to Okinawan resentment.) On 19 November 1968, Okinawans living near Kadena Air Base were awoken before dawn by a thunderous explosion that convinced many their islands had been invaded. A B-52 departing to bomb Southeast Asia had crashed on take-off, detonating its payload of explosives. The blast killed the crew, injured sixteen Okinawans, and damaged more than three hundred buildings. Just several hundred meters from the crash site lay Chibana Army Ammunition Depot and its bunkers of weapons of mass destruction.[36]

As with many instances of military abuses in Okinawa, only in later years has it become clear that even more serious problems had occurred, but they were hidden at the time. In December 1965, the US Navy was transporting nuclear weapons aboard aircraft carrier USS *Ticonderoga* between Southeast Asia and Yokosuka Naval Base, Japan. In seas some 130 kilometers from the Ryukyu Islands, one aircraft loaded with a B-43 bomb slid off the deck and plunged into the ocean. With a yield of one megaton, the weapon possessed some sixty-five times the power of the one that had obliterated Hiroshima, and to this day, it still lies on the seabed susceptible to corrosion and plate tectonics. The navy only revealed the incident in 1981, and even then, it prevaricated about just how near the incident had occurred to Okinawa.[37]

Another weapon that was brought to Okinawa unannounced by the United States was the herbicide Agent Orange. During the Vietnam War, the military and the CIA sprayed more than 75 million liters of the chemical and other rainbow herbicides (named after the color of the stripes around their barrels) over South Vietnam, Cambodia, and Laos to kill crops and jungles where enemy troops could hide. Because herbicides targeted vegetation not humans, the United States argued that they were not a chemical weapon and so were exempt from international prohibitions (a position supported by the Japanese government). But Agent Orange contained dioxin, triggering serious illnesses in those exposed and their subsequent children. In South Vietnam, when this first generation of deformed babies was born, the authorities blamed the defects on a sickness they named "Okinawa bacteria." Approximately three million Vietnamese people were sickened by Agent Orange, but the US government has continued to refuse to provide compensation. It acknowledges the damage to its own troops, though, and it pays support to veterans exposed in Vietnam, Laos, Cambodia, and elsewhere, such as Guam and Thailand, where Agent Orange was sprayed to kill vegetation around runways and perimeter fences.[38]

However, the US government denies the chemical was ever brought to its most important support site: Okinawa. Veterans, though, recall large stockpiles of Agent Orange at fifteen facilities, including Kadena Air Base, and they claim they sprayed it to clear roads, runways, and antenna farms. Prior to the incident at Gushikawa, which burned more than two hundred young swimmers, for example, US troops sprayed the substances along the shoreline. Veterans also claim to have sold excess stocks of Agent Orange to Okinawan farmers, who valued its weed-killing properties. According to one report funded by the US Army, there were 25,000 barrels of the chemical in Okinawa in 1972. Despite this overwhelming evidence, the Department of Defense insists Agent Orange was never in Okinawa—likely for fear of the compensation it would need to pay to the hundreds of thousands of

Americans stationed there during the Vietnam War, not to mention the political backlash from Okinawans working or living near the bases.[39]

"We've Got a Leaker"

The military first started storing chemical weapons at Chibana Army Ammunition Depot in the early 1950s, and in the following years, the stockpile grew to some 300,000 rockets, mines, and bombs packed with mustard gas and nerve agents. Because Okinawa's climate was so humid, though, the munitions were quick to corrode and required frequent maintenance.[40] On 8 July 1969, soldiers were ordered to sandblast some of the nerve-agent bombs ready for repainting. One of the men tasked with the work was nineteen-year-old Daniel Plemons. Five decades later, he recalled what happened that day:

> I started having trouble breathing and my vision became strange. Thinking it was just the dust, I stepped outside for a moment but when I went back inside, everybody was gone. I found them out the back of the building and they yelled at me to inject myself with my automatic spring-loaded antidote. I injected it into my upper thigh. It hurt—but that's what saved my life.[41]

Plemons and twenty-two other Americans were hospitalized for exposure to sarin, and Plemons suffered long-term aftereffects.

On the evening of the accident, the head of the army's Second Logistical Command telephoned High Commissioner James Lampert. After explaining, "We've got a leaker," he asked for permission to dump the sarin bomb at sea, but Lampert told him they would need the green light from the Pentagon.[42] (According to US veterans, the army did dump some of the munitions in the ocean, where, experts warn, they still pose a risk.) The military attempted to hide news of the leak, but journalists found out. On 18 July, the *Wall Street Journal* ran a front-page story, "Nerve Gas Accident: Okinawa Mishap Bares Overseas Deployment of Chemical Weapons." Although the article was short on specifics, it was more than enough to spark outrage among Okinawans, who had long suspected the storage of *nuclear* weapons at Chibana but had not imagined other weapons of mass destruction were there, too.[43]

The accident forced the US government to rethink its policy on chemical weapons. It announced a halt on production and a promise it would only use its existing arsenal in retaliation. The military also declared that it would remove the weapons from the island, but its refusal to specify a time frame incited further Okinawan anger. On 29 July, residents held a *kenmin taikai* mass rally to demand the immediate withdrawal of the munitions.[44]

Again, the CIA was more concerned with public image than public health. In a top-secret memo, it wrote, "Japanese leftists... are hurting for a good rallying cause in their lagging campaign against the Sato government's handling of the Okinawan and Mutual Security Treaty issues with the US. They may well be tempted to try to give this present incident a good propaganda ride."[45]

Victories at Konbu, Iejima, and Kunigami

What the CIA attributed to leftists looking to gain political clout overlooked the very real anger that broad sections of Okinawan society felt about American crimes, accidents, and environmental degradation. In democratic societies, citizens turn to the police, courts, and ballot box to right injustices and implement change, but such pathways were denied to Okinawans living under military administration. Instead, residents applied the forms of nonviolent civil disobedience born from the 1950s period of bayonets and bulldozers, and during the Vietnam War years, they won several notable successes.

In 1965, the military announced plans to seize 70,000 square meters of land in Konbu, Gushikawa Village. Much of this property belonged to war widows who, if dispossessed, would have no means to support their families. Residents united to create the Konbu Association to Protect the Land. They erected a hut from which they conducted sit-ins to thwart attempts to take away their farms. In the following months, US troops attacked the hut, but the villagers persisted in their nonviolent resistance, penning a song called "We Will Not Surrender Even a Single *Tsubo* [3.3 square meters] of Land." The lyrics encapsulated both landowners' opposition to the seizure of their property and resistance to the use of Okinawa for attacks on Vietnam. The Konbu struggle received the support of many people in mainland Japan, and following five and a half years of protests, the military abandoned plans to seize the land.[46]

On the island of Iejima, given their own history of US oppression, farmers felt strong affinity toward Vietnamese peasants. The bombings, arrests and imprisonments made them "understand the feelings of the Vietnamese people as if they were our own," wrote Ahagon Shōkō. At the same time, villagers also showed compassion toward the US conscripts stationed on their island, listening attentively to their stories of combat trauma. In 1966, the military unveiled plans to bring surface-to-air Hawk missiles to Iejima. To preempt residents' opposition, the Okinawa LDP distributed gifts to village officials, and the military made assurances that the missiles would only be deployed temporarily. But Ahagon and the farmers saw through such tricks, organizing hundreds of residents to block the arrival of the weapons. When the army responded by sending reinforcements, villagers calmly confronted them, explaining American missiles were not wanted there, and they ought to go home to their families. Three days later, the military canceled the missile deployment, and almost the entire village triumphantly escorted the departing trucks back to the port.[47]

Between December 1970 and March 1971, Okinawans won another significant victory, this time in the Yanbaru forests, where the military conducted guerrilla training. Now the marine corps was attempting to build a new artillery range in Kunigami Village to fire shells at a hillside, a source of drinking water and home to rare flora and fauna. Some six hundred residents, including the local mayor and school pupils, mobilized to protest. Clambering over barbed wire, the adults occupied both the launch site and the target, raising flags and lighting fires to signal their presence. The protests forced the military to abandon its plans to build the artillery range. In 2009, the village erected a monument to commemorate the residents' victory.[48]

Solidarity and Concessions

Alongside the misconception that Okinawan resistance was fomented by outside agitators, there was an equally erroneous belief that they hated Americans, but then, as today, there is a clear difference between antimilitarism and anti-Americanism. Many Okinawans married US service members. Others struck up lifetime friendships with troops and their families, often mentoring them in karate (upon their return to the States, some students opened their own dojos, helping to spread the 1970s boom in martial arts). In particular, solidarity arose between residents and service members who had been involuntarily drafted into uniform and shared Okinawans' resentment against the military. US troops tipped off journalists with classified information and supported demonstrators by buying their antiwar flyers. African American service members were especially supportive, recognizing in Okinawans parallel patterns of discrimination and resistance. The Black Panther Party had a strong presence, and in January 1969, its newspaper praised students' demonstrations: "The forceful action of the students threw the U.S. and Japanese reactionary pigs into a panic. . . . Braving the pigs' brutal suppression, the students stormed the base several times and fought bravely with the police."[49]

During the Vietnam War, Okinawa was a stop-off point for military entertainment tours by both establishment and antiestablishment performers. In 1971, Bob Hope visited the bases. When the high commissioner came onstage to introduce the performer, he was heckled by the audience. Hope's jokes included one where he suggested US troops should develop "meaningful relationships" with

Asians by smuggling prostitutes home in their duffel bags. Much better received was the Free the Army tour featuring the actors and anti–Vietnam War activists Donald Sutherland and Jane Fonda. After performing to packed crowds—including one show at an Okinawan bullring—they joined local union members striking at Kadena Air Base, where they urged American troops to support the action.[50]

Okinawans' unrelenting resistance to USCAR oppression forced the American government to make concessions. In 1965, thanks to the hard work of the Okinawa Human Rights Association and other groups, Congress finally agreed to provide $21 million compensation for the deaths, injuries, and land seizures suffered by Okinawans during the period between the end of World War II and the Treaty of San Francisco. USCAR also slackened some of its more oppressive measures, partly lifting restrictions on publications, displays of the Japanese flag, and travel. By 1970, the number of direct decrees had dropped to seventy-three, roughly half compared to a decade previously. Accompanying this diluted authoritarianism, the United States now allowed the Japanese government to increase economic aid to Okinawa. As a result, via the GRI, Okinawans were able to receive medical insurance, unemployment benefits, and pensions.[51]

Despite these concessions, though, the fundamental status of Okinawa as a military colony was unchanged. Most Okinawans were convinced there was only one effective way to secure such civil rights and economic opportunities: reversion to Japan.

7

Reversion

Subterfuge has been the bedrock of postwar US-Japan relations, from the rehabilitation of Emperor Hirohito and the amnesty of his army's bioweapon scientists, through the Central Intelligence Agency's (CIA) sponsorship of the Liberal Democratic Party (LDP) and US undermining of Japan's highest judiciary in the Sunagawa Supreme Court trial. So deep has American interference been that in 1996, the State Department's Historical Office complained that the CIA's refusal to release information makes it impossible to compile a thorough history of US-Japan relations in the 1960s.[1]

Notwithstanding the plethora of such interventions, few other matters have been buried beneath as much secrecy as Okinawa's reversion to Japanese administration. Negotiations took place behind closed doors in Washington and Tokyo, where officials struck a series of secret agreements (*mitsuyaku*) surrounding nuclear weapons, Japanese government pay-offs totaling hundreds of millions of dollars, and retention of the military's rights to use the bases. The existence of these deals stayed hidden for decades, and some details remain murky today, denied by the US and Japanese governments. Although reversion was necessitated by Okinawans' relentless opposition to American rule, the negotiations excluded them almost entirely, taking place without the input—or regard—for the islanders themselves. Ultimately, the scale of the betrayal was enormous, laying a path for the problems Okinawans still face and residents' ongoing resistance.

Essential to understanding this period is a recognition that the US and Japanese governments sought the same fundamental goal: to preserve American bases in Okinawa. Tokyo believed the US military was important for the defense of Japan, but because stationing American troops on the mainland was unpopular, concentrating them on Okinawa was a convenient solution for all but the Okinawans. For the US government, the islands provided a hub from which it could stage covert and overt operations in Southeast Asia while preparing for possible wars in Korea, Taiwan, China, and elsewhere. Although the United States and Japan differed in their aims over *how* Okinawa's bases should be managed postreversion—notably the number of facilities to retain and whether they should possess nuclear weapons—both countries agreed that Okinawa should remain militarized after its return to Japanese administration. This set the two governments at loggerheads with the desires of Okinawans, who demanded the removal of the bases consistent with the pacifist guarantees of the Japanese constitution.

For both nations' leaders, inseparable from the reversion issue was the renewal of the United States–Japan Security Treaty (a.k.a. Anpo), which, with its ten-year limit, was due to be abrogated or renewed in 1970. The two governments recalled the humiliation of the 1960 Tokyo protests that forced President Eisenhower to cancel his visit to Japan. Now, they feared that the combined might of Okinawa's Reversion Council and the mainland anti–Vietnam War movement would threaten Anpo's renewal. The longer the Okinawa issue remained undecided, the higher the potential for such trouble to occur. As early as 1965, US Ambassador to Japan Edwin O. Reischauer had warned "time is running out on us," and the "Okinawan problem would come to the explosion point before 1970." With the clock ticking, the Japanese and US governments realized they had only a few years to achieve Okinawa's reversion. If they waited any longer, the bases—and perhaps Anpo itself—might be swept away by the resistance of one million Okinawans compounded with the wrath of mainland Japanese. As a first step, US and Japanese authorities decided to buy some time.[2]

The 1968 Elections

For two decades, Okinawans had been demanding the right to elect the chief executive, the highest-level local official, but the US military had refused. Instead, it handpicked the executive due to fears that a popular vote would return a vocally proreversion leader. In 1968, though, the US Civil Administration of the Ryukyu Islands (USCAR) agreed to allow residents to choose the executive themselves. "A palliative might momentarily satisfy Okinawan aspirations and thereby give us more time in putting off the day when our freedom of military operations would be circumscribed," recalled High Commissioner Lieutenant General Ferdinand T. Unger. The Americans had another reason to allow the election: They felt certain they could rig a favorable outcome. Since the ouster of Senaga Kamejiro in the mid-1950s, the CIA had been channeling money into the Okinawa LDP to sway local polls. By 1965, Ambassador Reischauer concluded such tactics had grown too risky—"If the U.S. is caught with its hand in the cookie jar there will be a serious blow-up in Japan"—so he advised injecting American monies through the Japanese LDP, who in turn would pump the funds into Okinawan election campaigns. In 1968, during the run-up to the vote for chief executive, the CIA and the LDP spent the staggering sum of approximately $1.6 million to sway the result.³

Two main candidates were standing for the post: Yara Chōbyō, the left-wing head of the Okinawa Teachers' Association and Reversion Council stalwart, and conservative Nishime Junji, president of the Okinawa LDP. Although both politicians advocated reversion, Yara argued for immediate return to Japan and elimination of the bases; Nishime, in contrast, proposed a more gradual process of integration with the mainland without a concrete timeline. On 10 November, almost 90 percent of the electorate cast their votes, an exceptionally high turnout. The CIA-LDP funds almost tipped the win for Nishime, but Yara scraped to victory with a margin of 30,000 votes (roughly 7 percent of the ballots). (A third candidate, whose manifesto called for Okinawan independence, received fewer than three hundred votes, a sign of how effectively the reversion movement had convinced Okinawans that their future lay with Japan, not self-rule.)

The collaboration between the CIA and the LDP to manipulate the election was an ugly sign of how far they were prepared to subvert Okinawans' popular will, aligning two of the most powerful nations on the planet against the residents of the small islands. But unlike the election of Senaga, this time USCAR did not attempt to overturn the results. The backlash would have been too strong. Instead, the high commissioner declared Yara's victory a "landmark in the Okinawan movement for reversion." The military had finally started to understand that the days of its direct rule were numbered.⁴

Nixon, Kissinger, and Okinawa

In the same month as the Okinawa election, American voters also went to the polls to choose a new president. They selected Richard Milhous Nixon, who promised to tackle crime, calm public protests, and achieve peace in Vietnam (although he did not explain how to achieve this, and his record of bombing North and South Vietnam did not inspire confidence in US victory). As for Japan, Nixon possessed some awareness about Okinawa. In 1953, he had visited as vice president and asserted, "The United States will control Okinawa so long as the communist threat exists."⁵ More recently, in the lead-up to the 1968 election, he had told Japanese journalists that he supported reversion. US rule over Okinawa, he later wrote, was a "constant irritant" in relations between Japan and the United States.⁶

Within the US government, there remained a long-running schism between the military, which wanted to retain full control of the islands, and the Department of State, which was more amenable toward reversion. Nixon tasked National Security Advisor Dr. Henry A. Kissinger to investigate. In his own words, Kissinger's knowledge was poor—"When I first came to office, there was no major country I understood less than Japan"—so he convened an interagency group of advisors. By April 1969, Kissinger had been brought up to speed on the Okinawa issue and concluded that unless the islands were returned to Japanese administration forthwith while preserving the bases and their troops, the military presence would be at risk. For many years, American leaders had believed the most effective way to secure the bases was to retain administration of Okinawa, but now they understood that local opposition was so strong that ongoing USCAR rule had become a liability. "Popular agitation not only posed a physical danger to the bases but also constituted a political threat to Prime Minister Sato and his governing Liberal Democratic Party," summarized the Joint Chiefs of Staff. It was an astute assessment. Sato had staked his political future on reversion, so Washington, having invested so much time and money into the LDP, prioritized ensuring that he remained in power.[7]

In May 1969, Kissinger signed top-secret National Security Decision Memorandum 13 spelling out the US bargaining position on reversion. First, as long as agreement was reached within 1969, the United States would be willing to return the administration of Okinawa in 1972. Second, it would assert its "desire for maximum free conventional use of the military bases, particularly with respect to Korea, Taiwan and Vietnam." Third, although the United States wanted to retain its nuclear arsenal, the "President is prepared to consider, at the final stages of negotiation, the withdrawal of the weapons while retaining emergency storage and transit rights."[8]

Throughout the summer of 1969, Japanese and US representatives held official and back-channel meetings to discuss the preliminary logistics of how to revert Okinawa to Japan. In November, Sato traveled to Washington, and after three days of talks, on 21 November, the prime minister and Nixon released their joint announcement on the future of the islands. According to the statement, Sato believed, the "time had come to respond to the strong desire of the people of Japan, of both the mainland and Okinawa," for reversion, which, the two countries announced, would occur in 1972. Accompanying this promise was the obligatory recognition by Japan of the need for the US military: "The presence of United States forces in the Far East constituted a mainstay for the stability of the area." As for the postreversion fate of the bases, "the United States would retain under the terms of the Treaty of Mutual Cooperation and Security such military facilities and areas in Okinawa as required in the mutual security of both countries." When it came to the nuclear issue, the prime minister explained the "particular sentiment of the Japanese people against nuclear weapons and the policy of the Japanese Government reflecting such sentiment." In response, the United States agreed that reversion "would be carried out in a manner consistent with the policy of the Japanese Government as described by the Prime Minister." The statement confirmed that, as the two nations negotiated the finer details of reversion in the coming months, Okinawans would be relegated to the sidelines. The sole input would come from the chief executive, who would only be allowed to advise a preparatory commission on the transfer of administrative rights.[9]

President Nixon announced, "We have resolved the last major issue which came out of World War II, the Okinawa problem."[10] After this, Sato held a press conference to clarify the agreement's details to the Japanese public and silence suspicions that he had made any secret deals with the Americans. In the statement, he promised, "There are no particular conditions attached to the reversion." [11] Many listeners remained dubious.

In Okinawa, reactions to the announcement were bittersweet. On one hand, Japan and the United States had finally agreed to what islanders had been demanding for so many years: reversion to Japan and the removal of nuclear weapons. But on the other hand, their elation was tinged by the realization that the bases would stay. In the run-up to the November announcement, Prime Minister Sato had assured Okinawans that reversion would adhere to the principle of *hondo nami*: The proportion of bases in the newly returned prefecture would be equal to that in the rest of the country. With Okinawa's land mass comprising less than 1 percent of the nation, this ought to translate into only a handful of US bases remaining in Okinawa, but the joint statement's pledge that the United States would retain "such military facilities . . . as required in the mutual security of both countries" made clear that many more would remain.[12]

The Nixon-Sato announcement had painful parallels with the prewar years, when Okinawans' patriotic efforts to assimilate as Japanese were repaid with the sacrifice of their islands. Now again, they had done all they could to embrace the motherland—flying the Hinomaru flag and abandoning their own languages—but once again, they had been betrayed. Many Okinawans wanted the world to understand their wrath.

Days of Rage

From January 1970, Zengunrō (the All-Okinawan Military Workers' Union) staged a series of strikes that threatened to paralyze military operations. Base workers had to contend with a contradiction that tore at their consciences. While many opposed the use of the bases to launch wars that would involve Okinawa and Japan in Southeast Asian and US conflicts, the bases offered some of the few stable employment opportunities in the islands. Under Nixon's policies, the United States was downsizing its overseas military presence, resulting in the threat of mass layoffs for Okinawa employees. At the same time, Zengunrō was demanding better working conditions and higher wages. Many segments of society sympathized with the base workers. The strikes were supported by civil servants, teachers, and university students. To undermine this solidarity, USCAR resorted to the usual tactic of issuing off-limits orders to its troops to turn communities dependent on military patrons against the union. This encouraged a motley coalition of the Okinawa LDP, business owners, far rightists, and the yakuza to launch assaults and arson attacks on the strikers.[13]

Against this backdrop of organized right-wing violence, during the three-year wait between the Nixon-Sato announcement and scheduled reversion, the US military crime wave continued unabated. In 1969, five Okinawans were murdered and six killed in traffic accidents. Punishments for perpetrators were rare. In 1970, only 20 percent of Americans accused of crimes were prosecuted, compared to an 80 percent arraignment rate for Okinawans. Throughout the quarter-century of US rule, Okinawans had almost unanimously eschewed violence against their occupiers, but on 20 December 1970, in Koza City, this was upended in a fiery manner. Two incidents added to an already-tense mood. At the start of December, a court-martial had delivered a "not guilty" verdict to a soldier who had drunkenly run over and killed a woman in Itoman City. Meanwhile, the military was still stalling its removal of chemical weapons from the Chibana Army Depot, where nerve agent had leaked more than one year prior and another suspected spill on 3 December sickened Okinawans at a nearby dam. On 19 December, 10,000 people attended a mass rally (*kenmin taikai*) outside the Chibana base to demand the immediate withdrawal of the deadly stockpile.[14]

That night at 1.00 a.m. in Koza, there was another traffic accident involving a drunk US driver who struck a pedestrian. As the civilian police arrived on the scene, Okinawans emerged from the neighborhood bars. Some urged the police not to allow a repeat of the Itoman injustice and demanded the American be tried in a people's court. The police managed to escort the driver to safety, but the crowd swelled to five hundred, many of whom railed against the unfairness of the US courts and delays in removing chemicals weapons.[15]

Just as more Okinawans were pouring into the street from local bars, another American service member crashed his car. The furious crowd surrounded the vehicle and threw a cement block through its windshield, seriously injuring the driver. Military police (MPs) rushed to the scene, but when they attempted to rescue the American, they were surrounded. The MPs fired warning shots to disperse the crowd. Then they bundled the wounded driver into one of their cars and fled, leaving behind another vehicle. Okinawans flipped the abandoned patrol car onto its roof and set it afire. This was the start of five hours of rioting, the likes of which the island had never seen. More than one thousand Okinawans flooded the streets, rolling US-owned vehicles—identifiable by their yellow number plates—from parking lots and setting them ablaze. They stopped passing American cars, dragged out their occupants, and burned their vehicles. If the drivers were Black, they were allowed to pass, a sign of the solidarity many Okinawans felt toward African Americans.[16]

The crowd hurled rocks and blocks at the civilian police and MPs. Female bar workers filled bottles with gasoline to make Molotov cocktails. The rioters smashed up a local police station and then stormed Kadena Air Base, burning American cars and buildings, including the employment office and middle school. At 5:30 a.m., as the rioters drew near a US housing area, MPs received orders to use tear gas. Finally, the crowds dispersed.[17]

According to official calculations, the riot had injured fifty-six Americans, destroyed some eighty US-owned vehicles, and caused $20,000 damage to Kadena Air Base. But as philosopher Annmaria Shimabuku explains, for US authorities, "more than simply the cost of property damaged, they sensed a small tear in sovereign power with potentially catastrophic consequences." The rioters were those whom the military could normally count on—the bar workers who had previously been co-opted to intimidate antibase demonstrators—but by December 1970, even they had reached their breaking point. One Department of Defense intelligence report identified widespread public sympathy with the rioters: "Though the majority of Okinawans did not participate, their significant lack of condemnation or abhorrence of the actions of the crowd could indicate that they identify with and give consent to the actions of those few." The riot won support from African American troops in Okinawa. In the following days, they distributed leaflets, stating, "The Black GI's are aware of the situation that brought about the riot, and this was truly a RIGHT-ON-MOVE. That's the only way they'll bend."[18]

The riot persuaded the military to finally clear out its chemical weapons from Okinawa. In January 1971, it removed nine truckloads. Then in August, it withdrew the remaining stockpile in a thirty-eight-day mission it dubbed Operation Red Hat. Because governors in the United States refused to accept the munitions, they were taken to the American territory of Johnston Atoll, where previously failed nuclear launches had caused severe contamination. Once again, the US military was using one of its Pacific colonies as a dumping ground to do what would be unacceptable in the mainland United States.[19]

Back in Okinawa, the violence did not end with the Koza riot. In November 1971, residents staged a general strike to coincide with the second anniversary of Nixon and Sato's reversion announcement. Schools shut down, and the gates to the bases were blocked. Ninety thousand people participated in rallies and actions, the largest number to date. The protests sometimes turned violent, and one student hit a police officer with a petrol bomb. Witnessing the attack was the young photographer Ishikawa Mao, who later recalled her horror: "I saw an Okinawan policeman get hit by a bottle filled with gasoline.... The policeman just

FIGURE 7.1 *On 20 December 1970, Okinawans rioted in Koza City in an unprecedented display of violence that injured fifty-six Americans and destroyed dozens of US-owned vehicles. Courtesy of Larry Gray*

lay down and died. I ran away crying. I ran and ran. Then I stopped to vomit at the side of the road. 'Why do Okinawans fight Okinawans?' I thought." The killing of the policeman was a pivotal moment for many islanders, which accentuated how reversion tensions had spurred chaos even between Okinawans. In its wake, many residents' commitment to absolute pacifism was reinforced.[20]

Reversion Day

To prepare for Okinawa's reintegration into Japan's body politic, prior to reversion, residents were permitted to participate in elections for the national parliament. In November 1970, with seven seats up for grabs, islanders voted left-wing candidates into power, including those formerly blacklisted, such as Senaga Kamejiro and union founder Uehara Kōsuke. Representatives' main concerns centered on the military's ongoing covert and overt operations: broadcasts from the Voice of America antennas (with their accompanying bizarre effects on neighbors); supersonic spy flights from Kadena Air Base; and the Seventh Psychological Operations Group, which in the run-up to reversion was producing TV and radio shows to persuade Okinawans of the need for military bases to defend their islands from communism.[21]

Although Okinawan politicians had finally been permitted to return to the national Diet, this did not mean the LDP government would pay any attention to them. In November 1971, when parliament met to confirm the reversion agreement, the LDP steamrolled through the vote, ignoring scheduled questions by Okinawan parliamentarians. In a last-ditch attempt, Yara rushed to Tokyo brandishing a list of Okinawans' demands, but before he could disembark from his flight at Haneda Airport, the vote had already been passed. Such scorn sent an early message to Okinawans that even after rejoining Japan, their voices and their legitimate rights could be ignored.[22]

On 15 May 1972, Okinawa became a prefecture again—twenty-seven years after the Nimitz Proclamation had suspended Japanese administration. Under the finalized terms of the reversion agreement, the United States relinquished the rights granted by Article 3 of the Treaty of San Francisco, and the Japanese government agreed to pay $320 million for the transfer of US assets and unspecified "extra costs." Additionally, Japan waived all claims for damages caused by the military during its administration, and it recognized the judgments passed down by the USCAR courts, despite their opacity and unfairness. As for the military presence, the United States would keep eighty-eight bases (including almost all of the major ones, such as Naha Military Port, Makiminato Service Area, and Kadena Air Base), hand twelve to Japan for use by the Self-Defense Forces or Ministry of Transport, and return thirty-four facilities in "whole or part." (The agreement also permitted Voice of America to keep operating for five more years.)[23]

The Japanese government heralded reversion as a "historic accomplishment." On 15 May, it held a ceremony at the Nippon Budōkan Arena, Tokyo, where, after lauding the islands' return, LDP politicians ended with an ad-libbed "*Tennō heika banzai!*" (Long live the emperor!). The following year, when Prime Minister Sato met Nixon at the White House, he apologized for not having shouted "*Banzai*" for the US president, too.[24]

Yara, whose title had now been updated from chief executive to governor, boycotted the Tokyo ceremony. None of Okinawa's seven Diet members attended, either. Instead in Naha City, the Reversion Council staged a 10,000-person rally in which they decried the return as a repeat of the Ryukyu Disposal of the early Meiji Period. Once again, the Japanese government had swept aside Okinawans' rights. What ought to have been a moment for celebration was instead a time of disillusionment. The *Ryukyu Shimpo* newspaper captured islanders' emotions with its headline "The Bases Unchanged, the Suffering Continues" (*Kawaranu kichi tsudzuku kunō*). When Prime Minister Sato visited Naha in 1965, he had famously declared the postwar era would not be over until Okinawa had been returned. Yara countered with his own statement: "As long as there are military bases in Okinawa, we must continue to question their presence and deal with the numerous problems that they cause. So, while these bases remain in Okinawa, it cannot be said that reversion is complete."[25]

According to opinion polls, almost two-thirds of Okinawans shared Yara's frustrations, expressing uneasiness about the postreversion future of their islands. But the number of people feeling concern would certainly have been far, far higher if they had been aware of the true extent of the secret deals struck behind closed doors in Washington and Tokyo.[26]

The Mitsuyaku

The US and Japanese governments' *mitsuyaku* (secret agreements) centered on three main issues: nuclear weapons, money, and how Okinawa's bases could be used post-1972. For many years, their existence was concealed, and some details remain unknown, but thanks to the research of Okinawan and Japanese journalists and academics, now we have a clearer understanding of how Washington and Tokyo conspired to thwart Okinawans' desires for the return of their islands without military bases.

The Nuclear Weapons

The question of whether the US military could store nuclear weapons in Okinawa after reversion was the most sensitive. Throughout USCAR rule, Okinawans had protested the presence of these munitions, and in mainland Japan, there was overwhelming antinuclear sentiment engendered by the bombings of Hiroshima and Nagasaki and the 1954 exposure of Japanese fishing crews to fallout near the Marshall Islands. LDP leaders had long been at odds with public opinion on nuclear weapons. Sato had supported Japan possessing its own nuclear arsenal, and successive national governments had turned a blind eye to US Navy vessels retaining their munitions when visiting Japanese ports. Well aware that the electorate was averse to nuclear weapons, in 1967, Sato pandered to public sentiment with a parliamentary address in which he promised to follow the "Three Non-Nuclear Principles of not possessing, not producing and not permitting the introduction of nuclear weapons." In 1970, the prime minister reiterated his stance when he signed Japan onto the Treaty on the Non-Proliferation of Nuclear Weapons, which sought to control the spread of such munitions and eventually eliminate them. As Japanese officials entered negotiations with their US counterparts over the terms of Okinawa's reversion, the nuclear question was foremost in their minds.[27]

At its peak, the United States had housed some 1,200 nuclear weapons in Okinawa, but by the late 1960s, technological advances had rendered many of them obsolete. With this in mind, some US military officers believed that relinquishing the right to retain nuclear weapons in Okinawa might be an acceptable concession—but only if they could be reintroduced in circumstances deemed necessary. As American and Japanese officials prepared to discuss the conditions of reversion, the US position was bolstered by the presence of a CIA source within a Japanese subcommittee studying the return, fruit borne from the agency's years of payments to LDP politicians. The uproar over the 1969 leak of nerve agent reminded both sides of the sensitivities of storing weapons of mass destruction in Okinawa. Any agreement to allow the return of nuclear weapons would need to be carefully hidden. Behind the scenes, Wakaizumi Kei, Sato's secret envoy in reversion negotiations, and Kissinger choreographed a convoluted charade for their bosses to follow at the moment of the deal.[28]

On 21 November 1969, when Nixon and Sato met at the White House, the US president uttered a prearranged phrase—an invitation to see photographs he'd brought from his Californian hometown—so the two could meet privately in a side room.[29] There, with only Kissinger as a witness, Nixon and Sato signed an agreement that stated, "In time of great emergency the United States Government will require the re-entry of nuclear weapons and transit rights in Okinawa with prior consultation with the Government of Japan." To enable this, the United States needed the "standby retention and activation in time of great emergency" of facilities at Kadena, Naha, Henoko, and elsewhere. Under the terms of the deal, Sato promised to "meet these requirements without delay when such prior consultation takes place."[30]

Soon after striking the agreement, the two leaders stood on the White House lawn to announce that reversion "would be carried out in a manner consistent with the policy of the Japanese Government" on nuclear weapons.[31] To hide the deal, Sato and Nixon agreed to store the signed document in their private offices so it would not enter publicly accessible archives. The ploy worked for twenty-five years, until Wakaizumi revealed the existence of the agreement in his memoirs. Then in 2009, Sato's son released the documents signed by his father and Nixon. Notably, the same memorandum has never been released by the State Department.[32]

In December 1971, the US ambassador to Tokyo suggested that Nixon might repeat the promise that no nuclear weapons would remain in Okinawa after reversion, but the assistant to the secretary of defense rejected the idea, instead recommending an "oriental-type" assertion that Okinawa will be "returned in a state consistent with Japanese policy."[33] As it turned out, the United States broke its pledge. On 15 May, there were still eight different types of nuclear devices in Okinawa that were not removed until the following month. For his part, Sato's antinuclear pretense won him the 1974 Nobel Peace Prize. In later years, an official historian of the award called it the committee's largest-ever mistake.[34]

The Money

According to the official text of the reversion agreement, Japan would pay the United States $320 million in compensation for assets transferred to Japan and other costs, but this was only a fraction of the actual amount, as behind the scenes, Tokyo made a slew of secret payments. The first of these came to light in June 1971, when *Mainichi Shinbun* journalist Nishiyama Takichi published a scoop revealing that Japan had paid the United States $4 million to clean up some land formerly occupied by the military. Nishiyama had obtained the information from a Ministry of Foreign Affairs employee with whom he had been having an extramarital relationship, and the following year, both were arrested on charges related to the leak of state secrets. The Japanese government successfully manipulated the issue to ensure the public was more outraged about the pair's personal lives than revelations of the secret payment. Both the journalist and bureaucrat suffered widespread vilification—spreading a chilling effect on others who might have been tempted to lift the lid on similar *mitsuyaku*.[35]

As it turned out, $4 million was only the tip of the iceberg. In the coming years, researchers discovered that Japan had agreed to pay the United States some $685 million—more than double the officially acknowledged amount. Tokyo had agreed to pay for roads and buildings "constructed for civilian and joint civil-military use" as well as "land rental payments, social security obligations to Okinawans employed by the U.S. and [Washington's] obligation to restore leased land ... to its original condition." Finally, it agreed to fund "any costs of relocation of facilities made necessary by the reversion agreement." Tokyo and Washington agreed to keep these extra payments "secret forever."[36]

Both governments had portrayed reversion negotiations as amicable and fair, but in reality, they had been a buy back, and the government of Japan was a willing customer. For LDP politicians, $685 million was a small price to pay to keep the unpopular bases in Okinawa far away from their mainland constituencies. These moneys set a precedent for the coming years, whereby Japanese taxpayers would proffer large sums to keep the US military in Japan in the form of *omoiyari* (sympathy) payments (described in chapter 8). The secret moneys also presaged Japanese government funding for environmental remediation of shuttered bases and the costs of relocating military facilities, most egregiously in the 2000s, when Tokyo agreed to foot the bill to construct two new bases: one atop Okinawa's pristine Oura Bay and the other in the US territory Guam.

The Bases

One minute after midnight on 15 May 1972, representatives from the Japanese government and the US military convened a meeting in Tokyo of the US-Japan Joint Committee, the organization that had been established in 1960 under the terms of Status of Forces Agreement (SOFA) and, due to its lack of civilian oversight or transparency, embodied all that was wrong with Japan's client-state relationship. Now in the moments after reversion, the committee met to outline how the US military would be able to use the eighty-eight bases still under its control in Okinawa. In the minutes from that meeting—"The 5/15 memo"—one statement repeatedly appears: "The USG will continue to use the facility and area as during the period preceding reversion." With some minor exceptions, such as bans on using underwater explosives, the committee provided the military with carte blanche to continue using its bases as it always had. The Joint Committee session ended at 1:00 a.m., but during the single hour it had convened, Okinawa's burden was cemented for the coming decades. If the 5/15 memo had been made public at the time of its agreement, the public backlash would have been furious, so details of the memo were kept under wraps for the next twenty-five years.[37]

Now that Okinawa was once again a prefecture, it would be natural to assume that Japanese laws would apply there, but few of these covered the bases. Under SOFA, which postreversion was applied to Okinawa, the US military enjoyed exceptional freedom: exclusive rights to manage its bases and deny access to Japanese and Okinawans officials, exemption from cleaning up contamination on returned land, and jurisdiction of US suspects accused of committing crimes while on duty. Further adding to American troops' extraterritoriality was yet another secret agreement, this one signed in 1953, under which Japanese prosecutors waived the rights to indict US suspects except in cases "of material importance to Japan." As a result, the prosecution rates of accused US personnel remained far below national averages, affording Americans a degree of legal impunity akin to that enjoyed by their predecessors under the unfair treaties of the nineteenth century. (The existence of the 1953 deal was only made public in 2011.)[38]

Still more proof that postreversion Okinawa would not receive full constitutional protections was evinced by how the government dealt with the properties occupied by US bases. Following reversion, the government of Japan would take over leases formerly paid by USCAR, so to ensure a smooth transition, it decided to block potential disputes by Okinawan landowners. On 15 May, the Law on the Provisional Public Use of Land in Okinawa took effect, granting the Japanese government the right to continue using all land that had previously been seized by the US military. As the name suggests, the legislation was limited to Okinawa, so it violated Article 95 of the constitution, which forbade laws from applying only to a specific area without a local referendum. (The government had sidestepped the constitutional requirements by passing the law just before Okinawa returned to Japanese control.)[39]

For Okinawans in this era, the constitution held an almost-sacred significance. Unlike mainland Japan, where in 1947 the United States had bestowed the constitution on the nation, Okinawans were the only people who had to struggle for the freedoms it guaranteed. As a result, Okinawans appreciated the Kenpo more than many mainland Japanese, and they still do today. Nonetheless, reversion proved that Okinawans would not receive their full protections because constitutionally guaranteed rights were overridden by the US-Japan security agreement. The Kenpo was subordinate to Anpo.

Given the deep injustices of the *mitsuyaku* and the scale of the subversion of Okinawans' rights, the US military and Japanese government made concerted efforts to destroy as much incriminating evidence as possible. In December 1972, US military headquarters in Japan completed a review of its classified documents and concluded that 85 percent of its top-secret files would be destroyed. Meanwhile, after Japan passed its first national Freedom of Information law in 1999, the Ministry of Foreign Affairs proceeded to destroy two tons of documents a day. Some were recycled into toilet paper that was then provided to the same ministry—a fitting analogy for many Japanese bureaucrats' attitudes toward transparency and the public's right to know.[40]

8

Broken Promises

The Okinawa that returned to Japan on 15 May 1972 was an impoverished backwater. During its twenty-seven years of rule, the US military had seized vast tracts of land, depriving hundreds of thousands of residents of the means to support themselves, and it had woefully neglected civilian development, so the islands lacked sufficient schools, hospitals, nursing homes, and public housing. The electrical grid and water and sewage lines were ineffective. Unlike mainland Japan, which possessed extensive train and highway networks, Okinawa lacked a railway, and the roads in some communities remained unpaved. The economy was severely underdeveloped due to failure by the United States to nurture the industrial sector or capitalize on the islands' potential as a hub for regional trade. In 1972, Okinawans' per-capita income was less than half that of mainland Japanese. Exacerbating poverty was inflation, which, compounded by conversion of the dollar to the yen at a rate lower than prereversion, rose significantly in the coming years.[1]

The government of Japan had its work cut out to bring the prefecture up to national standards. In December 1972, it implemented the first ten-year Okinawa Promotion and Development Plan to boost the economy, improve infrastructure, and provide residents with the full welfare benefits enjoyed by other prefectures. By 1996, it had invested some ¥6 trillion into the islands, which gradually raised residents' quality of life—though not to the same level as mainland Japanese and not without some drawbacks. Tokyo's schemes for the main island envisaged a geographical divide, whereby the east coast would be developed for industry, and the west coast, for tourism. Sea-reclamation projects were launched in Kin Bay, pivoting on a large-scale oil storage facility, and there were plans to build an aluminum refinery. While some Okinawans welcomed the schemes as a boost to the economy, others quickly realized they threatened to degrade their environment and cause severe pollution similar to that on the mainland. Residents created civic groups that succeeded in halting some of the projects. In the coming years, these members also led campaigns to block the US military's destruction of forests and coral reefs to expand its bases.[2]

On the west coast, the Japanese government and business leaders planned to tap into mainlanders' growing disposable income and hunger for travel by transforming Okinawa into a discount Hawai'i, an exotic, nearby island destination accessible without a passport. Prior to reversion, much of Okinawa's tourist trade had catered to Japanese military veterans and their families, who visited the islands' battle sites. But now, to kickstart new sightseeing ventures and commemorate reversion, the authorities planned to stage the Okinawa International Ocean Exposition— Expo '75—on Motobu Peninsula. In preparation, the Japanese government and mainland construction firms built a stretch of the islands' first highway, hotels, and artificial beaches. Within the Expo grounds, they set up pavilions to showcase Japanese corporations and a massive oil-rig-like Aquapolis. The six-month event attracted far fewer visitors than hoped and triggered so many financial problems that residents coined the phrase *Expo bankruptcies* (*kaiyōhaku tōsan*). In many ways Expo '75 encapsulated the weaknesses of focusing Okinawa's postreversion economy on tourism. Money flowed off the islands to mainland Japanese companies that built and owned the hotels; work for residents was unskilled, underpaid, and temporary; and unsustainable projects damaged the environment. Nonetheless, in the coming years, Okinawa's tourist trade boomed. In 1978, it reached a significant milestone when it surpassed the economic contribution of the military, belying fears that the prefecture could not survive a reduction in the bases.[3]

Maintaining the Burden

Throughout its administration, the US government had insisted the military would remain in Okinawa as long as the regional security situation required. By the early 1970s, the time seemed ripe for its removal. In February 1972, Richard Nixon became the first US president to visit the People's Republic of China. Then in May, he visited the Soviet Union. The following year, the United States withdrew the last of its combat troops from Vietnam. Accompanying this deescalation in global tensions, Washington sought to cut costs in its defense budget by slashing the number of military facilities at home and overseas. In mainland Japan, the two governments agreed to the Kanto Plan, whereby six US facilities would be closed and their operations consolidated at Yokota Air Base, Tokyo, with Japanese taxpayers footing the bill. Thus, by the mid-1970s, the military footprint in mainland Japan was reduced by approximately one-third.[4]

In 1973, within the US government, there were discussions about downsizing the military presence in Okinawa, too. The Department of State and the US embassy in Tokyo supported a reduction, but some Department of Defense officials opposed it. However, Assistant Secretary of Defense Robert Hill, who had visited the prefecture, was convinced that maintaining the current scale was politically and economically untenable. As a result, the US government considered withdrawing marine corps facilities from the prefecture and relocating them to Hawai'i, California, or South Korea. If this plan had been realized, the overall military footprint in Okinawa would have dropped by more than two-thirds, fulfilling islanders' long-held hopes of a more equitable base burden.[5]

So why didn't the shift materialize? At least some of the blame lies with the Japanese government. In 1973, during bilateral meetings over the future of US bases in Okinawa, the Japanese Ministry of Foreign Affairs and the Defense Agency expressed concerns about the security situation in the Korean Peninsula and Southeast Asia. Defense Bureau Chief Kubo Takuya told his US counterparts, "Due to the need for mobile forces in Asia, the US Marine Corps should be maintained." Some members of the Japanese government valued the marines in Okinawa as the most visible evidence of US commitment to security of Japan. Until this moment, the Department of State had supported a reduction in Okinawa's bases, but the Japanese government's intervention provided the US government with the necessary justification to retain them. In August 1973, the Nixon administration issued National Security Decision Memorandum 230, wherein it announced it would maintain its current military strength in Okinawa and Japan. Once again, the Japanese government had betrayed Okinawans' wishes to demilitarize their islands. In public, it had promoted the principle of *hondo nami*—proportionate hosting—but behind closed doors, it was lobbying for the marines to stay in Okinawa. Nozoe Fumiaki, a professor at Okinawa International University who unearthed the details and revealed them in 2013, described Tokyo's intervention as a pivotal moment with long-term repercussions: "The opportunity to significantly downsize the US military presence in Okinawa was lost and thus the bases became more permanent."[6]

Because the US military had reduced its facilities in mainland Japan but retained them in Okinawa, during the 1970s, the islands' burden vis-à-vis the rest of Japan increased. In the 1960s, the split had been approximately 50–50, but by 1974, Okinawa was hosting three-quarters of US military bases in Japan, a huge imbalance, given the fact that Okinawa comprises only 0.6 percent of the nation's total land mass.[7]

Although the Department of State once again had deferred to the military, this did not prevent it from using the Japanese government's appeal to retain the marines as, what it called, "negotiation leverage." Perceiving how much Tokyo valued the presence of the marine corps, the US government pushed for increased funding for the bases. The 1960 US-Japan Status of Forces Agreement (SOFA) had set out the financial split for the military presence in Japan: The US government was responsible for "all expenditures incident to the maintenance" of its forces except for rents to landowners, which would be provided by Japanese taxpayers. During reversion negotiations, the United States tried to whittle this division by insisting that Japan pay for the social-security costs of base workers. In the 1970s, with the trade deficit between Japan and the United States growing, some American politicians accused Japan of receiving a free ride in defense. In 1977, the Carter administration asked Tokyo to pay the labor costs of military employees, and the Japanese government agreed to share the outlay. The following year, when the US military threatened to make redundant 850 base workers from the Makiminato Service Area, the Japanese government, fearful of the economic impact on Okinawa, agreed to pay for some of their welfare benefits. As a result, far fewer employees were laid off.[8]

To convince a skeptical Japanese public of the need for larger payments to the US military, the Director General of the Defense Agency said they were made "in sympathy" toward the cash-strapped US government. As a result, they became known as the "sympathy budgets" (*omoiyari yosan*). Initially, the payments were made in a provisional manner, but as time passed, they became an official part of the budget, and they were greatly expanded to cover a larger share of base workers' salaries, the construction of on-base apartment blocks (with rooms far more spacious than those inhabited by the average Okinawan family), and service members' utility bills. By the end of the century, Japan was paying approximately half of the costs to host the US military—more than any other country.[9]

At the same time as the Japanese government was showering taxpayers' money on the US military, it used a similar approach to buy the silence of some of the Okinawans so strenuously opposing their presence. Under its 1972 constitutionally questionable land law, it claimed the right to grant the US military the authority to continue to occupy residents' property. Next, the government upped the rents it paid to landowners by 600 percent. The Japanese version of the saying "the carrot and the stick" is *ame to muchi* ("the candy and the whip"), and the phrase applies to many of Tokyo's policies toward Okinawa, particularly the land issue. Property owners who rejected the government's *ame* in the form of higher rental payments were subjected to its *muchi*. Those who refused to sign contracts were subjected to intimidating telephone calls and punitive taxes. The tactic worked, and between 1972 and 1977, the number of defiant landowners dropped from 2,900 to fewer than 500. To further undermine resistance, the Japanese government introduced a system whereby if the landowner refused to sign a lease, the responsibility was passed on to the local mayor, and if they refused, too, the governor of Okinawa served as a proxy. All these measures empowered the Japanese government—on behalf of the US military—to occupy Okinawans' land without their consent.[10]

The Problems Persist

With the Japanese government doing all it could to maintain the military presence in Okinawa, the problems caused by the bases persisted, and for the residents of Kin Town, in northern Okinawa, conditions worsened. In April 1973, the marines embarked on a new method of artillery training that lobbed shells over a civilian road. Roughly once a month, the marines shut down Prefectural Route 104 and fired ordnance at a hillside four kilometers away, shattering trees, stripping soil, and causing erosion that flowed into the ocean. The blasts were so powerful they shook Kin Town and terrified residents. Between 1973 and the early 1990s, the marines shot some 30,000 shells, and machine-gun training caused widespread forest fires.[11]

Aircraft accidents continued as before reversion. Between 1972 and 1995, there were at least twenty-two incidents where airplanes or helicopters crashed or dropped objects, including weaponry and fuel tanks. Throughout this period, too, Okinawans living near the bases experienced severe environmental damage from leaks of fuel, sewage, and firefighting foam. At Makiminato Service Area, surplus chemicals brought back from the Vietnam War seeped into the soil and sea, killing marine life. In a bungled attempt to resolve the problem, in 1974, the army buried large volumes of hazardous substances within the base; four and a half decades later, some areas were still found to be contaminated, but commanders opted not to alert service members or their families living there. The military displayed similar disregard for human health on the island of Iejima, where residents were still asserting their moral authority to farm their stolen land. In October 1973, the army used a technique it had utilized with devastating effect in Vietnam: spraying the farmers' fields with herbicides, damaging two thousand square meters of land. The villagers filed a furious protest with the military, to no effect. Under SOFA, Okinawan government officials were powerless to investigate environmental problems. They had no right to enter the bases, nor did the military need to report accidents to civilian authorities.[12]

Islanders had hoped that reversion would reduce the number of offenses committed by US service members, but crimes continued relentlessly. Within one year of reversion, three Okinawan women and one man had been killed by American military personnel. By 1996, the number of postreversion crimes committed by US service members, their dependents, and contractors had reached approximately 4,800. Also, during the postreversion period, military personnel and veterans continued to use the island as a conduit for drug smuggling under the so-called Okinawa System. Islanders' addiction to heroin soared—particularly among workers in the bar areas, such as Koza City. In tandem, there was a rise in robberies committed by Americans against Okinawans to pay for their fixes.[13]

Reversion, Okinawans thought, was supposed to reduce their base burden, but post-1972, there was a new military presence: the Japanese Self-Defense Forces (SDF), who moved into some of the facilities returned by the United States. The Japanese government claimed their dispatch would protect Okinawa, but residents learned from World War II that the presence of bases makes their communities targets and soldiers commit atrocities against women and children. Most Okinawans opposed the SDF deployment to their islands, and their fears seemed justified when one member assaulted a woman in October 1972. Opposition ran so strong that Naha City prevented Japanese service members from registering as residents, and the prefectural government was the only one in Japan that refused to participate in SDF recruitment drives. Tokyo attempted to assuage Okinawans' antipathy by tasking its troops with the clearance of wartime unexploded ordnance (UXO). In the following years, this helped to convince some residents that the SDF might be able to contribute in a peaceful, positive way to their islands.[14]

Resisting the United States . . .

Faced with such a constant wave of military crime and other abuses, Okinawans continued to engage in sustained nonviolent resistance. Some of this was grounded in the tactics developed prior to reversion, such as sit-ins, marches, and mass rallies, but they also applied methods previously unavailable under US rule.

To protest the marines' artillery training over Prefectural Route 104, Okinawans blocked access roads with their cars and occupied the bombing sites, temporarily forcing cancelation of some drills. The authorities responded by dispatching hundreds of riot police to arrest the demonstrators. Yomitan Village emerged as the front line of the postreversion peace movement. US forces landed on its beaches in 1945, precipitating the forced suicides at Chibichiri Gama. Then throughout American rule, it had been used for missile tests and parachute drops. In the mid-1980s, half the village was still occupied by bases. Residents' experiences of earlier Japanese militarism and ongoing US militarism gave rise to a resolute pacifist consciousness. In 1983, hundreds of villagers assembled to disrupt army parachute drills, flying kites, blocking runways with cars, and setting off fireworks. Village mayor Yamauchi Tokushin was a key figure in the demonstrations. Insisting that the role of his administration was to protect residents' lives, he instructed his staff to obstruct the military drills. In neighboring Onna Village, residents also deployed nonviolent civil disobedience to block construction of an urban-guerrilla-training facility, forcing the American military to cancel the project.[15]

Under US rule, Okinawans had been unable to pursue legal challenges against the military, but now that the islands had reverted to Japan and were (theoretically) protected by its constitution, they turned to the courts as one avenue of resistance to the bases. One of their main targets was Kadena Air Base, where round-the-clock flights disturbed sleep; drowned out classes; and caused serious health damage, including heart and hearing problems. In 1982, 601 residents filed a lawsuit against the Japanese government calling for the end of nighttime flights at the base and compensation for past and future damages. It took sixteen years for the court to reach a decision, finally ruling in favor of the plaintiffs and awarding them compensation. But the judges refrained from ordering a halt to nocturnal use, arguing it was unable to control a third party (i.e., the US military). The verdict infuriated residents, who argued that because the US air force was operating in Japan under the bilateral security treaty and the Japanese government provided the United States with the land for the bases, Tokyo ought to share responsibility for the problem. For many Okinawans, this was another example of the new realities of double subjugation, whereby the Japanese government shirked responsibility and claimed to be unable to rein in US military excesses. The noise ruling reinforced how Anpo overrode residents' right to a peaceful life.[16]

Realizing the limits of conventional approaches, Okinawans developed innovative ways to oppose the largest military on the planet. Because the Japanese government maintained the bases through leases with the landowners, in 1982, Okinawans decided to express their solidarity for landowners resisting the bases by launching the Hitotsutsubo Anti-War Landlord Association, whereby they paid a ¥10,000 membership fee to jointly purchase land within Kadena Air Base (*Hitotsutsubo* means one *tsubo*, an area of 3.3 square meters). Participants included students, homemakers, and members of religious communities. The system symbolized support for the original owners to continue their resistance against the Japanese government's attempts to force them to sign leases against their will, and it shared the responsibility with future generations.[17]

. . . And Resisting Japan

During US occupation, Okinawans had seen reversion as the swiftest way to secure civil rights, thus many residents had muffled criticism of Japan so as not to delay return. Now, as the new realities became clear, islanders expressed their anger, particularly toward the three aspects of Japan unchanged since wartime: the emperor; the Hinomaru flag; and the anthem, "*Kimi ga Yo*" ("His Majesty's Reign"), which celebrated imperial rule "for eternity until pebbles grow into boulders covered in moss."

Following the war, Hirohito visited every prefecture in carefully stage-managed attempts to rehabilitate his reputation and display his humanity (which ironically often highlighted his awkwardness in dealing with mere mortals). The only area he had not visited was Okinawa. One reason for royal planners' trepidation was islanders' attitudes toward the emperor. According to one 1978 opinion poll, only in Okinawa did people harbor more negative feelings for the emperor than positive. In light of such sentiment, the authorities decided the first postreversion royal visitor to Okinawa should not be the emperor himself but his son, Crown Prince Akihito. They decided that he would attend the opening ceremony of Expo '75 in Motobu, but like many other aspects of that spectacle, the visit did not go as organizers had hoped.[18]

On 17 July 1975, as the crown prince's car was driving past a hospital, two protestors—who had checked themselves into the facility under false pretenses—rained bottles and other projectiles onto the motorcade. Nobody was injured, and the police quickly arrested the perpetrators. (After spending three years in prison, one of the assailants was elected to the Nago City Assembly, suggesting a measure of sympathy among some Okinawans for his anti-imperial actions.) Soon after, Akihito and his entourage visited the memorial to the Himeyuri Student Corps who had died in the final days of the Battle of Okinawa in Itoman City. As they laid a wreath at the entrance to the cave, two young protestors emerged from the darkness, threw a petrol bomb and fireworks, and swung nunchaku (an Okinawa-born martial arts weapon). One police officer was injured, but the suspects were promptly apprehended.[19]

Although most Okinawans denounced the violence against the crown prince, four years later, many islanders were united in their fury toward the imperial institution. In 1979, scholar Shindō Eiichi broke the news of Hirohito's 1947 suggestion to US occupiers that they ought to retain control of Okinawa for "25 to 50 years or more" in an article for the magazine *Sekai*. For the first time, Okinawans understood that their islands had been sold out by the emperor to save his own skin, and he bore at least partial blame for their twenty-seven years of US military administration. (Not until 1988 was the true depth of Hirohito's betrayal revealed when an Okinawan TV station reported his February 1945 call for one last, decisive victory, triggering the military to sacrifice Okinawa to secure a stronger position at the negotiating table and so preserve the imperial throne.)[20]

At the same time, the Japanese government was attempting to instill patriotism in the youth reminiscent of the wartime era. In 1985, the Ministry of Education issued an instruction to public schools over the "proper management" of the Hinomaru and "*Kimi ga Yo*" at entrance and graduation ceremonies. Whereas in mainland Japan, most primary schools displayed these patriotic trappings, in Okinawa, only 7 percent of primary schools flew the flag, and no schools sang the anthem. The Ministry of Education issued a veiled warning to Okinawan schools, and when teachers continued to resist, thirty-five were disciplined with suspensions, pay cuts, or other punishments. Okinawan students also opposed the Japanese government's demands. High schoolers boycotted one graduation ceremony that flew the flag and held their own alternative event outdoors, leaving their principal to address an empty auditorium. Resistance was strongest in Yomitan Village, where during one high school opening ceremony, a student tore down the Hinomaru and flung it into a ditch. Onlookers applauded her actions.[21]

It was an extraordinary turnaround. During the prereversion era, Okinawans had campaigned for the freedom to fly the Japanese flag; now they protested for the right *not* to display it. It was a clear sign of how the Japanese government's mistreatment of Okinawa had alienated large sections of the population with policies that failed to acknowledge its own wartime abuses while buttressing US military exploitation. For many Okinawans, the Hinomaru had transformed from a symbol of liberation to one of oppression.

The issue came to a head in autumn 1987, when school sports teams from across Japan convened at the National Athletic Meet, held in Okinawa for the first time. The Japanese event organizers announced the crown prince would attend the event to read out a message from his father, who was too sick to visit in person. When Akihito arrived, he was met with a large banner reading, "Return the blood which 200,000 people shed for the Emperor." Hirohito's message consisted of only generic platitudes with no hint of remorse—let alone responsibility—for the wartime slaughter.[22]

The signature event of the meet, the softball tournament, was scheduled to be held in Yomitan. Prior to the opening, villagers created a petition, and the local assembly passed a resolution not to play "*Kimi ga Yo*" or fly the Hinomaru for the event, but at the last minute, the mainland organizers threatened to cancel the tournament unless they relented. To ensure villagers' compliance, 5,000 riot police were dispatched to Yomitan (population: 30,000) in a show of force resembling martial law. During the opening ceremony, some junior high school band members refused to play their instruments for "*Kimi ga Yo*" and others sat in silence instead of standing and singing.[23]

Among the crowd was Chibana Shōichi, a supermarket owner, whose actions that day showed the world what many Okinawans felt about Japan. Born in Yomitan, from an early age, Chibana had been acutely aware of discrimination. During the war, his mother had worked at a mainland factory, where her supervisor had trivialized the damage from US attacks on Okinawa because the islands were "not originally Japan." After the war, Chibana's father worked on the US bases until one day, he was arbitrarily dismissed for attending a speech by Senaga Kamejiro. Chibana's own schooldays had been interrupted by the roar of missile tests along Yomitan's shoreline, and as he grew older, he became active in the islands' reversion and peace movement.[24]

On 26 October 1987, when Chibana saw the Hinomaru flying over his village at the softball tournament, he scaled the ten-meter-tall podium and cut through the ropes with a pocketknife. Then he lowered the flag and set it on fire with a lighter. The backlash was ferocious. Chibana was arrested and detained, and during his interrogations, he was denounced as a traitor. Far-right thugs descended on Yomitan, tried to burn down his supermarket, and picketed the store to scare away customers. In response, the community rallied to Chibana's support and set up a twenty-four-hour watch to protect the shop, forcing the rightists to give up.[25]

The following year, Chibana appeared in court. He described the psychological impact of *tennoism* (emperor worship) on Okinawans and Japan's wartime oppression, not shying from islanders' own participation in atrocities against other Asians. He told the judges, "In our eagerness to be accepted, we tried to be 'good Japanese,' and so willingly accepted our 'education'; but this resulted in our 'animal-like loyalty.' Okinawans were mobilized for murder and supported the aggression in Asia, which ultimately led to the Battle of Okinawa and the group suicides." Explaining why he had burned the Hinomaru, Chibana told the court, "Japan has laid aside the question of the Emperor's responsibility in war as supreme officer, has not taken steps to change its national flag and national anthem. Japan has never reflected upon the historical crimes in which 'Hinomaru and Kimigayo' played a part, and again today, is enforcing them on us."[26] Unswayed by Chibana's defense, the judge found him guilty and handed down a one-year suspended sentence. The charge: disrupting business.

The trial illuminated a surprising incongruency in Japan's postwar history. After World War II, the other defeated Axis nations abandoned their wartime symbols: Germany scrapped its swastika flag and deleted stanzas from its national anthem evoking militarism and expansionism; Italy, too, removed the royal crest from its tricolor and jettisoned its previous anthem. In contrast, Japan retained both its flag and anthem, but as a sop to domestic opposition, particularly from teachers, and the Asian nations it had invaded, it did not designate them as its official symbols. Following Chibana's court case, Japanese authorities moved to formalize the recognition of these signs of war and empire. In 1999, it passed the Act on the National Flag and Anthem, which recognized the official status of the Hinomaru and "*Kimi ga Yo.*"

The Japanese government's glorification of the anthem and flag was part of a wider campaign to rewrite the history of its wartime atrocities and imperial conquests. Japanese conservatives repudiated projections of their nation as an aggressor, instead portraying itself as a victim, pointing to the atomic attacks as proof. Such narratives, though, derailed when it came to describing the Battle of Okinawa, where the Japanese military had slaughtered civilians and forced them to commit suicide. In the early 1980s, the Ministry of Education attempted to downplay the realities of the battle in school textbooks by reducing the number of civilian deaths, erasing references to Japanese soldiers' atrocities and glorifying the group suicides as noble and brave actions. Okinawans protested vehemently.[27]

Seeking the Truth

The Japanese government's attempts to rewrite history combined with its deployment of the SDF and imposition of the flag and anthem prompted many Okinawans to reconsider what had happened to their islands during World War II and instilled a desire to teach its lessons to those too young to have experienced the battle firsthand.

Among the many activists was Nakamura Fumiko, who became known as the mother of the Okinawan peace movement. Born in 1913, she trained as an elementary school teacher, and like her colleagues, during the war, she encouraged her pupils to be loyal subjects and fight for Hirohito. Some later lost their lives in the Himeyuri Student Corps and the Emperor's Blood and Iron Corps. After the war, Nakamura reflected deeply on teachers' responsibility for having promoted militarism and dedicated herself to peace education, lecturing her students about the horrors of the Battle of Okinawa and the importance of *Nuchi du Takara*. The Okinawan proverb is often translated as "Life is precious," but this fails to fully capture the essence of the original, which encapsulates how Okinawans' love of life arose from centuries of Japanese attempts to eradicate their culture and, in World War II, their very existence. Today the phrase galvanizes a vociferous dedication to pacifism rarely found elsewhere in the world.[28]

Following her retirement, Nakamura became secretary general of the Okinawa Historical Film Society (a.k.a. the One Foot Association). The group took its name from its crowdfunding activities, which gathered donations to purchase unedited reels of American military film of the Battle of Okinawa—one foot at a time—from the US National Archives. The association screened the film, which depicted American landings, combat, and civilian suffering, at community venues throughout Okinawa, giving residents their first look at footage of the battle through which they had lived. The screenings provided survivors with a safe venue to share their own experiences of the battle, memories that some had suppressed for decades. By the time the One Foot Association wrapped up its work in 2013, it had collected 110,000 feet of film, lasting some fifty hours. Soon after its completion, Nakamura passed away at the age of ninety-nine.

During this period, too, survivors of the Chibichiri Gama group suicides broke their silence, encouraged to speak up by researchers, including supermarket owner Chibana. As an act of community catharsis, every villager donated to build a memorial outside the cave—the *Statue of Peace Through Generations*, designed by renowned Yomitan sculptor Kinjo Minoru. In the wave of violence following Chibana's flag burning, rightists destroyed the statue. "The victims were killed twice," lamented one relative upon learning of its destruction. *Tennoism* had created the conditions that had led to the deaths of Chibichiri Gama's 84 evacuees; now its modern counterparts desecrated their memory.[29]

Okinawans also confronted the Japanese military's system of sexual exploitation in their islands. Triggering their investigations was Bae Pong-I, a Korean comfort woman who had been brought to Okinawa by the Japanese army in 1944. Following the war, she remained there without revealing her past to the USCAR or local authorities. After reversion, however, the Japanese government required all foreign residents to register themselves or face deportation. This compelled Bae to reveal her existence and her background. Reacting with a combination of guilt and compassion, Okinawans persuaded the prefectural government to grant her the official paperwork to remain in Japan. Subsequently, islanders scoured Imperial Army documents and conducted extensive field research to uncover the extent of comfort stations in their islands. In 1994, the Okinawan Women's Research Group made public their findings: The Japanese military had established at least 130 comfort stations in Okinawa. The announcement horrified many islanders, who had not realized the scale of the abuse. The findings reinforced how militarism harmed women, resonating powerfully with female Okinawans, who continued to suffer sexual violence from US military servicemen.[30]

The 1980s

During US colonial rule, the high commissioner had wielded control over local municipalities via a secret slush fund. Communities that endured the military in relative silence were awarded with investments; those that were more confrontational were denied such moneys. From the 1980s, the Japanese government adopted a similar approach but on a far grander scale. It pumped moneys into places that cooperated with hosting the bases but denied them to those that opposed the military. This encouraged voters to elect officials who could keep such funds flowing, and electoral candidates vied for the approval of the central government. As a result, during the late 1970s and '80s, conservatives were elected to office, including Nishime Junji, the former Okinawa LDP chief who had lost in his 1968 bid to become the chief executive but ten years later succeeded in becoming governor.[31]

Despite the large amounts of government money entering Okinawa, many islanders only experienced limited improvements to their lives. Much of the investment was siphoned off the island as infrastructure development contracts were awarded to mainland construction firms, and national hotel, shopping mall, and airline corporations dominated the Okinawan market. By 1998, Okinawans' average income was still less than 70 percent of mainlanders', and proportionally little changed since 1964, the year of the Tokyo Olympics.[32]

In 1990, Iraq invaded Kuwait, and the United States assembled a coalition of countries to expel Saddam Hussein's forces. Japan's constitution prevented it from sending the SDF, so instead it paid $13 billion in support of the military operations, but this was not enough for the United States, which demanded that Japan dispatch SDF transport aircraft to the region. The issue triggered heated debate in Japan over its commitment to Article 9 pacifism. Although it declined to send aircraft, it sent minesweepers to the Persian Gulf in 1991, the Japanese military's first foreign deployment since World War II. The problem was particularly sensitive in Okinawa, where residents had suffered the consequences of Japan's last overseas ventures. It became one of the key issues in the prefecture's 1990 gubernatorial election which pitted the incumbent, Nishime, who supported the dispatch, against rival candidate, Ota Masahide, who knew firsthand the horrors of war.

At the age of nineteen, Ota had been mustered into the Emperor's Blood and Iron Corps, handed a rifle and two grenades, and ordered to run messages between military shelters. Most of his comrades were killed in deaths he described as "more like those of worms than humans." Ota, too, was wounded by shrapnel, but when he sought refuge in a cave, Japanese soldiers accused him of being a spy, and he narrowly avoided execution. Following his eventual surrender, Ota convinced the internment camp guards to allow him to lead searches to recover the bones of his teachers and classmates. During the US occupation, Ota received American funds to study in the United States, and in 1956, he completed his master's in journalism from Syracuse University. Upon his return to Okinawa, he became a professor at the University of the Ryukyus, traveling frequently to the US National Archives to gather documents and photographs of the Battle of Okinawa and USCAR administration. Based on these materials and his own experiences, Ota established himself as the prefecture's best-known historian, writing unflinchingly about Japanese and US discrimination against Okinawans.[33]

In his 1990 bid to become governor, Ota adopted a manifesto with an inclusive vision of pacifism that incorporated both a reduction of the military presence with respect for dignity and human rights, notably improving the welfare and medical systems, and advocating for the empowerment of women. The manifesto struck a chord with voters, and Ota was elected governor.

As a Battle of Okinawa survivor and historian, Ota was keenly aware of how the islands' past had been obliterated by World War II and manipulated under American rule to justify its occupation, so he dedicated himself to ensuring Okinawans knew their islands' history. His administration opened the Okinawa Prefectural Archives to preserve documents and hold exhibitions, some of which focused on issues that the US and Japanese governments would prefer forgotten, such as farmers' struggles against land seizures and the deployment of nuclear weapons. The most prominent achievement of Ota's administration was construction of the memorial to the Battle of Okinawa—the Cornerstone of Peace (*Heiwa no Ishiji*)—located on the southern shoreline of Itoman, the town where so many civilians had been slaughtered in the final weeks of fighting. Unveiled on 23 June 1995, near the fiftieth anniversary of the official end of the battle, the memorial consists of concentric waves of black granite slabs inscribed with the names of all those known to have died in the battle, regardless of nationality, including Japanese; Americans; Koreans; and, of course the largest number, Okinawans. Unlike the Vietnam Veterans Memorial, Washington, DC, which lists only the US dead, or Yasukuni Shrine, Tokyo, which glorifies the kamikaze and war gods, the Cornerstone of Peace was designed as a site to reflect on how war destroys the lives of those on all sides. At the opening ceremony, four children—one each from Okinawa, the United States, South Korea, and Taiwan—lit a "Flame of Peace" collected from the Kerama Islands, where US forces had initially landed, and the two targets of atomic bombings, Hiroshima and Nagasaki. Testament to Ota's staunch pacifism, the prefecture banned members of the US military from attending in uniform. During the day, Okinawan families walked the stone rows searching for the names of friends and relatives who had died. Many broke down in tears when they found them and offered prayers in their memories.[34]

The creation of the Cornerstone of Peace provided many Okinawans with a site to remember those they'd lost and reflect on the spirit of *Nuchi du Takara* while giving some survivors a degree of closure on the tragedy that had occurred a half-century earlier. With the prefecture guided by a resolutely pacifist governor, optimism that the islands might finally enjoy a more peaceful future prevailed. But two months later, any sense of hope was rent asunder.

4 September 1995

On 4 September 1995—Labor Day—four US servicemen hired a Subaru sedan from a rental shop in Camp Hansen and drove south to Naha City to buy CDs. On the way back to base, they started discussing ways to kidnap and rape a woman. One suggested targeting a schoolgirl because her skirt would be easier to roll up. Another asked who had the hardest punch to knock their victim unconscious. The Americans drove into Kadena Air Base to purchase duct tape and condoms. The cashier later told police she felt suspicious but did not raise the alarm. At this point, one of the men backed out of the plot. That evening, the three remaining service members, two marines and a sailor, drove out of Camp Hansen, searching for potential victims in a bar district known by Americans since the Vietnam War as "the Ville." Unable to find anyone, they headed toward the shopping streets nearby.[35]

Just before 8:00 p.m., a twelve-year-old girl told her mother she needed a new notebook for her primary school, which had just begun its autumn semester. After receiving ¥150, she walked to the stationery store, bought the book, and headed back home. On the way, she was approached by an American who spoke to her as if asking for directions. While figuring out what he wanted, she was choked from behind by another man, then the first American punched her in the jaw. The girl shouted for help. The man hit her again twice and dragged her into a parked car. In the driver's seat, there was a third man, who handed the others a roll of duct tape, which they wrapped around her eyes and mouth. The Americans drove toward a US Marine Corps training area, Blue Beach, but before they arrived, they pulled into a deserted lane surrounded by sugarcane fields and chicken farms. One of the men punched the girl twice in the stomach; then they took off her clothes and duct tape and raped her. After the assault, they pushed her out of the car and drove away. The girl went to a nearby house, where she telephoned her parents. They picked her up, took her home, and called the police.

Within forty-eight hours, US military law enforcement agencies had identified the suspects. The American who had backed out of the plan provided testimony, and one of the perpetrator's bloodstained boxer shorts had been recovered in an on-base garbage can alongside the girl's new notebook. When Okinawan police attempted to investigate, however, they were thwarted by the barriers of SOFA. Citing Article 17, the military refused to hand over the suspects to Japanese jurisdiction. The Okinawan police were angry. Although the military agreed to bring the men off-base for interrogations, not until 29 September, when Japanese prosecutors officially indicted the suspects, were the three Americans handed over to Japanese custody.[36]

Initially, Okinawa newspapers published only a small article about the crime. While some defended this low-key coverage as necessary to protect the victim's privacy, others saw it as part of a wider trend whereby military sexual violence was overlooked by the male-dominated media and peace movement. Okinawan women had long been fighting to break this silence and show how militarism affected females the most. One of those leading this movement was Takazato Suzuyo, who supported victims of military violence as a social worker in the 1980s and sought to improve women's rights after becoming a Naha City assembly member. Takazato and her colleagues argued that military sexual violence against Okinawan women was not a crime of individual soldiers; it was structural. They located sexual violence alongside decades of US occupation to show it had been pervasive from Commodore Perry's arrival to the present day. Exactly forty years before the 1995 Labor Day rape, the mutilated body of six-year-old Nagayama Yumiko was discovered near Kadena Air Base. Since 1990, there had been at least five other rapes by US servicemen, and in 1995, a marine had beaten an Okinawan woman to death with a hammer. Likewise, within the American military in Japan and Okinawa, the sexual assault rate was far higher than in other countries where US forces were stationed.[37]

Following the September 1995 rape, Takazato and her colleagues were at the forefront of a powerful antibase movement as Okinawan women demanded justice for the twelve-year-old girl and recognition that the crime must be understood within the context of the US military presence in Okinawa. (They also founded Okinawa's first rape counseling center to help survivors of sexual violence committed by military and civilians alike.) As awareness of the crime spread, anger surged throughout Okinawan society. On 28 September, Governor Ota threatened to undermine the bedrock of the military presence in Okinawa: the leases for the land where the bases stood. Normally, the local mayors or governor had signed these rental agreements in a perfunctory manner, and the Japanese government had taken for granted their renewal—but now, first the mayors, then Ota himself, refused to sign them. It was an unprecedented step that jeopardized the legality of the US military presence. The majority of Okinawans supported his stance.[38]

In October 1995, Okinawans held the largest citizens' mass meeting (*kenmin taikai*) since reversion, where, before an 85,000-strong crowd, Governor Ota apologized for not having been able to protect the girl. Then he proclaimed that islanders' anger had reached its limit: "Until now, Okinawa has been forced to cooperate. Now is the time for the Japanese and US governments to cooperate. We have clearly said that things will not continue as they have been."[39]

One female high school student gave a speech that reflected the reticence felt by some Okinawans about participating in the demonstration:

> I wondered whether to protest for fear it might violate the girl's feelings or privacy. . . . But because of her courage and the courage of her family, the incident was made public, and now it has created a historic vortex. We could not possibly waste her courage. . . . I would like us, the young generation, to start a new Okinawa. . . . Please return Okinawa without the military and without the tragedies—return the peaceful islands to us.[40]

Okinawans were united in their opposition to the bases. In September 1996, near the one-year anniversary of the rape, the islands held a prefectural-wide referendum. Some 540,000 people cast their votes, 90 percent in favor of rewriting SOFA and reducing the US military presence. Throughout late 1995 and 1996, Okinawans' anger was so incandescent that it threatened the very existence of the US bases in the prefecture. Historian Arasaki Moriteru framed this period as the third wave of all-island protest; the first had been triggered by US land seizures in the mid-1950s, and the second was the mass movement for reversion in the 1960s. Now again, Okinawans were galvanized against the unfair military burden they bore and the two governments that perpetuated its presence.[41]

FIGURE 8.1 *On 21 October 1995, 85,000 people attended an all-island demonstration in Ginowan City to protest the rape of a twelve-year-old girl by three US service members and demand the downsizing of the military presence. Courtesy of Okinawa Times*

Washington and Tokyo realized they needed to take drastic action to dampen public anger. On 25 October, four days after the *kenmin taikai*, the United States announced that it would give "sympathetic consideration" to Japanese police requests to hand over military personnel suspected of rape or murder. Then the following month, the two nations stated they would discuss how to reduce the islands' military burden via a new body, the Special Action Committee on Okinawa (SACO). Any breathing space these announcements might have bought, however, was extinguished when head of the US Pacific Command, Admiral Richard Macke, held a meeting with journalists during which he offered his thoughts on the Labor Day rape: Hiring a prostitute, he stated, would have been cheaper than renting the car to abduct the girl. The comment provided proof of the misogyny pervasive throughout the US military and the levity with which even senior officials regarded crimes against residents. The admiral's forced retirement did little to soften Okinawans' fury. So strong was their anger that it contributed to the cancellation of President Bill Clinton's trip to Japan scheduled for the end of 1995.[42]

In March 1996, all three accused servicemen were found guilty by a civilian court in Naha City. Two received sentences of seven years' incarceration, and the third received six and a half years. They were sent to Yokosuka Prison in mainland Japan, where thanks to (yet) another behind-the-scenes bilateral deal struck in the 1950s, US military prisoners received special privileges: higher-quality food and bedding and more frequent showers. After his release, one of the three criminals murdered a woman in her apartment in Kennesaw City, Georgia, and then committed suicide.[43]

In April 1996, Japan and the United States made public an interim SACO report on how to reduce the scale of the US presence in Okinawa by some 20 percent. Facilities to be closed included Yomitan Auxiliary Airfield and parts of the Northern Training Area and Makiminato Service Area. Most surprising was a promise to return Futenma Air Station "within the next five to seven years." The pledge surpassed Okinawans' most optimistic expectations. Accompanying these large land returns, the two governments announced a halt to the artillery training over Prefectural Route 104 and measures to reduce noise at Kadena Air Base.

The proposals heralded very real advances in Okinawans' quality of life. Residents of Kin, Kadena, and Yomitan would be able to live peaceful days, and once again, people would be able to experience the pristine environment of the Yanbaru forest. The decision to shutter the Futenma base—and *so soon*—would restore the heart to the city of Ginowan. For the first time since the army had bulldozed their bustling community, residents would be able to return to their land, replant their farms, and visit their ancestral graves. Almost a quarter-century earlier, reversion had failed to bring these improvements, instead prolonging the occupation of their land and the corresponding crime, noise, and pollution. Now, it had taken a heinous crime and an all-island uprising to convince Tokyo and Washington that urgent change could no longer be delayed. Finally, Okinawans would be able to experience the long-anticipated and long-overdue peace dividend they had been demanding.

9

Relieving the Burden

Around the globe, the early 1990s witnessed an unparalleled easing of military tensions. Since the end of World War II, the United States and the Soviet Union had attempted to cleave the world along the ideological lines of capitalism versus communism, engaging in nuclear brinkmanship and bloody proxy conflicts from Vietnam to Afghanistan that killed, wounded, and displaced millions, rendering the term *Cold War* a misnomer. The economic toll for both superpowers was incalculable. In 1967, Martin Luther King Jr. warned that a nation that spent more on its military "than on programs of social uplift is approaching spiritual death," words that must have resonated with Soviet citizens where, by the late 1980s, defense spending consumed more than 20 percent of its gross national product. It would take a leader with vision to break this cycle, not President Ronald Reagan, who in 1983 likened the nuclear arms race to a "struggle between right and wrong and good and evil." Fortunately, in 1985, a more innovative figure emerged from the opposite side of the Iron Curtain: Mikhail Gorbachev. With the Soviet leader's encouragement, free elections were held in Warsaw Pact countries, ending much authoritarian rule. In November 1989, Berliners tore down the wall that had symbolized US-Soviet rivalries, and in 1991, the Soviet Union itself dissolved into fifteen independent states. The Cold War, which many feared would end in nuclear apocalypse, had come to a (largely) peaceful conclusion.[1]

These upheavals left the United States, now the world's sole superpower, to decide the future of its global network of military bases originally constructed to impede the communist spread. In Europe, it halved the number of US soldiers, and both the United States and Russia conducted large-scale reductions in their nuclear arsenals. As for US relations with China, the picture was more complex. Since the Nixon administration, the United States had pursued closer relations with Beijing to undermine solidarity between China and the Soviet Union. In 1982, the Reagan government officially normalized relations, and two years later, it permitted the sale of US military equipment to China. But in 1989, the Chinese authorities' massacre of prodemocracy demonstrators in Tiananmen Square,

Beijing, temporarily derailed closer ties. Washington froze high-level diplomatic relations and halted the transfer of military technology to China. (Still, the US reaction was rudimentary, and it did not impose wider economic sanctions.) Soon after, the US government felt that the overall outlook in East Asia was trending more peaceably, so in 1990 and 1992, it announced it would shrink its military presence in the region. By 1994, it had slashed the number of troops from 135,000 to 100,000 (most reductions occurred in South Korea and mainland Japan) and announced more cuts would continue until the end of the decade.[2]

In February 1995, however, the Department of Defense halted plans for further reductions when it published the *United States Security Strategy for the East Asia-Pacific Region*, better known as the Nye Report, after its architect, Assistant Secretary of Defense for International Security Affairs Joseph S. Nye. The document pronounced that the US military presence would be maintained "at the existing level of about 100,000 troops, for the foreseeable future." Justifying this decision, it asserted the military was essential for regional stability: "Security is like oxygen: you do not tend to notice it until you begin to lose it. The American security presence has helped provide this 'oxygen' for East Asian development." (It was a dubious assertion given how, in the previous decades, US covert and overt interventions had choked out democratic movements and supported brutal dictators in Taiwan, South Korea, the Philippines, and elsewhere and cost the lives of millions of Vietnamese, Laotians, and Cambodians.)[3]

The report claimed that East Asians welcomed the American military because the United States served as an "'honest broker' among nervous neighbors, historical enemies, and potential antagonists." As far as naming possible adversaries, the report labeled North Korea a "source of unpredictability and potential danger," but its criticism of China was weaker. While noting its desire for Beijing to be more transparent, it highlighted strengthening ties between the USA and China, notably the secretary of defense's visit to China in 1994 and exchanges between the two nations' militaries. In its conclusion, the authors proclaimed, "The Asia-Pacific region is now more at peace than it has been at any time in this century."[4]

So why didn't the Nye Report advocate withdrawing troops from Japan? It offered three reasons. First and most tellingly, it lauded the sympathy budget: "Japan supplies by far the most generous host nation support of any of our allies," and due to these payments by Japan (and South Korea), "it is actually less expensive to the American taxpayer to maintain our forces forward deployed than in the United States." By this time, Tokyo was paying more than $5 billion per year to cover base workers' salaries, rent to landowners, service members' utility bills, and other (often obscure) benefits. The second reason was also economic: weapon sales. The close relationship between the US military and the Self-Defense Forces (SDF) guaranteed that Japan bought interoperable equipment from American defense companies, which, according to the report, included helicopters, fighter jets, and missile systems. The third rationale for stationing US troops was political: Japan "provides a stable, secure environment for our military operations and training."⁵

When the report was published, many people in Japan and Okinawa were disappointed that the end of the Cold War would not usher in an accompanying demilitarization of East Asia. So to sell his initiative to a skeptical public, Nye traveled to Tokyo to give a press conference at the Foreign Correspondents' Club of Japan. The date of that talk: Labor Day, 4 September 1995.

Muchi to Ame

After the rape of the twelve-year-old girl, Okinawans' fury reached levels unseen since the 1970 Koza Riot, challenging Nye's assurances of Japan providing US troops with a stable and secure environment. Antimilitary sentiment engulfed the prefecture, as 85,000 people gathered at the *kenmin taikai*; assembly members and mayors demanded reforms to the Status of Forces Agreement (SOFA); and Governor Ota Masahide refused to sign the leases for the bases, rendering the American presence illegal. In April 1996, the land issue peaked in dramatic fashion at Sobe Communications Site, Yomitan, where the military and National Security Agency operated a huge ringlike antenna nicknamed *Zō no Ori*, the Elephant's Cage. For decades the facility had been an imposing symbol of US power, but on 1 April, the military's lease expired, effectively reverting it back to civilian use. Among the landowners was the peace campaigner Chibana Shōichi, who now seized the opportunity to assert the illegality of the military's occupation of his property. While TV cameras rolled, he approached the gates of the base and demanded the security guards allow him to enter. With no legitimate grounds for denial, they granted permission. Accompanied by pacifist popstar Kina Shōkichi and some thirty friends and relatives, Chibana held a two-hour picnic in the sprawling base. It was a victorious display of nonviolent resistance in the very heart of the military machine—and a humiliating moment for US and Japanese authorities.⁶

Faced with such opposition, Washington and Tokyo scrambled to regain control, adopting tactics honed during decades of coercion. And just like past processes to shape the islands' future—notably the Treaty of San Francisco and reversion—Okinawans were excluded from the decision making. First, Japan and the United States attempted to douse public fury with ostensibly major concessions. Then, having placated some of the anger, they rolled back their promises. When it came to amending SOFA, Washington initially vowed that the Japanese police would receive "sympathetic consideration" in the handover of military suspects, but such decisions were left to the discretion of the US military, which subsequently rejected almost all requests. SOFA itself was not revised. Likewise, the Special

Action Committee on Okinawa (SACO) Interim Report released in April 1996 was engineered to satisfy Okinawans' demands to reduce the military footprint, yet when the final version was published in December, it axed their expectations. The return of military land would be contingent on constructing upgraded facilities within bases elsewhere in the prefecture. For the US government, this was a win-win. It could abandon rundown facilities and make Japanese taxpayers fund new ones, and the military was not required to clean up contaminated land. The masterstroke of deception had been the promise to shutter Futenma Air Station "within the next five to seven years," which had fooled Okinawans into believing their burden would genuinely be reduced. But the final SACO announcement described a replacement facility that would be built "off the east coast of the main island of Okinawa," merely shifting its problems elsewhere in the prefecture. Although the report tried to soften the blow by describing the new facility as temporary (it could be "removed when no longer necessary"), the claim was belied by a US government paper that revealed the base would be built to last two hundred years.[7]

As for Governor Ota's refusal to sign the proxy land leases, the central government sued him on the grounds of neglecting professional duty. Ota lost his first trial, so he appealed to the Supreme Court, where, on 10 July 1996, he delivered a remarkable statement that drew on his full repertoire of historian's knowledge to school the Japanese judges on the roots of mainland discrimination against Okinawa and how it facilitated the ongoing US military occupation. The Ryukyu Kingdom had been a pacifist culture, he explained, and today the prefecture was "dedicated to a way of life that shuns and abhors armed conflict." Okinawan lands had been illegally appropriated—first by Japanese soldiers and then by US troops, whose postwar use of the bases to wage conflicts in Korea, Vietnam, and the Middle East violated Okinawans' peaceful principles. Turning to the issue of the leases, Ota explained to the judges Okinawans' special relationship to their land: "It is not a commodity.... Land is an irreplaceable heritage graciously bequeathed to us by our ancestors or a spiritual string that ties us to them. My people's attachment to their land is firmly rooted, and their resistance against the forcible taking of their land is similarly strong."[8]

Ota called out Japanese NIMBY-ism, arguing that if the government held the US-Japan Security Treaty in such high regard, then the bases should be dispersed throughout the country. The concentration of bases in Okinawa was discriminatory, and the "responsibility and burdens under the treaty should be assumed by all Japanese citizens." In conclusion, Ota urged the Supreme Court judges to uphold the law and protect Okinawans' "constitutionally guaranteed property rights, people's rights to a life in peace, and the right to home rule."[9]

It was an impassioned testimony that convinced many Okinawans the judges would rule in Ota's favor. The following month, the Supreme Court summoned the governor to hear its verdict in a session that lasted approximately one minute: "We reject and dismiss the appeal. The court expenses shall be borne by the appellant." As short as the two lines were, they spoke volumes to the scorn the Japanese authorities harbored toward the governor and, by extension, Okinawans as a whole. The islands existed outside the protections of Japanese law, and the rights of residents were overridden by military necessities. The constitution still did not extend as far south as Okinawa almost a quarter-century after residents had struggled so tirelessly to win its protections.[10]

Ota now faced a stark decision: refuse to sign the leases and risk being removed from office or back down on the issue that was supported by most islanders. The governor capitulated. Soon after, the national government passed a new law that granted itself the power to sign proxy leases, thus ensuring that Ota and future Okinawan governors would never again be able to repeat such dissent and, despite constitutional guarantees of the inviolability of land ownership, resisting owners would not be able to retain the right to use their property as they wished.

Ota's concession lost him considerable support among Okinawans, but he threw his energies into resisting construction of the new base planned to be built in the prefecture's north to replace Futenma Air Station. Infuriated by Ota's recalcitrance, the central government launched economic warfare against the prefecture, cutting subsidies. Then in the lead-up to the 1998 gubernatorial election, Tokyo adopted tactics reminiscent of USCAR's campaign to dislodge left-wing Naha mayor Senaga Kamejiro. The LDP channeled millions of dollars from the chief cabinet secretary's clandestine slush fund into publicity to smear Ota as incompetent and idealistic, while his opponent, LDP-backed Inamine Keiichi, was portrayed as a candidate who would boost the prefecture's economy and restart subsidies from Tokyo. As a result of these underhanded tactics—many of them not revealed until 2010—Ota lost the election.[11]

Having used the *muchi* against Ota, the LDP now supplied the *ame* to Inamine's administration, pumping billions of yen of so-called development funds into the islands, particularly in Nago City, where it planned to build the new base. Much of the money wound up profiting mainland construction firms and benefited little the lives of most Okinawans. Unemployment remained high and salaries lower than in the rest of Japan.[12]

The Battle for Oura Bay: Part I

Okinawa Prefecture is the poorest in Japan, and within the main island itself, there are degrees of poverty. The north is poorer than the south, and in the north, the east coast is less affluent than the west. Thus, the Japanese government chose this area, one of the most impoverished in the nation, as the site for the new base to replace Futenma Air Station. The Henoko District of Nago City might be financially lacking, but ecologically, it is one of the richest places in the world. Rivers carry nutrients from the Yanbaru forests, depositing them in mangrove thickets and into the deep waters of Oura Bay. Over millennia, a unique ecosystem has evolved, consisting of more than 5,000 species—260 of them endangered—including corals, sea turtles, and submerged meadows of sea grass. The most precious inhabitant is the dugong, a relative of the manatee, which holds a sacred significance in the islands' creation myths and indigenous religion. So important is the dugong that some legends blame its mistreatment for the 1771 tsunami that swept across Miyako and Yaeyama.[13]

During the Battle of Okinawa, the US military established a large internment camp in Henoko, where, as elsewhere, conditions were squalid, but here the shellfish and marine life from Oura Bay provided sustenance, and many Okinawans came to regard it as a hallowed, life-saving area. During the mid-1950s, when marine corps violence in Japan triggered protests, forcing removal of the troops, the US government chose Henoko as one of the sites for relocation. In 1956, it opened Camp Schwab to house and train the marines and the adjacent Henoko Ordnance Ammunition Depot to store nuclear warheads.

During the Vietnam War, the marine corps had considered building an air base and runway atop Oura Bay, but the US government balked at the costs. Now, under SACO, it resurrected the plan because the multi-billion-dollar project would be funded by Japanese taxpayers. The Pentagon envisaged a megabase that would bury the reefs beneath a landfill to construct twin airstrips, helipads, and ammunition dumps. The new facility might also store nuclear weapons because Nixon and Sato had listed Henoko in their secret agreement of 1969.[14]

In 1997, Nago City held a referendum on whether to accept the base, and despite Tokyo's attempts to manipulate the outcome, a majority of voters rejected the plan. International environmental organizations also decried the proposed destruction of such precious biodiversity. Ignoring this opposition, the Japanese government dispatched survey teams to Henoko, so Okinawans vowed to resist by any (peaceful) means necessary. On land, protestors blocked official trucks. On the sea, they sailed canoes to obstruct the survey boats and chained themselves to drilling platforms. Even beneath the water, Okinawans in scuba gear confronted the surveyors. Although these protestors came from all generations and all walks of life, at their core were the elderly war survivors, who recalled how Oura Bay had saved internees from starvation—and now they vowed to protect the bay from becoming a base from which future wars could be waged.

Once again, Okinawans proved the power of persistent nonviolent civil disobedience. In October 2005, Prime Minister Koizumi Junichirō was forced to shelve the plan to build the base, announcing that his government "was unable to implement the relocation because of a lot of opposition."[15]

Relieving the Burden?

During this period, the US and Japanese governments made good on some of the promises of SACO. Yomitan Airfield was shuttered, fulfilling the efforts of the villagers who'd protested so long for its return, and Tokyo paid for the US Marine Corps to relocate its artillery training to a gunnery range in mainland Japan, but unexploded shells littered the hillsides near Kin Town, which, due to SOFA, the military did not need to clean up. As more parcels of land were returned, there were discoveries of severe contamination from arsenic, dioxin, and other hazardous substances. Again, the financial costs for remediation were borne by Japanese taxpayers—some ¥12.9 billion by 2018. Cleanup work delayed the redevelopment of the land, causing a financial strain on the owners, who had hoped to use their property as soon as possible. Throughout this period, too, military negligence caused large spills of fuel, sewage, and firefighting foam into communities near the bases.[16]

Overall, the military crime wave had subsided since its peak during the Vietnam War, and drug testing plus stricter customs controls had reduced narcotics use and smuggling. But Okinawans still became victims of military violence, and American suspects evaded punishment because Japanese prosecutors often failed to aggressively pursue indictments. Senior military officers, too, continued to show indifference to offenses against Okinawans. In 2001, when a marine was arrested for taking photographs up a high school girl's skirt, Okinawan legislators passed a protest resolution. In response, the US Marine Corps chief in Japan called them "nuts and a bunch of wimps." He was forced to apologize—but kept his job.[17]

Such attitudes might be attributed to the mandatory orientation lectures attended by marines upon their arrival in the islands. Known as Okinawa Culture Awareness Training (OCAT), the talks disparaged residents and their elected officials as ungrateful freeloaders whose grievances were specious. OCAT called public opinion "self-serving" and the antibase protests were "more emotional than logical." They claimed money was at the root of Okinawans' opposition: "It pays to complain. Anywhere offense can be taken it will be used." As for military crime, the lectures explained, "We get carried-away with our sudden 'gaijin power' (charisma man effect) and tend to go over-board by doing things that is [sic] not acceptable to the majority in society."[18]

OCAT belittled Okinawans' very real criticisms and downplayed military crimes as exuberance, placing the blame on the victims who could not resist

Americans' charms. The lectures, released via the US Freedom of Information Act, offered a telling window into how the marines perceived Okinawans. The governor slammed them as a "prime example of [the US military's] arrogant attitude."[19]

There was no clearer sign of this occupation mentality than what occurred on 13 August 2004. At this time, marines at Futenma Air Station were training for deployment to the war in Iraq. Just after 2:00 p.m., one of their helicopters—a thirty-meter-long CH-53D Sea Stallion—crashed into the campus of Okinawa International University and caught fire. The impact sent chunks of the aircraft over a wide area, damaging cars and homes. The three crew members were injured, but because the university was on summer vacation, nobody on the ground was hurt.[20]

As shocking as the initial accident was, the response by the military proved even worse: Marines immediately cordoned off the crash site and refused to allow local police or firefighters to enter. For one week, the military continued to block access by local elected officials or representatives from Japan's Ministry of Foreign Affairs. The only civilians allowed entry were the delivery drivers bringing pizzas ordered by US crash investigators. In Okinawa, the accident made headlines across the media, but on mainland Japan, it barely warranted mention. State broadcaster Nippon Hōsō Kyōkai (NHK) ran the story fourth in its nightly news—after its baseball and Olympics coverage.[21]

For many islanders, the crash was a wake-up call. Witnessing arrogant young marines block the paths of senior elected officials, many residents asked themselves if US colonial rule had ever actually ended. At the same time, the lack of mainland news coverage—let alone public outrage—reinforced Okinawans' suspicions that Japan cared little for the daily dangers they faced bearing the burden of national defense obligations. So egregious were the visuals of marines blocking the police but waving through delivery drivers that they inspired artwork and a hip-hop track. *New York Times* labeled the blunt display of colonialism a "Pizzatocracy."[22]

Rewriting History

Okinawans felt not only their present was under attack but also their past. In the 1980s, LDP politicians had moved to rewrite school history books to downplay Japan's World War II atrocities. In the 2000s, they expanded their efforts. Among these revisionists was Prime Minister Abe Shinzo, grandson of Kishi Nobusuke (and great-nephew of Sato Eisaku), whose administration advocated a patriotic education for Japan's youth and pride in the nation's past that would pave the way to strengthen the current military and scrap the pacifist principles extolled under Article 9 of the constitution. (Japan was encouraged in these attempts to

FIGURE 9.1 *Following the crash of a marine corps helicopter onto the campus of Okinawa International University, Ginowan City, on 13 August 2004, the military refused access to local police and firefighters. Courtesy of Okinawa Times*

remilitarize by Nye and fellow "Japan handler" Richard Armitage, whose security recommendations were adopted by Tokyo one after another between 1996 and 2009.) To rearm the nation, many LDP members believed it would be necessary first to erase memories of the sins of their forefathers, especially the Rape of Nanking, the comfort-woman system, and military mistreatment of civilians during the Battle of Okinawa.[23]

In 2006, the Japanese government ordered publishers of high school history textbooks to rewrite descriptions of the Battle of Okinawa to downplay references to the military's role in forced suicides. Critics understood this as an act of censorship to obscure Okinawans' suffering and prepare for future militarization. The revisions aimed to "extinguish from people's consciousness the important lesson of the Battle of Okinawa that 'armies do not protect people,' and by protecting the 'honor' of the emperor's army, to raise a people who will serve country and army and thus mobilize them again for war." In September 2007, some 117,000 Okinawans gathered in the largest *kenmin taikai* of the postreversion era to protest the textbook revisions. The rally was a success, prompting the Japanese government to rescind its order and allow at least partial reference to the army's responsibility for the forced suicides of civilians. Once again, Okinawans had proven that a united front could win change.[24]

Complementing attempts to erase memories of the nation's World War II aggression, Japanese conservatives also glorified members of the imperial military. Their focus was Yasukuni Shrine, which honored as heroes those who had died fighting for the emperor and Class A war criminals sentenced to death at the Tokyo Trials. Article 20 of Japan's constitution affirms, "The State and its organs shall refrain from religious education or any other religious activity," but despite this, Japanese prime ministers and cabinet members repeatedly visited Yasukuni, angering many people domestically and in the Asian countries that had been brutalized during wartime occupation. Without their knowledge or assent, Yasukuni had also enshrined more than 55,000 Okinawan civilians alongside Japanese military personnel. The reason dates to the 1950s, when the relatives of those killed in the battle sought compensation from the Japanese government. Tokyo agreed—but only if family members designated the dead as "combat participants." The authorities devised twenty categories into which they had to assign their killed relatives: For instance, civilians who had died after Japanese soldiers had stolen their supplies were listed as "donors of food," and those executed as spies had died "preserving military secrets." At the time, many Okinawans were unaware that the categorization signaled their agreement that their relatives had died supporting the Japanese military. For the Japanese government, the process enabled them to whitewash wartime atrocities against Okinawans. Adding to these horrors, Tokyo subsequently provided these lists to Yasukuni's priests, who enshrined the dead civilians as "fallen war heroes" alongside the Japanese soldiers who had robbed, raped, and murdered them.[25]

The Japanese government did not inform Okinawans about the enshrinement, and many families did not discover the truth until decades later. In 2008, relatives sued Yasukuni and the Japanese government over the enshrinement of their family members. The plaintiffs included a man whose mother had been forced from her shelter by Japanese soldiers. The shrine described her as an "unpaid employee of the military." Among the other reputed combat participants was a two-year-old boy.[26]

Once again, the Japanese judiciary trampled on Okinawans' concerns when it dismissed the lawsuit, ruling that it could not interfere with the shrine's freedom of religion. "Yasukuni officials ignore the rights of individuals, claiming that the consent of bereaved families is not required and that they are only exercising their religious freedom," responded the litigating son. "This is because they are confident they enjoy the same kind of special status and privileges granted by the state before and during the war to designated government shrines."[27]

UN Intervention

During USCAR rule, the United States had controlled access to the islands to conceal its mistreatment of Okinawans from the international community.

Similarly, postreversion, the Japanese government worried that its abuses against the islanders would attract global condemnation. In 2006, their fears were confirmed when the United Nations special rapporteur on contemporary forms of racism, racial discrimination, xenophobia, and related intolerance published a report lambasting Japan for its treatment of Okinawans.

"The most serious discrimination they presently endure is linked to the presence of the American military bases in their island. The Government justifies the presence of the bases in the name of 'public interest.' However, the people of Okinawa explained that they suffered daily from the consequences of the military bases," wrote rapporteur Doudou Diène. Among the problems he highlighted were environmental contamination, aircraft crashes, and crimes. He urged the Japanese government to investigate whether the immense US military presence was "compatible with the respect of the fundamental human rights of the people of Okinawa."[28]

The UN references to discrimination touched a nerve with Japanese conservatives. Since the Meiji Era, to buttress their vision of national identity, government officials had promulgated the myth that Okinawa had always been an integral part of Japan and the nation was racially and linguistically homogenous. Such beliefs were reinforced in the postwar years by a surge in popular culture extolling *nihonjin ron*, the theory that Japan was a uniform nation that enjoyed social cohesion unlike anywhere else in the world. The notion was underscored in 2005, when Foreign Minister Asō Tarō declared, "Japan is one nation, one civilization, one language, one culture, and one race, the like of which there is no other." The UN's comments about Okinawa fractured this myth, exposing the hypocrisy at the heart of the government's discrimination. While asserting that Japan was one nation, it did not afford equal rights to residents of its southernmost prefecture, instead treating the islands as places it could do things impermissible elsewhere.[29]

In 2008, the UN's Human Rights Committee criticized the government's failure to recognize Okinawans as "indigenous peoples entitled to special rights and protection." The committee recommended that Tokyo improve its treatment of Okinawans, including provisions to allow children to learn their native languages and study their culture and history. Coming on the heels of LDP attempts to rewrite textbook descriptions of the Battle of Okinawa, this was a strong admonition against the Japanese government. The committee further instructed Tokyo to "recognize [Okinawans'] land rights"—a direct criticism of the government's laws that targeted antibase landowners in likely violation of the constitution.[30]

In 2009, the United Nations continued to advocate for Okinawans when it broached the language issue. Ever since Meiji Era bureaucrats had classified Okinawa's languages as mere dialects (*hogen*) of Japanese, many mainlanders—and some islanders—had maligned them as substandard, leading to the proliferation of the *hogen fuda* (dialect plaque), a badge of humiliation for students who spoke the island's languages in school. This sense of inferiority persisted into the twenty-first century. But in 2009, the United Nations Educational, Scientific and Cultural Organization (UNESCO) boosted awareness when it published an atlas detailing the global languages it categorized as "endangered" (defined as "not being passed on to younger generations"). Included in its list were six languages of Okinawa Prefecture and neighboring Amami. UNESCO classified four of the languages as "definitely endangered"—Amami, Kunigami, Miyako, and Okinawan (a.k.a. Uchinaaguchi)—and two as "severely endangered"—Yaeyama and Yonaguni. UNESCO's categorization provided international recognition that Okinawans' languages were distinct from Japanese, they were under threat of extinction, and they needed to be preserved. Moreover, it reinforced previous UN calls for Okinawans to be recognized as indigenous peoples, further eroding the myth of Japan's racial and linguistic homogeneity.[31]

Accompanying its admonitions to recognize Okinawans as indigenous, the United Nations urged Japan to extend similar recognition to residents of the other region seized during the Meiji Era, Hokkaido. Following the annexation of their island in 1869, Ainu had experienced extreme discrimination, and during the twentieth century, they suffered forced assimilation and the loss of their land. At the start of the twenty-first century, the United Nations repeatedly urged Tokyo to recognize Ainu as indigenous. Finally, in 2008, the government buckled to domestic and international pressure and agreed to do so. But the Japanese government still refused to follow UN recommendations for its southernmost prefecture. In 2012, it told the United Nations, "People who live in Okinawa and natives of Okinawa are Japanese nationals." (It seemed to misunderstand the distinction between race and nationality.) Then in 2016, Tokyo equivocated, "We understand that people in Okinawa have inherited a unique culture and tradition over their long history. However, the Government of Japan recognizes only the Ainu people as indigenous people in Japan."[32]

So why was Japan so reluctant to recognize Okinawans as indigenous? One reason was the opinions of some residents themselves. The word *indigenous* carries the taint of backwardness and stirs uncomfortable reminders of the 1903 Human Pavilion incident, where Okinawans were displayed alongside Ainu and Taiwanese tribespeople. Some municipal councils adopted resolutions urging the United Nations to retract its recommendations. The first of these, produced by Tomigusuku City in 2015, stated, "Most people of Okinawa do not consider themselves to be indigenous," and expressed concern that if Okinawans declared themselves as such, "we will be seen as non-Japanese minority by the rest of the Japanese, thus promoting reverse discrimination." As for the government of Japan, its reluctance was very likely rooted in the realization that recognition of Okinawan indigeneity might threaten national sovereignty and challenge the presence of the American military bases in the prefecture. Under the UN Declaration on the Rights of Indigenous Peoples (2007), Okinawans would be granted the right to self-government, opening the possibility for a referendum on independence or semiautonomous rule, accompanied by control of their own economy, education, and religious customs. As for land, the declaration prohibits the removal of indigenous people from their properties without their "free, prior and informed consent" and affords those dispossessed "fair compensation and, where possible, with the option of return." Thus, granting indigenous status to Okinawans would imperil the existence of the US—and SDF—bases under international law, a risk the Japanese government was unwilling to take. Tokyo's refusal to respect Okinawan indigeneity exemplified—once again—how it valued the US-Japan Security Treaty over the rights of Okinawans and international norms.[33]

The Okinawa Boom

At the end of the twentieth century, there emerged in Japan what became known as the "Okinawa boom," whereby mainland residents grew more aware of the islands. Some of this was manufactured by the national government and corporations, who ensured that portrayals of the islands were stripped of crucial context, but at the same time, Okinawan artists were able to parlay this surge in interest into increased understanding of their islands' culture as well as historical and contemporary patterns of exploitation.

In the summer of 2000, Japan hosted the G8 summit in Nago City. While touted as a way to showcase the government's "passionate compassion" and Okinawa's distinct culture, it primarily served as an attempt to buy local support for the new base. To insulate world leaders from potential protests, the summit was staged on the coast opposite Oura Bay, and 22,000 riot police were imported to the islands. The government also brought in all the summit's meals from Tokyo because, as one foreign office spokesperson explained, "we didn't want the press corps and world leaders to suffer from stomach upset." Equally dismissive was another gesture by the national government: To commemorate the G8 summit, Tokyo introduced a new ¥2,000 bank note featuring an image of Shuri Castle. The notes were widely circulated within the prefecture, but Japan's ubiquitous vending machines could not accept them, and by 2004, the Bank of Japan had ceased printing them.[34]

At the same time, in 2000, NHK began airing a TV drama called *Churasan* set on a small island in the prefecture. "The actors portraying Okinawans were predominantly Japanese mainlanders who used insultingly fake Okinawan accents. *Churasan* also depicted Okinawan men as lazy and more apt to drink sake and play the sanshin than work," writes Wesley Ueunten, professor of Asian

American studies. The scriptwriters steered clear of describing Japan's 1879 annexation of the Ryukyu Kingdom, the sacrifice of the islands in World War II, and ongoing discrimination. "The cameras deftly avoid capturing any sign that US military bases cover one-fifth of the main island of Okinawa," Ueunten writes. *Churasan*—and other Japanese representations of Okinawans as carefree and happy-go-lucky—perpetuated USCAR-era stereotypes of the islands' residents, silencing their long history of resilience and resistance.[35]

During this rush to exoticize and defang Okinawans, some artists were able to insert voices of dissent. Kina Shōkichi, the musician who had picnicked within the Elephant's Cage, led the trend in *uchinaa* pop featuring lyrics sung in the islands' languages. Kina coined the motto "Turn all weapons into musical instruments and the bases into flower gardens. Hold festivals not wars." (In 2003, he staged a peace concert in Baghdad to protest the upcoming US-led invasion of Iraq. The following year, he won a seat in Japan's upper-house election.) At the same time, Okinawan authors were winning national acclaim. In 1996, Matayoshi Eiki won Japan's most prestigious literary award, the Akutagawa Prize, for his tragicomedy *Buta no Mukui* (*The Pig's Retribution*). The following year, Medoruma Shun won the same prize for his novella *Suiteki* (*Droplets*), a magical-realist exploration of the Battle of Okinawa in which the spirits of dead soldiers visit a surviving comrade to sip the waters from his swollen leg. As well as being an award-winning author, Medoruma was an outspoken opponent of the Henoko base, taking to a canoe together with other demonstrators to block construction and experiencing detention by US and Japanese authorities.

At the same time its artists were receiving national acclaim, in the summer of 1999, Okinawan youths won the National High School Baseball Tournament for the first time. Not only a source of sporting pride, Shōgaku's victory exorcised a moment of colonial trauma for many Okinawans. In 1958, a team from the occupied islands had been allowed to travel to the mainland to participate in the tournament, and despite being knocked out in the first round, their appearance garnered much support. As tradition dictates, following their game, the students scooped up small samples of the field's soil to remember their experience, but when their ship arrived back in US-occupied Okinawa, customs officials dumped the souvenirs into the sea, claiming that they violated quarantine protocols. Four decades later, the 1999 victory offered a poignant moment of resolution.[36]

Many residents recall the year 2000 with pride, not because of the national government's token offer of the G8 summit and new ¥2,000 bill but because it was the year when UNESCO recognized the importance of Okinawa's pre-Japanese history by adding nine Ryukyu Kingdom sites to its World Heritage list. Five of these were castles, including Shuri Castle, the royal home, which had been rebuilt and opened to the public in 1992; the royal mausoleum, Tamaudun; and Shikinaen, the site of a royal villa and garden. In explaining its decision, UNESCO lauded the monuments for demonstrating how the Ryukyu Islands had "served as a centre of economic and cultural interchange between south-east Asia, China, Korea, and Japan" and the kingdom "flourished in a special political and economic environment, which gave its culture a unique quality." UNESCO also listed two religious sites, Sonohyan Utaki Ishimon, the gateway to a sacred grove in the grounds of Shuri Castle, and Sēfa Utaki, a wooded hilltop where, according to Ryukyuan beliefs, the goddess of creation arrived on the island. In its explanation for listing these two sites, UNESCO wrote, "They constitute an exceptional example of an indigenous form of nature and ancestor worship that has survived intact into the modern age alongside other established world religions." Okinawans were overjoyed by international recognition of their precolonial history, but UNESCO's use of the word *indigenous* likely caused some teeth grinding among Japanese conservatives.[37]

10

All Okinawa vs. Japan and the United States

In the 2000s, historic changes were afoot in mainland Japanese politics. Since 1955, the Liberal Democratic Party (LDP) had governed the nation (except for a short spell on the sidelines between 1993 and 1994), a prolonged rule that transformed Japan into essentially a single-party state, during which its politicians took their reelection for granted. The electorate had supported the LDP for as long as it provided economic growth and strong social security. Besides, a fragmented opposition offered few viable alternatives to lead. Now, though, with the gap between rich and poor widening due to the LDP's business-first policies and the party rife with corruption, nepotism, and incompetency, Japanese voters were growing frustrated with LDP politicians' sense of entitlement. In 2007, they displayed their dissatisfaction by wiping out the LDP's majority in the upper-house election.

As it became evident that the party's five-decade rule might soon end, the United States grew alarmed that influence over its number 1 Asian ally was in jeopardy. Before this could occur, Washington and Tokyo rushed to settle some unfinished business. In 2006, the two nations had announced the US-Japan Roadmap for Realignment Implementation, a plan they claimed would lessen Okinawa's military burden via Japan building two new bases for the US marines. One would be at Oura Bay, reversing Prime Minister Koizumi Junichirō's earlier decision to abandon the project. The cost to Japanese taxpayers: an estimated $2–22 billion. The second would be in the US territory Guam, where, just like Okinawa, construction would ignore widespread opposition by indigenous residents and decimate an environmentally unique habitat. Japan's bill: $6 billion. On the US side, Washington promised to close Futenma Air Station and relocate some marines to Guam. At the time, both governments extoled the Roadmap as a major reduction of Okinawa's military burden, but this was a falsehood. Shuttering the

Futenma base merely shifted its problems to residents of northern Okinawa while destroying one of the most biodiverse bays on the planet. As for the relocation of marines, the governments fudged the numbers of personnel involved to pretend the Japanese public was getting a better deal than it really was.[1]

With lower-house elections set for some time in 2009, Tokyo and Washington realized that if the LDP lost power, the incoming government might scrap the plans. So between February and May, they transformed the Roadmap into the Guam International Agreement, a treaty that bound Japan to the terms, rendering it almost impossible for a new government to reverse. The move displayed contempt for Japanese democratic processes. As historian Gavan McCormack wrote, the treaty was "not only unequal but also unconstitutional, illegal, colonial, and deceitful."[2]

In August, Japan went to the polls and voted into power the Democratic Party of Japan (DPJ) by the largest margin in the country's postwar history. DPJ leader Hatoyama Yukio had campaigned on a center-left manifesto that promised more government openness and accountability to the public. As for relations with the United States, the party acknowledged the importance of the US-Japan Security Agreement but promised to work toward a more equal relationship.

Due to its position at the fulcrum of Japan-US relations, Okinawa featured prominently in the new government's priorities. Long neglected by the LDP, now the islands' past and present dominated national politics. Keeping its promise for greater transparency, the DPJ launched an investigation into the Cold War secret agreements, including those related to the islands. The search confirmed that prior LDP governments had allowed US ships to carry nuclear weapons into Japanese ports and granted the military free use of bases in the event of a war in Korea. The inquiry substantiated that Japan had agreed to fund the cleanup of some former military land in Okinawa, an admission that exonerated journalist Nishiyama Takichi, who four decades earlier had been vilified for reporting such claims. The DPJ investigation also uncovered the 1953 agreement whereby Japan waived its right to arrest US military suspects unless the case was of "material importance," the effects of which ensured that prosecution rates against American service members remained low into the twenty-first century.[3]

In addition to more transparency, the DPJ pledged to scrap construction of the new base on Oura Bay. Instead it would attempt to relocate Futenma's operations outside Okinawa and, if possible, outside Japan entirely. Fourteen years had passed since the announcement to close the Futenma base, but here at last was a national government that seemed to respect Okinawans' will. The DPJ, though, had severely underestimated how the United States would react to a Japanese government that dared to place the desires of its people over those of Washington. For decades, the US government had worked with the LDP to ensure its military wielded free rein in Okinawa—overriding the Japanese constitution if necessary—and now

Hatoyama and his upstarts threatened such unfettered US dominance. So the United States moved to block the DPJ's policies and ensure it kept to the terms of the Guam Treaty. In the autumn and winter of 2009, members of the Obama administration and advisors subjected the DPJ government to a litany of insults and intimidation, threatening to halt land returns in Okinawa if the Oura base was not built. Obama refused to meet Hatoyama to consider any alternative plans, and Washington think tankers and former officials exerted additional pressure on the DPJ. Ex-defense official Richard Lawless, who had been an architect of the 2006 Roadmap, likened Hatoyama's administration to a "group of boys and girls playing with a box of matches as they sit in a room of dynamite. . . . When you have dug yourself a great big hole, it is usually wise to stop digging, or somebody has to take away the shovel." Muddled metaphors aside, the message was clear: America would tolerate zero disobedience from its formerly loyal client state.[4]

At the same time as Prime Minister Hatoyama's plans came under attack from Washington, they were also sabotaged from within his own administration. Secret diplomatic cables released by WikiLeaks showed DPJ officials were advising their US counterparts not to pander to their leader's policies on the base. They called Hatoyama "weak" and his government "inexperienced," "stupid," and "chaotic." The head of DPJ Diet affairs, Yamaoka Kenji, displayed a scorn toward Okinawans identical to the LDP: "It's all about opposing for its own sake. . . . If Okinawa's will is respected, nothing will ever happen." As Hatoyama faced such attacks from outside and within, the Japanese and US media added their own criticism. The *Washington Post* branded him "hapless" and "increasingly loopy."[5]

In April 2010, 90,000 Okinawans, including the governor and all municipal mayors or their representatives, held a mass rally in Yomitan Village in a last-ditch effort to persuade the DPJ to keep its electoral pledge, but it was too late. As WikiLeaks cables later revealed, by December 2009, the DPJ government had already told the United States that they would follow through on the Henoko plan, but to assuage political backlash, they would need a few months before making public the decision. For six months, Hatoyama maintained the pretense of seeking an alternative relocation site outside Okinawa, before settling on a way to justify his volte-face: The marine presence in Okinawa was important for purposes of "deterrence." (He later admitted the reason had merely been a pretext to justify his failure to fulfill his promise.) In May 2010, Hatoyama announced that he would agree to construction of the new base atop Oura Bay—then he immediately resigned.[6]

It is impossible to overstate the sense of betrayal felt by many Okinawans toward the United States and Japan. They had hoped the Obama administration might herald a more egalitarian foreign policy, while the departure of the LDP, which had caused their islands so much suffering, raised their expectations that demilitarization might become reality. The events of 2010, however, signaled that regardless of who governed the United States and Japan, the results were the same: Okinawan voices were irrelevant. In July, the Prefectural Assembly passed a unanimous resolution condemning Hatoyama's capitulation as a "violent, democracy-trampling act" that "treated Okinawans as stupid."[7]

In the coming months, two incidents seemed to confirm just how deeply American and Japanese disdain was ingrained. In December 2010, the Department of State's top advisor for Japan, Kevin Maher, met with US students, where he unleashed a string of slurs against Okinawans reminiscent of those uttered by high commissioners of yore. They were "lazy" and "masters in extorting Tokyo for money," and antibase protests were designed to "jack up the price on the rent." When the comments became public, Maher was removed from his post. He later accused the students of a "kind of fabrication."[8]

Then, in November 2011, Japanese journalists attended an informal dinner with Tanaka Satoshi, head of the Okinawa Defense Bureau, the agency in charge of building the new base at Oura Bay. Asked when the government would commence environmental assessments, a prelude to construction, Tanaka replied, "Before you commit a rape, do you say you're going to do so?" The journalists were flabbergasted. Not only did the comment make light of the destruction of the bay, but it also touched a raw nerve, given the islands' decades of sexual assaults. Tanaka was punished with a forty-day pay cut, a slap on the wrist.[9]

As for the DPJ, following its retreat on the new base, it never regained its credibility, nor did it risk further attempts to rebalance the US-Japan alliance. Adding to its woes, in March 2011, Japan was struck by a magnitude 9 earthquake and tsunami, killing some 20,000 in its worst postwar disaster and triggering meltdowns at the Fukushima Daiichi nuclear power plant. The DPJ's mishandling of the crisis made a traumatized public long for the perceived stability of the LDP era, its crookedness and cronyism notwithstanding.

The Revenge of the LDP

The 2012 general election was overwhelmingly won by the LDP, with Abe Shinzo at its helm. In 2007, he had resigned from the post citing health problems, but now, given a second shot at power, he vowed to fulfill his campaign slogan to "Take back Japan" (*"Nippon o torimodosu"*). In the coming months, the true meaning of the words became apparent as he returned the nation to the policies prescribed by US handlers for Japan. In 2012, Richard Armitage and Joseph Nye published a report for the Center for Strategic and International Studies, *The U.S.-Japan Alliance: Anchoring Stability in Asia*, which outlined the path Japan's defense should take in the coming years. Many of these recommendations aligned with views already held by senior members of the LDP, so under Abe 2.0, the government began implementing US requests one by one. In 2013, parliament passed the State Secrecy Law, granting the government the power to classify indefinitely any information related to security and diplomacy with zero independent oversight. Under the new law, government whistleblowers could be jailed for ten years, and journalists who published leaked information faced five years' imprisonment. Whereas Japanese public opposition to the bill stood at some 80 percent, US Ambassador Caroline Kennedy lauded it as an "evolution of Japan's security policies." The following year, Japan rescinded its ban on arms exports, which since the 1960s had stopped it from selling weapons overseas. Now, with the green light from the United States, it planned to export military equipment to kickstart its stalled economy.[10]

The ultimate goal of Prime Minister Abe and his LDP cohort had always been to scrap the pacifist clause of the constitution, but this put them at odds with the public who supported it. So instead of a direct attack to eliminate Article 9, the LDP set out to circumvent it. The 2015 Legislation for Peace and Security consisted of a package of ambiguously worded laws that would allow Japan to send military forces to fight overseas. Even if Japan itself was not under direct attack, they allowed it to deploy forces in what it called "collective self-defense." These troops would fight alongside, or more likely *under* the command of, the US military. As the LDP strove to pass the bills, inside the Diet there were punch-ups between lawmakers, while outside there were huge protests, including large numbers of university students for the first time since the Vietnam War. The Japan Federation of Bar Associations decried the contents of the legislation as unconstitutional—"The Bills have the effect of fundamentally overturning Japan's status as a nation of peace"—and the LDP's tactics to pass them, which "fly directly in the face of the basic principle of the sovereignty of the people." Nevertheless, Prime Minister Abe shunted the bills through parliament just as his grandfather Nobusuke Kishi had railroaded Anpo in 1960. The US State Department reacted to the bill's passage with enthusiasm: "We welcome Japan's ongoing efforts to strengthen the alliance and play a more active role in regional and international security activities."[11]

The whirlwind of changes enacted between 2012 and 2015 fundamentally altered the pacifist foundations of the nation that had been constitutionally stipulated since the end of World War II. And nowhere was the immediate impact felt as strongly as in Okinawa, where the return of Japan to LDP rule signaled to the US government there would be no official opposition to further militarization. The islands had always been a site for the Pentagon to deploy dangerous, new equipment—bioweapon tests, nerve agent, and supersonic spy planes—so the marines decided to send MV-22 Ospreys. During development of the aircraft, which take off like helicopters but fly like planes, thirty service members had lost their lives, earning it the nickname "the Widowmaker," but in 2012, the marines announced they were sending Ospreys to Futenma Air Station, in the crowded heart of Ginowan City.¹²

Horrified by the plan, in late September 2012, Okinawans blocked the gates of the base, effectively shutting it down for several days. Then, with the Japanese and US governments ignoring Okinawan demands to halt the deployment, the prefecture's elected officials declared they would travel to Tokyo to protest the Ospreys and push for the immediate, unconditional closure of the Futenma base. In an unparallelled show of unity, in January 2013, a delegation consisting of the mayors or representatives of all forty-one Okinawan municipalities gathered in Hibiya Park, a stone's throw from the Imperial Palace. After welcoming the assembled crowds in the Okinawan language, the officials demanded removal of the aircraft: "It is outright discrimination against Okinawans to deploy to the dangerous air station the unsafe Osprey. . . . Forty years after reversion, US forces continue to be arrogant as if Okinawa is still under their occupation. Japan's national sovereignty is being challenged." Tokyo had never witnessed such a spectacle. Some of the Okinawan delegation were members of the LDP, but here they were, making demands against the national government—and in a foreign language, no less.¹³

From Hibiya Park, the Okinawans marched through the glitzy shopping district of Ginza, where they were met by an outpouring of hate. Japanese right-wingers lined the boulevards, waving Japanese and American flags. Some lunged at the Okinawans, forcing the police to step in. The nationalists hurled insults: The delegation was comprised of traitors and Chinese Communist Party stooges who ought to go back to Beijing. It was a card taken from the USCAR playbook to delegitimize righteous grievances. Any Okinawan unhappy with their mistreatment must be funded by outside agitators.

Throughout 2013, Prime Minister Abe's government continued to exert pressure on Okinawan officials to agree to the construction of the new base on Oura Bay. In December, Governor Nakaima Hirokazu, who had been elected on a promise to oppose the base, buckled and approved Tokyo's requests to start landfilling the bay. The public reaction was best summed up by the *Ryukyu Shimpo*, which called Nakaima's about-face an "act of sacrilege not only towards the Okinawans alive now, but also to those who died in the war, and to the generations yet to come. It is a crime of historic proportions."¹⁴

In November 2014, Okinawans went to the polls in the gubernatorial election. They kicked out Nakaima by a margin of some 100,000 votes. In his place, they elected Onaga Takeshi. Throughout his political career, Onaga had been a staunch conservative—a former secretary general of the prefecture's LDP, with close ties to the islands' business elite—but, in 2013, he had led the Okinawan delegation to Tokyo, marched through the Japanese nationalists' venom, and emerged at the forefront of a broad movement that brought together Okinawans from the left and right wings, business and civic leaders. The All Okinawa Council pledged to put "identity over ideology" and unite the prefecture against the governments of Japan and the United States. Displaying his Okinawan pride, Onaga frequently addressed audiences in the Okinawan language, further shedding long-held misconceptions of it as a backward and inferior dialect.

Three days after his election win, Onaga joined protestors outside the gates of the new base, thanked them for their struggle, and pledged to do all in his power to protect Oura Bay. True to his word, his administration launched a series of lawsuits against Tokyo to challenge the legality of the new base. In reprisal for Onaga and his fellow Okinawans' resistance, the national government reduced the prefecture's annual budget by around 10 percent, scrapped plans for building a railroad there, and accelerated preparations to construct the new US Marine Corps base in Henoko.[15]

If Japan and the United States refused to respect Okinawans' wishes, then perhaps the international community would be more receptive. Onaga's father had been the mayor of Naha who had announced the Government of the Ryukyu Islands' resolution based on the UN's Declaration of Decolonization in 1961. Now, the son was the first governor of a Japanese prefecture to travel to Geneva to petition the United Nations for global support to block construction of the new base. On 21 September 2015, Onaga appeared before the Human Rights Commission, where he explained Okinawans' opposition:

> After World War II, the US military took our land by force and constructed military bases in Okinawa. We have never provided our land willingly.... Now, the Japanese government is about to go ahead with a new base construction at Henoko by reclaiming our beautiful ocean ignoring the people's will expressed in all Okinawan elections last year. I am determined to stop the new base construction using every possible and legitimate means.[16]

The Battle for Oura Bay: Part II

As Onaga appealed to the international community, outside the entrance to the construction site at Camp Schwab, Okinawans put their bodies on the line to protect Oura Bay. Every morning, protestors of all ages and social classes blocked government trucks from delivering rocks and concrete. Some days saw hundreds of demonstrators, while other days saw dozens—but one permanent fixture was Yamashiro Hiroji, head of the Okinawa Peace Movement Center. If Onaga was the respectable face of the All Okinawa movement, Yamashiro was its grittier side. Born into a farming family, his father had been a child soldier wounded in the Battle of Okinawa, and his mother survived the US invasion of Tinian too traumatized to talk about her experiences. In his youth, Yamashiro had been expelled from high school after leading a hunger strike and lockdown to protest US injustices (his mother told him she was proud of him). Then in later years, he helped to lead protests against military construction in the Yanbaru forests and the temporary closure of Futenma Air Station in 2012.[17]

Every morning in rain or sun, Yamashiro orchestrated the battle to save Oura Bay. Wrapped in his trademark powder-blue poncho, he directed demonstrators on where to place themselves for maximum disruption and how to minimize injuries when the riot police moved in. First, he issued the instructions in the Okinawan language, followed by Japanese to enable demonstrators from the mainland to understand. At around 5:00 a.m., the first of the government trucks would approach the site, so Yamashiro linked arms with those around him, led chants of "Save the sea! Stop construction!" and sometimes launched into a spontaneous rendition of the reversion-era anthem *"Okinawa o kaese"* ("Return Okinawa"). Then the Japanese police would pour out from their riot vans, many of the men brought from the mainland in the hope they would be less sympathetic to the demonstrators. As the elderly Okinawans confronted the officers, they recounted their experiences of the war, describing how the last uniformed mainlanders to come here had been Imperial Japanese Army soldiers who had murdered Okinawans. The demonstrators said they were exercising their constitutionally protected right to free speech and the police ought to go home to *Yamato* (the mainland). Most of the officers were unswayed by the appeals. After issuing warnings, they waded into the crowd, lifting demonstrators by their arms and legs and dragging them to the sides of the road. No concessions were made for age. The riot police manhandled protestors old enough to be their own great-grandparents.

Take, for example, Shimabukuro Fumiko. During the Battle of Okinawa, she had been fifteen years old, fleeing from cave to cave with her blind mother and ten-year-old brother, witnessing horrific civilian deaths, and being chased from shelters by Japanese troops. Toward the end of the battle, she hid in a trench, when US soldiers used a flamethrower to clear the occupants. Severely burned, Shimabukuro surrendered. During US occupation, she worked as a maid within Camp Schwab, but she quit in protest of American aggression in Vietnam, which she felt echoed the wartime suffering of Okinawan civilians. Now, the eighty-five-year-old demonstrated outside the same base where she had once worked, a stalwart of the protests to save Oura Bay. Japanese police, though, showed Shimabukuro no leniency. In November 2014, while attempting to block a truck, she was knocked unconscious and hospitalized. Upon recovering, she returned to the protests, welcomed back with a standing ovation by fellow demonstrators.[18]

Shimabukuro was one of dozens of demonstrators injured by the police in a war of attrition played out daily. Sometimes, the authorities managed to clear the protestors, enabling the construction trucks to enter the base. Other times, the crowds were so large that the police had to abandon their attempts to disperse them, and the trucks turned around. As demonstrators blocked the construction of the new base on land, others took to the sea. The Japanese government had created a maritime exclusion zone in Oura Bay, packing it with so many coast guard vessels that it reminded elderly Okinawans of spring 1945, when the ocean was black with US battleships. Protestors who sailed into the zone were repelled by the Japanese coast guard with a ruthlessness verging on homicidal: They rammed small boats; assaulted crews; and towed canoeists into the treacherous depths beyond the outer reefs, abandoning them to paddle several kilometers back to shore.[19]

Anti-Okinawan Hate

Okinawans' defiance against the central government enraged many Japanese nationalists. In September 2015, a group of twenty attacked the demonstrators' tent outside Camp Schwab, destroying banners and menacing the occupants. Meanwhile, online, Japanese rightists conducted a concerted disinformation campaign echoing the slander flung at the delegation during its Ginza march: Demonstrators received daily stipends, they were organized by Beijing, and the governor's daughter was married to a Chinese Communist Party cadre. During this period, there was a boom in magazine articles and books smearing Okinawans, with such titles as *Okinawa, Don't Be So Spoiled!* (2015) and *If You Truly Love Okinawa, Please Don't Feed the People* (2017). In 2017, mainland TV station Tokyo MX TV broadcasted a program encapsulating disinformation about the peace movement. It called the protestors "terrorists," claimed they were paid, and alleged that one of the masterminds behind the protests was a Korean Japanese agitator.[20]

Members of the marine corps joined the assaults. One deputy assistant chief of staff appeared on a Japanese neonationalist TV network, branding Okinawan demonstrations as "hate speech" and leaking on-base surveillance footage to one of the channel's presenters. Consequently, he was fired. Another senior public affairs officer accused protestors of faking their wounds—"the attempt to appear injured is laughable"—and a base commander repeated the well-worn trope that demonstrators were receiving daily payments.[21]

Such attacks were replays of Cold War claims blaming outside instigators for riling up the docile islanders. New, though, was how fiercely Japanese nationalists had aligned themselves with the American military against Okinawans, a reflection of how, in the halls of power, Prime Minister Abe's government was doing the same with Washington. Structural discrimination bubbled over into overt discrimination with a severity not seen in a century or more. And just as Okinawans were targeted by the United States and Japan, they found themselves threatened from yet another direction: China.

"The Ryukyus Do Not Belong to Japan"

In June 2013, the *New York Times* published an article headlined "Calls Grow in China to Press Claim for Okinawa" that quoted a senior People's Liberation Army officer—Major General Luo Yuan—who had proclaimed, "We can say with certainty that the Ryukyus do not belong to Japan."[22] The comment alarmed many in Okinawa and around the world.

Triggering the announcement was an issue dating back some 120 years that had just flared into an international dispute: ownership of the Senkaku Islands, known in China as the Diaoyu Islands and in Taiwan as the Diaoyutai Islands. Located some 170 kilometers equidistant from Ishigaki Island and Taiwan, they consist of five tiny islands and three outcrops of rocks, with a total area of some six square kilometers. In the days of the Ryukyu Kingdom, the Senkakus had served as navigation aids for tribute ships, but they had not been settled for habitation. During the First Sino-Japanese War (1894–1895), Japan declared the islands as terra nullius and made them part of Okinawa Prefecture. The subsequent Treaty of Shimonoseki ceded Taiwan to Japan but made no specific mention of the Senkakus. In the following years, some 250 Japanese people resided on the islands and conducted such small-scale industry as collecting feathers and making bonito, but the operations had petered out by the late 1920s.[23]

In 1952, the Treaty of San Francisco granted the United States control of the Nansei Shoto south of 29°N, an area that encompassed Okinawa—the military's main prize—and also the Senkakus. At the time, the islands did not warrant specific mention. There was scant debate about their sovereignty, and under US control, two of them were used as bombing ranges. The islands might have remained unimportant, but in 1968, the UN Economic Commission for Asia and the Far East made a discovery that put them in the spotlight. Near the islands there was the possibility of vast oil and gas reserves. Suddenly these once-neglected outcrops were seen as a potential bounty of natural resources, and they became the target of territorial claims by Taipei and, by extension, Beijing, which perceived the islands as part of Taiwan.[24]

The Chinese government argued that the islands were discovered by the Ming dynasty in 1372, so they were an "inherent part of Chinese territory since ancient times." It also contended that because they had been seized by the Meiji government during the First Sino-Japanese War, they ought to have been returned to China when Japan ceded control of Taiwan after World War II. Both Taiwan and China pointed out that the Potsdam Declaration limited Japan's sovereignty to the four main islands and "minor islands," so Tokyo's claim to the Senkaku Islands ought to have been voided in 1945.[25]

Dispute over sovereignty of the Senkaku Islands coincided with Japan-US negotiations over the reversion of Okinawa, but the United States opted not to side with any of the claimants, instead stating in 1971 it "considers that any conflicting claims to the islands are a matter for resolution by the parties concerned." According to political scientist Kimie Hara, US logic was twofold: First, the Nixon administration wanted to avoid derailing the détente it was seeking with China. Second, Washington perceived potential benefits in allowing a territorial dispute to fester. Hara describes this as a "wedge" in Japan-China relations that "rendered the US military presence in Okinawa more acceptable to Japan."[26]

In 1972, the Senkaku Islands returned to Japanese administration, again becoming part of Okinawa Prefecture (four of the islands were privately owned by one Japanese family). Tensions over international sovereignty simmered through the 1970s, but then in 1978, Chinese leader Deng Xiaoping attempted to lay the problem aside with the pronouncement "Our generation is not wise enough to find a common language on this question. Our next generation will certainly be wiser. They will surely find a solution acceptable to all."[27]

Three decades later, events unfurled that proved the current generation had no more wisdom than the previous. In the background, there was a historic shift in the geopolitical balance, as by the early twenty-first century, China had transformed itself into an economic and military powerhouse. Its 2001 entry into the World Trade Organization supercharged its export economy, providing annual GDP growth in the double digits. In 2010, China overtook Japan as the world's second-largest economy. Between 1990 and 2005, China increased its military spending by 15 percent annually. In 2007, it officially reached $45 billion for the year. (Pentagon experts estimated that figure was likely only one-third of the actual total, but it still paled compared to the US defense budget of $623 billion for the same year.) Accompanying this military build-up, China asserted territorial claims over large areas of the South China Sea, bringing it into disputes with neighboring nations, especially the Philippines. At the same time, China still declared its sovereignty over Taiwan, threatening military intervention if the island proclaimed formal independence. China's increased nationalism clashed with Japan, particularly revolving around Tokyo's failure to recognize the brutality of its World War II occupation. China was angered by Japanese leaders' visits to Yasukuni Shrine and their attempts to erase accounts of wartime atrocities from school textbooks, as well as delays in Japan's cleanup of chemical weapons abandoned during the war in China.[28]

In 2010, tensions came to a head when a Chinese fishing trawler collided with Japanese coast guard vessels near the Senkaku Islands and its captain was detained. The minor incident ripped the scab off the territorial dispute, and in the coming weeks, the issue quickly cascaded. Although Japanese authorities released the Chinese captain, at the same time, they pronounced the Senkaku Islands were part of Japan's sovereign territory and denied there was any dispute over their ownership. The assertion sparked angry responses in China and Taiwan, which in turn provoked Japanese nationalists, notably Tokyo's governor, Ishihara Shintarō, a notorious revisionist. Ishihara escalated tensions over the Senkaku dispute by recommending that the Tokyo government buy the islands from the Japanese family who still owned them. His proposal proved popular with the Japanese public, and they donated almost $20 million to the purchase. In Okinawa, too, the Prefectural Assembly and the local assemblies of Ishigaki and Miyako adopted resolutions declaring Japanese ownership of the Senkaku Islands. Moreover, members of the antibase movement urged the Japanese government to take a strong stance against Beijing, belying right-wing accusations they were beholden to the Chinese Communist Party. Potential oil reserves aside, the Senkakus were important grounds for Okinawa fishing crews.[29]

In an attempt to calm the furor, the DPJ government purchased three of the privately owned Senkaku Islands in 2012, but the plan rebounded. Taiwanese citizens were furious, and in China, there were anti-Japanese riots. To assert its sovereignty, Beijing adopted so-called gray-zone operations, whereby it dispatched coast guard ships and military flights in the vicinity of the islands. The Chinese Communist Party paired these displays of hard power with a soft-power push to undermine Japan's claims. One such tactic was to problematize Japan's ownership of other islands in the East China Sea, namely Okinawa.

In the spring of 2013, Major General Luo Yuan, citing the Ryukyu Kingdom's tributary relationship with China, declared, "We can say with certainty that the Ryukyus do not belong to Japan." Although the general was well known for making such inflammatory statements, the following week, Chinese government researchers and retired senior army officers met at Renmin University, Beijing, where they discussed how China could question Japan's rule over Okinawa to improve their nation's international influence.[30]

On 11 May 2013, the Chinese government-run *Global Times* outlined a three-step approach to challenge Japan's claims to sovereignty: First, initiate public debate on the Okinawa issue; for example, by allowing the establishment of "research organizations." Second, raise the matter "in the international arena." And finally, sponsor groups within Okinawa to seek independence. The article described how Okinawa's sovereignty could be "played as a powerful card," and if Japan threatened China's future, such a tactic was "fair game."[31]

Many Okinawans reacted to the news of the Chinese claims with revulsion. Sick of being a pawn in the games of superpowers, they understood that China had no intention of annexing the prefecture. It was an attempt to lay claim to the natural resources that might lie beneath the Senkaku Islands. Blatantly, throughout the article, the Chinese writers used the term *Ryukyu* instead of *Okinawa*, reminiscent of the USCAR's policy of *rinichi* (separation from Japan). As for Beijing's call to support the independence movement, some actual proponents of self-rule have long been aghast. Matsushima Yasukatsu, an advocate of Okinawan independence, cited China's persecution of Tibetans, Uighurs, and other minority groups. Any decisions on Okinawa's future must be made by Okinawans themselves, he explained:

> Ryūkyū does not belong to either China or Japan. Okinawa has learned from the post-war history and liberation struggles of former colonies to stand on its own feet, take back its language and teach its children in their own language as legitimate subjects in school Okinawan culture, history, language, economy, environment, property rights, peace, and human rights as Okinawans.[32]

2016

In Okinawa, not a year goes by without US military brutality, but there are certain years when the slew of injustices is so intense it leaves residents reeling. In 1955, troops stormed Iejima and Isahama, forcing villagers from their land. Then a soldier raped and murdered a six-year-old girl. Another abominable year was 1969: Americans murdered five Okinawans and killed another six in traffic accidents, and a leak of nerve agent struck terror into residents. And then there was 2016.[33]

The year began with the realization that the US Air Force had polluted Okinawa's primary aquifer with per- and polyfluoroalkyl substances (PFAS)—"forever chemicals"—which cause cancers, developmental delays, and harm the human immune system. Decades of training with toxic firefighting foam at Kadena Air Base had seeped PFAS into the groundwater, a source of drinking water for 450,000 residents. Although Okinawans had long been aware of the base's potential risks—in the 1960s, fuel leaks had made water from nearby wells catch fire—nobody had envisioned this scale of impact, one of the largest cases of environmental contamination in Japanese history. Further checks by the Okinawa prefectural government also discovered dangerous PFAS levels near Camp Hansen, where the drinking water for Kin Town residents was affected, and near Futenma Air Station, where the grounds of an elementary school and sacred springs were polluted. Okinawan officials demanded access to the bases to inspect the sources of contamination, but the US military refused; SOFA enabled it to pollute with impunity.[34]

As Okinawans began to grapple with the fact that Kadena Air Base had poisoned their drinking water, an American from the same facility was arrested for murder.

On the evening of 28 April, Kenneth Gadson, a former marine employed as a civilian contractor, drove through Uruma City seeking a woman to rape. He was not afraid of arrest, he later explained, because he believed that Japanese females tended not to report sexual assaults. At approximately 8:00 p.m., Gadson spotted a twenty-year-old woman walking along the roadside. Military police files describe what Gadson did next: "He kidnapped, bound, raped, bludgeoned, stabbed, and strangled (the victim). Subsequently, he placed (the victim) into a suitcase which he placed into the trunk of his vehicle." Gadson drove to woodland and disposed of her corpse. Then he dumped the suitcase inside Camp Hansen, where he thought Japanese police would not be able to investigate. If Gadson had been living on-base, he might have evaded arrest by Japanese police due to SOFA, but because he resided in a civilian area, local police were able to detain him. In interviews, he confessed he had fantasized about raping and killing women for many years, and during enlistment, he had told recruiters that his motivation to join the marines was to kill people.[35]

In response to the murder, the Okinawa Prefectural Assembly passed its first-ever resolution to demand the removal of the marine corps from the islands, and 65,000 people staged a mass rally. Once again, Washington and Tokyo attempted to quell the anger with promises of reform. In July, they announced limits to the protections contractors received under SOFA, but when the changes were announced the following January, they proved merely cosmetic, leaving the text of SOFA unchanged. In December, Gadson was sentenced by a Japanese court to life in Yokosuka Prison.[36]

Given Okinawans' levels of grief, the Japanese government might have been expected to dial back its oppression, but instead it rubbed salt into residents' wounds with the construction of yet more US military facilities in the Yanbaru forests. The region hosts the Northern Training Area, where the military had tested Agent Orange and built mock Vietnamese villages in the 1960s, but under SACO, the two governments promised to release approximately half of its land. Just like the closure of Futenma Air Station, however, there was a catch: Before it could be returned, new facilities had to be built elsewhere. Six landing pads for helicopters and MV-22 Ospreys—each around the size of a baseball field—would be constructed around the tiny hamlet of Takae.[37]

Even in an area as ecologically significant as the Yanbaru, Takae was unique. Nearby lived Japan's highest concentration of endangered and rare species; among the 126 varieties was the Okinawa rail (*Yanbaru kuina*), a flightless bird only officially recognized in 1978. Residents vowed to protect this biodiversity from military construction projects, and since 2007, they had staged sit-ins against the helipads. The Japanese government had tried to thwart the demonstrators with "strategic lawsuits against public participation" (SLAPP), including one filed against an eight-year-old child.[38]

Refusing to buckle to such intimidation, residents had successfully blocked construction of four of the helipads. But in 2016, Prime Minister Abe's administration decided to proceed with construction by force. Wary of potential blowback from voters, the government waited until 11 July, the day after the upper-house elections, to launch its attack. Then it deployed more than five hundred riot police—many from mainland Japan—who dragged away the citizens attempting to protect the forest. Scuffles between the police and demonstrators led to arrests and injuries. Journalists were corralled, hindering their ability to report on the violence.[39]

The authorities felled some 30,000 trees and brought in thousands of truckloads of gravel to build the helipads. particularly galling to many residents was the use of Self-Defense Forces helicopters to fly in materials. Okinawans clambered atop the construction fences and appealed for the workers to halt their operations. Veteran environmental activist Iha Yoshiyasu explained the forest was a "treasure of humanity"; reminded them how military bases had already devastated Okinawa's environment; and emphasized, "This forest belongs to *Uchinaanchu*."[40]

Mainland police responded to the resistance by hurling racial slurs. In an encounter caught on video, one officer from Osaka Prefecture called demonstrators *dojin*, the derogatory term for *indigenous people* harking back to Meiji Era insults against Okinawans. Forced to comment on the matter, the minister of state for Okinawa and northern territories affairs refused to denounce the word as discriminatory, instead defending the police officer: "Everyone has freedom of speech." Another officer called demonstrators *shinajin* (a racist word for *Chinese people*) in a comment that followed a familiar pattern of blaming Okinawans' civil disobedience on outsiders. (Both officers received reprimands from their police departments.)[41]

With international attention on Takae, the Japanese government decided to send a message to islanders that further resistance would not be tolerated by moving against its nemesis, the charismatic leader of the Okinawa Peace Movement Center, Yamashiro Hiroji. On 17 October, police arrested and detained him on charges of snipping barbed wire set by the Okinawa Defense Bureau. The estimated cost of the damage: ¥2,000. Under Japanese law, the police can hold suspects for twenty-three days before indictment. So to prolong his detention, Japanese prosecutors pressed additional charges for incidents allegedly occurring many months previously: interference of official duties and bodily injury (in which an Okinawa Defense Bureau officer received a cut to his leg) and blocking the gates of Camp Schwab with 1,500 bricks, an action the police witnessed but ignored as it happened. Yamashiro had previously been diagnosed with malignant lymphoma, but he was not allowed visits by his doctor or family during the five months of his detention before finally being released on bail. On 14 March 2018, Yamashiro appeared in court, where he received a two-year suspended sentence.

Among the human rights organizations condemning his treatment was Amnesty International, which stated, "The arrest of Hiroji Yamashiro, a symbolic opposition figure, has had a chilling effect on others who are peacefully exercising their rights to freedom of expression, association and peaceful assembly. Some activists now hesitate to join the protest for fear of reprisals."[42]

Okinawans' year of abominations was still not over. In December, what many residents had feared became a reality when a marine corps Osprey crash-landed into shallow seas in Nago City. Fortunately, nobody was injured among the crew or on the ground, but it was a stark reminder of the dangers of the aircraft for which the Japanese government was building new landing pads in the nearby Yanbaru forests. By 2024, another two Japan-based Ospreys had been destroyed in crashes: One in 2017 killed three marines during training in Australia, and the other in 2023, involving an air force Osprey, killed eight service members near Yakushima, Kyushu Prefecture. The aircraft's moniker was proven tragically appropriate: the Widowmaker.

11

Islands of Peace?

The fiftieth anniversary of Okinawa's reversion to Japan was 15 May 2022. Under coronavirus restrictions, official commemorations were divided between Tokyo and Okinawa, where, in Ginowan City, Japanese and American dignitaries gathered to listen to an address by prefectural leader Tamaki Denny. The eighth governor elected since reversion, Tamaki was the son of an Okinawan mother and an American marine father who had left the islands before his birth. In his younger days, Tamaki had been a well-known radio DJ—popular for speaking Okinawan on air—who then entered politics, serving as a left-wing member of the lower house for nine years. Unfortunate circumstances propelled Tamaki into the gubernatorial post. In 2018, Onaga Takeshi, the leader of the All Okinawa movement, was diagnosed with pancreatic cancer, and as his health rapidly deteriorated, he designated Tamaki as a potential successor. In the election that followed Onaga's death, Tamaki pledged to pursue his predecessor's antimilitary policies, and he injected a streak of indigenous pride by adopting the slogan "Okinawans ought to decide what happens in Okinawa" (*"Uchinaa no koto wa Uchinaanchu ga kimeru"*). It was an immensely popular platform. Tamaki received almost 400,000 votes, the highest in the prefecture's history.[1]

Taking the stage at the ceremony in Ginowan to commemorate the fiftieth anniversary of reversion, Tamaki was representing a prefecture that had undergone significant demographic changes since 1972. The population had increased by 50 percent to almost 1.5 million, most of whom were born after the Battle of Okinawa and lacked firsthand experience of life without civil rights under US colonial rule. Tamaki opened his address with a greeting in Okinawan. Then he outlined the significant problems the islands still faced: lack of industrial development, depressed incomes (the nation's lowest), and child poverty (Japan's worst).[2]

The governor offered blunt criticism of the ongoing US military presence:

Okinawa Prefecture accounts for only 0.6 percent of Japan's land mass—but 70.3 percent of the total area of facilities exclusively used by the US military in Japan are concentrated here. Prefectural residents continue to bear this heavy burden, including crimes and accidents caused by American service members and civilian employees, noise pollution, and environmental contamination.³

Due to such problems, Okinawa had failed to become islands of peace, said Tamaki, who then outlined his vision for the prefecture's future, describing the history of the Ryukyu Kingdom and the notion of *chimugukuru*, an Okinawan word meaning *a sense of compassion*: "We, the people of Okinawa Prefecture, will protect our abundant nature for our children and grandchildren, ensure that every resident relishes a sense of purpose in life, cherishes human connections and *chimugukuru*, and contributes to peace and stability in the Asia-Pacific region in the spirit of the Bridge of Nations."⁴

It was a heartfelt oratory that on one hand outlined the broken promises of reversion and criticized the shortcomings of Japanese administration and on the other expressed an optimistic vision for an Okinawa-led future anchored in its historical experiences as an independent kingdom. In many aspects, Tamaki's speech reflected the contradictory emotions shared by many prefectural residents, as evinced by a wide-ranging survey conducted by state broadcaster Nippon Hōsō Kyōkai (NHK) to coincide with the anniversary. According to the poll, most Okinawan respondents—84 percent—regarded return to Japan in a favorable light, but the ongoing presence of the US military undercut such positivity: 63 percent wanted the bases reduced to the same level as mainland Japan, and 16 percent wanted them removed entirely from their islands. The NHK poll also surveyed mainland Japanese on their attitudes toward Okinawa, and the results revealed major disparities. Although the respondents sympathized with islanders' military burden [79 percent said it was unusual or improper (*okashī*)], only 14 percent supported transferring the bases to mainland Japan. In contrast, 40 percent of Okinawans favored such a redistribution. In the 1950s, the US bases had been relocated from Japan to Okinawa, but mainlanders were not keen to take them back. NIMBY-ism was very much alive and well in 2022.⁵

Despite Okinawans' overwhelming desire to reduce the number of bases in their prefecture, this did not correspond with outright opposition to the US-Japan Security Treaty. Fifty-eight percent of respondents said they believed Anpo contributed to the nation's peace and safety. But Okinawans questioned why they ought to be burdened with such a high concentration of bases. Moreover, 82 percent wanted a revision of the US-Japan Status of Forces Agreement (SOFA), with its enshrinement of extraterritoriality and lack of environmental accountability. The number of mainland respondents supporting the security treaty was even higher (82 percent). Clearly it is easier to endorse a system in theory when your daily lives are not endangered by its actual practice.

To highlight how little Okinawa's demilitarization had progressed since reversion, the newspaper *Ryukyu Shimpo* published its 15 May 2022 edition with

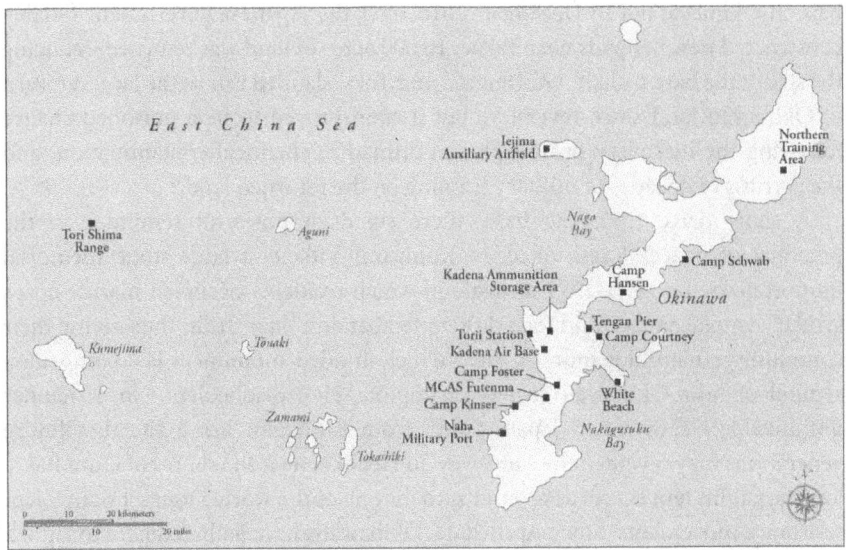

MAP 11.1 *Main US military bases in Okinawa*

the identical page 1 headline of a half-century earlier: "The Bases Unchanged, the Suffering Continues" ("*Kawaranu kichi tsudzuku kunō*"). So how did Okinawa look fifty years after its return to Japanese administration?

Okinawa Island: From North to South

Okinawa remains one of the most militarized places on the planet. Its landscape is dominated by the current bases—thirty-one US and fifty-seven Japanese Self-Defense Force (SDF) facilities—alongside hundreds of memorials and museums to World War II. Threaded through this geography runs a vibrant river of resistance in the form of demonstrations, sit-ins, and teach-ins that embody how persistent, nonviolent resistance can bend the will of even the most powerful governments.

In Okinawa's main island, the northernmost US base is Camp Gonsalves (a.k.a. the Jungle Warfare Training Center), named by the military after a marine corps private who died during the Battle of Okinawa. In few other allied nations (perhaps with the exception of South Korea) does the US military dedicate its facilities to those who died killing local nationals, but different rules apply here. The marines seem to think Okinawans must be reminded which side won the war and why their land is still occupied. Camp Gonsalves used to be the largest US base in Okinawa, but in December 2016, after the Japanese government forcibly constructed new helipads near Takae, 10,000 acres of land was returned, reducing the size of the base by half. Washington and Tokyo lauded this as the largest return of Okinawan land since reversion, but it soon proved to be a poisoned chalice following the discovery of unexploded ordnance, chemical contamination, and the detritus of decades of military training on the returned land.[6]

A short drive from the base, there stands a powerful reminder to the potential of peaceful resistance. In Kunigami Village, a large stone memorial immortalizes the 1970–1971 struggle in which residents occupied marine corps artillery emplacements and forced them to abandon their drills, thus saving their community's natural resources. The publicly funded monument is a compelling symbol of how Okinawan society champions civil disobedience in a manner unthinkable elsewhere in Japan. South from Kunigami lies a site that future generations may revere in the same way. In Henoko, near the shores of Oura Bay, a long tarpaulin tent serves as ground zero for one of the world's longest nonviolent resistance movements. Since April 2004, Okinawans have gathered here to launch canoes to block construction of the new US Marine Corps base. These protestors represent the citizens' struggle, while at the same time, Governor Tamaki and his colleagues at Okinawa Prefectural Government have fought to cancel the base via the legal system. Repeatedly, though, the Japanese courts have sided with the national government, signaling how Anpo still trumps the Kenpo. In 2018, construction trucks began to dump rocks and dirt into the pristine bay, the start of a landfill expected to take until the mid-2030s to complete. Environmental desecration aside, even senior US military officers have deemed the project unfeasible due to its too-short runways and proximity to mountains. Moreover the new base sits on two fault lines, and the seabed is as soft as mayonnaise, making construction extremely challenging.[7]

Westward to Motobu Port, a short ferry ride connects to the island of Iejima. Roughly one-third is still controlled by the military and, under the terms of the Special Action Committee on Okinawa (SACO), parachute training was moved here from the main island. Sometimes stray service members drift onto farmers' fields, crushing their crops of sugarcane and tobacco. Such infractions bolster residents' opposition to the military, keeping alive the spirit of their island's most famous leader, Ahagon Shōkō. In 1984, he founded the House of Nuchi du Takara Anti-War Peace Museum, installing displays to explain why islanders so strongly oppose militarism: the bloodied clothes of a baby bayoneted by a Japanese soldier to silence its cries; photographs of the Beggars' March; and, most strikingly, several dummy H-bombs dropped by the Americans and purloined by farmers. Ahagon welcomed thousands of visitors to the museum and gave lectures about the peace movement until his death in 2002 at the age of 101. Within the prefecture, almost everyone knows about the Gandhi of Okinawa, but few people in mainland Japan are aware of his work, or even his name; ignorance itself is a form of violence.

Back on the main island, driving south one soon arrives at Yomitan Village, where the US military still occupies more than one-third of civilian land, too. At the entrance of the army base, Torii Station, stand two huge US-built vermillion gates that resemble those marking Shinto shrines. It is a bizarre display signaling the sacredness with which the military deems its presence in Okinawa. Elsewhere in Yomitan, thanks to residents' resistance, the United States was forced to close some bases. In 2007, it dismantled the colossal Elephant's Cage antenna—but not before it extracted $500 million from the Japanese government to build a better version within Camp Hansen. Near Yomitan's sea, where the military used to stage expensive missile exercises, today tourist resorts occupy the shoreline, but one reminder of the Cold War still exists in nearby Onna Village, where the Monument to World Peace preserves Okinawa's sole surviving nuclear-missile silo. The vast concrete bunker, with six gaping launch tubes facing China, has been transformed into a museum to teach visitors about the islands' role in US plans for Armageddon. Back in Yomitan, the village has erected Okinawa's largest *shīsā* lion-dog statue to remind residents of the Ryukyu Kingdom's peaceful relations with Beijing. The statue was designed by Kinjo Minoru, the renowned sculptor who designed the memorial outside Chibichiri Gama, and his other works dot the village, including the Monument to Grief and Anger (Han no Hi), depicting the wartime suffering of the thousands of Korean laborers brought by the Japanese military to Okinawa.[8]

Driving south from Yomitan brings us to Kadena Air Base and its adjacent Ammunition Storage Area, site of the 1969 nerve-agent leak. The air base resembles an American suburb, replete with a shopping mall; two golf courses; and seven schools, one named after comedian Bob Hope, who, during his 1971 visit to the base, joked that soldiers ought to smuggle home Asian prostitutes in their luggage. The twenty square kilometers that Kadena Air Base occupies belongs to 12,000 landowners, and some 620 family graves still lie behind its fences. According to one air force report, service members and dependents have defaced the tombs with graffiti, and "it is not uncommon to [sic] for human bones to be found in proximity to deteriorating or vandalized tombs." Okinawans wishing to visit their ancestral graves require special permission. Equally inaccessible are at least sixteen *utaki* (sacred sites).[9]

A quick glance at any aerial map of Kadena Air Base (and other US installations in Okinawa) reveals the stark disparity in living conditions between military personnel and their neighbors. Whereas on-base housing consists of widely spaced houses with sprawling lawns, Okinawans' homes are crammed along narrow lanes. Thanks to Japanese taxpayers' *omoiyari* funding, service members pay heavily discounted utility bills, allowing them to water their yards and run air-conditioning 24/7, oblivious to the costs. Because service personnel are exempt from paying many local taxes, the national government is forced to make up the difference. Overall, the military presence in Okinawa is estimated to hobble the economy to the tune of ¥1 trillion.[10]

As for Kadena Air Base, in addition to the constant roar of aircraft, the base exposes Okinawans and service members to a plethora of toxins. In 2013, near US schools, construction workers unearthed 108 rusty barrels containing the ingredients of Agent Orange and arsenic, but base commanders tried to hide the discovery from parents. The military has been equally secretive about its contamination of 450,000 Okinawans' drinking water with per- and polyfluoroalkyl substances (PFAS) "forever chemicals." No local officials have been allowed to inspect the base, nor has the Japanese government pushed the military for transparency. The environmental loopholes of SOFA, combined with Tokyo's complacency, ensures the US military can poison without fear of punishment.[11]

Eight kilometers south from Kadena Air Base lies Ginowan City. Blessed with an abundance of natural springs, humans have inhabited the area since prehistoric times, and in the early twentieth century, it was a major transport and administrative hub. But in the Battle of Okinawa, the US military expelled residents, bulldozed their homes, and built the air base still dominating the city. In 2018, Ginowan's long and rich history was ignored by the head of the marine corps, General Robert B. Neller, who proclaimed at a Pentagon press briefing, "Futenma [Base] when it was built was—there were no people living within several kilometers. Now the cities around Futenma are right up to the fence." The implication that the base had been built on empty space echoed tabula rasa excuses deployed by other colonizers to seize indigenous lands, and its blame on Okinawans for living near the base disguised how military occupation caused chronic land shortages. Thirty-two percent of Ginowan is occupied by Futenma Air Station, and 4,200 residents own the land beneath the base, which contains tombs and sacred sites to which they are denied access. Neller's comment was a mistruth piled on the earlier US-Japan lie from 1996 that the base would be closed within five to seven years. That promise had precipitated grand Okinawan plans to redevelop the site into a verdant residential and business hub. The current facility employs some 200 civilians, but the redeveloped land would have provided work for almost 35,000 and produced thirty-two times the economic benefit. Almost three decades after that promise had been made, the base was still there, its closure contingent on the construction of a replacement facility at the expense of destroying Oura Bay.[12]

For some tourists, the US bases contribute to Okinawa's exotic appeal. Visitors gawk at low-flying MV-22 Ospreys, shop for surplus military clothes, and punch their names into souvenir dog tags. The American Village, located between Kadena Air Base and Futenma Air Station, embodies this fantasy, consisting of a Vegas-esque sprawl of hotels, restaurants, and souvenir shops. Gaudiness aside, the area highlights the financial benefits of shuttering bases. The land used to be occupied by the military, who, according to prefectural records, had not employed any local workers there. But after the bases' closure and redevelopment for civilian use, by the 2010s, the area created 3,400 new jobs, and the direct economic impact rose 108-fold to almost ¥34 billion per year. This reflects a wider shift in Okinawa's postreversion finances. Today, tourism contributes approximately one-quarter to the prefecture's economy, compared to 5 percent created by the military.[13]

The Japanese government had long envisaged that Okinawa would rival Hawai'i as a tourist destination. This goal was finally achieved in 2019 when 10 million people visited the islands, matching for the first time the number of tourists to the Aloha State. Such revenues, though, are notoriously unstable. In 2020, coronavirus travel bans slashed the numbers of visitors to Okinawa to 3.7 million. A similar drop had occurred in 2001 after the 9/11 attacks, when Japanese schools canceled visits to Okinawa for fears the bases would become terrorist targets. Moreover, the benefits of tourism to Okinawans tend to be illusory: poverty-line wages, seasonal employment, and profits funneled to mainland corporations. Tourism also damages an environment already blighted by the military, as landfill projects and artificial beaches disrupt the ecosystem, and visitors' demands for swimming pools and lush golf greens strain already-precarious supplies of freshwater.[14]

Continuing south brings us to the site where in 1955 US missionary Harold Rickard declared, "I watched a village die," after witnessing soldiers drag Okinawans from their land and drown their fields in silt. Today, Camp Foster, the base that took their homes, is still there, and one of the only signs of the village is a bus stop named Isahama along a roadside of tattoo shops, strip clubs, and other businesses catering to US military personnel. Isahama used to be famous for its fields of rice, and the army's seizure was mirrored across the main island as bases occupied 20 percent of agricultural land. The traditional Okinawan diet—rich in sweet potatoes, tofu, and *goya*—is acclaimed as one of the healthiest on the planet (it even spawned a 2004 *New York Times* best-seller). But the theft of farmland forced many residents to subsist on imported—usually processed—foods. (Spam is a staple of Okinawan larders, just like in other US colonies, such as Guam and Hawai'i.) In 2015, Okinawans under the age of sixty-five had the worst mortality rate in Japan, and in 2022, Okinawans' healthy-life expectancy (i.e., the period of time people can live without nursing care or becoming bedridden) was almost the worst nationally. Most medical professionals attribute Okinawans' poor health to diet and an overreliance on cars, but some have also begun to assess the impact of exposure to PFAS and other military contaminants.[15]

One base in particular underscores the persistence of environmental pollution: Makiminato Service Area (now called Camp Kinser), where the army had stored Vietnam War chemicals. As recently as 2019, the soil was still contaminated with dangerous levels of dioxin and pesticides, but the military hid the information from service members, their families, and Okinawans. For base commanders, all too often public image still outweighs public health.[16]

From Camp Kinser to Okinawa's capital, Naha, is less than ten kilometers, but due to congested roads, the journey by car can sometimes take almost one hour. With a population of 310,000, Naha resembles mainland Japanese cities—tower apartment blocks, and franchised restaurants and convenience stores—but residents celebrate their Ryukyu roots. *Shīsā* dogs stand guard atop almost every roof, street junctions display *ishigantō* amulets to ward off ill spirits, and families hold annual *shīmī* feasts in the courtyards of their family tombs. Although the Battle of Okinawa obliterated Naha, sites from the Ryukyu Kingdom's glory days have been rebuilt, and numerous museums chronicle the islands' history of discrimination and resistance. Pride of place in the Okinawa Prefectural Museum and Art Museum hangs the fifteenth-century Bridge of Nations bell, scarred with bullet strikes and blackened from the combat of 1945. Fukutsu-kan is a museum overseen by the daughter of Senaga Kamejiro that chronicles the left-wing politician's struggles against US authorities, their dirty tricks to oust him, and his victories on behalf of Okinawa in the Japanese parliament.

When Commodore Matthew Calbraith Perry occupied the Ryukyu Kingdom, he demanded the construction of a cemetery for foreign nationals. Today, it still stands in Tomari, where among the graves is the tomb of William Board, the US sailor who allegedly raped a Naha resident in 1854. Along with the other graves, it is still carefully tended by volunteers from the American Legion. At the time of Perry's arrival, Okinawans could not have known that Board would be the first of countless Americans to assault residents, and today, SOFA enshrines a similar extraterritoriality foisted on the island 170 years earlier. Despite promises to rewrite SOFA, it has undergone only superficial amendments, and US service members' sense of impunity is bolstered by Japanese prosecutors, who often allow suspects to walk. Military-on-military crime within the bases is also rampant.[17]

Naha is home to Okinawa's mass media, which, unlike its mainland counterparts, is indomitably antiestablishment due to journalists' shame that their wartime predecessors wrote propaganda urging sacrifice for the emperor and their experiences of censorship under USCAR rule. The Memorial to Fallen Journalists, engraved with the names of the fourteen reporters killed during the Battle of Okinawa, stands in Asahi ga Oka Park, where each year members of the media gather to pledge not to glorify war again. Such commitment to pacifism and service to the Okinawan people often draws acrimony from mainland Liberal Democratic Party politicians and the US military.[18]

During US administration, the south of Okinawa Island had not been as heavily militarized as elsewhere—with the exception of Naha Air Base and the CIA logistical hub Camp Chinen. After reversion, the spy agency's facility was briefly operated by the army, before closing in 1974. Today, most of the site is a deluxe twenty-seven-hole golf course from which Japan's annual women's tour kicks off. (The golf club's home page makes no mention of its clandestine past.) Southwest from here lie the killing fields of Itoman City, where tens of thousands of Okinawans were driven after the Japanese army's retreat from Shuri in an effort to prolong the battle. These experiences underpin islanders' current conception of warfare: At times of conflict, the military does not protect civilians, and it adheres to its own priorities first, abandoning women, children, and the elderly to fend for themselves and slaughtering those who get in the way. In Itoman, there are some 250 war memorials, testament to the ferocity of the fighting that occurred here. Each year, busloads of schoolchildren arrive from prefectural and mainland schools to listen firsthand to the experiences of the battle's dwindling survivors. Among the most visited memorials is the Himeyuri Peace Museum, built adjacent to the cave where many student nurses died, which unflinchingly portrays the Japanese military's exploitation of the young women and the horrific waste of life. Equally uncompromising in its critique of militarism is the museum at Okinawa Peace Memorial Park, which locates the Pacific War within the context of Japanese colonialism in Eastern Asia and chronicles the injustices of Okinawa's postwar US occupation. A short walk from the museum, there is the Cornerstone of Peace, with its waves of stone slabs engraved with the names of all those known to have died in the Battle of Okinawa. As of 2024, the number totaled 242,225. In 1965, 23 June was inaugurated as a prefectural holiday (Irei no Hi), when schools and public offices are closed, allowing residents to reflect on the lessons from the battle. According to NHK's 2022 survey, fewer than one-third (27 percent) of Japanese respondents were aware of the day. Each year on Irei no Hi, Japanese prime ministers visit the park to deliver rote promises to reduce Okinawa's military burden. In 2019, when Abe Shinzo came here for the first time after green-lighting the landfill of Oura Bay, he was heckled with jeers of "Liar!" and "Go home!" At the podium, he gave a speech so similar to the previous year's that it boarded on self-plagiarism, callousness that deeply offended many Okinawans.[19]

Offshore from Okinawa's main island, other monuments keep alive wartime memories that the Japanese government would rather be forgotten. In the Keramas, where US troops first landed in March 1945, residents erected a memorial to the victims of the forced suicide, *Shiratama no Tō*. But in 1960, the Americans requisitioned the land to build a missile base, forcing them to relocate it. Not even the souls of the departed were allowed to rest, displaced for the needs of a new military. Another memorial to what Tokyo would rather erase lies on Miyako Island, site of some seventeen wartime comfort stations. Following groundbreaking research by Korean historian Hong Yunshin, in the 2000s local assembly members called for an official investigation into their island's history of sexual slavery—only to be blocked by right-wing politicians. As a result, residents and historians from

Japan and South Korea took matters into their own hands, raising funds to build a monument. The Arirang Memorial is inscribed with a message in the eleven languages of those who had been comfort women, plus Vietnamese, to recognize the sacrifice of women in that country's war. It reads, "We remember the suffering of the individual women who were subjected to sexual violence by the Japanese military. Lament the victims of war-time sexual violence throughout the entire world. Pray for a peaceful world without any more war."[20]

As residents of Miyako Island fought to condemn past militarization, they faced a new build-up of Japanese troops. In 2019, the SDF established a missile unit there and brought in seven hundred soldiers to operate it, and islanders protested the deployment. Meanwhile, the SDF constructed new bases on Ishigaki Island and Yonaguni Island, where the mayor invited the troops, claiming they would help to reverse depopulation. At the time of reversion, most Okinawans opposed dispatching the SDF to the prefecture, but fifty years later, attitudes were more complex. According to NHK's 2022 poll, 31 percent of Okinawan respondents felt that the SDF build-up in the outer islands was needed, and 45 percent said it couldn't be helped (*yamu o enai*). In contrast, 11 percent replied the deployment was unnecessary, and 12 percent said it increased the risk of conflict. The reason for many Okinawans' acceptance of the SDF—albeit reluctant—was a rise in regional tensions that gave residents an ominous sense of déjà vu.[21]

At 4:00 a.m. on 24 August 2023, Okinawans were awoken by sirens in the streets and emergency alerts on their mobile phones, urging them to seek immediate shelter: North Korea had launched a missile toward the prefecture. The rocket passed between the main island and Miyako Island, and although landing in the sea without causing injuries, it frightened many residents. In 2006, North Korea claimed to successfully test an underground nuclear detonation. In the following years, it manufactured an estimated fifty warheads and conducted rocket tests to carry them to potential targets. The August 2023 alert was the latest in a series of launches that had overflown Japanese territory.[22]

Accompanying North Korea's intermittent missile tests, there was near-constant friction with China centered around the Senkakus, which, even after Japan's nationalization of the islands in 2012, Beijing continued to claim as its own. In December 2012, the Chinese government sent a survey plane over the Senkakus, the first intrusion into the airspace claimed by Japan. Then it waged gray-zone operations, dispatching aircraft and ships near the islands to chip away at Japan's assertion of undisputed sovereignty.

As political scientist Kimie Hara explained, the United States left its position on the ownership of the Senkaku Islands ambiguous to create a "wedge" that made Japan—and the Japanese public—more amenable to keeping US bases in the country. The tactic worked exactly as anticipated. Following Chinese incursions, Tokyo urged the United States to confirm that the Security Treaty encompassed the islands and US forces would protect them. In 2014, President Barack Obama specifically stated that the US-Japan Security Treaty indeed covered the Senkaku Islands, and subsequent presidents have repeated the assurance.[23]

For many Okinawans, the dispute over the Senkaku Islands soured sentiments toward China. At the start of the twenty-first century, the US consulate in Naha wrote, "Many Okinawans identify with China culturally. . . . Some also say Okinawa, over the centuries, has received better treatment from China than from Japan or the United States." By the time of the 2022 NHK poll, though, 87 percent of Okinawan respondents said they felt that China was a threat, a similar proportion to mainland Japanese respondents (89 percent). As for North Korea, some 84 percent of Okinawan and 89 percent of mainland Japanese respondents said it was a danger.[24]

However, residents of China and North Korea must have perceived with alarm the US and Japanese military build-up around their borders throughout the 2010s and 2020s. Although the expansion was not new—in 1949 General Douglas MacArthur boasted that the Pacific Ocean was an "Anglo-Saxon lake"— the expansion accelerated following President Barack Obama's announcement in 2011 to make "our presence and missions in the Asia-Pacific a top priority." In 2018, the US military expanded its domain even further when it added the prefix *Indo* to its Pacific command; the renamed USINDOPACOM described how its "Area of Responsibility (AOR) encompasses about half the earth's surface" and consists of approximately 375,000 US military and civilian personnel. The Japanese government had already promised to support the United States militarily under its revised guidelines on so-called collective self-defense. Then its 2022 National Security Statement described China as the "unprecedented and largest strategic challenge" to Japan, while North Korea was a threat "that had increased in seriousness and urgency from the past." If Chinese leaders were left with any doubts of the risks the United States (and Japan) posed, these were likely dispelled in 2023 by the four-star US Air Force general predicting war with China in 2025.[25]

The main flashpoint in US-China tensions was Taiwan. China saw the island as a renegade province to be reunited with the motherland, but Washington viewed it as a beacon of liberal democracy and, perhaps more importantly, a barrier to prevent Chinese expansion into the Pacific. Since Chiang Kai-shek and his Kuomintang fled to the island in 1949, the United States had provided military support, even considering the use of nuclear weapons from Kadena Air Base against Mao's forces in the 1958 Taiwan Straits Crisis. (Meanwhile, it turned a blind eye to the human-rights abuses of the Taipei regime that imprisoned and executed tens of thousands.) Following Nixon's détente with mainland China, the United States acknowledged, "There is but one China," and there ought to be a "peaceful settlement" of the Taiwan issue. Soon after, the United States removed its troops from the island but continued to provide arms for "defensive purposes."[26]

In the following years, Taiwan transitioned into a thriving democracy, allowing legislature and presidential elections (1992 and 1996, respectively). At the same time, many residents sought independence. These calls angered the Chinese government, which believed retaking the island was the "core of the core interests of China." Successive US administrations walked a thin line as they followed a policy of "strategic ambiguity" (not specifying whether the United States would defend Taiwan in a war with China), a strategy that it hoped would deter Beijing from taking military action. As China became more assertive in the South China Sea in the 2010s, it also became more aggressive in its claims on Taiwan. In the 2020s, too, Washington adopted confrontational tactics, such as sailing warships between Taiwan and the mainland, and in 2021, Biden expressly stated that the United States would militarily intervene in a "Taiwan contingency." In response, China escalated tensions. In 2022, President Xi Jinping called the capture of Taiwan essential for the "rejuvenation of the Chinese nation" and refused to renounce military means. As Washington, DC, and Beijing rattled their sabers, Prime Minister Abe cranked up tensions when he announced, "A Taiwan contingency is a Japan contingency." More accurately, given how close Taiwan is located to Japan's southernmost prefecture, he ought to have said, it is an *Okinawan* contingency.[27]

In August 2022, Okinawans experienced a precursor of how a war might play out when China fired five missiles into waters off Hateruma Island, in the southernmost part of their prefecture, within Japan's Exclusive Economic Zone. The launch signaled Chinese anger at a visit by US House of Representatives Speaker Nancy Pelosi to Taipei. In the case of an actual US-China war over Taiwan, US bases in Okinawa are within reach of Chinese short- to midrange missiles. According to American military experts, Kadena Air Base will be a "priority target," and they point to how China has created mock-ups of the facility in its western deserts. Simulated strikes are one thing, but the real base is surrounded by Okinawan communities that would be devastated by even a relatively small-scale attack.[28]

In the event of a Taiwan contingency, the Japanese government plans to assign civilian airports and ports in Okinawa and mainland Japan to military use, a designation that would make them potential targets. Moreover, Japan and the United States indicated they would declare the prefecture (and such neighboring islands as Amami-Ōshima) a war zone, which, as Okinawa specialist and political scientist Douglas Lummis explains, carries definite meanings under international law as a "region where killing is not murder, so long as it is carried out in accordance with the laws of war." This would put Okinawans at risk from both sides: Not only might Chinese forces who killed civilians be able to claim some immunity from prosecution, but also residents who refused to support US-Japan military operations could be designated as enemy sympathizers. "On the one hand, we can say that's just how it is with war. On the other hand, it's remarkable to be declared killable by one's own government," concluded Lummis.[29]

In the mid-2020s, the Japanese government outlined plans for civilians in case of conflict. From Ishigaki and nearby islands, private aircraft and ships would evacuate 110,000 residents and tourists to the mainland, plus underground shelters would be constructed with food supplies to last a minimum of two weeks. As for people in the main island of Okinawa, the government advised them to remain indoors. The countermeasures were frighteningly reminiscent of the build-up to the Battle of Okinawa: inadequate evacuation plans, insufficient shelters and food reserves, the merger of civilian and military infrastructure, and the imposition of martial law, under which dissenters could be punished as spies. Okinawans knew how previous plans turned out the last time their islands were dragged into global conflict, but it seemed no lessons had been learned in the ensuing eighty years.[30]

Coda

So Why Are We Really in Okinawa?

As a journalist for the newspaper *Okinawa Times*, the main tool of my trade is the US Freedom of Information Act, which permits access to documents from the American federal government, including those entities most active in Japan: the Department of Defense, the State Department, and the Central Intelligence Agency (CIA). In 2017, I obtained a sixty-page manual from the CIA, *A Master Narratives Approach to Understanding Base Politics in Okinawa* (2012), which details decades of the agency's information gathering on the islands' current events, culture, and public figures. According to the guide, the purpose of this undertaking was to identify "actionable opportunities for US communicators to connect with the Okinawan public" and flag "potential communication pitfalls." In plain English, this was the CIA's manual for American policymakers on how to shape islanders' opinions on why the US military was still in Okinawa.[1]

The agency advised officials to claim that the bases benefit Okinawa's economy and promote cultural exchange. As for residents' feelings of discrimination, it exonerated Americans of any blame and attributed the problem solely to the Japanese government: "Tokyo can be tone-deaf to the narratives and historical events that have shaped Okinawan attitudes." The manual accuses mainland Japanese groups of exploiting Okinawa's peace movement, while at the same time, the CIA advises US policymakers to leverage islanders' pacifism by asserting its troops could support disaster-relief efforts.[2]

When *Okinawa Times* reported on the existence of the manual, readers expressed anger about the attempts to manipulate public sentiment, and they were shocked by its recentness. This was not some relic from the dark days of the high commissioners; this was produced in 2012. After further research, it became evident that, in the same time frame, the CIA had published similar guides (known as *Master Narratives*) for US officials about Afghanistan, al-Qaeda, and Syria. It was a unique window into just how much of a threat the agency perceived Okinawans and, presumably, the government of the Democratic Party of Japan (DPJ), which held power at the time.

One more aspect of the manual that readers found eye-opening was the CIA's discussion of the role of the bases in providing deterrence. American and Japanese government officials have long been adamant that deterrence was the primary reason for the military presence in Okinawa, but the CIA guide warned against drawing on this argument because it might exacerbate residents' resentment of bearing such a disproportionate burden: "Okinawans may react with frustration to messages about the deterrence value of U.S. forces because that does not answer their 'why us' question."[3] The CIA also cautioned US policymakers that "skeptics of the deterrence argument will almost certainly look for ways to undermine it."[4] In this last point, at least, the CIA was correct.

The D Word

The United States and Japan insist that the American military in Japan furnishes indispensable deterrence, which dissuades potential enemies from attacking the nation. US Forces Japan (USFJ) describes how its presence "provides a ready and lethal capability that deters adversary aggression, protects the Homeland, aids in Japan's defense, and enhances regional peace and security." Japan's Ministry of Defense echoes the assertion: "The military presence of USFJ provides deterrence against unexpected contingencies caused by various security issues or destabilizing factors."[5]

Given that 70 percent of the US military presence can be found in Okinawa Prefecture, it would be natural to assume that the weight of deterrence lies there, too. But a closer examination shows that the elements with the most ability to deter attack are located on mainland Japan and elsewhere. Yokosuka City, Kanagawa Prefecture, is host to the largest US Navy base overseas, home to more than fifty ships and submarines, notably the only US nuclear-powered aircraft carrier homeported outside the United States. In Tokyo, Yokota Air Base is headquarters to USFJ and the Fifth Air Force. Meanwhile Camp Zama, Kanagawa Prefecture, houses the US Army's headquarters in Japan, serving four thousand soldiers and their families. Covering these bases—and Japan as a whole—is a network of defensive missiles, while above stands the US nuclear umbrella. Since the Cold War, Tokyo has sought—and received—assurances from the United States that if Japan came under threat by a nuclear-armed foe, Washington would use its nuclear arsenal to defend it. Assessing the situation militarily, then, Japan's deterrence appears as watertight as it could possibly be.

So how do the thirty-one US bases in Okinawa serve to deter potential enemy aggression? Arguably, the facility with the largest role is Kadena Air Base. Used to launch attacks in the Korean and Vietnam Wars, the Pentagon still refers to it as the "Keystone of the Pacific," and it hosts the largest combat wing in the air force. Despite its size, noise, and environmental damage, the possibility of shutting the base is not raised by Japanese politicians in discussions to reduce the military footprint, such as the Special Action Committee on Okinawa (SACO) negotiations in the mid-1990s. As Okinawa International University professor Maedomari Hiromori argued, "The reason is clear. It's because 'Kadena is off limits.' And the solution to the problem lies beyond the wall of difficult negotiations with the US government." Asking the Americans to remove their keystone, Japanese officials believe, would become tantamount to suggesting the dissolution of the US-Japan Security Treaty itself.[6]

Besides Kadena, though, the deterrent role of Okinawa's other thirty US bases is more dubious. The army occupies a handful of facilities, but its main mission is relegated to maintaining fuel supplies for the other services, plus the management of Naha Military Port, which is only seldom used (much to the chagrin of residents, who lament the waste of waterfront real estate). The navy has five facilities, notably a port at White Beach (shared with the army), where no vessels are permanently stationed. So that brings us to the marine corps, the most prominent military presence in Okinawa, not only in terms of land usage (130 square kilometers), but also in how its members provoke residents with crimes, accidents, and US Marine Corps commanders' occupation mentality. Forced from mainland Japan by protests in the 1950s, today the marines have thirteen bases in Okinawa, including Futenma Air Station in the middle of Ginowan City. When Prime Minister Hatoyama Yukio broke his pledge to remove the facility from the prefecture in 2010, he gave the reason (later admitted as a pretext) that the marines were vital for deterrence. Since then, experts have attempted to assess the extent of deterrence the marines truly provide—and most have concluded the answer is very little. Professor Mike Mochizuki, George Washington University's Elliott School of International Affairs, contended that Japanese policymakers' assertions of the marines' deterrence were vague and the roles of the US Air Force and Navy—plus the nuclear umbrella—were more important. According to Yanagisawa Kyōji, former head of Japan's National Institute of Defense Studies, too, US nuclear weapons and conventional missile-defense systems have a more powerful deterrent effect: "The US Marine Corps troops are ready to be deployed anywhere in the world. By the nature of their mission, they are not to stay and defend a specific region."[7]

The most thorough exploration of the deterrence provided by the marines in Okinawa was conducted by Paul O'Shea of the Center for East and Southeast Asian Studies, Lund University, Sweden. After examining the marines' effect in terms of central and extended deterrence—and deterrence as denial or punishment—he discovered that "in contrast to the official Japanese discourse, the Marines' role in deterrence is overstated at best, and relatively insignificant at worst." Their deployment in the event of a conflict in the East China Sea would be unlikely or difficult due to the stationing of their transport ships in mainland Japan, found O'Shea. Moreover, compared to the larger deterrence created by the US Air Force and Navy and joint operations with the Japanese Self-Defense Forces (SDF), stationing marines in Okinawa added little to the overall effect. "The marines in Okinawa are not 'crucial' to either defence or deterrence," O'Shea concluded. Both Mochizuki and O'Shea argued that instead of providing essential deterrence, the preponderance of marine (and other bases) in Okinawa might conversely have the opposite result. O'Shea wrote, "As far as Okinawa is concerned, one could argue that the Marines play as much a 'magnet' role as a deterrent one."[8]

"Sitting Ducks"

Long before China and North Korea developed missiles capable of reaching Okinawa, American officials questioned the wisdom of cramming so many bases into such a tight space. During the mid-1950s, even as the United States was forcibly expanding its facilities in Okinawa, the chairman of the Joint Chiefs of Staff warned they were "sitting ducks—difficult if not impossible to defend, likely to be knocked out completely in a one-shot operation." In the following years, the Soviet Union and China developed their own nuclear arsenals, heightening the risks. One US Air Force technician stationed in a nuclear-weapon silo there during the 1962 Cuban missile crisis described his fears of the "evaporation of Okinawa in a preemptive or retaliatory strike." As well as enemy attack, the military's own negligence posed an equally catastrophic threat, as shown by the 1959 Nike Hercules misfire at Naha Air Base and the hydrogen bomb lost from the USS *Ticonderoga* in 1965. (And then there are the natural dangers posed by typhoons, earthquakes, and tsunami.)[9]

Fast forward to 2000. The folly of overconcentration was again raised by a senior US official. One of the delegates who had been involved in SACO, ex–Deputy Assistant Secretary of Defense Kurt Campbell, warned, "It is neither smart nor stable for the United States to have . . . so many of our eggs in one basket on Okinawa. It is in our strategic interests to diversify, to be more flexible, and simultaneously, to reduce the burden on the people of Okinawa." As China developed its missile capabilities and staged strikes against a mocked-up Kadena Air Base in its western deserts, even military commanders were ringing alarm bells. In 2020, the Indo-Pacific Command told US Congress, "It is not strategically prudent, nor operationally viable to physically concentrate on large, close-in bases that are highly vulnerable to a potential adversary's strike capability." Then in 2023, the Congressional Research Service published an assessment of military infrastructure, quoting specialists who surmised that Kadena Air Base was "uniquely ill-positioned for permanently basing large numbers of American aircraft" and urged rotating and dispersing US forces in the region.[10]

Responding to these assessments, the Department of Defense reconsidered the overconcentration of assets in Okinawa. Between 2022 and 2024, the US Air Force withdrew outdated F-15 fighter aircraft that had been permanently stationed at Kadena Air Base and replaced some of them with temporary assignments of newer jets. Also, the US Navy and Marine Corps edged away from a reliance on large, permanent bases toward dispersing them more widely into temporary positions. The marines conducted short-term deployments to Darwin, Australia, out of reach of most Chinese missiles, and the Pentagon announced plans to build runways there for US Air Force bombers. It is a stark irony that, as of the mid-2020s, many military officials finally aligned their thinking with what Okinawans had been demanding for decades: the relocation of the bases away from their islands. Nevertheless, the US military still possessed thirty-one military bases in Okinawa, consisting of 70 percent of its presence in Japan.[11]

So Why Are We Really in Okinawa?

Responsibility for the ongoing overconcentration of bases in Okinawa must be apportioned between the United States and Japan. For America, the islands provide three advantages: the projection of power; the ability to train forces without civilian interference; and, most importantly, money. For Japan, Okinawa serves as a national sacrifice zone, a place geographically distant from the mainland that can be forced to bear the dangers that the rest of the nation refuses to tolerate.

Power Projection

For eight decades, the United States has used Okinawa to stage military, covert, and psychological warfare around the world. Initially, it used the veneer of UN trusteeship to control Okinawa, alongside islands in Micronesia, from which to run CIA operations, test and stockpile weapons of mass destruction, and fight wars throughout Asia (while denying these islands' residents the freedoms it was claiming to promote). These aggressions compelled Okinawans to campaign for reversion, but after 1972, the United States continued to use its bases to dispatch troops to wars in the Persian Gulf, Afghanistan, and Iraq. Such operations violate Article 6 of the US-Japan Security Treaty, which limits American use of its bases for the "security of Japan and the maintenance of international peace and security *in the Far East*" (italics added). But few—if any—Japanese leaders lodged protests.

Instead, successive Liberal Democratic Party (LDP) governments have backed American wars, for example contributing $13 billion toward the US-led Gulf War. Just like its domestic judiciary and implementation of constitutional guarantees, Japanese foreign policy is subordinate to the security treaty: national sovereignty sacrificed for the Pax Americana.[12]

Freedom to Train

The US military regards Okinawa Prefecture as one big training site, teaching jungle and urban warfare, beach assaults, parachute drops, and air-to-ground bombings. Unlike within the United States, where such exercises tend to occur far from residential areas and the Pentagon (sometimes) heeds local communities' complaints, it routinely ignores Okinawans' objections. Due to the US-Japan Status of Forces Agreement (SOFA), military training can skirt domestic laws. Inbound troops do not need to follow immigration or quarantine procedures, so the United States has been able to train third-nation forces in Okinawa (apparently unbeknownst to the Japanese government) and move freely during COVID-19 restrictions. When training goes wrong (as it often does), SOFA allows the military to escape the consequences, covering up aircraft accidents and blocking local officials from accessing crash sites. Military exercises take a heavy toll on the environment, and Japanese taxpayers are left with the tab to clean up unexploded ordnance, depleted uranium, and drinking water contaminated by decades of on-base firefighter training.[13]

The Money

In 1935, decorated marine General Smedley D. Butler wrote the best-selling booklet *War Is a Racket*, in which he railed against arms manufacturers profiting from conflict and US colonialism. "For a very few this racket, like bootlegging and other underworld rackets, brings fancy profits, but the cost of operations is always transferred to the people—who do not profit," he wrote. Ninety years later, the general's name adorns marine corps bases in Okinawa, the collective title for six facilities: Camp Smedley D. Butler. Whether intended or not, the naming rubs Japanese taxpayers' noses in the fact that they pay ¥211 billion a year in host-nation support, an estimated 75 percent of the cost of stationing US troops in Japan and almost double the ratio paid by South Korea. As Joseph S. Nye explained in 1995, it is cheaper for the United States to keep its troops in Japan than at home.[14]

Between 1978 and 2010, Japan paid some $22 billion in improvements to US facilities. then it funded the $500 million NSA listening post at Camp Hansen and MV-22 Osprey landing pads in the Yanbaru forests. Under the 2009 Guam Agreement—slammed by historian Gavan McCormack as "illegal, colonial, and deceitful"—Tokyo also promised to build two new marine corps bases: one atop Oura Bay ($2–22 billion) and the other in Guam ($6 billion). Tokyo's funding is so generous that even when the US military breaks the law, Japanese taxpayers foot the costs. In the court rulings for illegal noise from air bases, the compensation comes from the Japanese government, and after US service personnel commit crimes against local nationals, much of the financial redress is provided by Japan.[15]

With US policymakers and LDP politicians colluding to erode the pacifist constitution and integrate the SDF with US forces, American arms manufacturers have enjoyed a windfall. According to the Department of State, as of 2021, Japan was paying at least $32.5 billion for US weaponry and other military equipment, such as fighter jets, surveillance drones, and ballistic missiles. Signaling its fealty to the United States, Japan is the only overseas nation to purchase Ospreys. If war is a racket, then Japanese taxpayers are the marks.[16]

Structural Discrimination

Although the three aforementioned factors make it attractive for the United States to locate its military in Japan, this still leaves unanswered the fundamental question of why the bases need to be in Okinawa. Under the terms of the US-Japan Security Treaty, the United States would enjoy these benefits wherever in Japan its troops were stationed. Ultimately, then, the answer to why the bases are in *Okinawa* must lie with the Japanese government. As previous chapters explain, Tokyo has spurned repeated US suggestions to move the bases from the islands. An especially revelatory moment occurred in the uproar following the 1995 rape, when top American officials made it clear that the marines could be relocated to mainland Japan, but Tokyo rebuffed the proposal due to fears of local opposition. Even when faced with Okinawans' visceral grief, the Japanese government prioritized the sentiments of mainland residents. Whoever is in charge of the nation, Japan's leaders treat Okinawans with the same disregard. When the opposition Democratic Party of Japan took power, its secretary general in 2011 admitted that the marines could not be moved from the island because nowhere else wanted to host them. Mainland politicians are unwilling to force military bases on their constituents; such treatment is reserved solely for Okinawans. The hypocrisy was highlighted by Governor Onaga Takeshi, who said, "If the majority of the citizens of Japan feel that the US-Japan Security Treaty is necessary, then the government should fairly distribute the burden of the US bases to the rest of Japan."[17]

Mainlanders' refusal to accept military bases is not unique to Japan. Around the world, NIMBY-ism is a common phenomenon when it comes to situating dangerous facilities, such as nuclear reactors, waste-disposal plants, and detention centers (incidentally all of which can be found inside military bases). In the United States, these tend to be located in marginalized communities, too. In Japan, government officials and the media often refer to the overconcentration of bases as the "Okinawa problem," suggesting the issue is limited to the islands with no relevance to—or blame on—mainland Japan. Many Okinawans, though, argue the phrase obscures the reality, preferring the term *structural discrimination* (*kōzōteki sabetsu*). In addition to the overt discrimination experienced by Okinawans (slurs; signs barring them from businesses; and racist, colonial-era wage scales), *structural discrimination* refers to the ways in which US and Japanese government policies have colluded to keep the bases there. Many prominent Okinawans argue this is a form of double subjugation: The United States oppresses Japan, which in turn oppresses Okinawa.

The Okinawa Human Rights Association attributed structural discrimination to the "coexistence of the US government's self-righteousness and the Japanese government's abnormal subordination towards the United States." Under the client-state relationship, Japan is subjugated by the United States, so in turn, Japan deflects this oppression onto Okinawa, which as a result suffers from a twofold subjugation.[18]

Historian Arasaki Moriteru takes the argument further, asserting that structural discrimination against Okinawans was a fundamental pillar of Japan-US relations: "What has supported postwar Japanese politics—particularly the US-dependent Japan-US relationship, which forms its core—has been structural discrimination against Okinawa. This mechanism was created by the United States, the victor and occupier, and was carried over even after Japan's independence." The oppression of Okinawa is the glue that binds the US-Japan alliance, according to Arasaki's argument.[19]

Meanwhile, independence advocate Matsushima Yasukatsu draws a reptilian analogy to illustrate Japan's treatment of the islands: Okinawa "can be sacrificed like the cut-off tail of a lizard. Whenever Japan faces an inconvenient situation, it makes use of Okinawa, historically as negotiator with China, or as a commodity to sell, as a place to fight her battles or to establish military bases."[20]

As these arguments—and the preceding chapters of this book—demonstrate, without the sacrifice of Okinawa, modern Japan would not exist as it is. The nation is predicated on the past and present exploitation of the islands' residents. Since the 1879 Ryukyu Disposal through World War II, Japan used the islands to secure its own safety. In 1951, Japan ceded Okinawa in exchange for the return of its own sovereignty (albeit nominal). Then, thanks to base-construction contracts and the sieve economy, Japan was able to boost its dollar reserves. Much of this money emanated from the islands' prostitution industry. In the words of peace activist Takazato Suzuyo, postwar Japan used "its 'Okinawan' daughter as a breakwater of flesh and then subsequently sold her body to gain economic prosperity." Today, because more than two-thirds of US bases are shunted onto Okinawa, mainland Japanese residents—myself included—are largely safe from military crimes, accidents, and environmental damage. Likewise, many enjoy the (illusory) sense of security provided by the bases located out of sight and mind far away to the south. Accordingly, the happiness of mainland Japan remains rooted in the exploitation of Okinawans, but you would be hard-pressed to find mainland residents of any political stripe who would willingly acknowledge this fact.[21]

Part and parcel of Japan's ongoing exploitation is the erasure of Okinawan identity. Although the government and media are happy to celebrate islanders' exoticness—the dances! the costumes! the food!—they are careful to keep their depictions within narrow parameters for fear of opening the Pandora's box of independence or indigeneity. In 2015, Prime Minister Abe Shinzo told an Okinawan Diet member that "it was difficult to answer clearly" whether the Ryukyu Kingdom had been an independent, sovereign nation, and the Japanese government still refuses UN recommendations to recognize Okinawans as indigenous. In 2018, Japan reiterated its position that the only native people in the country were the Ainu but explained, "There were colourful traditions in Okinawa and the Government recognized and respected that fact. In order to deal with the unemployment among youth in Okinawa, the authorities had encouraged tourist activity." If any other developed nation dismissed centuries of traditions as colorful and sanctioned impoverished native youth to engage in tourism, there would be an international uproar. The statement itself highlights the urgent need for recognition of Okinawan indigeneity and the rights under international law such status might provide.[22]

Persistent discrimination against Okinawans begs the question, Why is there not more international acknowledgment of the problem? For certain, some blame lies with the global media's poor track record of covering indigenous movements that clash with US defense priorities. Rarely reported are the struggles of other Pacific peoples to protect their lands from military occupation and desecration in Micronesia, Hawai'i, and elsewhere. Another factor is the extent to which the two governments have been able to limit knowledge about Okinawa. In the past, the US military controlled travel to its colony, and after reversion, both countries destroyed vast volumes of official documents. Today, the CIA's *A Master Narratives Approach to Understanding Base Politics in Okinawa* and marine corps orientation lectures gloss over American mistreatment, and base home pages omit historical information that might cause service members to question the legitimacy of their own presence (and the health implications of living on bases atop decades of accumulated contamination.) The Japanese government, too, pushes to erase evidence of its wartime atrocities from history textbooks, paving the way for a new generation to embrace a remilitarized Japan. Because the media, the military, and schools are failing to report about Okinawa, misinformation often seeps in to fill the vacuum. On the internet, rumors spread that Okinawan demonstrators receive regular stipends, and they are led by foreign agitators. Meanwhile the head of the marine corps can claim Futenma Air Station was built on empty land. This confusion provides fertile ground for Chinese nationalists to launch their own claims that Okinawa does not belong to Japan and the Senkaku Islands have always been an inherent part of Chinese territory.[23]

Occasionally, glimpses emerge of how some in the corridors of power perceive Okinawans: On the US side, the top marine calling Okinawan legislators "nuts and wimps" and the diplomat decrying islanders as "masters of manipulation"; on the Japanese side, the DPJ official's warning that "if Okinawa's will is respected, nothing will ever happen" and the LDP minister defending the police officer's use of the slur *dojin*. Elsewhere in Japanese society, there runs an undercurrent of anti-Okinawan hate in books, magazines, and online message boards akin to the abuse hurled at the islands' delegates on the streets of Ginza in 2013.

Rarely do American officials make these kinds of inflammatory comments about residents of its allied "partners." Japan also does not often experience such aggression from the public or public officials (except when targeted at the long-discriminated Korean-Japanese community). The levels of vitriol toward Okinawans run so raw that they suggest something deeper is going on. Okinawans' resistance and, at times, their very *existence* challenge some of the beliefs that the United States and Japan hold so sacred. For Americans, their government's oppression of Okinawans—like the treatment of Chamorro, Hawaiians, Native Americans, and other indigenous groups—runs counter to the principles of self-determination, democracy, and respect for the international rule of law and human rights. Okinawa in particular belies two of the most hallowed American myths: World War II was a just war, and today the military is a force for good with service members who act with bravery and honor. For many Japanese, the questions Okinawa poses are even more disruptive. Okinawa makes Japan reexamine its belief in racial homogeneity, the notion it was a victim in World War II, and the fallacy that Japan is a sovereign nation with a healthy democracy, independent judiciary, and control over its foreign policy. The greatest myth that Okinawa challenges is the sanctity of the emperor and his ablution of responsibility for the catastrophe of World War II. The issue remains so taboo that very few in the Japanese media—and academia—dare to address it.

Some Lessons

In Okinawa's subversion of the beliefs held so dear by many Japanese people lies the seeds of potential change. For one and a half centuries, Japan has sought to assimilate Okinawa, but in contrast, the islands can help to forge a new model of Japanese identity—one that embraces racial heterogeneity, critical creativity, historical awareness, and political engagement.

Decades of the *nihonjin ron* discourse have encouraged many Japanese people to envisage their country as uniquely homogenous. In 2005, you'll recall, the foreign minister announced, "Japan is one nation, one civilization, one language, one culture, and one race." Conversely, Okinawa has a long history of diversity. The Ryukyu Kingdom had large numbers of Chinese, Korean, and Japanese residents; perspectives were broadened by the diaspora; and international marriages increased with the arrival of US service members. In some ways, these factors have encouraged a more-encompassing view of identity. This was evinced in the 1980s, when Okinawans campaigned for changes in Japanese laws on nationality. Formerly, Japanese nationality could solely be passed paternally, meaning only children born to Japanese men could receive it. This created problems in Okinawa, where many babies were born to American fathers who, if they left the family, rendered the children stateless and unable to automatically access Japanese health care or education. Recognizing these dire problems, residents worked with the Okinawa Prefectural Department of Education to overhaul the system. As a result, in 1985, the law was changed, granting Japanese nationality to children from Japanese mothers. Nowadays, each year, between two hundred and three hundred children are born from mixed US-Japanese couples in Okinawa. Although, as elsewhere in Japan, they often experience discrimination, thanks to the efforts of campaigners, they are at least able to enjoy the full range of rights that nationality guarantees. This has implications for the rest of Japan. In recent years, the government has relaxed immigration laws to counter the ageing population. As of 2024, foreign residents stood at 3.5 million (approximately 2.8 percent of the total population), more than double the number (1.6 million) in 2005, when the foreign minister made his "one race" speech. With Japan fast becoming an immigrant nation, other children born to mixed-nationality parents can benefit from the legal revision achieved by Okinawans.[24]

Not only within their home islands but also outside, Okinawans have been exposed to international perspectives via the diaspora. In the prewar years, almost one in ten lived overseas. Then during US occupation, many more left, and these migrations bestowed on some Okinawans a global outlook and, thanks to international marriages, a flexible sense of racial identity. "Unlike exclusive and fixed identities established through national agendas, diasporic Okinawan identities may be nonessential, decentered, nonexclusive, transnational, and fluid, even for those from the Okinawan homeland," wrote Arakaki Makoto. Today, some 420,000 people of Okinawan descent live overseas, and many of them keep close contact with their home communities. Every five years, Okinawa's prefectural government celebrates the diversity of Okinawan identity by staging the Worldwide Uchinanchu Festival, replete with reunions, parades, and concerts. So important is the diaspora to Okinawans that in 2016 the prefecture designated 10 October as World Uchinanchu Day. Throughout the rest of the year, too, the worldwide network of more than one hundred *kenjin kai* keeps connections alive, bestowing some Okinawans a broader international identity that extends beyond their own prefecture's borders.[25]

At the core of the Japanese myth of homogeneity is the assertion that the nation possesses only one language. As chapter 9 describes, in 2009, UNESCO fought this fallacy by recognizing six Ryukyuan languages and declaring them endangered. Despite this warning, the Japanese government appears content to wait and watch the languages die. It has not initiated programs to ensure their survival, nor has there been sustained support from private institutions, such as universities. Leading the struggle for revival has been linguist Fija Byron, the son of an American father and an Okinawan mother who lectures and writes about the need for the revitalization of Uchinaaguchi (the language predominantly spoken on the main island). In a 2009 article coauthored with two European researchers, he described how "even speaking about Luchuan 'languages', to [some Japanese linguists] is almost a rebellious act, challenging no less than the unity of the Japanese nation state." For Fija, the islands' languages possess the revolutionary potential to bolster Okinawan identity and the ability to prize open the thinking of the rest of Japan. "The Luchu Islands can serve as an important means for the 'de-parochialization' of Japan's majority, which recognizes only their language and culture. It can serve as a means to create more tolerant orders and attitudes, more befitting today's diversifying and globalizing world," wrote Fija and his colleagues.[26]

Critical Creativity

During US colonial rule, Okinawans believed that reversion to Japan would enable their voices to be heard via the ballot box, but since 1972, despite countless elections, demonstrations, and referendums, their wishes have been largely ignored. This has propelled Okinawans to seek alternative ways to express their resistance and seek change. One result has been an abundance of cutting-edge artists. In literature, Okinawan authors continue to produce groundbreaking works questioning Japanese and US hegemony. In 1999, Medoruma Shun sparked heated debate with the short story "Hope," depicting the fictional killing of an American child by an Okinawan man. Then, in *Me no Oku no Mori* (*In the Woods of Memory*; 2009), Medoruma explored the generational ramifications of a US military rape during the Battle of Okinawa. Another award-winning Okinawan is nonfiction writer Uema Yōko, whose *Hadashi de Nigeru* (*Barefoot Runaways*; 2017) explores the violence faced by young Okinawan women and *Umi o Ageru* (*I'll Give You the Sea*; 2020), in which she writes about her young daughter and the impacts of militarization, including per- and polyfluoroalkyl substances (PFAS) contamination.[27]

Music has always been a key medium for Okinawans to express their opposition. Kina Shōkichi, you'll recall, led a 1990s boom in Okinawan music under the slogan "Turn all weapons into musical instruments." In the 2000s, just like other marginalized peoples, Okinawans embraced rap to express their resistance. Prompted by the scenes of occupation after the marine corps helicopter crash into Okinawa International University in 2004, DUTY FREE SHOPP. x Kakumakushaka produced the blistering "*Tami no Domino*" ("People's Dominos"), punning on President Eisenhower's 1954 "falling domino principle" and the public anger over the US military permitting access to the crash site only to pizza delivery drivers. Another accident near Futenma Air Station—the 2017 drop of a helicopter window among children playing in the grounds of a primary school—triggered rapper Awich to record "*Tsubasa*" ("Wings"), featuring lyrics from her daughter, a pupil at the school.

Despite laughter being one of the most powerful weapons available to oppressed communities, mainland Japan lacks the political comedy often found in the United States and Great Britain. In contrast, satirical humor has thrived in Okinawa. Comedy troupe Owarai Beigun Kichi (Laughing at the US Bases) was founded by Kohatsu Masamitsu in reaction to the paucity of mainland media coverage of the 2004 helicopter crash. Throughout the 2010s and '20s, the group played sold-out shows across the prefecture, performing skits lampooning life near the bases—the noise, crime, and environmental contamination. One well-known routine features a faux TV shopping salesman trying to persuade mainland Japanese to buy back the military facilities.[28]

Humor permeates the work of Okinawa's visual artists. In the video installation *My Father's Favorite Game* (2018), Yuken Teruya presents two ten-member teams engaged in a joyous recreation of the Koza Riot. Surrounded by cheering onlookers, they tip and roll wrecked cars while flinging brightly colored powder in scenes reminiscent of Indian Holi festivities. The artist also employs the traditional dyeing technique *bingata* to produce works incorporating such classic motifs as flowers and streams alongside US military hardware and heroes of the peace movement. Teruya's *bingata* robe *You-I, You-I* (2002–2022) was the first work of Okinawan contemporary art to be acquired by the British Museum. Meanwhile, in her three-part series *Okinawa Tourist* (2004), videographer Chikako Yamashiro plays on the disconnect between Japanese and Okinawan perceptions of the islands. In one of the scenes, she stands outside the national parliament, holding a placard in protest. Her mouth moves, but the only phrases we hear are mis-synched banalities from government and tourist campaigns, such as descriptions of Shuri Castle, beautiful beaches, and mangos. Another part sees her in tight close-up outside a US base's wire fence as she gorges on ice cream cones passed from someone off-camera while a sultry porno soundtrack plays in the background. The juxtaposition makes viewers question how Japanese government hand-outs—the *ame*—sicken Okinawans physically, financially, and morally.

Okinawa's most famous photographer is Ishikawa Mao, who captured the fiery killing of the local police officer in the 1971 protests. Since then, her work has explored the experiences of Okinawans living with the military, such as candid photographs of the female bar staff she worked alongside near the bases in the 1970s. In 2013, Ishikawa embarked on the epic project *The Great Ryukyu Photo Scroll*, in which her friends and acquaintances recreated key moments from the islands' history, many of which were injected with Ishikawa's satirical humor. In one photo, Commodore Matthew Perry holds up the 1854 compact between the United States and the Kingdom of Lew-Chew, but on closer inspection, you can see the text reads, "We would like to stay here forever because we love Omoiyari." In another, a giant *shīsā* lion-dog and Okinawans chase Prime Minister Abe along the shoreline of Oura Bay. For exhibitions, Ishikawa prints dozens of the scenes onto tall, serpentine scrolls, measuring more than one hundred meters, to wrap venues and their visitors in centuries of Okinawans' humor, pain, and indefatigable resistance.

Historically Aware and Politically Engaged

Japan's mistreatment of Okinawa mirrors American mistreatment of Hawai'i: annexation, discrimination, and imposition of military bases. But in 1993, the US government officially apologized for its role in the illegal overthrow of the Hawaiian Kingdom a century earlier and pledged to provide reconciliation for Native Hawaiians. Although the benefits for islanders have been slow to materialize, the apology made many Americans aware of their nation's unjust seizure of Hawai'i and triggered debate on self-determination and land returns. In 2021, a similar approach was proposed by political scientist Ōshiro Shōko, who recommended to the UN Human Rights Commission's special rapporteur on truth, justice and reparation, "The Japanese government should officially and immediately admit the historical existence of Okinawa as an independent nation and apologize for its forced assimilation of Okinawa into Japan in the 1870s."[29]

Let's consider Ōshiro's two recommendations in turn. First, it is important to understand that in today's Japan, discussions including the terms *Okinawa* and *independence* (whether in historical or future contexts) can be perilous. Proponents of Prime Minister Abe's hedging on the Ryukyu Kingdom's sovereign status argue that since the 1609 Satsuma samurai invasion, the kingdom had been under Japanese control, proof that the islands had not been independent. Outweighing such arguments, though, are the three international trade agreements signed by the Shuri government and the fact that the 1879 disposal was tantamount to an invasion, forcefully conducted by hundreds of armed Japanese police and soldiers. (The similarities with the US illegal annexation of Hawai'i are striking.)

As for the possibility of modern-day independence for Okinawa, Japanese right-wingers often accuse its advocates of geopolitical or economic naivete (a self-ruled Okinawa could not defend itself or survive economically) or outright treachery against the Japanese state. Consequently, as of 2022, only some 3 percent of respondents to an *Okinawa Times* survey expressed support for independence. Recommendations by the Chinese government's newspaper *Global Times* in 2013 to fund groups seeking Okinawan independence provided extra fuel for critics to allege that advocates of self-rule are in the pockets of Beijing, an accusation that holds no water. Although only a small proportion of residents want full independence, the 2022 poll found that 48 percent desired more local autonomy. The high number is likely a reaction to national government attempts to impose laws that only apply to the prefecture (in breach of Article 95 of the Japanese constitution) and the judiciary's refusal to side with Okinawans in legal cases, especially regarding the new US base on Oura Bay. Time and time again, Okinawans have pushed back against these moves, and while not always successful, such resistance serves as a model for other prefectures opposing Tokyo's imposition of dangerous projects on their communities, such as radioactive waste disposal sites and environmentally harmful dams.[30]

As for Ōshiro's second suggestion—an apology for forced assimilation—implementation would open national debate on Okinawa's history and potentially more accurate representations of the islands in government materials, school textbooks, and the media. The public would be confronted with the illegality of the 1879 disposal, wartime atrocities committed against civilians by Japanese troops, and the emperor's dual responsibility for prolonging the conflict and the islands' postwar occupation. None of these topics would come easy for many mainland Japanese, inured to narratives of their nation as a wartime victim and the innocence of Hirohito, but this reflection is long overdue and, given Japanese politicians' efforts to remilitarize, more important today than ever.

At the same time, an honest review of the nation's wartime past could lead to renewed appreciation of the postwar constitution. Many people in Japan and the United States have forgotten the radicalness of the 1947 document: the sweeping guarantees of equality and righteousness of Article 9's renunciation of warfare. Okinawa can help people to remember. Unlike mainland Japanese, who were bequeathed the constitution by the United States, islanders had to struggle long and hard to obtain its rights. As former CIA-advisor-turned-Okinawa-ally Chalmers Johnson wrote, "Okinawa is the only Japanese community whose residents have fought for the democracy they enjoy." Okinawans, disenfranchised during American occupation and denied the freedom of speech, can help mainland Japanese to appreciate universal suffrage and the power of peaceful protest.[31]

Finally, with LDP governments sliding the nation toward remilitarization, Okinawa can offer an alternative path. In 2019, the prefectural government convened economic, defense, and political experts in a panel it named after the bridge of nations, the Bankoku Shinryō Council on US Military Base Issues, to consider other options to armed buildup in the region. The panel explored the overreliance on military deterrence, labeling it a "mental block" for Japan policymakers that prevented them from perceiving other approaches. Deterrence alone could not ensure regional peace. There needed to be more active promotion of diplomacy and trust building, the panel concluded. The prefecture ought to play a key role in such efforts: "Taking advantage of its geographical conditions and historical background, Okinawa should be a network hub of regional cooperation," asserted the council. The islands ought to extend the definition of security beyond pure militarism to encompass the environment, health care, and human rights—all of which have been undermined by the bases in the prefecture.[32]

Dedication to peace—and peaceful *resistance*—pervades Okinawan society, from elected officials to grassroots activists and the wider public. Okinawa has politicians who listen to the will of their constituents and convey their voices to the governments of Japan, the United States, and the United Nations. Current leaders' commitment is rooted in predecessors who struggled so hard during the dark days of US colonial rule—recall Senaga Kamejiro, who urged Okinawans to shout in unison so their voices could cross the stormy seas to reach Washington, DC—and today's elected officials persevere in the face of relentless pressure from the Japanese and US governments. Alongside these politicians are the organizers of the peace movement—many of them Battle of Okinawa survivors or their children—who work diligently to keep the lessons of the war alive and ensure their islands are not engulfed by conflict again. Experiences from the battle have instilled the spirit of *Nuchi du Takara* ("Life is an incomparable treasure") into Okinawans from all backgrounds. When life comes under threat, residents, from the youngest to the oldest, are ready to resist, even if it endangers their own personal safety or liberty. Remember the children who blocked marine corps artillery drills in the Kunigami forests in 1970–1971, the Yomitan schoolgirl in the 1980s who tore down her school's Hinomaru flag, and her fellow young villagers who stood up for peace by refusing to stand for the Japanese anthem at the national sports meet. In addition to these children, thousands of demonstrators have joined road blocks and sit-ins—near Kin Town and in Yomitan, Henoko, and Takae—and taken to canoes to halt the destruction of their islands' nature, despite the risk of arrest or police brutality. Behind those participating in direct civil disobedience, there are the tens of thousands of islanders who join mass *kenmin taikai* demonstrations against base expansion, military crimes, and the erasure of their history and the hundreds of thousands who expressed their opposition through elections, referendums, and petition drives.

Okinawans began organized all-island resistance in 1955. More than seventy years later, they have not given up their struggles for justice, equality, and peace. Okinawa is a model of participatory civic involvement. It embodies the resilience of peaceful resistance, and the struggles of these small islands deserve to be known—and *supported*—around the globe.

NOTES

An Introduction

1. G. Ward Price, "Pacific Now Anglo-Saxon Lake," *Daily Mail*, 3 March 1949, 1.
2. Quoted in Thomas R. H. Havens, *Fire Across the Sea: The Vietnam War and Japan, 1965–1975* (Princeton University Press, 1987), 85.
3. "US Military Base Issues in Okinawa," Okinawa Prefectural Government, accessed 24 June 2024, https://dc-office.org/basedata; David Vine, *Base Nation: How US Military Bases Abroad Harm America and the World* (Metropolitan Books, 2015), 306; Jon Mitchell, "Okinawa: U.S. Marines Corps Training Lectures Denigrate Local Residents, Hide Military Crimes," *Asia-Pacific Journal* 14, iss. 13, no. 4 (1 July 2016): 1–5, https://apjjf.org/2016/13/mitchell.
4. Information Office, Headquarters, US Army Ryukyu Islands, *Why We Are Here* (US Army, 1969). For a detailed discussion of how the US military attempted to control information about Okinawa, see chapter 5.
5. Consulate General Naha, "Okinawan Exceptionalism: The China Threat or Lack Thereof," WikiLeaks, 26 April 2006, https://wikileaks.org/plusd/cables/06NAHA103_a.html; Jane Perlez, "Calls Grow in China to Press Claim for Okinawa," *New York Times*, 14 June 2013, 4; "Ryukyu Issue Offers Leverage to China," *Global Times*, 11 May 2013, https://www.globaltimes.cn/content/780732.shtml; Kanematsu Yuichiro, "Social Media Fuel Pro-Okinawa Independence Disinformation Blitz," *Nikkei Asia*, 3 October 2024, https://asia.nikkei.com/Spotlight/Cybersecurity/Social-media-fuel-pro-Okinawa-independence-disinformation-blitz.

Chapter 1

1. Personal visit to Okinawa Prefectural Museum and Art Museum, Naha City, 14 September 2023.
2. John M'Leod, *Narrative of a Voyage, in His Majesty's Late Ship Alceste, to the Yellow Sea, along the Coast of Corea, and through its Numerous Hitherto Undiscovered Islands, to the Island of Lewchew; with an Account of her Shipwreck in the Straits of Gaspar* (M. Carey and Son, 1818), 75; Akamine Mamoru, *The Ryukyu Kingdom: Cornerstone of East Asia*, ed. Robert Huey, trans. Lina Terrell (University of Hawai'i Press, 2018), 31.
3. Takara Kurayoshi, *Ryūkyū Ōkoku* (Iwanami Shoten, 1993), 96–98; Akamine, *Ryukyu Kingdom*, 21.
4. Takara, *Ryūkyū Ōkoku*, 81; Akamine, *Ryukyu Kingdom*, 22–23.
5. Akamine, *Ryukyu Kingdom*, 30–31; Takara, *Ryūkyū Ōkoku*, 84–85.

6 Akamine, *Ryukyu Kingdom*, 32–36; Takara, *Ryūkyū Ōkoku*, 82–85.
7 Tomé Pires, *The Suma Oriental of Tomé Pires and the Book of Francisco Rodrigues*, trans. Armando Cortesão (Hakluyt Society, 1944), 130.
8 Akamine, *Ryukyu Kingdom*, 123–24.
9 Akamine, *Ryukyu Kingdom*, 40–44.
10 Personal visit to Okinawa Prefectural Museum and Art Museum, Naha City, 14 September 2023; Akamine, *Ryukyu Kingdom*, 105; Takara, *Ryūkyū Ōkoku*, 86.
11 Gregory Smits, *Maritime Ryukyu, 1050–1650* (University of Hawai'i Press, 2018), 206–7.
12 Akamine, *Ryukyu Kingdom*, 59–61.
13 Smits, *Maritime Ryukyu*, 221; Akamine, *Ryukyu Kingdom*, 63.
14 This account of the 1609 invasion is based on the thorough description in Smits, *Maritime Ryukyu*, 223–33.
15 Smits, *Maritime Ryukyu*, 233–37. According to Smits, when it comes to Ryukyuan deaths, "records are insufficient even to approximate a figure" (233).
16 Akamine, *Ryukyu Kingdom*, 73–74.
17 George H. Kerr, *Okinawa: The History of an Island People*, rev. ed. (Tuttle, 2000), 178; Akamine, *Ryukyu Kingdom*, 84–95; personal visit to Okinawa Karate Kaikan, Tomigusuku City, 2 December 2023.
18 Akamine, *Ryukyu Kingdom*, 84, 96–98.
19 Akamine, *Ryukyu Kingdom*, 8.
20 M'Leod, *Narrative of a Voyage*, 69–75.
21 Ryukyuans' genuine hospitality notwithstanding, some visitors' reports tended to hyperbole, such as assertions the islanders did not possess money or weapons or fight wars. Famously, in 1817, when the latter myth reached Napoleon Bonaparte in exile in St. Helena, "he shook his head, as if the supposition were monstrous and unnatural" (Basil Hall, "Notes of an Interview with Bonaparte at St. Helena on the 13th August 1817," in the collections of Royal Navy National Army Museum, London)
22 Kerr, *Okinawa*, 283–87.
23 Kerr, *Okinawa*, 283–92.
24 Peter Booth Wiley, with Korogi Ichiro, *Yankees in the Land of the Gods: Commodore Perry and the Opening of Japan* (Viking, 1990), 34–36; Kerr, *Okinawa*, 294–95.
25 John W. Dower, "Black Ships and Samurai: Commodore Perry and the Opening of Japan (1853–1854)," MIT Visualizing Cultures, accessed 5 May 2024, https://visualizingcultures.mit.edu/black_ships_and_samurai/bss_essay01.html.
26 Wiley, *Yankees in the Land*, 102–26; Kerr, *Okinawa*, 303–4.
27 Quoted in Kerr, *Okinawa*, 304–5.
28 Kerr, *Okinawa*, 307.
29 Personal visit to Okinawa Prefectural Museum and Art Museum, Naha City, 14 September 2023; Wiley, *Yankees in the Land*, 182.
30 Kerr, *Okinawa*, 309–15.
31 Kerr, *Okinawa*, 308–12; Samuel Wells Williams, *A Journal of the Perry Expedition to Japan (1853–1854)* (Kelly & Walsh, 1910), 12–13.
32 Kerr, *Okinawa*, 315–17.
33 Wiley, *Yankees in the Land*, 288–316.
34 Wiley, *Yankees in the Land*, 320–27.
35 Matthew Calbraith Perry, *Narrative of the Expedition of an American Squadron to the China Seas and Japan Performed in the Years 1852, 1853, and 1854, Under the*

Command of Commodore M. C. Perry, ed. Francis Lister Hawks (Beverley Tucker, Senate Printer, 1856), 275–79; J. W. Spalding, *The Japan Expedition: Japan and Around the World* (Redfield, 1855), 174. During Perry's stay in Japan, the elderly regent had been replaced by the Shuri government.

36 Commodore Perry to the secretary of the navy, 24 December 1853, in *Message of the President of the United States Transmitting a Report of the Secretary of the Navy, in Compliance with a Resolution of the Senate of December 6, 1854, Calling for Correspondence, &c., Relative to the Naval Expedition to Japan* (US Government Printing Office, 1855), 81.

37 Commodore Perry to the secretary of the navy, 25 January 1854, in *Message of the President*, 109.

38 Secretary of the navy to Commodore Perry, 30 May 1854, in *Message of the President*, 112–13.

39 Kerr, *Okinawa*, 329.

40 C. Andrew Gerstle and Timothy Clark, "Introduction," *Japan Review*, no. 26 (2013): 3–14; Wiley, *Yankees in the Land*, 416–17.

41 Williams, *Journal of Perry Expedition*, 192, 224.

42 Wiley, *Yankees in the Land*, 445–46; Williams, *Journal of Perry Expedition*, 229–31.

43 Wiley, *Land of the Gods*, 446; Williams, *Journal of Perry Expedition*, 236.

44 Commodore Perry to the secretary of the navy, 20 July 1854, in *Message of the President*, 171–73.

45 Commodore Perry to the secretary of the navy, 19 and 20 July 1854, in *Message of the President*, 169–73; Perry, *Narrative of the Expedition*, 495; Williams, *Journal of Perry Expedition*, 244.

46 Perry, *Narrative of the Expedition*, 496; Williams, *Journal of Perry Expedition*, 242; Spalding, *Japan Expedition*, 339–42.

47 Spalding, *Japan Expedition*, 341–42.

48 The full text of the compact can be read in *Message of the President*, 174–75.

49 Williams, *Journal of Perry Expedition*, 243, 245, 251; Patrice Gaines-Carter, "Okinawa Stone Makes Up for Monumental 135-Year Loss," *Washington Post*, 5 August 1989, https://www.washingtonpost.com/archive/local/1989/08/05/okinawa-stone-makes-up-for-monumental-135-year-loss/c619b06b-1317-41af-bef4-b6ef8a77eb45/; Samuel Limneos, "The Japanese Bell and Its Many Travels," US Naval Academy Nimitz Library, 5 November 2020, https://libguides.usna.edu/c.php?g=472716&p=6628899&t=62929. Following a request from the prefectural governor, the broken bell was eventually returned to Okinawa in 1987 ("Historic Bell Goes Back to Okinawa," Associated Press, 28 July 1987).

Chapter 2

1 Historian John W. Dower called the revolution a "masterpiece of political spin," in which the "rebels . . . argued that they were not really rebels at all, but simply 'restoring' power and authority to its original and proper source" (John W. Dower, "Throwing Off Asia 1: The Meiji Emperor and Invention of the Modern Emperor System," MIT Visualizing Cultures, accessed 24 September 2025, https://visualizingcultures.mit.edu/throwing_off_asia_01/toa_vis_01.html).

2. The most comprehensive English-language exploration of Japan's colonization of Ainu and the role of foreigners is Michael Randall Marcel Roellinghoff, "No Man's Land: De-Indigenization and the Doctrine of Terra Nullius in the Japanese Colonization of Hokkaido, 1869–1905" (PhD diss., University of Toronto, 2020).
3. Ōhama Ikuko, "'Botanshajiken' wa naze okotta no ka 'Genjūmin' Ryūkyū tōmin kyakuya hito kara mita jiken no hottan ni kansuru kentō," *Third Taiwan-Japan Conference on Indigenous Peoples Studies* (August 2010): 101–12.
4. George H. Kerr, *Okinawa: The History of an Island People*, rev. ed. (Tuttle, 2000), 356–60; Gregory Smits, *Visions of Ryukyu: Identity and Ideology in Early-Modern Thought and Politics* (University of Hawai'i Press, 1999), 144.
5. Kerr, *Okinawa*, 358; Roger D. Cunningham, "'Recreant to His Trust': The Disappointing Career of Major James R. Wasson," *Army History*, no. 60 (Winter–Spring 2004): 8–11.
6. Kerr, *Okinawa*, 359–360; Smits, *Visions of Ryukyu*, 145.
7. Yanagihara Masaharu, "Treaties Concluded by the Kingdom of Ryukyu," Oxford Public International Law, accessed 24 September 2025, https://opil.ouplaw.com/page/485; Kerr, *Okinawa*, 350, 546; Smits, *Visions of Ryukyu*, 141.
8. Kerr, *Okinawa*, 362–66; Smits, *Visions of Ryukyu*, 145; "Treaties Show That Japan's Annexation of the Ryukyu Kingdom Was an Unjustified Act," *Ryukyu Shimpo*, 12 July 2014, https://english.ryukyushimpo.jp/2014/07/21/14644/.
9. Arakawa Akira, *Ryūkyū Shobun Ikō*, vol. 1 (Asahi Shinbunsha, 1981), 11–13; Kerr, *Okinawa*, 367–70; *Ginowan Shigikai Shi* (Ginowan City Office, 2006), 384–85.
10. Kerr, *Okinawa*, 373–74; Arakawa, *Ryūkyū Shobun Ikō*, 13–14.
11. Kerr, *Okinawa*, 371–75.
12. Kerr, *Okinawa*, 376.
13. Arakawa, *Ryūkyū Shobun Ikō*, 26–29; Kerr, *Okinawa*, 378–82; Akamine Mamoru, *The Ryukyu Kingdom: Cornerstone of East Asia*, ed. Robert Huey, trans. Lina Terrell (University of Hawai'i Press, 2018), 8.
14. Arakawa, *Ryūkyū Shobun Ikō*, 28; Kerr, *Okinawa*, 383, 394.
15. Among the writers who emphasize the illegitimacy of Japan's annexation of the Ryukyu Kingdom are Takara Kurayoshi, Arakawa Akira, and Ota Masahide. For a comprehensive English exploration of the issue, see Ai Abe, "An Outstanding Claim: The Ryukyu/Okinawa Peoples' Right to Self-Determination Under International Human Rights Law," *Asian Journal of International Law* (2022): 1–24.
16. For example, on its website for the 2000 Kyushu-Okinawa Summit, the Ministry of Foreign Affairs describes "The Birth of Okinawa Prefecture" thus: "The Meiji Government, which came into being as a result of the Meiji Restoration of 1868, transformed the Ryukyu Kingdom, first into the domain of Ryukyu in 1872, and later into the prefecture of Okinawa in 1879. The Ryukyu Kingdom was thus brought to a close. This is known as the 'Ryukyu Disposition'" ("Kyushu-Okinawa Summit 2000: Outline of Kyushu-Okinawa Summit Meeting," Ministry of Foreign Affairs of Japan, accessed 24 September 2025, https://www.mofa.go.jp/policy/economy/summit/2000/outline/eng/okinawa/oki0302.html).
17. Kerr, *Okinawa*, 386.
18. Richard T. Chang, "General Grant's 1879 Visit to Japan," *Monumenta Nipponica* 24, no. 4 (1969): 379–81; Kerr, *Okinawa*, 387–88.
19. Kerr, *Okinawa*, 388–89; Chang, "General Grant's 1879 Visit," 381.
20. Chang, "General Grant's 1879 Visit," 381; Smits, *Visions of Ryukyu*, 146.

21 Nishizato Kikō, *Shinmatsu Chūryūnichi Kankeishi no Kenkyū* (Kyoto University Press, 2005), 363–73; Chang, "General Grant's 1879 Visit," 382; Kerr, *Okinawa*, 390–91.
22 Kerr, *Okinawa*, 396–98; Arakawa, *Ryūkyū Shobun Ikō*, 31–32.
23 Arakawa, *Ryūkyū Shobun Ikō*, 99–101; Smits, *Visions of Ryukyu*, 147–49.
24 Arakawa, *Ryūkyū Shobun Ikō*, 103–9, 118.
25 Arakawa, *Ryūkyū Shobun Ikō*, 113–18, 125–38.
26 For example, see Dower, "Throwing Off Asia 1."
27 Kerr, *Okinawa*, 403–7; Ota Masahide, *Okinawa no Minshū Ishiki* (Shinsensha, 1976), 267–71; personal visit to Okinawa Karate Kaikan, Tomigusuku City, 2 December 2023; Matsushima Yasukatsu, "Minzoku no jiko ketteiken ni yoru ikotsu henkan undō: Ryūkyū no datsushokuminchika o mezashite," *Ainu Senjūmin Kenkyū* 4 (29 March 2024): 241–48, https://doi.org/10.14943/Jais.4.241.
28 Ota, *Okinawa no Minshū Ishiki*, 289–91.
29 *Ryukyu Shimpo*, 11 April 1903.
30 Gregory Smits, "New Cultures, New Identities: Becoming Okinawan and Japanese in Nineteenth-Century Ryukyu," in *Values, Identity, and Equality in Eighteenth- and Nineteenth-Century Japan*, ed. James E. Ketelaar, Yasunori Kojima, and Peter Nosco (Brill, 2015), 168–69.
31 Yonaha Satoko, "Okinawa josei no irezumi 'hajichi' kinshirei kara kotoshi de 120 nen," *Okinawa Times*, 26 August 2019, https://www.okinawatimes.co.jp/articles/-/462429. For a wider discussion of the Meiji-Era prohibition on tattoos, see Jon Mitchell, "Japan Inked: Is It Time for Japan to Reclaim Its Tattoo Culture?" *Japan Times*, 4 May 2014, 13–15.
32 Arakawa, *Ryūkyū Shobun Ikō*, 29; Stanisław Meyer, "Between a Forgotten Colony and an Abandoned Prefecture: Okinawa's Experience of Becoming Japanese in the Meiji and Taishō Eras," *Asia-Pacific Journal* 18, iss. 20, no. 7 (15 October 2020): 1–16, https://apjjf.org/2020/20/Meyer.
33 Arakawa, *Ryūkyū Shobun Ikō*, 203–9; Ota Masahide, *Essays on Okinawa Problems* (Yui Shuppan, 2000), 163. Strong resistance to conscription also erupted in mainland Japan, where many people regarded it as a "blood tax."
34 Also the six groups of Ryukyu languages are so distinct from one another that they are mutually unintelligible. Patrick Heinrich, "Language Loss and Revitalization in the Ryukyu Islands," *Asia-Pacific Journal* 3, iss. 11 (24 November 2005): 1–12, https://apjjf.org/Patrick-Heinrich/1596/article.
35 Fija Bairon and Patrick Heinrich, "'Wanne Uchinanchu—I Am Okinawan': Japan, the US and Okinawa's Endangered Languages," *Asia-Pacific Journal* 5, iss. 11 (3 November 2007): 1–19, https://apjjf.org/Patrick-Heinrich/2586/article; personal visit to Okinawa Prefectural Peace Memorial Museum, Itoman City, 4 December 2023.
36 For a discussion of these reforms, see Smits, *Visions of Ryukyu*, 149.
37 Ota, *Okinawa no Minshū Ishiki*, 271; Meyer, "Between a Forgotten Colony."
38 Steve Rabson, *The Okinawan Diaspora in Japan: Crossing the Borders Within* (University of Hawai'i Press, 2012), 64–65; Wesley Iwao Ueunten, "Rising Up from a Sea of Discontent: The 1970 Koza Uprising in U.S.-Occupied Okinawa," in *Militarized Currents: Toward a Decolonized Future in Asia and the Pacific*, ed. Setsu Shigematsu and Keith L. Camacho (University of Minnesota Press, 2010), 99–100; personal visit to Okinawa Prefectural Museum and Art Museum, 14 September 2023.

39 Rabson, *Okinawan Diaspora*, 49, 71–73, 99; Akamine, *Ryukyu Kingdom*, 8; Takara Ben, "Kantō daishinsai 100 nen Ryūkyūjin e no sabetsu ya gyakusatsu wa kenkyū sukunaku," *Okinawa Times*, 2 September 2023, https://www.okinawatimes.co.jp/articles/-/1214675.
40 "Ōshiro Takayuki-san (27)—Seitan 150 nen sai de Tōyama Kyūzō yaku," *Okinawa Times*, 20 October 2018, https://www.okinawatimes.co.jp/articles/-/333580.
41 "Uchinā no kizuna jidai e keishō," *Okinawa Times*, 22 July 2022, 16–17; Brandon Marc Higa and Kelli Y. Nakamura, "The Hawai'i Connection: Okinawa's Postwar Reconstruction and Uchinanchu Identity," *Asia-Pacific Journal* 20, iss. 17, no. 3 (1 October 2022): 1–24, https://apjjf.org/2022/17/Nakamura-Higa.
42 "Sekai ni hirogaru Uchinā nettowāku," Ministry of Foreign Affairs of Japan, 20 April 2021, https://www.mofa.go.jp/mofaj/gaiko/local/page23_003410.html.
43 Rabson, *Okinawan Diaspora*, 77–82.

Chapter 3

1 Araragi Shinzo, "Lost Homeland: Colonial Memories of Manchuria in Okinawa After WWII," *Center for Okinawa Migration Studies* 9 (2013): 169–78; "Manchuria: A 'Utopia' Created by Opium," *Asahi Shimbun*, 20 December 2023, https://www.asahi.com/special/manchukuo-opium/en/.
2 Jon Mitchell, *Poisoning the Pacific: The US Military's Secret Dumping of Plutonium, Chemical Weapons, and Agent Orange* (Rowman & Littlefield, 2000), 13–25.
3 Peter Kuznick and Oliver Stone, *The Untold History of the United States* (Gallery Books, 2012), 87; Satoko Oka Norimatsu, "From Nanjing to Okinawa—Two Massacres, Two Commanders," trans. Mark Ealey, *Asia-Pacific Journal* 16, iss. 2, no. 2 (15 January 2018): 1–7, https://apjjf.org/2018/2/norimatsu.
4 Between the reigns of Emperor Meiji and Hirohito (a.k.a. Emperor Shōwa), there was the rule of Emperor Taishō (1912–1926), who, following a childhood bout of cerebral meningitis, suffered from lifelong mental impairment. So severe was his disability that he was unable to perform public duties. His son Hirohito was appointed regent in 1921. *Field Service Code (Senjinkun)* (Ministry of War, 1941).
5 Personal visit to Okinawa Prefectural Peace Memorial Museum, Itoman City, 4 December 2023; Patrick Heinrich, "Language Loss and Revitalization in the Ryukyu Islands," *Asia-Pacific Journal* 3, iss. 11 (24 November 2005): 1–12, https://apjjf.org/patrick-heinrich/1596/article.
6 Ryukyu Shimpo, *Descent into Hell: Civilian Memories of the Battle of Okinawa*, trans. Mark Ealey and Alastair McLauchlan (Merwin Asia, 2014), 465–66; quoted in Steve Rabson, "Okinawan Perspectives on Japan's Imperial Institution," *Asia-Pacific Journal* 6, iss. 2 (1 February 2008): 1–23, https://apjjf.org/steve-rabson/2667/article.
7 Gavan Daws, *Prisoners of the Japanese: POWs of World War II in the Pacific* (William Morrow, 1994), 360–61.
8 John W. Dower, *War Without Mercy: Race and Power in the Pacific War* (Pantheon Books, 1986), 79–81.
9 Miyagi Osamu, "Uwagaki ni sarasareru Okinawa-sen no kyōkun," *Gendai no Riron*, 15 March 2015; "Kīwādo Okinawa-sen (8) Ōmasu seishin," *Okinawa Times*, 10 April 2015, https://www.okinawatimes.co.jp/articles/-/13190.

10 Mitchell, *Poisoning the Pacific*, 25; Alastair A. McLauchlan, "War Crimes and Crimes Against Humanity on Okinawa: Guilt on Both Sides," *Journal of Military Ethics*, 13, no. 4 (2014): 363–80; personal visit to Okinawa Prefectural Peace Memorial Museum, Itoman City, 4 December 2023.
11 Ryukyu Shimpo, *Descent into Hell*, 241–43; Norimatsu, "From Nanjing to Okinawa."
12 Hong Yunshin, *"Comfort Stations" as Remembered by Okinawans During World War II*, trans. and ed. Robert Ricketts (Brill, 2020), 1, 21, 86.
13 Ryukyu Shimpo, *Descent into Hell*, 17. USS *Bowfin*, the submarine that sunk the *Tsushima Maru*, is on display at the Pearl Harbor National Memorial. Due to its launch date one year after the 1941 Japanese attack, it was nicknamed the "Pearl Harbor Avenger."
14 Roy E. Appleman, James M. Burns, Russell A. Gugeler, and John Stevens, *Okinawa: The Last Battle* (Department of the Army, Office of the Chief of Military History, 1948), 44–45; personal visit to Okinawa Prefectural Peace Memorial Museum, Itoman City, 4 December 2023; Ota Masahide, *Essays on Okinawa Problems* (Yui Shuppan, 2000), 35–38.
15 Hong, *"Comfort Stations,"* 8; Ota, *Essays on Okinawa Problems*, 31; Ryukyu Shimpo, *Descent into Hell*, 221; quoted in Ota, *Essays on Okinawa Problems*, 33.
16 Arasaki Moriteru, *Okinawa Gendai Shi* (Iwanami Shoten, 1996), 120–21.
17 Ota, *Essays on Okinawa Problems*, 42; Ryukyu Shimpo, *Descent into Hell*, 221; quoted in Ota, *Essays on Okinawa Problems*, 56.
18 Appleman et al., *Okinawa*, 35–52.
19 Office of the Chief of Naval Operations, *Civil Affairs Handbook: Ryukyu (Loochoo) Islands*, (Navy Department, 1944), 43.
20 Arnold G. Fisch Jr., *Military Government in the Ryukyu Islands, 1945–1950* (Center of Military History, US Army, 1988), 42.
21 Ryukyu Shimpo, *Descent into Hell*, 33–34.
22 Kinjo Shigeaki, interview by Michael Bradley, "'Banzai!' The Compulsory Mass Suicide of Kerama Islanders in the Battle of Okinawa," *Asia-Pacific Journal* 11, iss. 22, no. 3 (2 June 2013): 1–3, https://apjjf.org/2014/11/22/michael-bradley/4125/article.
23 Ryukyu Shimpo, *Descent into Hell*, 33; Miyume Tanji, *Myth, Protest, and Struggle in Okinawa* (Routledge, 2006), 38.
24 Chibana Shoichi, *Burning the Rising Sun: From Yomitan Village, Okinawa: Islands of U.S. Bases*, trans. South Wind (South Wind, 1992), 82, 127. For an in-depth exploration of the tragedy, see Shimojima Tetsurō, *Okinawa: Chibichiri Gama no "Shūdan Jiketsu"* (Iwanami Shoten, 1992).
25 Chibana, *Burning the Rising Sun*, 82–83, 127.
26 Ryukyu Shimpo, *Descent into Hell*, 31; Chibana, *Burning the Rising Sun*, 83, 127.
27 *War Without Mercy*, 232; Kameda Sanae, "Booklet Details History of Meth Chocolates Wrapped by Students for Japanese Suicide Pilots," *Mainichi*, 10 January 2022, https://mainichi.jp/english/articles/20220107/p2a/00m/0na/018000c; Yokoi Toshiyuki, "Kamikazes and the Okinawa Campaign," *United States Naval Institute Proceedings* 80, iss. 5, no. 615 (May 1954).
28 Appleman et al., *Okinawa*, 364.
29 "Who Decided to Send Japan's Battleship Yamato on Ill-Fated WWII Suicide Mission?" *Mainichi*, 21 April 2021, https://mainichi.jp/english/articles/20210408/p2a/00m/0na/024000c.

30. Appleman et al., *Okinawa*, 173–182; Ryukyu Shimpo, *Descent into Hell*, 246. Among the dead was US war correspondent Ernie Pyle, shot by a Japanese machine gunner on 18 April. Discovered in his pocket was the text of an unpublished article that offered a glimpse into the mental toll the war had taken on him: "Dead men by mass production—in one country after another—month after month and year after year.... Dead men in such familiar promiscuity that they become monotonous. Dead men in such monstrous infinity that you come almost to hate them" (Ernie Pyle, "On Victory in Europe," Indiana University, 18 April 1945, https://erniepyle.iu.edu/wartime-columns/on-victory.html).
31. Kabira Nario, "Okinawa-sen mō hitotsu no higeki," *Tokyo Shimbun*, 19 June 2016, 13.
32. McLauchlan, "War Crimes," 363–80; In one bizarre atrocity, sailors carved "souvenir rings" from the leg bone of a kamikaze pilot who had crashed into their ship. Peter Schrivjers, *The GI War Against Japan: American Soldiers in Asia and the Pacific During World War II* (New York University Press, 2002), 209–12; Okinawa Women Act Against Military Violence, *Okinawa Beihei ni yoru Josei he no Seihanzai*, 13th ed. (Kichi Guntai o Yurusanai kōdō suru Onnatachi no Kai, 2023), 2–4.
33. Ryukyu Shimpo, *Descent into Hell*, 280–82; Ota Masahide, *The Battle of Okinawa: The Typhoon of Steel and Bombs* (Takeda Printing, 1984), 240.
34. Dower, *War Without Mercy*, 11.
35. McLauchlan, "War Crimes," 375; Ota, *Essays on Okinawa Problems*, 60.
36. McLauchlan, "War Crimes," 375; Ota, *Essays on Okinawa Problems*, 58; quoted in Ota, *Essays on Okinawa Problems*, 265.
37. Ota Masahide, interview by author, 3 February 2012; McLauchlan, "War Crimes," 374; Ryukyu Shimpo, *Descent into Hell*, 432.
38. The description of the nursing corps is based on my visit to the Himeyuri Peace Museum, Itoman City, 4 December 2023.
39. Eugene Sledge, *With the Old Breed: At Peleliu and Okinawa* (Presidio Press, 1981), 253; *A Guide to Battle Sites and Military Bases in Okinawa City* (Okinawa City Office, 2012) 4. Some translators also render *Tetsu no Bōfū* as *Typhoon of Steel*.
40. Ota, *Battle of Okinawa*, 123.
41. Quoted in Ryukyu Shimpo, *Descent into Hell*, 223.
42. Ota, *Battle of Okinawa*, x–xi.
43. Ota, *Essays on Okinawa Problems*, 42.
44. Ryukyu Shimpo, *Descent into Hell*, 369, 392, 455.
45. Quoted in Appleman et al., *Okinawa*, 462.
46. Quoted in Schrivjers, *GI War Against Japan*, 252.
47. McLauchlan, "War Crimes," 365.
48. Personal visit to Himeyuri Peace Museum, Itoman City, 4 December 2023.
49. Nicholas Evan Sarantakes, *Keystone: The American Occupation of Okinawa and US-Japanese Relations* (Texas A&M University Press, 2000), 18–19; Appleman et al., *Okinawa*, 470–71; Ryukyu Shimpo, *Descent into Hell*, 222.
50. Appleman et al., *Okinawa*, 473; McLauchlan, "War Crimes," 375; Ota, *Essays on Okinawa Problems*, 58.
51. Henry Stanley Bennett, "The Impact of Invasion and Occupation on the Civilians on Okinawa," *US Naval Institute Proceedings* 72, iss. 2, no. 516 (February 1946); "Ginowan shi ni okeru sensai no jōkyō (Okinawa ken)," Ministry of Internal Affairs and Communications, accessed 24 June 2024, https://www.soumu.go.jp/main_sosiki/daijinkanbou/sensai/situation/state/okinawa_12.html.

52 Mitchell, *Poisoning the Pacific*, 12; Ota, *Essays on Okinawa Problems*, 69; display by Executive Committee of the Construction of the Memorial to the Korean Victims in Building Matsushiro Headquarters, Matsushiro, 1995. See also Aoki Takaju, *Matsushiro Dai Hon Ei: Rekishi no Shōgen* (Shin Nihon Shuppansha, 1997).
53 For a detailed description of Japan's suggestions to surrender and US responses—including the War Department official's "poor damn Japanese" comment—see Kuznick and Stone, *Untold History*, 161–62; United States, United Kingdom, and China, Potsdam Declaration: Proclamation Defining Terms for Japanese Surrender, Office of the Historian, 26 July 1945, https://history.state.gov/historicaldocuments/frus1945Berlinv02/d1382.
54 Mitchell, *Poisoning the Pacific*, 33–36.
55 Mitchell, *Poisoning the Pacific*, 33–36.
56 Henry L. Stimson, "The Decision to Use the Atomic Bomb," *Harper's Magazine*, February 1947, 97–107; Mitchell, *Poisoning the Pacific*, 39–40; quoted in Kuznick and Stone, *Untold History*, 164.
57 "Text of Hirohito's Radio Rescript," *New York Times*, 15 August 1945, 3.
58 John W. Dower, *Embracing Defeat: Japan in the Wake of World War II* (W. W. Norton, 1999), 36–39; Okinawa Times, *Okinawa no Shōgen*, vol. 1 (Okinawa Times, 1971), 43–54; Samuel Limneos, "The Japanese Bell and Its Many Travels," United States Naval Academy Nimitz Library, 5 November 2020, https://libguides.usna.edu/c.php?g=472716&p=6628899&t=62929. The bell was finally returned to Okinawa in 1987.
59 Douglas MacArthur and Center of Military History, *Reports of General MacArthur: The Campaigns of MacArthur in the Pacific*, vol. 1 (Center of Military History United States Army, 1966), 455–58.
60 Ota, *Battle of Okinawa*, 231; personal visit to Okinawa Prefectural Peace Memorial Museum, Itoman City, 4 December 2023; Ota, *Essays on Okinawa Problems*, 67; personal visit to Himeyuri Peace Museum, Itoman City, 4 December 2023; Ryukyu Shimpo, *Descent into Hell*, 31; McLauchlan, "War Crimes," 375.
61 Ryukyu Shimpo, *Descent into Hell*, 433; McLauchlan, "War Crimes," 365; Okinawa Women Act Against Military Violence, *Okinawa Beihei*, 4.
62 Douglas E. Nash Sr., *Battle of Okinawa: III MEF Staff Ride, Battle Book* (US Marine Corps, History Division, 2015), 142; Fujiko Toyama, Misuzu Takahara, Mariko Oshiro, Mayumi Taba, Ryouji Arizuka, Haruo Nakamoto, and Megumi Ogimi, "Shūsen kara 67 nen me ni miru Okinawa-sen taikensha no seishin hoken: Kaigo yobō jigyō e no sankasha o taishō toshite," *Journal of Okinawa Prefectural College of Nursing*, no.14 (March 2013): 1–12.
63 Appleman et al., *Okinawa*, 498–500; Mitchell, *Poisoning the Pacific*, 57; Yonaha Satoko, "Fuhatsudan, subete no shori ni ato 100 nen ka," *Okinawa Times*, 13 December 2022, https://www.okinawatimes.co.jp/articles/-/1072759.
64 Bennett, "Impact of Invasion"; personal visits to Okinawa Prefectural Peace Memorial Museum, Itoman City, 14 September and 4 December 2023; Steve Leblanc, "22 Artifacts Looted After the Battle of Okinawa Returned to Japan," Associated Press, 16 March 2024, https://apnews.com/article/japanese-okinawa-historic-looted-artifacts-recovered-wwii-b0245ad46ac07a752cd09b28ce00ee7f. In one egregious case of vandalism during the battle, US troops took an eighteenth-century plaque inscribed by King Shō Kei, carved a hole into the center, and used it as a latrine (display at Okinawa Prefectural Museum and Art Museum).

Chapter 4

1. United States, United Kingdom, and China, Cairo Declaration (Communiqué), National Diet Library, 1 December 1943, https://www.ndl.go.jp/constitution/e/shiryo/01/002_46/002_46tx.html.
2. Yoshida Kensei, *Democracy Betrayed: Okinawa Under US Occupation* (Western Washington University, 2001), 17–18.
3. Kimie Hara, "Okinawa, Taiwan, and the Senkaku/Diaoyu Islands in United States–Japan–China Relations," *Asia-Pacific Journal* 13, iss. 28, no. 2 (13 July 2015): 1–18, https://apjjf.org/2015/13/28/kimie-hara/4341.
4. Yoshida, *Democracy Betrayed*, 19; quoted in Nicholas Evan Sarantakes, *Keystone: The American Occupation of Okinawa and US-Japanese Relations* (Texas A&M University Press, 2000), 25, 204. Buckner's racism is well-documented. During his service in Alaska, he ordered indigenous villages razed and opposed the stationing of African American soldiers, citing the possibility they would "interbreed with the Indians and the Eskimos and produce an astonishingly objectionable race of mongrels" [quoted in Greg Grandin, *The End of the Myth: From the Frontier to the Border Wall in the Mind of America* (Metropolitan Books, 2019), 146].
5. Harry S. Truman, radio report to the American people on the Potsdam Conference, 9 August 1945.
6. Quoted in Yoshida, *Democracy Betrayed*, 22.
7. Kabira Nario, "Okinawa-sen mō hitotsu no higeki," *Tokyo Shimbun*, 19 June 2016, 13; Yoshida, *Democracy Betrayed*, 27–32; "'Pigs from the Sea' Commemorative Monument," Okinawa Prefectural Government, accessed 27 September 2025, https://www.pref.okinawa.jp/_res/projects/default_project/_page_/001/009/859/monument.pdf.
8. Arnold G. Fisch Jr., *Military Government in the Ryukyu Islands, 1945–1950* (Center of Military History, US Army, 1988), 98–114; Yoshida, *Democracy Betrayed*, 32–34.
9. Fisch, *Military Government*, 109; Yoshida, *Democracy Betrayed*, 33; Mizoguchi So, "Narratives of the Early Stage of American Occupation in Okinawa," *Japanese Studies Review* 22 (2018): 69.
10. Fisch, *Military Government*, 182.
11. Miyume Tanji, *Myth, Protest, and Struggle in Okinawa* (Routledge, 2006), 45.
12. Fisch, *Military Government*, 127.
13. "Big Picture: Okinawa: Keystone of the Pacific," National Archives and Records Administration, Department of Defense, n.d.
14. Frank Gibney, "Okinawa: Forgotten Island," *Time*, 28 November 1949, http://content.time.com/time/magazine/article/0,9171,856392,00.html.
15. Fukuchi Hiroaki, *Okinawa ni okeru Beigun no Hanzai* (Dojidai-sha, 1995), 99–104.
16. Okinawa Women Act Against Military Violence, *Okinawa Beihei ni yoru Josei he no Seihanzai*, 13th ed. (Kichi Guntai o Yurusanai kōdō suru Onnatachi no Kai, 2023), 4–17; Takazato Suzuyo, founding member of Okinawa Women Act Against Military Violence, interview by author, 1 September 2015.
17. Okinawa Women Act Against Military Violence, *Okinawa Beihei*, 3; Calvin Simms, "3 Dead Marines and a Secret of Wartime Okinawa," *New York Times*, 1 June 2000, 12.
18. "Beigunki jiko ni yoru omona jūmin higai," *Okinawa Times*, 6 August 2013, 6; Jon Mitchell, *Poisoning the Pacific: The US Military's Secret Dumping of Plutonium, Chemical Weapons, and Agent Orange* (Rowman & Littlefield, 2020), 58–59.

19 Shimabukuro Seitoku, "Ie Island: A Battered Island," Videos Testimonies of War Survivors During and After World War II, Okinawa Prefectural Peace Memorial Museum, 2022, http://www.peace-museum.okinawa.jp/testimony/en/archive/148/.
20 "Bakuhatsu jiko kara 61 nen: Minato de nani ga okotta no ka," Ryūkyū Asahi Hōsō, 5 August 2009, https://www.qab.co.jp/news/2009080511048.html; Headquarters Ryukyus Command, *Report of Proceedings of Board of Officers: Explosion of LCT #1141, Near Ie Shima* (Headquarters Ryukyus Command, 10 September 1948).
21 Shimabukuro, "A Battered Island." Shimabukuro later served as Iejima's mayor between 1989 and 2005.
22 Personal visit to Monument to the Iejima LCT Explosion, Ie Village, 17 September 2023; Headquarters Ryukyus Command, *Report of Proceedings*; Jahana Naomi, *Chinmoku no Kioku 1948 nen: Hōdan no Shima Iejima Beigun LCT Bakuhatsu Jiken* (Impact Shuppankai, 2022), 206, 233–34. The military's compensation for the deaths of those tasked with loading the explosives was fifty-eight dollars and a blanket.
23 John W. Dower, *Embracing Defeat: Japan in the Wake of World War II* (W. W. Norton, 1999), 324, 326–27.
24 W. J. Sebald, "Emperor of Japan's Opinion Concerning the Future of the Ryukyu Islands," dispatch 1293 to secretary of state, 22 September 1947.
25 Yonaha Keiko, "Okinawa Under US Occupation: The Chaotic Situation of Okinawa from 1945 to 1952: How Was It and Why Was It?" *Meiō Daigaku Sōgō Kenkyū* 23 (March 2014): 5–7.
26 Central Intelligence Agency, *The Ryukyu Islands and Their Significance* (Central Intelligence Agency, 6 August 1948).
27 National Security Council, *Report by the National Security Council on Recommendations with Respect to United States Policy Toward Japan*, NSC 13/3 (National Security Council, 6 May 1949); Mitchell, *Poisoning the Pacific*, 26–29; Dower, *Embracing Defeat*, 272.
28 Fisch, *Military Government*, 183.
29 UN Security Council, Trusteeship Agreement for the Former Japanese Mandated Islands Approved at the One Hundred and Twenty-Fourth Meeting of the Security Council, 2 April 1947.
30 Quoted in Walter J. Hickel, *Who Owns America?* (Prentice-Hall, 1971), 208.
31 Mitchell, *Poisoning the Pacific*, 41–48, 188–89.
32 Dower, *Embracing Defeat*, 541–42.
33 China and Japan signed a peace treaty in 1978, but Russia and Japan still have not done so.
34 Yoshida, *Democracy Betrayed*, 48–50; Hara, "Okinawa, Taiwan."
35 John Foster Dulles, address to the San Francisco Peace Conference, 5 September 1951.
36 Tanji, *Myth, Protest, and Struggle*, 61.
37 Fisch, *Military Government*, 169.
38 *Okinawa Times* Chūbūshisha Henshūbu, *Kichi de Hataraku: Gunsagyōin no Sengo* (Okinawa Times, 2013), 54; Tanji, *Myth, Protest, and Struggle*, 58–59.
39 Fisch, *Military Government*, 174; Okinawa Jinken Kyōkai, *Sengo Okinawa no Jinkenshi*, (Kōbunken, 2012), 34–35; Yoshida, *Democracy Betrayed*, 64–65.
40 Chizuru Saeki, "The Perry Centennial of 1953 in Okinawa: U.S. Cultural Policy in Cold War Okinawa," *Journal of International and Area Studies* 19, no. 3 (2012): 19–20.

41 Ahagon Shōkō, *The Island Where People Live*, trans. C. Harold Rickard (Christian Conference of Asia Communications, 1989), 9, 160.
42 Personal visit to Wabiai no Sato, Ie Village, 27 July 2013; Ahagon, *Island Where People Live*, 23.
43 Ahagon, *Island Where People Live*, 9–10, 22, 162.
44 Ahagon, *Island Where People Live*, 69, 71, 93–99.
45 Ahagon, *Island Where People Live*, 23, 100–101, 168.
46 Ginowanshiritsu Hakubutsukan, ed., *Isahama no Tochi Tōsō (Kaisetsuhen)*, Ginowan Shishi, vol. 8, Shiryōhen 7, Sengoshiryōhen 2 (Okinawaken Ginowanshi Kyōiku Iinkai Kyōikubu, 2021) 3, 18–21; Ginowanshiritsu Hakubutsukan, ed., *Isahama no Tochi Tōsō (Shiryōhen)*, Ginowan Shishi, vol. 8, Shiryōhen 7, Sengoshiryōhen 2 (Okinawaken Ginowanshi Kyōiku Iinkai Kyōikubu, 2019), 231–32.
47 *Summary of Hearings by Subcommittee of House Armed Services Committee: Regarding Land Acquisition by the United States in the Ryukyu Islands*, 24–25 October 1955, in *Isahama (Shiryōhen)*, 378–80; Ginowanshiritsu Hakubutsukan, *Isahama (Kaisetsuhen)*, 20–23.
48 Ginowanshiritsu Hakubutsukan, *Isahama (Kaisetsuhen)*, 26–36; Ginowanshiritsu Hakubutsukan, *Isahama (Shiryōhen)*, 237–39; Harold Rickard, "The Okinawa Land Problem," *Japan Christian Quarterly* 37 (1971).
49 Okinawa Women Act Against Military Violence, *Okinawa Beihei*, 30.
50 "Kadena de shōjo o satsugai," *Okinawa Times*, 4 September 1955, 1.
51 Quoted in Richard A. Serrano, *Summoned at Midnight: A Story of Race and the Last Military Executions at Fort Leavenworth* (Beacon Press, 2019), 96–98.
52 Serrano, *Summoned at Midnight*, 95. In only September 1955, US military personnel committed three attempted gang rapes, one home invasion resulting in rape, and the abduction and rape of a nine-year-old girl. "Inochi, songen mō ubawasenai," *Okinawa Times*, 19 June 2016, 30.
53 "Okinawa Sergeant Found Guilty," *Stars and Stripes*, 8 December 1955; Serrano, *Summoned at Midnight*, 97–99.
54 Quoted in Serrano, *Summoned at Midnight*, 99.
55 Jon Mitchell and Richard A. Serrano, "Okinawa: Race, Military Justice and the Yumiko-Chan Incident," *Asia-Pacific Journal* 19, iss. 22, no. 2 (15 November 2021): 1–8, https://apjjf.org/2021/22/mitchell.

Chapter 5

1 Major General David Ogden, "Keystone of the Pacific," *Army Information Digest*, January 1954, 42–43.
2 Yoshida Kensei, *Democracy Betrayed: Okinawa Under US Occupation* (Western Washington University, 2001), 69–70.
3 *Summary of Hearings by Subcommittee of House Armed Services Committee: Regarding Land Acquisition by the United States in the Ryukyu Islands*, 24–25 October 1955, in *Isahama no Tochi Tōsō (Shiryōhen)*, Ginowan Shishi, vol. 8, Shiryōhen 7, Sengoshiryōhen 2, ed. Ginowanshiritsu Hakubutsukan (Okinawaken Ginowanshi Kyōiku Iinkai Bunkaka, 2019), 374–91.

4   *Summary of Hearings*, 374, 380, 411.
5   House of Representatives, *Report of a Special Subcommittee of the Armed Services Committee: Following an Inspection Tour, October 14 to November 23, 1955* (US Government Printing Office, 1956).
6   House of Representatives, *Report of a Special Subcommittee*.
7   House of Representatives, *Report of a Special Subcommittee*.
8   Ginowanshiritsu Hakubutsukan, ed., *Isahama no Tochi Tōsō (Kaisetsuhen)*, Ginowan Shishi, vol. 8, Shiryōhen 7, Sengoshiryōhen 2 (Okinawaken Ginowanshi Kyōiku Iinkai Bunkaka, 2021), 48; Arasaki Moriteru, interview by author, 17 April 2016.
9   Yoshida, *Democracy Betrayed*, 72–73; Okinawa Jinken Kyōkai, *Sengo Okinawa no Jinkenshi* (Kōbunken, 2012), 43–44.
10 Quoted in Kozy K. Amemiya, "The Bolivan Connection: U.S. Bases and Okinawan Emigration," Japan Policy Research Institute, working paper no. 25 (October 1996): 5–6.
11 Ginowanshiritsu Hakubutsukan, *Isahama (Kaisetsuhen)*, 36; Jon Mitchell, "Okinawan Diaspora," *Japan Times*, 23 October 2016, 15.
12 Personal visit to Fukutsu-kan: Kamejiro Senaga and the People's History Museum, Naha City, 27 February 2016. One of the most comprehensive Japanese sources in Senaga's own words is Senaga Kamejiro, *Mimokuno Ikari: Moeagaru Okinawa* (Shin Nihon Press, 1971).
13 Okinawa Jinken Kyōkai, *Sengo Okinawa*, 42; Fukutsu-kan; Nicholas Evan Sarantakes, *Keystone: The American Occupation of Okinawa and US-Japanese Relations* (Texas A&M University Press, 2000), 97; Yoshimoto Hideko, "A Historical Perspective on Press Freedom in Okinawa," in *Press Freedom in Contemporary Japan*, ed. Jeff Kingston (Routledge, 2017), 245–46.
14 Yoshimoto, "Historical Perspective," 246; Okinawa Jinken Kyōkai, *Sengo Okinawa*, 49.
15 One US tabloid, the *New York Daily Mirror*, argued that USCAR should have gone further than merely removing Senaga. It ought to tell Okinawans "that we shall have no more nonsense, that we shall tolerate no communists and that spies will be hanged on lampposts" (quoted in Sarantakes, *Keystone*, 99); Yoshida, *Democracy Betrayed*, 81–83.
16 Annmaria M. Shimabuku, *Alegal: Biopolitics and the Unintelligibility of Okinawan Life* (Fordham University Press, 2019), 116.
17 Yoshimoto Hideko, *U.S. Occupation of Okinawa: A Soft Power Theory Approach* (Kyoto University Press, 2019), 5, 64. According to the US military, the trusteeship issue became moot when Japan joined the United Nations in 1956 because "under the Charter of the United Nations, trusteeship cannot be imposed on the territory of a member state" [*A History of the Special Representative of the Secretary of Defense and Chairman Joint Chiefs of Staff and Senior U.S. Military Representative Okinawa Negotiating Team* (USMILRONT Staff, 15 June 1972), 2].
18 Patrick Heinrich, "Language Loss and Revitalization in the Ryukyu Islands," *Asia-Pacific Journal* 3, iss. 11 (24 November 2005): 1–12, https://apjjf.org/patrick-heinrich/1596/article; Miyume Tanji, *Myth, Protest, and Struggle in Okinawa* (Routledge, 2006), 88; Fija Bairon, Matthias Brenzinger, and Patrick Heinrich, "The Ryukyus and the New, but Endangered, Languages of Japan," *Asia-Pacific Journal* 7, iss. 19, no. 2 (9 May 2009): 1–20, https://apjjf.org/patrick-heinrich/3138/article. According to Heinrich (2005), reasons for USCAR abandoning plans to create textbooks in Okinawan languages included the "absence of a modern written Ryukyuan style since

official records had been written in classical Chinese prior to the Japanese seizure of the Ryukyus, . . . a fixed orthography did not exist, nor resources and materials on which such textbooks could be based."
19 Yoshimoto, *U.S. Occupation*, 108, 119.
20 Personal visit to Okinawa Prefectural Peace Memorial Museum, Itoman City, 4 December 2023; Yoshimoto, *U.S. Occupation*, 122, 151.
21 "Isahama Goes to U.S. with Little Opposition," *Okinawa Morning Star*, 20 July 1955, 1.
22 "Worldwide Propaganda Network Built by the C.I.A.," *New York Times*, 27 December 1977, 41; "Varying Ties to C. I. A. Confirmed in Inquiry," *New York Times*, 26 December 1977, 1.
23 Yoshida, *Democracy Betrayed*, xx; Yoshimoto, *U.S. Occupation*, 153; Sarantakes, *Keystone*, 106–7.
24 Joint Chiefs of Staff, "Future of the Ryukyu Islands," memorandum for the secretary of defense, 23 December 1965.
25 Roger B. Jeans, *The CIA and Third Force Movements in China During the Early Cold War: The Great American Dream* (Lexington, 2018), 123; Jon Mitchell, "Ajia bōryaku sakusen no kyoten mori ni kakurega, tokushu kunren mo," *Okinawa Times*, 17 August 2017, 1.
26 "*Okinawa Times* Article Reveals CIA Island Base," FBIS daily report, 28 September 1971; Joe F. Leeker, "Smaller Operations: Kadena Air Base, Clark Air Base," in *The History of Air America* (University of Texas, 2015), 1–6; Jeans, *Third Force Movements*, 126.
27 Leeker, "Smaller Operations," 1; Joe F. Leeker, "Scheduled Air Services Ryukyus," in *The History of Air America* (University of Texas, 2015), 1–2; United States Senate, *Final Report of the Select Committee to Study Governmental Operations with Respect to Intelligence Activities* (US Government Printing Office, 14 April 1976), 223–24.
28 Jon Mitchell, "Ajia zen'iki no hōdō, Okinawa de bōju 2006 nen henkan no beigun shisetsu wa CIA kyoten," *Okinawa Times*, 6 April 2018, https://www.okinawatimes.co.jp/articles/-/233430; "Hondo fukki to Beikokuei hōsō," RBC, 1 August 2022, https://www.rbc.co.jp/special_contents/yuu/voice-of-america/.
29 Sarantakes, *Keystone*, 97, 100.
30 Jon Mitchell, *Poisoning the Pacific: The US Military's Secret Dumping of Plutonium, Chemical Weapons, and Agent Orange* (Rowman & Littlefield, 2000), 73.
31 Mitchell, *Poisoning the Pacific*, 26–27, 71, 82.
32 Mitchell, *Poisoning the Pacific*, 45–47, 67; House of Representatives, *Report of a Special Subcommittee*.
33 Mitchell, *Poisoning the Pacific*, 67; "Japs Aroused as Atomic Guns Reach Okinawa," *Chicago Tribune*, 30 July 1955, 32; Mitchell, *Poisoning the Pacific*, 69.
34 "Taikensha no shōgen," Ishikawa Miyamori 630 Kai, accessed 27 September 2025, https://ishikawamiyamori630kai.cloud-line.com/syougen/.
35 "Taikensha no shōgen."
36 Ishikawa Miyamori 630 Kai, ed., *Inochi to Heiwa no Kataribe: "Okinawa no Sora no Shita de: Shogen Ā kono Hisan: Ishikawa Miyamori Jettoki Tsuiraku Jiko,"* vol. 4 (Ishikawa Miyamori 630 Kai, 2019), 9.
37 "The Ishikawa Tragedy," in *History of the 313th Air Division: January–June 1959* (Kadena Air Base, 313th Air Division Historical Division, 1960), 84–85; "Jiko no gaiyō," Ishikawa Miyamori 630 Kai, accessed 27 September 2025, https://ishikawamiyamiy

amori630kai.cloud-line.com/gaiyou/. Included in the official death toll is one student, Arakaki Akira, who died aged twenty-three from injuries sustained as a young boy in the crash.

38 "1959 nen 6 gatsu 30 nichi: Miyamori shōgakkō jettoki tsuiraku jiko," Okinawa Prefectural Archives, accessed 27 September 2025, https://www.archives.pref.okinawa.jp/news/that_day/4606; "Ishikawa Tragedy," 77–79, 122–24.

39 "Ishikawa Tragedy," 80, 129. See also Jon Mitchell, "Error at CIA-Owned Facility Contributed to '59 School Tragedy, Current USAF Website Plays Down Casualties, Plays Up Military Relief," *Okinawa Times*, 18 July 2024, https://www.okinawatimes.co.jp/articles/-/1395979.

40 "Ishikawa Tragedy," 79, 99, 106. For further primary-source documents on the accident, see Ishikawa Miyamori 630 Kai, ed., *Ishikawa Miyamori no Sangeki: Beikoku Kōbunshokan Bunsho ni Miru Jettoki Tsuiraku Jiken* (Ishikawa Miyamori 630 Kai, 2019).

41 Yoshida, *Democracy Betrayed*, 104.

42 Justin Jesty, "Tokyo 1960: Days of Rage and Grief," MIT Visualizing Cultures, accessed 27 September 2025, https://visualizingcultures.mit.edu/tokyo_1960/anp2_essay01.html; Jennifer M. Miller, "Fractured Alliance: Anti-Base Protests and Postwar U.S.-Japanese Relations," *Diplomatic History* 38, no. 5 (2014): 963–71.

43 Arasaki Moriteru, *Okinawa Gendai Shi* (Iwanami Shoten, 1996), 26.

44 Ginowanshiritsu Hakubutsukan, *Isahama (Kaisetsuhen)*, 48.

45 Miller "Fractured Alliance," 982; "Editorial: Top Court Chief's Behavior During Sunagawa Case Crossed the Line," *Asahi Shimbun*, 23 January 2024, https://www.asahi.com/ajw/articles/15125438; cable from MacArthur II to the secretary of state, 31 March 1959, quoted in "U.S. Ambassador Pressed Japan's Top Court to Reject Lower Court Ruling That U.S. Forces in Japan Are Unconstitutional," *Japan Press Weekly*, 11 May 2008, https://www.japan-press.co.jp/s/news/?id=4761.

46 Tim Weiner, *Legacy of Ashes: The History of the CIA* (Doubleday, 2007), 138.

47 Weiner, *Legacy of Ashes*, 136.

48 Weiner, *Legacy of Ashes*, 136–38.

49 Yoshida, *Democracy Betrayed*, 80.

50 For a concise exploration of this tumultuous period, see Jesty, "Tokyo 1960."

51 Nick Kapur, *Japan at the Crossroads: Conflict and Compromise After Anpo* (Harvard University Press, 2018), 22–24.

52 Dwight D. Eisenhower, remarks upon arrival at Kadena Air Force Base, Okinawa, 19 June 1960; Naha-shi Kikakubu Ichishi Henshūshitsuhen, ed., *Shashinshū Naha Hyaku nen no Ayumi* (Naha-shi Kikakubu Ichishi Henshūshitsuhen, 1980), 184; "Okinawa: Winner: The U.S.," *Time*, 28 November 1960; Yoshida, *Democracy Betrayed*, ix, 115–16.

53 Yoshida, *Democracy Betrayed*, 116–17.

54 Tanji, *Myth, Protest, and Struggle*, 83; Yoshida, *Democracy Betrayed*, 92.

55 Okinawa Jinken Kyōkai, *Sengo Okinawa*, 54–56.

56 *Okinawa Times* Chūbūshisha Henshūbu, *Kichi de Hataraku: Gunsagyōin no Sengo* (Okinawa Times, 2013), 230–31; Tanji, *Myth, Protest, and Struggle*, 84. For a chronicle of the struggles faced by base workers, see Uehara Kōsuke, *Kichi Okinawa no Kutō: Zengunrō Tōsōshi* (Sōkō, 1982).

57 Quoted in Ai Abe, "An Outstanding Claim: The Ryukyu/Okinawa Peoples' Right to Self-Determination Under International Human Rights Law," *Asian Journal of*

International Law (2022): 15; Ota Masahide, *Minikui Nihonjin: Nihon no Okinawa Ishiki (Shinpan)* (Iwanami Gendai Bunko, 2000), 248.
58 Quoted in Abe, "Outstanding Claim," 15.

Chapter 6

1 *Report and Recommendation of the Task Force Ryukyus*, presidential papers of John F. Kennedy, president's office files, December 1961. For many Okinawans, there was no clearer sign of military priorities than the annual service practice, Yomitan Village, during which dozens of Hawk and Nike missiles were test-fired in the presence of US and Okinawan dignitaries. The eight-day drills cost $10 million, a "sum the Okinawan VIPs feel could much better be spent, even in part, on their health and welfare" [M. D. Morris, *Okinawa: A Tiger by the Tail* (Hawthorn, 1968), 97–98]. In 1956, the Ryukyu legislature passed a law to grant access to abortions, but it was vetoed by the high commissioner [Kozy K. Amemiya, "The Bolivan Connection: U.S. Bases and Okinawan Emigration," Japan Policy Research Institute, working paper no. 25 (October 1996), 4].
2 *Report and Recommendation*, 108; Makino Hirotaka, "Senryoka no keizai: Doru no seijigaku," in *Shimpojiumu: Okinawa Senryo: Mirai e mukete*, ed. Miyagi Etsujiro (Hirugisha, 1993), 327.
3 John Fitzgerald Kennedy, statement by the president upon signing order relating to the administration of the Ryukyu Islands, 19 March 1962.
4 *Report and Recommendation*, 6–7, 18, 23, 56, 67.
5 *Report and Recommendation*, 25.
6 Nicholas Evan Sarantakes, *Keystone: The American Occupation of Okinawa and US-Japanese Relations* (Texas A&M University Press, 2000), 116–24; Yoshida Kensei, *Democracy Betrayed: Okinawa Under US Occupation* (Western Washington University, 2001), 124–27.
7 Paul W. Caraway, remarks by the high commissioner of the Ryukyu Islands at the regular monthly dinner meeting of the Golden Gate Club, Harborview Club, Naha, 5 March 1963.
8 Rafael Steinberg, "Our Unhappy Asia Bastion," *Washington Post*, 3 May 1964, quoted in Yoshida, *Democracy Betrayed*, 171.
9 Quoted in Tim Weiner, *Legacy of Ashes: The History of the CIA* (Doubleday, 2007), 135.
10 Tim Weiner, "C.I.A. Spent Millions to Support Japanese Right in 50's and 60's," *New York Times*, 9 October 1994, 1; Department of State, "Your Meetings with Prime Minister Sato, January 11–14, 1965," memorandum for the president, 9 January 1965, 1, 6. Sato was married to his own first cousin, who described him as taciturn with a propensity for domestic violence: "He beat me and smashed things . . . before he opened his mouth, his hand came out" ("Japan: The Wife Tells All," *Time*, 10 January 1969).
11 Sarantakes, *Keystone*, 135–37; Central Intelligence Agency, "Weekly Summary: Special Report: The Okinawan Issue in Japanese Politics," 5 May 1967, 6.

12 Lyndon B. Johnson, joint statement following meetings with the prime minister of Japan, 13 January 1965.
13 Yoshimoto Hideko, "A Historical Perspective on Press Freedom in Okinawa," in *Press Freedom in Contemporary Japan*, ed. Jeff Kingston (Routledge, 2017), 246–47; "Okinawa no sokokufukki undō to Satō sōri no hōmon," Nippon Hōsō Kyōkai, 1965, https://www2.nhk.or.jp/archives/movies/?id=D0009030504_00000; Sarantakes, *Keystone*, 137–39; Miyume Tanji, *Myth, Protest, and Struggle in Okinawa* (Routledge, 2006), 90.
14 Sato Eisaku, remarks upon prime ministerial visit to Okinawa, 19 August 1965.
15 Prime Minister Sato's commitment to the US military was always firm but still not enough for the US government. Prior to his visit to Okinawa, Washington insisted that he make explicit reference to the need for US bases. As a result, he added to his speech, "The Ryukyu Islands are playing a very important role for peace and security of the Far East" ("US Pressed Sato to Soften 1965 Okinawa Speech," *Japan Times*, 16 January 2015, 1).
16 *Public Papers of the Presidents of the United States: Dwight D. Eisenhower (1954)* (US National Archives, 1960), 381–90.
17 Information Office, Headquarters, US Army Ryukyu Islands, *Why We Are Here* (US Army, 1969).
18 Thomas R. H. Havens, *Fire Across the Sea: The Vietnam War and Japan, 1965–1975* (Princeton University Press, 1987), 119; Jon Mitchell, "Vietnam: Okinawa's Forgotten War," *Asia-Pacific Journal* 13, iss. 16, no. 1 (20 April 2015): 1–7, https://apjjf.org/jon-mitchell/4308; quoted in Edwin O. Reischauer, telegram from the embassy in Japan to the Department of State, 15 June 1965.
19 Joint Chiefs of Staff, "Future of the Ryukyu Islands," memorandum for the secretary of defense, 23 December 1965; quoted in Yoshida, *Democracy Betrayed*, 112.
20 Mitchell, "Vietnam"; Okinawa Times Chūbūshisha Henshūbu, *Kichi de Hataraku: Gunsagyōin no Sengo* (Okinawa Times, 2013), 83–84, 266–70.
21 Mitchell, "Vietnam"; "A-12 Oxcart," Central Intelligence Agency, accessed 28 September 2025, https://www.cia.gov/legacy/museum/exhibit/a-12-oxcart/.
22 Quoted in Havens, *Fire Across the Sea*, 85.
23 John Hughes, "Okinawa," *Atlantic*, October 1969, 42; Jon Mitchell, *Tsuiseki: Okinawa no Karehazai*, trans. Abe Kosuzu (Kōbunken, 2014), 144–45; quoted in *Okinawa Times* Chūbūshisha Henshūbu, *Kichi de Hataraku*, 276; Mark Selden, "Okinawa and American Colonialism," *Bulletin of Concerned Asian Scholars* 3, no. 1 (1970):50–63.
24 Beijing NGO Forum Workshop, *Military Violence and Women in Okinawa* (NGO Forum on Women Beijing, 7 September 1995); Tanji, *Myth, Protest, and Struggle*, 80; quoted in Annmaria M. Shimabuku, *Alegal: Biopolitics and the Unintelligibility of Okinawan Life* (Fordham University Press, 2019), 118.
25 Jon Mitchell, *Poisoning the Pacific: The US Military's Secret Dumping of Plutonium, Chemical Weapons, and Agent Orange* (Rowman & Littlefield, 2020), 61–62; "Inochi, songen mō ubawasenai," *Okinawa Times*, 19 June 2016, 31.
26 "Inochi, songen mō ubawasenai," 31.
27 Quoted in Jon Mitchell, "Late Marine's Message Lives On in Okinawa and Vietnam," *Japan Times*, 9 July 2015, 8.
28 Jon Mitchell, "On the Ground: Military Police Turn to Crime to Support Their Heroin Habits on Okinawa," *Okinawa Times*, 25 July 2022, https://www.okinawatimes.co

.jp/articles/-/992212; Tanji, *Myth, Protest, and Struggle*, 102–3; "Inochi, songen mō ubawasenai," 31; Selden, "Okinawa and American Colonialism," 61–62.
29. Committee on Foreign Affairs, *The World Heroin Problem* (US Government Printing Office, 1971), 21.
30. Committee on Foreign Affairs, *World Heroin Problem*, 21.
31. *Alleged Drug Abuse in the Armed Services: Hearings*, 91st Cong., 2nd sess. (US Government Printing Office, 1971), 1386–87, 1702; General Accounting Office, *Drug Abuse Control Program Activities in Okinawa* (General Accounting Office, 11 August 1972), 2, 6, 15–17.
32. Quoted in Mitchell, "On the Ground."
33. Mitchell, *Poisoning the Pacific*, 63, 149–50; Jon Mitchell and Shimabukuro Natsuko, dirs., *Nuchi nu Miji: Okinawa's Water of Life* (Ryūkyū Asahi Hōsō, 2022).
34. Mitchell, *Poisoning the Pacific*, 69, 93.
35. Central Intelligence Agency, "Nerve Gas Incident on Okinawa," memorandum from Chief North Asia Branch to director of current intelligence, 18 July 1969.
36. Mitchell, *Poisoning the Pacific*, 236.
37. Mitchell, *Poisoning the Pacific*, 69.
38. Mitchell, *Poisoning the Pacific*, 83–89; "Agent Orange Exposure and Disability Compensation," US Department of Veterans Affairs, 3 May 2024, https://www.va.gov/disability/eligibility/hazardous-materials-exposure/agent-orange/.
39. Mitchell, *Poisoning the Pacific*, 90–93.
40. Mitchell, *Poisoning the Pacific*, 73–76.
41. Quoted in Jon Mitchell, "'I Was Exposed to Nerve Agent on Okinawa'—US Soldier Sickened by Chemical Weapon Leak at Chibana Ammunition Depot in 1969 Breaks Silence on What Happened That Day," *Asia-Pacific Journal* 17, iss. 20, no. 2 (15 October 2019): 1–7, https://apjjf.org/2019/20/mitchell.
42. James B. Lampert, US Military History Institute, senior officers debriefing papers, James and Williams Bolote Papers.
43. Mitchell, *Poisoning the Pacific*, 77–78; "Nerve Gas Accident: Okinawa Mishap Bares Overseas Deployment of Chemical Weapons," *Wall Street Journal*, 18 July 1969, 1.
44. Mitchell, *Poisoning the Pacific*, 76; personal visit to "Kaku to misairu to Yomitan son," Yuntanza Museum, Yomitan Village, 19 August 2022.
45. Central Intelligence Agency, "Nerve Gas Incident."
46. "Beigun sesshū ni go nen han teikō shi tsudzuketa koya," *Okinawa Times*, 11 July 2021, https://www.okinawatimes.co.jp/articles/-/784502.
47. Ahagon Shōkō, *Beigun to Nōmin: Okinawa ken Iejima* (Iwanami Shoten, 1973), 193–201.
48. Personal visit to Ibudake jitsudan shageki enshū soshi tōsō no ishibumi, Kunigami Village, 2 February 2012.
49. Personal visit to Okinawa Karate Kaikan, Tomigusuku City, 2 December 2023; Mitchell, *Tsuiseki*, 64; quoted in Wesley Iwao Ueunten, "Rising Up from a Sea of Discontent: The 1970 Koza Uprising in U.S.-Occupied Okinawa," in *Militarized Currents: Toward a Decolonized Future in Asia and the Pacific*, ed. Setsu Shigematsu and Keith L. Camacho (University of Minnesota Press, 2010), 115–16.
50. "Bob Hope versus FTA," *Camp News*, 15 February 1972. When *Okinawa Morning Star* reported about the FTA's support for striking base workers, the CIA-funded newspaper headlined its coverage "Jane Fonda Joins Dull Strike" and lambasted the movie star as "another 'Instant Okinawa Expert'" (*Okinawa Morning Star*, 16 December 1971, 1).
51. Yoshida, *Democracy Betrayed*, 142–45.

Chapter 7

1. National Security Archive, "State Department Document Reveals 'Secret Action Plan' to Influence 1965 Okinawan Elections," press release, 17 September 1996, https://nsarchive2.gwu.edu/nsa/archive/news/okinawa.htm.
2. US Department of State, "U.S. Policy in the Ryuku Islands," memorandum of conversation, 16 July 1965, 4–5.
3. US Army Military History Institute, "Senior Officers Debriefing Program: Lieutenant General Ferdinand T. Unger," 29 April 1975, 28; US Department of State, "U.S. Policy," 8–9; Gavan McCormack and Satoko Oka Norimatsu, *Resistant Islands: Okinawa Confronts Japan and the United States* (Rowman & Littlefield, 2012), 82.
4. Quoted in Yoshida Kensei, *Democracy Betrayed: Okinawa Under US Occupation* (Western Washington University, 2001), 141.
5. Quoted in Yoshida, *Democracy Betrayed*, 58.
6. Quoted in Komine Yukinori, "Okinawa Confidential, 1969: Exploring the Linkage Between the Nuclear Issue and the Base Issue," *Diplomatic History* 37, no. 4 (2013): 811; Yamamoto Akiko, *Nichibei Chiikyōtei: Zainichi Beigun to "Dōmei" no 70 nen* (Chūōkōron Shinsha, 2019), 96.
7. Quoted in Komine, "Okinawa Confidential," 811; Walter S. Poole, *The History of the Joint Chiefs of Staff* (Office of Joint History, Office of the Chairman of the Joint Chiefs of Staff, 2013), 233.
8. National Security Council, "Policy Toward Japan," memorandum 13, 28 May 1969.
9. Richard Nixon, joint statement following discussions with Prime Minister Sato of Japan, 21 November 1969.
10. Quoted in Wakaizumi Kei, *The Best Course Available: A Personal Account of the Secret U.S.-Japan Okinawa Reversion Negotiations* (University of Hawai'i Press, 2002), 301.
11. Quoted in Wakaizumi, *Best Course Available*, 303.
12. Yamamoto, *Nichibei Chiikyōtei*, 96. Some commentators have interpreted *hondo nami* only to mean that the usage of Okinawa's bases would be equivalent to mainland Japan and not the proportion. But in talks with Yara Chōbyō, Japan's Minister of Foreign Affairs Aichi Kiichi confirmed the phrase meant "After reversion, the bases will be reorganized and reduced to the same level as those on the mainland" ("Shōgen dokyumento 'Okinawa henkanshi,'" Nippon Hōsō Kyōkai, on air 15 May 2022).
13. Miyume Tanji, *Myth, Protest, and Struggle in Okinawa* (Routledge, 2006), 102–3; Annmaria M. Shimabuku, *Alegal: Biopolitics and the Unintelligibility of Okinawan Life* (Fordham University Press, 2019), 131.
14. "Inochi, songen mō ubawasenai," *Okinawa Times*, 19 June 2016, 31; Okinawa Women Act Against Military Violence, *Okinawa Beihei ni yoru Josei he no Seihanzai*, 13th ed. (Kichi Guntai o Yurusanai kōdō suru Onnatachi no Kai, 2023), 55; personal visit to "Joseitachi no Okinawa: Kōbunshokan shiryō ni miru josei no ayumi," Okinawa Prefectural Archives, Haebaru Town, 27 January 2023. In May 1970, a sixteen-year-old girl walking home from school was attacked by a US service member who attempted to rape her. When she resisted, she was stabbed in the neck, stomach, and head, leaving her with serious injuries. The American received a three-year prison sentence, a punishment many Okinawans felt too lenient. Okinawa Jinken Kyōkai, *Sengo Okinawa no Jinkenshi* (Kōbunken, 2012), 73–74; Jon Mitchell, *Poisoning the Pacific: The US Military's Secret Dumping of Plutonium, Chemical Weapons, and Agent*

Orange (Rowman & Littlefield, 2020), 78; "Omoi kichi futan teikō 70 nen," *Okinawa Times*, 17 May 2015, 6.

15 "Summary Police Report on Koza Riot of 20 December," memorandum of dissemination (source redacted), 16 January 1971, in *Beikoku ga Mita Koza Bōdō*, ed. Okinawa City Planning Department Peace Culture Promotion Division (Okinawa City Hall, 1999), 20–24.

16 "Summary Police Report," 26–28, 40; Shimabuku, *Alegal*, 156.

17 Commanding Officer, 1st Military Police Group, Department of the Army, "Koza Riot, 20 December 1970," n.d., in *Beikoku ga Mita Koza Bōdō*, ed. Okinawa City Planning Department Peace Culture Promotion Division (Okinawa City Hall, 1999), 120–22; Wesley Iwao Ueunten, "Rising Up from a Sea of Discontent: The 1970 Koza Uprising in U.S.-Occupied Okinawa," in *Militarized Currents: Toward a Decolonized Future in Asia and the Pacific*, ed. Setsu Shigematsu and Keith L. Camacho (University of Minnesota Press, 2010), 96; "Summary Police Report," 44–46, 76; Department of Defense, "Widespread Violence Directed at Kadena AB and U.S. Military Personnel in Koza City, 20 Dec. 70," Intelligence Information Report, 28 December 1970, in *Beikoku ga Mita Koza Bōdō*, ed. Okinawa City Planning Department Peace Culture Promotion Division (Okinawa City Hall, 1999), 102.

18 "Summary Police Report," 76; Shimabuku, *Alegal*, 158; Department of Defense, "Widespread Violence," 102–4; quoted in Ueunten, "Rising Up," 115.

19 Mitchell, *Poisoning the Pacific*, 75–79, 192–97.

20 Yoshida, *Democracy Betrayed*, 162; quoted in Jon Mitchell, "Okinawa Shutterbug Captures Varied Reactions to Hinomaru," *Japan Times*, 19 November 2011, 12.

21 Yoshida, *Democracy Betrayed*, 161; Yoshimoto Hideko, *U.S. Occupation of Okinawa: A Soft Power Theory Approach* (Kyoto University Press, 2019), 144.

22 Okinawa Jinken Kyōkai, *Sengo Okinawa*, 93.

23 US Government Printing Office, "Reversion to Japan of the Ryukyu and Daito Islands: Agreement Between the United States of America and Japan; With Related Arrangements," 1971.

24 Yoshida, *Democracy Betrayed*, 164; Memorandum of conversation, 31 January 1973, National Security Advisor's Memoranda of Conversation Collection at the Gerald R. Ford Presidential Library, also available at https://catalog.archives.gov/id/1552551.

25 Yoshida, *Democracy Betrayed*, 164; "Kawaranu kichi tsudzuku kunō," *Ryukyu Shimpo*, 15 May 1972, 1; quoted in Jon Mitchell and Shimabukuro Natsuko, dirs., *Nuchi nu Miji: Okinawa's Water of Life* (Ryūkyū Asahi Hōsō, 2022).

26 Yoshida, *Democracy Betrayed*, 162.

27 Mitchell, *Poisoning the Pacific*, 156–59; Sato Eisaku, statement at the Budget Committee in the House of Representatives, 11 December 1967.

28 Nicholas Evan Sarantakes, *Keystone: The American Occupation of Okinawa and US-Japanese Relations* (Texas A&M University Press, 2000), 170; Fujita Naotaka, "Sato Guided from Outset on Signing Secret Nuclear Pact with U.S.," *Asahi Shimbun*, 4 January 2023, https://www.asahi.com/ajw/articles/14807309.

29 Fujita, "Sato Guided from Outset."

30 All excerpts from "Agreed Minute to Joint Communique of United States President Nixon and Japanese Prime Minister Sato Issued on November 21, 1969," in Wakaizumi, *Best Course Available*, 236.

31 Nixon, joint statement.

32 Fujita, "Sato Guided from Outset"; Robert A. Wampler, ed., "Nuclear Noh Drama: Tokyo, Washington and the Case of the Missing Nuclear Agreements," National Security Archive, 13 October 2009, https://nsarchive2.gwu.edu/nukevault/ebb291/#7.
33 Office of Secretary of Defense, "Covering Brief: Issue of [redacted] from Okinawa," 17 December 1971.
34 Mitchell, *Poisoning the Pacific*, 70–71; "Sato's '74 Nobel Peace Prize Questioned," Kyodo News, 6 September 2001.
35 Okinawa Jinken Kyōkai, *Sengo Okinawa*, 93–94.
36 NSDM 13, "Background: Okinawa, Economic and Financial Issues of Reversion," 28 May 1969, quoted in Yoshida, *Democracy Betrayed*, 159.
37 US-Japan Joint Committee, minutes of the 251st meeting, 15 May 1972.
38 US-Japan Joint Committee, "Sub-Committee on Jurisdiction Administrative Agreement Matters Criminal Panel," 22 October 1953.
39 Okinawa Jinken Kyōkai, *Sengo Okinawa*, 91.
40 Office of the Secretary Joint Staff, "History of Headquarters United States Forces, Japan," 1974, 28; McCormack and Norimatsu, *Resistant Islands*, 58.

Chapter 8

1 Yoshida Kensei, *Democracy Betrayed: Okinawa Under US Occupation* (Western Washington University, 2001), 167. The US government had invested even less in the outlying Miyako and Yaeyama Islands, neglecting irrigation facilities for farms and protections against storms. When a devastating typhoon hit the region in September 1971, residents labeled it a man-made disaster (not a natural one), a result of USCAR's prioritization of military infrastructure at the expense of civilian projects.
2 Miyume Tanji, *Myth, Protest, and Struggle in Okinawa* (Routledge, 2006), 130–44; Okinawa Jinken Kyōkai, *Sengo Okinawa no Jinkenshi* (Kōbunken, 2012), 101–2.
3 Vivian Blaxell, "Preparing Okinawa for Reversion to Japan: The Okinawa International Ocean Exposition of 1975, the US Military and the Construction State," *Asia-Pacific Journal* 8, iss. 29, no. 2 (19 July 2010): 1–20, https://apjjf.org/vivian-blaxell/3386/article; Okinawa Jinken Kyōkai, *Sengo Okinawa*, 108; Nishime Junji, *Sengo Seiji o Ikite: Nikki* (Ryukyu Shimposha, 1998), 341.
4 "Bei, henkanji ni tettai kentō mo seifu ga hikitome," *Okinawa Times*, 15 June 2016, https://www.okinawatimes.co.jp/articles/-/5172; Nozoe Fumiaki, "Okinawa beigun kichi no seiri shukushō o meguru nichibei kyōgi 1970–1974 nen," *Kokusai Anzen Hosho* 41, no. 2 (2013): 99.
5 Nozoe, "Okinawa beigun kichi," 105.
6 "Bei, henkanji ni tettai"; Nozoe, "Okinawa beigun kichi," 107–11.
7 Arasaki Moriteru, *Okinawa Gendai Shi* (Iwanami Shoten, 1996), 26.
8 Nozoe, "Okinawa beigun kichi," 108; Yamamoto Akiko, *Nichibei Chiikyōtei: Zainichi Beigun to "Dōmei" no 70 nen* (Chūōkōron Shinsha, 2019), 119–25.
9 Chalmers Johnson, "Three Rapes: The Status of Forces Agreement and Okinawa," *Asia-Pacific Journal* 1, iss. 4 (10 April 2003): 1–19, https://apjjf.org/chalmers-johnson/2021/article.

10 Yoshida, *Democracy Betrayed*, 175; Tanji, *Myth, Protest, and Struggle*, 108–18; Iha Yōichi, speech at Okinawa Prefectural Assembly, 30 March 2000.
11 Hideki Yoshikawa, "Living with a Military Base: A Study of the Relationship Between a US Military Base and Kin Town, Okinawa, Japan" (master's thesis, Oregon State University, 1996), 62–72; Jon Mitchell, *Poisoning the Pacific: The US Military's Secret Dumping of Plutonium, Chemical Weapons, and Agent Orange* (Rowman & Littlefield, 2000), 132.
12 "Tsuiraku hashiru kinchō," *Okinawa Times*, 6 August 2013, 6. In July 1972, one of the USAF supersonic spy aircraft—which Okinawans had so vehemently protested—crashed at Kadena Air Base. Other collisions set fire to farmers' fields and snapped power lines, blacking out communities. In 1987, navy aircraft mistakenly dropped dummy bombs on a Malaysian cargo ship sailing near Okinawa, tearing off a sailor's arm (Jody Liliedahl, "Blackbird Down," *Air and Space Magazine*, October 2015, https://www.smithsonianmag.com/air-space-magazine/17_on2015-above-beyond-180956605/; "Navy Bombers Score Hits on Freighter—by Mistake," United Press International, 29 July 1987). Mitchell, *Poisoning the Pacific*, 50; Jon Mitchell, "Contamination at Camp Kinser: 2019 Report Detailed High Health Risks for Children, Base Workers—but Military Failed to Inform," *Okinawa Times*, 17 February 2023, https://www.okinawatimes.co.jp/articles/-/1103107; "Beigun ga kareha sakusen," *Okinawa Times*, 31 October 1973, 1.
13 As former CIA consultant and political scientist, Chalmers Johnson inveighed, "All servicemen in Okinawa know that if after committing a rape, a robbery, or an assault, they can make it back to the base before the police catch them, they will be free until indicted even though there is a Japanese arrest warrant out for their capture." Johnson, "Three Rapes"; "Inochi, songen mō ubawasenai," *Okinawa Times*, 19 June 2016, 31; Ota Masahide, address to the American Bar Association Section of International Law and Practice, 15 April 1997. What happened at a beach in Kin Town in April 1975 disturbed even those who had become numb to military violence. Two junior high school girls—one twelve, one thirteen—were changing into their swimwear when a service member knocked them unconscious with a rock and raped them. Initially, the military refused to hand over the suspect to Okinawan police, but after protests by citizens and the Prefectural Assembly, the military finally agreed to cede custody. The attacker received six years in prison. "Beihei, 2 joshi chūgakusei ni ranbō," *Okinawa Times*, 21 April 1975, 1; Okinawa Women Act Against Military Violence, *Okinawa Beihei ni yoru Josei he no Seihanzai*, 13th ed. (Kichi Guntai o Yurusanai kōdō suru Onnatachi no Kai, 2023), 61; Jon Mitchell, "Addiction and Crime—How the 'Okinawa System' Harmed Island's Residents," *Okinawa Times*, 26 July 2022, https://www.okinawatimes.co.jp/articles/-/992224.
14 In an August 1971 *Asahi Shimbun* poll, 22 percent of Okinawan respondents supported the dispatch of the SDF, whereas 56 percent expressed opposition. Arasaki, *Okinawa Gendai Shi*, 42–44; Okinawa Jinken Kyōkai, *Sengo Okinawa*, 98; Mitchell, *Poisoning the Pacific*, 234. Postreversion construction projects often unearthed UXO. In March 1974, for example, one bomb blew up near a kindergarten in Naha City, killing a three-year-old girl and three other people.
15 "Kisenbaru tōsō 50 nen: Taishū undō ga rekishi aita," *Ryukyu Shimpo*, 12 December 2023, https://ryukyushimpo.jp/editorial/entry-2571440.html; Chibana Shoichi, *Burning the Rising Sun: From Yomitan Village, Okinawa: Islands of U.S. Bases*, trans. South Wind (South Wind, 1992), 66; Tanji, *Myth, Protest, and Struggle*, 116.

16 Children living near Kadena Air Base lost an aggregate two years of education due to noise, and experts estimate the noise causes health problems contributing to an average of ten deaths per year. Carolyn Bowen Francis, "Women and Military Violence," in *Okinawa: Cold War Island*, ed. Chalmers Johnson (Japan Policy Research Institute, 1999), 201; Mitchell, *Poisoning the Pacific*, 97–99, 141; "Saiban no ashiato," Kadena kichi bakuon soshōdan, accessed 24 June 2024, https://kadena-bakuon.jp; Okinawa Jinken Kyōkai, *Sengo Okinawa*, 191–92.
17 Iha, speech at Okinawa Prefectural Assembly; Shinnosuke Takahashi, *The Translocal Island of Okinawa: Anti-Base Activism and Grassroots Regionalism* (Bloomsbury Academic, 2024), 64.
18 In one 1978 poll, Nippon Hōsō Kyōkai asked whether the emperor warranted respect. In Okinawa, 36 percent agreed and 37 percent disagreed. Nationwide, the responses were 56 percent and 25 percent, respectively. Arasaki, *Okinawa Gendai Shi*, 115.
19 The most detailed English description of the incidents was written by William Andrews, author of *Dissenting Japan* (Hurst, 2016), at "Himeyuri no Tō, 1975: The Memorial That Nearly Killed a Crown Prince," Throw Out Your Books, 23 February 2015, https://throwoutyourbooks.wordpress.com/2015/02/23/himeyuri-no-to-1975-incident-crown-prince-akihito-tower-lilies-okinawa/; "Prince and Princess of Japan Attacked by Okinawa Radicals," *New York Times*, 18 July 1975, 1.
20 Shindō Eiichi, "Bunkatsu sareta ryōdo," *Sekai*, April 1979, 31–51. Although the conversation between Hirohito and former Prime Minister Konoe Fumimaro was described in an academic publication in 1966, it only became widely known when Ryukyu Broadcasting Corporation aired a documentary about the issue in June 1988 (Arasaki, *Okinawa Gendai Shi*, 120–21).
21 For instance, in mainland Japan, 93 percent of primary schools displayed the flag, and 73 percent sung the anthem at graduation events. Arasaki, *Okinawa Gendai Shi*, 122–30; Chibana, *Burning the Rising Sun*, 18–19.
22 Chibana, *Burning the Rising Sun*, 28, 71.
23 Arasaki, *Okinawa Gendai Shi*, 134–36; Chibana, *Burning the Rising Sun*, 28.
24 Chibana, *Burning the Rising Sun*, 43–48.
25 Chibana, *Burning the Rising Sun*, 10–12, 30–35; Arasaki, *Okinawa Gendai Shi*, 135.
26 Chibana, *Burning the Rising Sun*, 126.
27 Tanji, *Myth, Protest, and Struggle*, 44.
28 "Ano hito ni aitai: Nakamura Fumiko," Nippon Hōsō Kyōkai, accessed 30 September 2025, https://www2.nhk.or.jp/archives/articles/?id=D0009250433_00000; Takehiko Kambayashi, "War Memories Drive Okinawa's Most Passionate Peace Activist," *Christian Science Monitor*, 2 May 2005, https://www.csmonitor.com/layout/set/amphtml/2005/0502/p07s01-woap.html.
29 Chibana, *Burning the Rising Sun*, 90.
30 Hong Yunshin and Tomiyama Ichiro, "When Violence Is No Longer Just Somebody Else's Pain: Reading Hong Yunshin's 'Comfort Stations' as Remembered by Okinawans During World War II," *Asia-Pacific Journal* 20, iss. 9, no. 1 (1 May 2022): 1–27, https://apjjf.org/2022/9/tomiyama. Today, the total number of comfort stations built by the Japanese military in Okinawa is estimated at 146.
31 Okinawa Jinken Kyōkai, *Sengo Okinawa*, 115–17.
32 Yoshida, *Democracy Betrayed*, 167–68.

33 Ota Masahide, interview by author, 3 February 2012 and 1 February 2015; Jon Mitchell, "The Battle of Okinawa: America's Good War Gone Bad," *Japan Times*, 31 March 2015, 10.
34 Sam Jameson, "Irony Pervades 50-Year Struggle over Okinawa," *Los Angeles Times*, 23 June 1995, https://www.latimes.com/archives/la-xpm-1995-06-23-mn-16345-story.html.
35 Unless otherwise noted, the description of the crime is based on US and Japanese law enforcement records from September 1995 – March 1996. Also, see Jon Mitchell, "US law enforcement records: Two assailants in notorious 1995 Okinawa assault had criminal histories before entering Marine Corps," *Okinawa Times*, 22 September 2025, https://www.okinawatimes.co.jp/articles/-/1672384.
36 Edward W. Desmond, "The Outrage on Okinawa," *Time*, 2 October 1995, 17.
37 "Inochi, songen mō ubawasenai," *Okinawa Times*, 19 June 2016, 31; Chalmers Johnson, "The 1995 Rape Incident and the Rekindling of Okinawan Protest Against the American Bases," in *Okinawa: Cold War Island*, ed. Chalmers Johnson (Japan Policy Research Institute, 1999), 114. Between 1988 and 1994, navy and marine corps bases in Japan had the highest number of courts-martial for sexual assaults of all US military bases worldwide. There had been 169 such cases compared to the second-highest location, San Diego (with 102 cases but double the number of personnel).
38 Tanji, *Myth, Protest, and Struggle*, 155–57. In an opinion poll conducted by *Ryukyu Shimpo* on 7 October 1995, 75 percent of respondents said they supported Governor Ota's refusal to sign the land leases.
39 Quoted in Okinawa Jinken Kyōkai, *Sengo Okinawa*, 155.
40 Quoted in Masamichi Inoue, *Okinawa and the U.S. Military: Identity Making in the Age of Globalization* (Columbia University Press, 2017), 69.
41 Ota, address; Arasaki Moriteru, interview by author, 17 April 2016.
42 US Embassy, "Joint Committee Reaches Agreement on Criminal Jurisdiction Procedures," press release, *Okinawa Marine*, 3 November 1995; Irvin Molotsky, "Admiral Has to Quit over His Comments on Okinawa Rape," *New York Times*, 18 November 1995, https://www.nytimes.com/1995/11/18/world/admiral-has-to-quit-over-his-comments-on-okinawa-rape.html.
43 Sano Tadashi, "US Military-Affiliated Personnel Receiving Special Treatment in Prison in Japan," *Mainichi*, 16 June 2020, https://mainichi.jp/english/articles/20200615/p2a/00m/0na/013000c; "University Student Killed in a Murder-Suicide," *Daily Citizen*, 23 August 2006, https://daltoncitizen.com/2006/08/23/university-student-killed-in-a-murder-suicide/.

Chapter 9

1 Martin Luther King Jr., "Beyond Vietnam," 4 April 1967, https://riverside.whirlihost.com/Detail/objects/13962; Peter Kuznick and Oliver Stone, *The Untold History of the United States* (Gallery Books, 2012), 467; Ronald Reagan, speech to National Association of Evangelicals, 8 March 1983.
2 The number of US soldiers decreased from approximately 213,000 in 1990 to 122,000 in 1992 ("US Army Europe and Africa Mission and History," US Army Europe and

Africa, accessed 30 September 2025, https://www.europeafrica.army.mil/Mission-History/). Under the Strategic Arms Reduction Treaty (signed in 1991 and fully implemented by 2001), "80 percent of all the world's strategic nuclear weapons were dismantled" (Strategic Arms Reduction Treaty, Center for Arms Control and Non-proliferation, 16 November 2022, https://armscontrolcenter.org/strategic-arms-reduction-treaty-start-i/). Department of Defense, Office of International Security Affairs, *United States Security Strategy for the East Asia-Pacific Region* (Department of Defense, February 1995).

3   Department of Defense, Office of International Security Affairs, *United States Security Strategy*.
4   Department of Defense, Office of International Security Affairs, *United States Security Strategy*.
5   Department of Defense, Office of International Security Affairs, *United States Security Strategy*.
6   Miyume Tanji, *Myth, Protest, and Struggle in Okinawa* (Routledge, 2006), 156.
7   Regarding jurisdiction, as of 2003, the United States "rejected all subsequent requests for early hand-over except one, a 1996 case in which a sailor pleaded guilty to American authorities for the attempted murder (slitting the throat) and robbery of a 20-year-old Japanese woman" [Chalmers Johnson, "Three Rapes: The Status of Forces Agreement and Okinawa," *Asia-Pacific Journal* 1, iss. 4 (10 April 2003): 1–19, https://apjjf.org/chalmers-johnson/2021/article]; Department of Defense, "Operational Requirements and Concept of Operations for MCAS Futenma Relocation, Okinawa, Japan" (Department of Defense, 29 September 1997).
8   Ota Masahide, "Governor Ota at the Supreme Court of Japan," in *Okinawa: Cold War Island*, ed. Chalmers Johnson (Japan Policy Research Institute, 1999), 205–14.
9   Quoted in Ota, "Governor Ota," 212–13.
10 Quoted in Ota, "Governor Ota," 205.
11 Gavan McCormack and Satoko Oka Norimatsu, *Resistant Islands: Okinawa Confronts Japan and the United States* (Rowman & Littlefield, 2012), 140–41.
12 McCormack and Norimatsu, *Resistant Islands*, 147.
13 Nago City Office, *Issues of US Military Bases and Relocation Marine Corps Air Station (MCAS) Futenma to Henoko, Nago City*, (Nago City Office, n.d.), https://www.city.nago.okinawa.jp/kurashi/2018083000044/file_contents/IssuesofUSmilitarybases.pdf; Tome Chie, "Legends Tell of Dugong Curses," *Ryukyu Shimpo*, 19 April 2017, https://english.ryukyushimpo.jp/2017/04/26/26871/.
14 McCormack and Norimatsu, *Resistant Islands*, 93.
15 Quoted in McCormack and Norimatsu, *Resistant Islands*, 98.
16 Shimabukuro Natsuko, "Kyū beigun yōchi no genjō kaifuku ni sosogareta Nihon no 129 oku en," *Webronza*, 18 November 2018, https://webronza.asahi.com/politics/articles/2018111400003.html. Between December 1995 and January 1996, the marine corps mistakenly fired hundreds of depleted uranium rounds at Tori Shima, an offshore training range, but they kept the incident secret for more than a year, likely for fear of exacerbating Okinawan rage in the aftermath of the rape [Jon Mitchell, *Poisoning the Pacific: The US Military's Secret Dumping of Plutonium, Chemical Weapons, and Agent Orange* (Rowman & Littlefield, 2000), 134–47].
17 Between 2007 and 2016, only 18 percent of SOFA-status suspects were prosecuted, compared to 41 percent of Japanese suspects. Shimabukuro Ryota, "US Military Crime's Low Indictment Rates Appear Affected by Secret Agreement," *Ryukyu*

Shimpo, 11 December 2017, https://english.ryukyushimpo.jp/2017/12/14/28195/; Paul Richter, "Officer in Japan Gets U.S. Support in E-Mail Snafu," *Los Angeles Times*, 7 February 2001, https://www.latimes.com/archives/la-xpm-2001-feb-07-mn-22235-story.html.

18 Jon Mitchell, "Okinawa: U.S. Marines Corps Training Lectures Denigrate Local Residents, Hide Military Crimes," *Asia-Pacific Journal* 14, iss. 13, no. 4 (1 July 2016): 1–5, https://apjjf.org/2016/13/mitchell.

19 Quoted in Mitchell, "Okinawa."

20 Yamamoto Akiko, *Nichibei Chiikyōtei: Zainichi Beigun to "Dōmei" no 70 nen* (Chūōkōron Shinsha, 2019), i–ii.

21 Yamamoto, *Nichibei Chiikyōtei*, ii; Maedomari Hiromori, ed., *Hontō wa Kenpō yori Taisetsu na "Nichibei Chii Kyōtei Nyūmon"* (Sōgensha, 2013), 107.

22 DUTY FREE SHOPP. X Kakumakushaka, "Tami no Domino," on *Oto Ashagi* (2006), https://kakumakushaka.com/discography/oto-ashagi/; Yuken Teruya, *For the World to Come* (2004) in Yuken Teruya, *Okinawa Heavy Pop* (Okinawa Prefectural Museum and Art Museum, 2023); James Brooke, "Ginowan Journal: A Crash, and the Scent of Pizzatocracy, Anger Okinawa," *New York Times*, 13 September 2004, 4.

23 McCormack and Norimatsu, *Resistant Islands*, 69–70.

24 McCormack and Norimatsu, *Resistant Islands*, 32–34, includes the quote from Ishiyama Hisao, *Kyokasho Kentei: Okinawa Sen "Shudan Jiketsu" Mondai kara Kangaeru* (Iwanami Shoten, 2008), 56.

25 Okinawa Jinken Kyōkai, *Sengo Okinawa no Jinkenshi* (Kōbunken, 2012), 198–99; McCormack and Norimatsu, *Resistant Islands*, 37–38.

26 Tanaka Nobumasa, "Desecration of the Dead: Bereaved Okinawan Families Sue Yasukuni to End Relatives' Enshrinement," trans. Steve Rabson, *Asia-Pacific Journal* 6, iss. 5 (3 May 2008): 1–4, https://apjjf.org/nobumasa-tanaka/2744/article; McCormack and Norimatsu, *Resistant Islands*, 38.

27 Quoted in Tanaka, "Desecration of the Dead." Taiwanese and Koreans filed similar lawsuits to remove the names of family members forced to serve in the imperial military from Yasukuni's rolls of war heroes, but Japanese courts likewise rejected their claims. Protecting the shrine's right to glorify imperial aggression was an important tool in right-wingers' culture war on historical memory, which attempted to sweep aside atrocities committed against the subjects of the imperial colonies or, in the case of Okinawa, a quasi-colony.

28 E/CN.4/2006/16/Add.2, United Nations, Economic and Social Council, Commission on Human Rights, Racism, Racial Discrimination, Xenophobia and All Forms of Discrimination: Report of the Special Rapporteur on Contemporary Forms of Racism, Racial Discrimination, Xenophobia and Related Intolerance, Doudou Diène: Mission to Japan (24 January 2006), https://digitallibrary.un.org/record/566139/usage?ln=en&v=pdf.

29 Quoted in Steve Rabson, "Being Okinawan in Japan: The Diaspora Experience," *Asia-Pacific Journal* 10, iss. 12, no. 2 (19 March 2012): 1–11, https://apjjf.org/2012/10/12/steve-rabson/3720/article.

30 CCPR/C/JPN/CO/5, United Nations, Human Rights Committee, Consideration of Reports Submitted by States Parties Under Article 40 of the Covenant: Japan (18 December 2008), https://docs.un.org/en/CCPR/C/JPN/CO/5.

31 UNESCO, *Interactive Atlas of the World's Languages in Danger* (UNESCO, 2009).

32 As for Japan's recognition of Ainu as indigenous, some critics have pointed out that it offers no recognition of mainland oppression or reparations for dispossessed communities [e.g., see Leni Charbonneau and Hiroshi Maruyama, "A Critique on the New Ainu Policy: How Japan's Politics of Recognition Fails to Fulfill the Ainu's Indigenous Rights," *Hurights Osaka: Focus* 96 (June 2019), https://www.hurights.or.jp/archives/focus/section3/2019/06/a-critique-on-the-new-ainu-policy-how-japans-politics-of-recognition-fails-to-fulfill-the-ainus-indi.html]. CCPR/C/JPN/6, United Nations, International Covenant on Civil and Political Rights, Human Rights Committee, Consideration of Reports Submitted by States Parties Under Article 40 of the Covenant: Sixth Periodic Report of States Parties: Japan (26 April 2012); Ministry of Foreign Affairs of Japan, "Comments by the Government of Japan Regarding the Concluding Observations of the Committee on the Elimination of Racial Discrimination," 20 June 2016.

33 Tomigusuku City Council, "Opinion Statement Requesting the UN Human Rights Treaty Bodies to Revise Their Understanding That the 'People of Okinawa Are Indigenous People of Japan' and to Retract Such Recommendations," 22 December 2015; G.A. Res. 295 A, United Nations Declaration on the Rights of Indigenous Peoples, A/RES/61/295 (13 September 2007).

34 Tanji, *Myth, Protest, and Struggle*, 49; Jonathan Watts, "Okinawa Diary," *Guardian*, 24 July 2000, https://www.theguardian.com/business/2000/jul/24/4. During the Okinawa boom, one proverb was often used to symbolize islanders' carefree attitude: "*Nankurunaisa*" ("Everything will turn out fine"). But it omitted the first half, which stated, "*Makutōsōkē*," meaning "If you persevere in an honest way." Like other depictions of Okinawans, mainlanders took what they wanted but left out what did not comply with their stereotypes.

35 Wesley Ueunten, "Making Sense of Diasporic Okinawan Identity Within US Global Militarisation," *Intersections: Gender and Sexuality in Asia and the Pacific*, iss. 37 (March 2015), http://intersections.anu.edu.au/issue37/ueunten1.htm.

36 For example, see Uranaka Taiga, "The Sacrificed Island's Dream Remains Deferred," *Japan Times*, 14 July 2000, 1, 3.

37 UNESCO Dec. 24 COM X.C.1, Report of the Twenty-Fourth Session of the World Heritage Committee: Gusuku Sites and Related Properties of the Kingdom of Ryukyu (Japan) (2000).

Chapter 10

1 Jon Mitchell, "These Two Islands, 1,400 Miles Apart, Are Banding Together Against U.S. Bases," Foreign Policy in Focus, 20 March 2018, https://fpif.org/these-two-islands-1400-miles-apart-are-banding-together-against-to-u-s-bases/; Emma Chanlett-Avery, Christopher T. Mann, and Joshua A. Williams, "U.S. Military Presence on Okinawa and Realignment to Guam," Congressional Research Service, 9 April 2019, https://www.congress.gov/crs-product/IF10672. "Both the supposed eight thousand [marines] to be transferred to Guam and the ten thousand to move to Henoko were phantom, groundless figures" because at the time, the total number of marines in Okinawa was some 13,000 [Gavan McCormack and Satoko Oka Norimatsu, *Resistant*

Islands: Okinawa Confronts Japan and the United States (Rowman & Littlefield, 2012), 104].

2 Quoted in McCormack and Norimatsu, *Resistant Islands*, 105.
3 McCormack and Norimatsu, *Resistant Islands*, 56, 62.
4 McCormack and Norimatsu, *Resistant Islands*, 115–21.
5 Quoted in McCormack and Norimatsu, *Resistant Islands*, 117–21; Al Kamen, "Among Leaders at Summit, Hu's First," *Washington Post*, 14 April 2010, http://www.washingtonpost.com/wp-dyn/content/article/2010/04/13/AR2010041304461.html.
6 McCormack and Norimatsu, *Resistant Islands*, 119, 128.
7 Quoted in McCormack and Norimatsu, *Resistant Islands*, 130.
8 David Vine, *Base Nation: How US Military Bases Abroad Harm America and the World* (Metropolitan Books, 2015), 304–8.
9 McCormack and Norimatsu, *Resistant Islands*, 259–60.
10 Jon Mitchell, "In Preparation to Join US Wars, Japan Dismantles Freedom of the Press," Freedom of the Press Foundation, 10 December 2015, https://freedom.press/news/in-preparation-to-join-us-wars-japan-dismantles-freedom-of-the-press/.
11 Japan Federation of Bar Associations, "Statement Opposing the Bills to Revise National Security Policies," 14 May 2015, https://www.nichibenren.or.jp/en/document/statements/150514.html; Mitchell, "In Preparation." The LDP government showered its gratitude on the US architects of the defense guidelines by awarding the Order of the Rising Sun to Armitage and Nye, the latest in a long line of American recipients dating back to Major James R. Wasson, the Civil War veteran who had orchestrated the Meiji government's invasion of Taiwan in 1874.
12 Graham Smith, "The Osprey: Good Reviews, but a Costly Program," NPR, 24 October 2011, https://www.npr.org/2011/10/24/141589693/the-osprey-good-reviews-but-a-costly-program.
13 Jon Mitchell, "Okinawan Leaders Carry Osprey Protest to Tokyo," *Asia-Pacific Journal* 10, iss. 54, no. 139 (31 January 2013): 1–4, https://apjjf.org/jon-mitchell/4749/article.
14 "Okinawa Governor Nakaima Should Resign for Betraying the Okinawan People by Approving the Henoko Landfill," *Ryukyu Shimpo*, 28 December 2013, https://english.ryukyushimpo.jp/2013/12/.
15 Gavan McCormack, "'All Japan' versus 'All Okinawa'—Abe Shinzo's Military-Firstism," *Asia-Pacific Journal* 13, iss. 11, no. 1 (16 March 2015): 1–18, https://apjjf.org/2015/13/10/gavan-mccormack/4299.
16 Onaga Takeshi, oral statement at the United Nations Human Rights Council by the governor of Okinawa, 21 September 2015.
17 Parts of this description appear in Jon Mitchell, "The Peacemakers of Okinawa," *Japan Times*, 12 June 2016, 13–15.
18 Shimabukuro Fumiko, *Watashi no Sensō Taiken: Jigoku no yō na Okinawa Sen o Ikinuite* (2014 Nen Kokusai Fujin Dē no Tsudoi Jikkō Iinkai, 2014); Jon Mitchell, "The Battle of Okinawa: America's Good War Gone Bad," *Japan Times*, 31 March 2015, 10; Jon Mitchell, "On Okinawa, U.S. Marines Raise Tensions with Accusations and Arrests of Peace Campaigners," *Asia-Pacific Journal* 13, iss. 9, no. 1 (2 March 2015): 1–8, https://apjjf.org/jon-mitchell/4819/article.
19 For a partial list of injuries, see International Movement Against All Forms of Discrimination and Racism and All Okinawa Council for Human Rights, *Joint Report: Silencing the Voices of Okinawans* (3 February 2017), 16–23; McCormack, "'All Japan.'"

20 Megumi Ryūnosuke, *Okinawa yo, Amaeruna!* (WAC Bunko, 2015); Megumi Ryūnosuke and Watanabe Tetsuya, *Okinawa o hontō ni Aishitekureru nonara Kenmin ni Esa o Ataenaide kudasai* (Business Sha, 2017); International Movement Against All Forms of Discrimination and Racism and All Okinawa Council for Human Rights, *Joint Report*, 7–8, 19.
21 Mitchell, "On Okinawa, U.S. Marines"; "US Marines Official Dismissed for Leaking Video of Arrest of Henoko Protesters," *Ryukyu Shimpo*, 20 March 2015, https://english.ryukyushimpo.jp/2015/03/27/17631/.
22 Jane Perlez, "Calls Grow in China to Press Claim for Okinawa," *New York Times*, 14 June 2013, 4.
23 Gisela Grieger, *Sino-Japanese Controversy over the Senkaku/Diaoyu/Diaoyutai Islands: An Imminent Flashpoint in the Indo-Pacific?* (European Parliamentary Research Service, July 2021); "About the Senkaku Islands," Ishigaki City Senkaku Islands Digital Portal, accessed 2 October 2025, https://www.senkaku-islands.jp/en/about/.
24 Grieger, *Sino-Japanese Controversy*.
25 Grieger, *Sino-Japanese Controversy*.
26 *The Agreement Between the United States of America and Japan Concerning the Ryukyu Islands and the Daito Islands: Hearing on the Okinawa Reversion Treaty*, 92nd Cong., 1st sess. (27 October 1971), 91; Kimie Hara, "Okinawa, Taiwan, and the Senkaku/Diaoyu Islands in United States–Japan–China Relations," *Asia-Pacific Journal* 13, iss. 28, no. 2 (13 July 2015), https://apjjf.org/2015/13/28/kimie-hara/4341.
27 Mark E. Manyin, *The Senkakus (Diaoyu/Diaoyutai) Dispute: U.S. Treaty Obligations* (Congressional Research Service, updated March 1, 2021); quoted in McCormack and Norimatsu, *Resistant Islands*, 217.
28 "US-China Relations," Council on Foreign Relations, accessed 2 October 2, 2025, https://www.cfr.org/timeline/us-china-relations; Edward Cody, "China Boosts Military Spending," *Washington Post*, 5 March 2007, https://www.washingtonpost.com/wp-dyn/content/article/2007/03/04/AR2007030400401.html; Jon Mitchell, *Poisoning the Pacific: The US Military's Secret Dumping of Plutonium, Chemical Weapons, and Agent Orange* (Rowman & Littlefield, 2000), 20–21.
29 McCormack and Norimatsu, *Resistant Islands*, 210–18; Elaine Lies, "Shintaro Ishihara, Japanese Politician Who Set Off Row with China, Dies at 89," Reuters, 1 February 2022, https://www.reuters.com/world/asia-pacific/shintaro-ishihara-japanese-politician-who-set-off-row-with-china-dies-89-nhk-2022-02-01/. Ishihara's provocations included denials of the Rape of Nanking and fearmongering that Korean and Chinese residents would commit crimes following a future large earthquake in the capital, particularly incendiary given the Japanese massacres of Koreans that had occurred after the 1923 Tokyo tremor.
30 Perlez, "Calls Grow."
31 "Ryukyu Issue Offers Leverage to China," *Global Times*, 11 May 2013, https://www.globaltimes.cn/content/780732.shtml.
32 Matsushima Yasukatsu, "Okinawa Is a Japanese Colony," trans. Kaneko Erika, *KAN: Quarterly for History, Environment, Civilization* 43 (Autumn 2010): 195.
33 "Inochi, songen mō ubawasenai," *Okinawa Times*, 19 June 2016, 31.
34 Jon Mitchell, "PFAS Contamination from US Military Facilities in Mainland Japan and Okinawa," *Asia-Pacific Journal* 18, iss. 16, no. 9 (15 August 2020): 1–19, https://apjjf.org/2020/16/jmitchell.

35 Brandon Marc Higa, "Unpacking Okinawa's 'Suitcase Murder': Revisiting Extraterritoriality Protections for Military Contractors Under the U.S.-Japan SOFA Supplementary Agreement," *Asian-Pacific Law and Policy Journal* 21, no. 2 (May 2020): 9–20; US Naval Criminal Investigative Service, Report of Investigation (Closed), 4 October 2016.
36 *Agreement Between the Government of Japan and the Government of the United States of America on Cooperation with Regard to Implementation Practices Relating to the Civilian Component of the United States Armed Forces in Japan*, Ministry of Foreign Affairs of Japan, 16 January 2017.
37 Tabuki Yoko, "Looking Back on the Distressful 12 Years in Takae Through Photos," *Ryukyu Shimpo*, 11 October 2019, https://english.ryukyushimpo.jp/2019/10/16/31132/.
38 Iha Yoshiyasu, "Kaisetsu: Yanbaru no mori to Takae heripaddo no kensetsu," in *Okinawa: Aragau Takae no Mori*, ed. Yamashiro Hiroaki (Kōbunken, 2017), 85; Tabuki, "Looking Back."
39 Iha, "Kaisetsu," 87; Tabuki, "Looking Back"; International Movement Against All Forms of Discrimination and Racism and All Okinawa Council for Human Rights, *Joint Report*, 24.
40 Iha, "Kaisetsu," 87–88.
41 International Movement Against All Forms of Discrimination and Racism and All Okinawa Council for Human Rights, *Joint Report*, 4–6.
42 G.A. Opinion No. 55/2018, United Nations Human Rights Council, Opinions Adopted by the Working Group on Arbitrary Detention at its Eighty-Second Session, 20–24 August 2018: Opinion No. 55/2018 Concerning Yamashiro Hiroji (Japan) (27 December 2018); "Open Space for Protest Must Be Created in Okinawa," International Movement Against All Forms of Discrimination and Racism, 16 June 2017, https://imadr.org/unhrc35-sideevent-summary-freedomofexpression-okinawa japan 16june2017/; "Prominent Peace Activist Detained Without Bail," Amnesty International, 26 January 2017, https://www.amnesty.org/en/documents/asa22/5552/2017/en/.

Chapter 11

1 Ai Abe, "An Outstanding Claim: The Ryukyu/Okinawa Peoples' Right to Self-Determination Under International Human Rights Law," *Asian Journal of International Law* (2022): 23.
2 Tamaki Denny, "'Okinawa fukki 50 shūnenkinen shikiten' shikiji," 15 May 2022, https://www.pref.okinawa.jp/kensei/kencho/1001519/1001521/1001527.html.
3 Tamaki, "Okinawa fukki."
4 Tamaki, "Okinawa fukki."
5 Nippon Hōsō Kyōkai, *Fukki 50 nen no Okinawa ni kansuru ishiki chōsa* (Nippon Hōsō Kyōkai, 2022), https://www.nhk.or.jp/bunken/research/yoron/pdf/20220516_1.pdf. The survey compiled responses from 812 residents of Okinawa and 1,115 residents of mainland Japan.

6   Janessa Pon, "US Forces Japan Returns 9,852 Acres of Okinawan Land," Marines, 22 December 2016, https://www.marines.mil/News/News-Display/Article/1036517/us-forces-japan-returns-9852-acres-of-okinawan-land/; "Hokubu kunrenjō ato kara PCB seikaiisan suisenchi doramukan hakken chiten de," *Ryukyu Shimpo*, 9 March 2019, https://ryukyushimpo.jp/news/entry-886156.html; "Bakuhatsu no kanōsei hikuikedo . . . shuryūdan doko ni kieta," *Okinawa Times*, 24 January 2024, https://www.okinawatimes.co.jp/articles/-/1296225.

7   "U.S. Experts Say Plan to Replace Futenma Is the 'Worst Solution,'" *Asahi Shimbun*, 23 September 2024, https://www.asahi.com/ajw/articles/15422915; Okinawa Prefectural Government, *What Okinawa Wants You to Understand About the US Military Bases* (Okinawa Prefectural Government, 2018), 21.

8   National Security Agency, "NSA SIGINT Site Relocated in Japan: The Story Behind the Move," 16 March 2007; Jon Mitchell, "Nuchi Du Takara, Okinawan Resistance and the Battle for Henoko Bay," *Asia-Pacific Journal* 11, iss. 35, no. 3 (1 September 2013): 1–10, https://apjjf.org/2014/11/35/jon-mitchell/4173/article.

9   US Air Force, *Integrated Cultural Resources Management Plan for Kadena Air Base* (US Air Force, January 2013), 3-14, 4-19, 2-12.

10 Maedomari Hiromori, "Okinawa Demands Democracy: The Heavy Hand of Japanese and American Rule," trans. Joseph Essertier, *Asia-Pacific Journal* 18, iss. 16, no. 4 (15 August 2020): 1–18, https://apjjf.org/2020/16/maedomari; Yoshida Kensei, *Democracy Betrayed: Okinawa Under US Occupation* (Western Washington University, 2001), 167.

11 Jon Mitchell, *Poisoning the Pacific: The US Military's Secret Dumping of Plutonium, Chemical Weapons, and Agent Orange* (Rowman & Littlefield, 2020), 97–99, 141.

12 Department of Defense, press briefing on the navy, 2 May 2018; US Marine Corps, *Integrated Natural Resources and Cultural Resources Management Plan* (US Marine Corps, April 2014), 281–83; Okinawa Prefectural Government, *What Okinawa Wants*, 12.

13 Okinawa Prefectural Government, *What Okinawa Wants*, 12; Eric Johnston, "Tourism and Logistics: Okinawa's Latest Plan to Boost Its Economy," *Japan Times*, 15 May 2022, https://www.japantimes.co.jp/news/2022/05/15/national/okinawa-economic-development-local-leaders/.

14 Kodama Shogo, "Okinawa Rivals Hawaii in Tourist Numbers but Not Spending," *NikkeiAsia*, 29 April 2022, https://asia.nikkei.com/Business/Travel-Leisure/Okinawa-rivals-Hawaii-in-tourist-numbers-but-not-spending; Kuniyoshi Mika, "Tourists Visiting Okinawa Drop 63% in 2020 amid Pandemic," *Asahi Shimbun*, 27 January 2021, https://www.asahi.com/ajw/articles/14140340.

15 Harold Rickard, "The Okinawa Land Problem," *Japan Christian Quarterly* 37 (1971); Arnold G. Fisch Jr., *Military Government in the Ryukyu Islands, 1945–1950* (Center of Military History, US Army, 1988), 127; "'Chōju no ken' shokku futatabi," *Okinawa Times*, 14 December 2017, https://www.okinawatimes.co.jp/articles/-/183880; "Okinawa kenmin no 'kenkō jumyō,'" *Okinawa Times*, 25 December 2024, https://www.okinawatimes.co.jp/articles/-/1496898. The average healthy-life expectancy for Okinawan men was 72.6 years (forty-fifth out of Japan's forty-seven prefectures), and for women, 75.5 years (forty-sixth in Japan); Jon Mitchell and Shimabukuro Natsuko, dirs., *Nuchi nu Miji: Okinawa's Water of Life* (Ryūkyū Asahi Hōsō, 2022).

16 Jon Mitchell, "Contamination at Camp Kinser: 2019 Report Detailed High Health Risks for Children, Base Workers—but Military Failed to Inform," *Okinawa Times*, 17 February 2023, https://www.okinawatimes.co.jp/articles/-/1103107.

17 "American Legion Post Awarded for Community Service at Okinawa Cemetery," *Stars and Stripes*, 5 July 2017, https://www.stripes.com/theaters/asia_pacific/american-legion-post-awarded-for-community-service-at-okinawa-cemetery-1.476686; Jon Mitchell, "NCIS Case Files Reveal Undisclosed US Military Sex Crimes in Okinawa," *Intercept*, 3 October 2021, https://theintercept.com/2021/10/03/okinawa-sexual-crimes-us-military/. Among recent military crimes, sixty-nine marines were convicted at courts-martial for sexual offenses targeting children between 2015 and 2020.

18 Jon Mitchell, "The Battle for Press Freedom on Okinawa," *FCCJ Number 1 Shimbun*, December 2016, 6–7.

19 Gavan McCormack and Satoko Oka Norimatsu, *Resistant Islands: Okinawa Confronts Japan and the United States* (Rowman & Littlefield, 2012), 39; "'Heiwanoishiji' koku meishasū ichiran," Okinawa Prefectural Government, updated 18 June 2025, https://www.pref.okinawa.jp/heiwakichi/jinken/1008269/1008287/1008288/1008292.html; "'Usotsuki' 'Kaere'—Abe shushō no aisatsuchū ni kōgi no koe," *Okinawa Times*, 24 June 2019, https://www.okinawatimes.co.jp/articles/-/436502; "Okinawa zen senbotsusha tsuitō shiki de dogō," *Nikkan Gendai*, 25 June 2019, https://www.nikkan-gendai.com/articles/view/news/256885.

20 "Japanese Professor Claims Comfort Women System Was a 'Crime of the State,'" *Hankyoreh*, 23 October 2019, https://english.hani.co.kr/arti/english_edition/e_international/914318.html; "Monument for 'Comfort Women' Tells the Truth," *Japan Press Weekly*, 27 May 2013, https://www.japan-press.co.jp/s/news/?id=5706.

21 "SDF's Pivot to Southwest a Cause for Concern in Okinawa," *Asahi Shimbun*, 14 May 2023, https://www.asahi.com/ajw/articles/14907701.

22 "Arms Control and Proliferation Profile: North Korea," Arms Control Association, June 2024, https://www.armscontrol.org/factsheets/arms-control-and-proliferation-profile-north-korea.

23 Mark E. Manyin, *The Senkakus (Diaoyu/Diaoyutai) Dispute: U.S. Treaty Obligations* (Congressional Research Service, updated 21 February 2017).

24 Consulate General Naha, "Okinawan Exceptionalism: The China Threat or Lack Thereof," cable, 26 April 2006.

25 "Barack Obama Says Asia-Pacific Is 'Top US Priority,'" BBC News, 17 November 2011, https://www.bbc.com/news/world-asia-15715446; "About USINDOPACOM," USINDOPACOM, accessed 2 October 2025, https://www.pacom.mil/about-usindopacom/; Matsuyama Naoki, "Cabinet Approves 3 New Security Documents to Bolster Defense," *Asahi Shimbun*, 16 December 2022, https://www.asahi.com/ajw/articles/14794341; Courtney Kube and Mosheh Gains, "Air Force General Predicts War with China in 2025, Tells Officers to Prep by Firing 'a Clip' at a Target, and 'Aim for the Head,'" NBC News, 28 January 2023, https://www.nbcnews.com/politics/national-security/us-air-force-general-predicts-war-china-2025-memo-rcna67967.

26 Hans Kristensen, "Nukes in the Taiwan Crisis," Federation of American Scientists, 13 May 2008, https://fas.org/publication/nukes-in-the-taiwan-crisis/.

27 Susan M. Gordon and Michael G. Mullen, chairs, "U.S.-Taiwan Relations in a New Era," Council on Foreign Relations, updated June 2023, https://www.cfr.org/task-force-report/us-taiwan-Relations-in-a-new-era; quoted in Gota Nishimura and Shukan Toyokeizai, "The Cost of the 'Taiwan Contingency' and Japan's Preparedness," Freeman Spogli Institute for International Studies, 14 August 2023, https://fsi.stanford.edu/news/cost-taiwan-contingency-and-japans-preparedness.

28 Oriana Skylar Mastro and Ian Easton, "Risk and Resiliency: China's Emerging Air Base Strike Threat," Project 2049 Institute, 8 November 2017, https://project2049.net/2017/11/08/risk-and-resiliency-chinas-emerging-air-base-strike-threat/; Ministry of Defense, *Chūgoku dandō misairu hassha ni tsuite* (Ministry of Defense, 4 August 2022), https://www.mod.go.jp/j/press/news/2022/08/04d.html.
29 "Japan Eyes Upgrade of 16 Airports, Ports for Possible Defense Use," Kyodo News, 27 March 2024, https://english.kyodonews.net/news/2024/03/c085935cd6cc-japan-eyes-upgrade-of-16-airports-ports-for-possible-defense-use.html; C. Douglas Lummis, "The People of Okinawa Don't Want to Be Pawns in a US-China Conflict," Jacobin, 3 November 2023, https://jacobin.com/2023/11/okinawa-japan-china-us-militarism-antiwar-activism.
30 "Challenges Crop Up After Practice Evacuation of Okinawa Islands," *Asahi Shimbun*, 31 January 2024, https://www.asahi.com/ajw/articles/15140184; "Japan to Build Shelters on Isles Near Taiwan in Case of Attack," *Asahi Shimbun*, 30 March 2024, https://www.asahi.com/ajw/articles/15215063.

Coda

1 Central Intelligence Agency, *A Master Narratives Approach to Understanding Base Politics in Okinawa* (Central Intelligence Agency, 2012).
2 The merits of US military-led relief operations came under scrutiny following the 11 March 2011 earthquake and tsunami in northeast Japan, when hundreds of American sailors aboard the USS *Ronald Reagan* were exposed to fallout from the Fukushima nuclear power plant meltdowns and the military disposed of low-level radioactive waste in the sewers beneath its mainland bases (Jon Mitchell, *Poisoning the Pacific: The US Military's Secret Dumping of Plutonium, Chemical Weapons, and Agent Orange* (Rowman & Littlefield, 2020), 166–69).
3 Central Intelligence Agency, *Understanding Base Politics*, 3.
4 Central Intelligence Agency, *Understanding Base Politics*, 20.
5 "Guidance from the Commander," U.S. Forces Japan, accessed 2 October 2025, https://www.usfj.mil/About-USFJ/; "Significance of the Japan-U.S. Security Arrangements," Ministry of Defense, accessed 2 October 2025, https://www.mod.go.jp/en/j-us-alliance/security-arrangements/index.html.
6 Maedomari Hiromori, "Okinawa Demands Democracy: The Heavy Hand of Japanese and American Rule," trans. Joseph Essertier, *Asia-Pacific Journal* 18, iss. 16, no. 4 (15 August 2020): 1–18, https://apjjf.org/2020/16/maedomari.
7 Mike Mochizuki, "Yokushiryoku to Zaioki Beikaiheitai," in *Kyozō no Yokushiryoku*, ed. Shin Gaikō Initiative (Junpōsha, 2014), 97–128; quoted in Satoko Oka Norimatsu, "Hatoyama's Confession: The Myth of Deterrence and the Failure to Move a Marine Base Outside Okinawa," *Asia-Pacific Journal* 9, iss. 9, no. 3, (28 February 2011): 1–15, https://apjjf.org/2011/9/9/satoko-norimatsu/3495/article.
8 Paul O'Shea, "The US-Japan Alliance and the Role of the US Marines on Okinawa in Extended Deterrence," *Social Science Japan Journal* 27, no. 1 (February 2024): 1–19; Mochizuki, "Yokushiryoku," 123.

9   Quoted in Yoshimoto Hideko, *U.S. Occupation of Okinawa: A Soft Power Theory Approach* (Kyoto University Press, 2019), 155–56; quoted in Jon Mitchell, "'Seconds Away from Midnight': U.S. Nuclear Missile Pioneers on Okinawa Break Fifty Year Silence on a Hidden Nuclear Crisis of 1962," *Asia-Pacific Journal* 10, iss. 30, no. 1 (22 July 2012): 1–10, https://apjjf.org/2012/10/30/jon-mitchell/3800/article.

10   Quoted in Yoshida Kensei, *Democracy Betrayed: Okinawa Under US Occupation* (Western Washington University, 2001), 188; National Defense Authorization Act: Section 1253 Assessment, "Regain the Advantage," US Indo-Pacific Command, 2020, https://int.nyt.com/data/documenthelper/6864-national-defense-strategy-summ/8851517f5e10106bc3b1/optimized/full.pdf; Luke A. Nicastro, "U.S. Defense Infrastructure in the IndoPacific: Background and Issues for Congress," Congressional Research Service, 6 June 2023, 21, https://www.congress.gov/crs-product/R47589.

11   For reports of this dispersal, see, for example, Stephen Losey, "F-22s Arrive at Kadena, as Aging F-15s Prepare to Depart," *Defense News*, 8 November 2022, https://www.defensenews.com/air/2022/11/07/f-22s-arrive-at-kadena-as-aging-f-15s-prepare-to-depart/, and Sam Roggeveen, "The Real Message B-52s Send from Northern Australia," *Interpreter*, 4 November 2022, https://www.lowyinstitute.org/the-interpreter/real-message-b-52s-send-northern-australia.

12   Nakanishi Hiroshi, "The Gulf War and Japanese Diplomacy," *Nippon.com*, 6 December 2011, https://www.nippon.com/en/features/c00202/#.

13   Jon Mitchell, "Igirisuhei ga Okinawa no beigun gun kichi de kunren: Hōteki ni mondai," *Okinawa Times*, 18 July 2016, https://www.okinawatimes.co.jp/articles/-/54456; Shioiri Yūichirō, "Orandagun ga kennai de kunren hokubu kunrenjō de beigun no nittei ni sanka," *Okinawa Times*, 28 April 2024, https://www.okinawatimes.co.jp/articles/-/1350654; Matthew M. Burke and Hana Kusumoto, "Okinawa Governor Blasts US Military Discipline as COVID-19 Cases Climb at Marine Base," *Stars and Stripes*, 27 December 2021, https://www.stripes.com/theaters/asia_pacific/2021-12-27/okinawa-governor-coronavirus-covid-19-camp-hansen-4097838.html; Jon Mitchell, "US Military Hid Discovery of Radioactive and PFAS Contamination at Scene of '17 Heli Crash," *Okinawa Times*, 30 July 2022, https://www.okinawatimes.co.jp/articles/-/997100.

14   Smedley D. Butler, *War Is a Racket* (Round Table Press, 1935), 1; "Host-Nation Deal Raises Prospect of Funding in Other Guises," *Asahi Shimbun*, 23 December 2021, https://www.asahi.com/ajw/articles/14508688; Department of Defense, Office of International Security Affairs, *United States Security Strategy for the East Asia-Pacific Region* (Department of Defense, February 1995).

15   Gavan McCormack and Satoko Oka Norimatsu, *Resistant Islands: Okinawa Confronts Japan and the United States* (Rowman & Littlefield, 2012), 105, 195.

16   "US Security Cooperation with Japan: Fact Sheet," Department of State, 20 January 2021, https://www.state.gov/u-s-security-cooperation-with-japan/.

17   Nozoe Fumiaki, "Okinawa beigun kichi no seiri shukushō o meguru nichibei kyōgi 1970–1974 nen," *Kokusai Anzen Hosho* 41, no. 2 (2013): 107–8. For US-Japan discussions to relocate USMC bases following the 1995 assault, see Yara Tomohiro, "Exploring Solutions to the US Military Base Issues in Okinawa," *Eurasia Border Review* 3, no. 2 (2012): 119–31; Maedomari Hiromori, "Okinawa Demands Democracy: The Heavy Hand of Japanese and American Rule," trans. Joseph

Essertier, *Asia-Pacific Journal* 18, iss. 16, no.4 (15 August 2020): 1–18, https://apjjf.org/2020/16/maedomari.

18 Okinawa Jinken Kyōkai, *Sengo Okinawa no Jinkenshi* (Kōbunken, 2012), 75.
19 Arasaki Moriteru, *Nihon ni totte Okinawa to wa nanika* (Iwanami Shoten, 2016), 206.
20 Matsushima Yasukatsu, "Okinawa Is a Japanese Colony," trans. Kaneko Erika, *KAN: Quarterly for History, Environment, Civilization* 43 (Autumn 2010): 190.
21 Quoted in Annmaria M. Shimabuku, *Alegal: Biopolitics and the Unintelligibility of Okinawan Life* (Fordham University Press, 2019), 118.
22 Quoted in Ōshiro Shōko, "Human Rights Violations in Colonial Contexts—Okinawa (Ryukyu-Lew Chew) Case," ed. Daniel Iwama, 13 May 2021, in *Call for Inputs: Transitional Justice Measures and the Legacy of Human Rights Violations in Colonial Contexts* (UN Human Rights Office of the High Commissioner, 19 July 2021), https://www.ohchr.org/sites/default/files/Documents/Issues/Truth/CallLegacyColonialism/CSO/Shoko-Oshiro.pdf; UN Human Rights Office of the High Commissioner, "Committee on the Elimination of Racial Discrimination Examines the Report of Japan," press release, 17 August 2018, https://www.ohchr.org/en/press-releases/2018/08/committee-elimination-racial-discrimination-examines-report-japan.
23 A prime example of the military's omissions of uncomfortable history was Kadena Air Base's online description of the 1959 Miyamori jet disaster (Jon Mitchell, "US Air Force Corrects Official Description of '59 Miyamori Elementary School Jet Crash, Stays Silent on Causes," *Okinawa Times*, 21 August 2024, https://www.okinawatimes.co.jp/articles/-/1418120). For an exploration of Chinese disinformation about Okinawa, see Kanematsu Yuichiro, "Social Media Fuel Pro-Okinawa Independence Disinformation Blitz," *NikkeiAsia*, 3 October 2024, https://asia.nikkei.com/Spotlight/Cybersecurity/Social-media-fuel-pro-Okinawa-independence-disinformation-blitz.
24 Quoted in Steve Rabson, "Being Okinawan in Japan: The Diaspora Experience," *Asia-Pacific Journal* 10, iss. 12, no. 2 (19 March 2012): 1–11, https://apjjf.org/2012/10/12/steve-rabson/3720/article; Okinawa Jinken Kyōkai, *Sengo Okinawa*, 127–32.
25 Arakaki Makoto, "Hawai'i *Uchinanchu* and Okinawa," in *Okinawan Diaspora*, ed. Ronald Y. Nakasone (University of Hawai'i Press, 2002), 141.
26 Jon Mitchell, "Campaigning to Save the Languages of Okinawa," *Japan Times*, 5 September 2010, 12; Fija Bairon, Matthias Brenzinger, and Patrick Heinrich, "The Ryukyus and the New, but Endangered, Languages of Japan," *Asia-Pacific Journal* 7, iss. 19, no. 2 (9 May 2009): 1–20, https://apjjf.org/patrick-heinrich/3138/article.
27 Medoruma Shun, "Hope," trans. Steve Rabson, *Asia-Pacific Journal* 14, iss. 12, no. 5 (15 June 2016): 1–4, https://apjjf.org/2016/12/medoruma; Medoruma's blog, *Uminari no Shima kara*, can be found at https://blog.goo.ne.jp/awamori777; Uema Yōko, "Clean Water," trans. Lisa Hofmann-Kuroda, *Guernica*, 1 May 2023, https://www.guernicamag.com/clean-water/.
28 Shawn De Haven attributes the lack of satirical comedy in mainland Japan to several factors, including media self-censorship and indirect pressure from the government. Shawn De Haven, "Comedians Who Dare: Political Satire in Contemporary Japan," *Asia-Pacific Journal* 18, iss. 16, no. 3, (15 August 2020): 1–19, https://apjjf.org/2020/16/dehaven.
29 Ōshiro, "Human Rights Violations."
30 "Okinawa ga mezasubeki sugata wa 'Tsuyoi kengen o motsu jichitai' ga 48% 'Genjō o iji' ga 42% 'Dokuritsu' wa 3%," *Okinawa Times*, 12 May 2022, https://www.okinawatimes.co.jp/articles/-/956771. The article notes that the proportion

of respondents supporting independence was almost identical to a similar survey in 2017. "Ryukyu Issue Offers Leverage to China," *Global Times*, 11 May 2013, https://www.globaltimes.cn/content/780732.shtml. Political scientist Shimabukuro Jun describes how Okinawa might learn from Scotland's model of devolution in "Okinawan Identity and the Struggle for Self-Determination," *Nippon.com*, 3 August 2015, https://www.nippon.com/en/in-depth/a04501/.

31 Chalmers Johnson, *Blowback: The Costs and Consequences of American Empire* (Little, Brown, 2000), 52.

32 Bankoku Shinryō Council on U.S. Military Base Issues, *Recommendations Toward Reducing the Burden of Military Bases on Okinawa in the New Security Environment* (Bankoku Shinryō Council on U.S. Military Base Issues, March 2021), https://storage.googleapis.com/studio-design-asset-files/projects/8dO8BMJran/s-1x1_848c07c5-ca47-4860-842e-e72a59ddd9d4.pdf.

BIBLIOGRAPHY

Ahagon Shōkō. *Beigun to Nōmin: Okinawaken Iejima*. Iwanami Shoten, 1973.
Ahagon Shōkō. *The Island Where People Live*. Translated by C. Harold Rickard. Christian Conference of Asia Communications, 1989.
Akamine Mamoru. *The Ryukyu Kingdom: Cornerstone of East Asia*. Edited by Robert Huey. Translated by Lina Terrell. University of Hawai'i Press, 2018.
Aoki, Takaju. *Matsushiro Dai Hon Ei: Rekishi no Shōgen*. Shin Nihon Shuppansha, 1997.
Appleman, Roy E., James M. Burns, Russell A. Gugeler, and John Stevens. *Okinawa: The Last Battle*. Department of the Army, Office of the Chief of Military History, 1948.
Arakawa Akira. *Ryūkyū Shobun Ikō*. Vol. 1. Asahi Shimbunsha, 1981.
Arasaki Moriteru. *Nihon ni totte Okinawa to wa nanika*. Iwanami Shoten, 2016.
Arasaki Moriteru. *Okinawa Gendai Shi*. Iwanami Shoten, 1996.
Beijing NGO Forum Workshop. *Military Violence and Women in Okinawa*. NGO Forum on Women Beijing, 7 September 1995.
Butler, Smedley D. *War Is a Racket*. Round Table Press, 1935.
Central Intelligence Agency. *A Master Narratives Approach to Understanding Base Politics in Okinawa*. Central Intelligence Agency, 2012.
Johnson, Chalmers. *Blowback: The Costs and Consequences of American Empire*. Little, Brown, 2000.
Chibana Shoichi. *Burning the Rising Sun: From Yomitan Village, Okinawa: Islands of U.S. Bases*. Translated by South Wind. South Wind, 1992.
Daws, Gavan. *Prisoners of the Japanese: POWs of World War II in the Pacific*. William Morrow, 1994.
Department of Defense, Office of International Security Affairs. *United States Security Strategy for the East Asia-Pacific Region*. Department of Defense, February 1995.
Dower, John W. *Embracing Defeat: Japan in the Wake of World War II*. W. W. Norton, 1999.
Dower, John W. *War Without Mercy: Race and Power in the Pacific War*. Pantheon Books, 1986.
Fisch, Arnold G., Jr. *Military Government in the Ryukyu Islands, 1945–1950*. Center of Military History, US Army, 1988.
Fukuchi Hiroaki. *Okinawa ni okeru Beigun no Hanzai*. Dōjidaisha, 1995.
Ginowan Shigikai Shi. Ginowan City Office, 2006.
Ginowanshiritsu Hakubutsukan, ed. *Isahama no Tochi Tōsō (Kaisetsuhen)*. Ginowan Shishi, vol. 8, Shiryōhen 7, Sengoshiryōhen 2. Okinawaken Ginowanshi Kyōiku Iinkai Kyōikubu, 2021.
Ginowanshiritsu Hakubutsukan, ed. *Isahama no Tochi Tōsō (Shiryōhen)*. Ginowan Shishi, vol. 8, Shiryōhen 7, Sengoshiryōhen 2. Okinawaken Ginowanshi Kyōiku Iinkai Bunkaka, 2019.
Grandin, Greg. *The End of the Myth: From the Frontier to the Border Wall in the Mind of America*. Metropolitan Books, 2019.

Grieger, Gisela. *Sino-Japanese Controversy over the Senkaku/Diaoyu/Diaoyutai Islands: An Imminent Flashpoint in the Indo-Pacific?* European Parliamentary Research Service, July 2021.

A Guide to Battle Sites and Military Bases in Okinawa City. Okinawa City Office, 2012.

Havens, Thomas R. H. *Fire Across the Sea: The Vietnam War and Japan, 1965–1975.* Princeton University Press, 1987.

Hickel, Walter J. *Who Owns America?* Prentice-Hall, 1971.

Hong Yunshin. *"Comfort Stations" as Remembered by Okinawans During World War II.* Translated and edited by Robert Ricketts. Brill, 2020.

Inoue Masamichi. *Okinawa and the U.S. Military: Identity Making in the Age of Globalization.* Columbia University Press, 2017.

Ishikawa Miyamori 630 Kai, ed. *Inochi to Heiwa no Kataribe: "Okinawa no Sora no Shita de: Shogen Ā kono Hisan: Ishikawa Miyamori Jettoki Tsuiraku Jiko."* Vol. 4. Ishikawa Miyamori 630 Kai, 2019.

Ishikawa Miyamori 630 Kai, ed. *Ishikawa Miyamori no Sangeki: Beikoku Kōbunshokan Bunsho ni Miru Jettoki Tsuiraku Jiken.* Ishikawa Miyamori 630 Kai, 2019.

Ishiyama Hisao. *Kyokasho Kentei: Okinawa Sen "Shudan Jiketsu" Mondai kara Kangaeru.* Iwanami Shoten, 2008.

Jahana, Naomi. *Chinmoku no Kioku 1948 nen: Hōdan no Shima Iejima Beigun LCT Bakuhatsu Jiken.* Impact Shuppankai, 2022.

Jeans, Roger B. *The CIA and Third Force Movements in China During the Early Cold War: The Great American Dream.* Lexington, 2018.

Johnson, Chalmers, ed. *Okinawa: Cold War Island.* Japan Policy Research Institute, 1999.

Kapur, Nick. *Japan at the Crossroads: Conflict and Compromise After Anpo.* Harvard University Press, 2018.

Kerr, George H. *Okinawa: The History of an Island People.* Rev. ed. Tuttle, 2000.

Kingston, Jeff, ed. *Press Freedom in Contemporary Japan.* Routledge, 2017.

Kuznick, Peter, and Oliver Stone. *The Untold History of the United States.* Gallery Books, 2012.

Leeker, Joe F. *The History of Air America.* University of Texas, 2015.

MacArthur, Douglas, and Center of Military History. *Reports of General MacArthur: The Campaigns of MacArthur in the Pacific.* Vol. 1. Center of Military History United States Army, 1966.

Maedomari, Hiromori, ed. *Hontō wa Kenpō yori Taisetsu na "Nichibei Chii Kyōtei Nyūmon."* Sōgensha, 2013.

Manyin, Mark E. *The Senkakus (Diaoyu/Diaoyutai) Dispute: U.S. Treaty Obligations.* Congressional Research Service, updated March 1, 2021.

McCormack, Gavan, and Satoko Oka Norimatsu. *Resistant Islands: Okinawa Confronts Japan and the United States.* Rowman & Littlefield, 2012.

Mitchell, Jon. *Poisoning the Pacific: The US Military's Secret Dumping of Plutonium, Chemical Weapons, and Agent Orange.* Rowman & Littlefield, 2020.

Mitchell, Jon. *Tsuiseki: Nichibei Chii Kyōtei to Kichi Kōgai.* Translated by Abe Kosuzu. Iwanami Shoten, 2018.

Mitchell, Jon. *Tsuiseki: Okinawa no Karehazai.* Translated by Abe Kosuzu. Kōbunken, 2014.

Miyagi Etsujiro, ed. *Shimpojiumu: Okinawa Senryo: Mirai e mukete.* Hirugisha, 1993.

M'Leod, John. *Narrative of a Voyage, in His Majesty's Late Ship Alceste, to the Yellow Sea, Along the Coast of Corea, and Through Its Numerous Hitherto Undiscovered Islands, to the Island of Lewchew; with an Account of Her Shipwreck in the Straits of Gaspar.* M. Carey and Son, 1818.

Morris, M. D. *Okinawa: A Tiger by the Tail*. Hawthorn, 1968.
Naha-shi Kikakubu Ichishi Henshūshitsuhen, ed. *Shashinshū Naha Hyaku nen no Ayumi*. Naha-shi Kikakubu Ichishi Henshūshitsuhen, 1980.
Nakasone, Ronald Y., ed. *Okinawan Diaspora*. University of Hawai'i Press, 2002.
Nash, Douglas E., Sr. *Battle of Okinawa: III MEF Staff Ride, Battle Book*. U.S. Marine Corps History Division, 2015.
Nippon Hōsō Kyōkai. *Fukki 50 nen no Okinawa ni kansuru Ishiki Chōsa*. Nippon Hōsō Kyōkai, 2022.
Nishime Junji. *Sengo Seiji o Ikite: Nikki*. Ryukyu Shimposha, 1998.
Nishizato Kikō. *Shinmatsu Chūryūnichi Kankeishi no Kenkyū*. Kyoto University Press, 2005.
Office of the Chief of Naval Operations. *Civil Affairs Handbook: Ryukyu (Loochoo) Islands*. Navy Department, 1944.
Okinawa City Planning Department Peace Culture Promotion Division, ed. *Beikoku ga Mita Koza Bōdō*. Okinawa City Hall, 1999.
Okinawa Jinken Kyōkai. *Sengo Okinawa no Jinkenshi*. Kōbunken, 2012.
Okinawa Prefectural Government. *What Okinawa Wants You to Understand About the US Military Bases*. Okinawa Prefectural Government, 2018.
Okinawa Times. *Okinawa no Shōgen: Gekidō no 25 Nenshi*. Vol. 1. Okinawa Times, 1971.
Okinawa Times Chūbūshisha Henshūbu. *Kichi de Hataraku: Gunsagyōin no Sengo*. Okinawa Times, 2013.
Okinawa Women Act Against Military Violence. *Okinawa Beihei ni yoru Josei he no Seihanzai*. 13th ed. Kichi Guntai o Yurusanai kōdō suru Onnatachi no Kai, 2023.
Ota Masahide. *The Battle of Okinawa: The Typhoon of Steel and Bombs*. Takeda Printing, 1984.
Ota Masahide. *Essays on Okinawa Problems*. Yui Shuppan, 2000.
Ota Masahide. *Minikui Nihonjin: Nihon no Okinawa Ishiki (Shinpan)*. Iwanami Gendai Bunko, 2000.
Ota Masahide. *Okinawa no Minshū Ishiki*. Shinsensha, 1976.
Perry, Matthew Calbraith. *Narrative of the Expedition of an American Squadron to the China Seas and Japan Performed in the Years 1852, 1853, and 1854, Under the Command of Commodore M. C. Perry*. Edited by Francis Lister Hawks. Beverley Tucker, Senate Printer, 1856.
Pires, Tomé. *The Suma Oriental of Tomé Pires and the Book of Francisco Rodrigues*. Translated by Armando Cortesão. Hakluyt Society, 1944.
Poole, Walter S. *The History of the Joint Chiefs of Staff*. Office of Joint History, Office of the Chairman of the Joint Chiefs of Staff, 2013.
Public Papers of the Presidents of the United States: Dwight D. Eisenhower (1954). US National Archives, 1960.
Rabson, Steve. *The Okinawan Diaspora in Japan: Crossing the Borders Within*. University of Hawai'i Press, 2011.
Ryūnosuke Megumi. *Okinawa yo, Amaeruna!* WAC Bunko, 2015.
Ryūnosuke Megumi and Watanabe Tetsuya. *Okinawa o hontō ni Aishitekureru nonara Kenmin ni Esa o Ataenaide kudasai*. Business Sha, 2017.
Ryukyu Shimpo. *Descent into Hell: Civilian Memories of the Battle of Okinawa*. Translated by Mark Ealey and Alastair McLauchlan. Merwin Asia, 2014.
Sarantakes, Nicholas Evan. *Keystone: The American Occupation of Okinawa and US–Japanese Relations*. Texas A&M University Press, 2000.

Schrivjers, Peter. *The GI War Against Japan: American Soldiers in Asia and the Pacific During World War II*. New York University Press, 2002.
Senaga Kamejiro. *Mimokuno Ikari: Moeagaru Okinawa*. Shin Nihon Press, 1971.
Serrano, Richard A. *Summoned at Midnight: A Story of Race and the Last Military Executions at Fort Leavenworth*. Beacon Press, 2019.
Setsu Shigematsu, and Keith L. Camacho, eds. *Militarized Currents: Toward a Decolonized Future in Asia and the Pacific*. University of Minnesota Press, 2010.
Shimabuku, Annmaria M. *Alegal: Biopolitics and the Unintelligibility of Okinawan Life*. Fordham University Press, 2019.
Shimabukuro Fumiko. *Watashi no Sensō Taiken: Jigoku no yō na Okinawa Sen o Ikinuite*. 2014 Nen Kokusai Fujin Dē no Tsudoi Jikkō Iinkai, 2014.
Shimojima Tetsurō. *Okinawa: Chibichiri Gama no "Shūdan Jiketsu."* Iwanami Shoten, 1992.
Shin Gaikō Initiative, ed. *Kyozō no Yokushiryoku*. Junpōsha, 2014.
Sledge, Eugene. *With the Old Breed: At Peleliu and Okinawa*. Presidio Press, 1981.
Smits, Gregory. *Maritime Ryukyu, 1050–1650*. University of Hawaiʻi Press, 2018.
Smits, Gregory. *Visions of Ryukyu: Identity and Ideology in Early-Modern Thought and Politics*. University of Hawaiʻi Press, 2017.
Spalding, J. W. *The Japan Expedition: Japan and Around the World*. Redfield, 1855.
Takahashi, Shinnosuke. *The Translocal Island of Okinawa: Anti-Base Activism and Grassroots Regionalism*. Bloomsbury Academic, 2024.
Takara Kurayoshi. *Ryūkyū Ōkoku*. Iwanami Shoten, 1993.
Tanji Miyume. *Myth, Protest, and Struggle in Okinawa*. Routledge, 2006.
Teruya Yuken. *Okinawa Heavy Pop*. Okinawa Prefectural Museum and Art Museum, 2023.
Uehara Kōsuke. *Kichi Okinawa no Kutō: Zengunrō Tōsōshi*. Sōkō, 1982.
US Air Force. *Integrated Cultural Resources Management Plan for Kadena Air Base*. US Air Force, January 2013.
US Marine Corps. *Integrated Natural Resources and Cultural Resources Management Plan*. US Marine Corps, April 2014.
Vine, David. *Base Nation: How U.S. Military Bases Abroad Harm America and the World*. Metropolitan Books, 2015.
Wakaizumi Kei. *The Best Course Available: A Personal Account of the Secret U.S.-Japan Okinawa Reversion Negotiations*. University of Hawaiʻi Press, 2002.
Weiner, Tim. *Legacy of Ashes: The History of the CIA*. Doubleday, 2007.
Wiley, Peter Booth, with Korogi Ichiro. *Yankees in the Land of the Gods: Commodore Perry and the Opening of Japan*. Viking, 1990.
Williams, Samuel Wells. *A Journal of the Perry Expedition to Japan (1853–1854)*. Kelly & Walsh, 1910.
Yamamoto Akiko. *Nichibei Chiikyōtei: Zainichi Beigun to "Dōmei" no 70 nen*. Chūōkōron Shinsha, 2019.
Yamashiro Hiroaki. *Okinawa: Aragau Takae no Mori*. Kōbunken, 2017.
Yoshida Kensei. *Democracy Betrayed: Okinawa Under US Occupation*. Western Washington University, 2001.
Yoshimoto Hideko. *U.S. Occupation of Okinawa: A Soft Power Theory Approach*. Kyoto University Press, 2019.

ACKNOWLEDGMENTS

Like many other colonies, the history of Okinawa has been partially erased by its occupiers through official policy or neglect. Since the mid-nineteenth century, the islands' records have been looted, destroyed, or otherwise disappeared by Japanese and US authorities. In reaction, many Okinawans place great value on documentation detailing their pasts, so researchers have done their utmost to gather and preserve primary sources. Based on these records, Okinawan scholars have produced an abundance of books and articles about their islands' history. Writing my own book would have been impossible without these indispensable works and researchers' generosity in making their archives public (or sharing them with me personally). During the sixteen years I have been writing about Okinawa, I have been fortunate to receive guidance from some of the prefecture's preeminent scholars. In particular, I am grateful to former Governor Ota Masahide, who took time to teach me about the inequities of Japan and US policy; Takazato Suzuyo, for her patient explanations of the appalling burden borne by Okinawan women; and Arasaki Moriteru, alongside whom I lectured in the spring of 2016. Among the other Okinawan and non-Okinawan researchers whose work has shaped my understanding are Ai Niimi-Abe, Arakawa Akira, Fukuchi Hiroaki, Gabe Masaaki, Hong Yunshin, Maedomari Hiromori, Miyume Tanji, Nozoe Fumiaki, Steve Rabson, Annmaria Shimabuku, Yamamoto Akiko, Yoshida Kensei, and Yoshimoto Hideko. I would especially like to thank Jahana Naomi for sharing with me the US investigations into the 1948 Iejima LCT explosion.

Ensuring that current and future generations do not forget the lessons of the past, Okinawan museums, archives, and nongovernmental organizations fuse history with the spirit of absolute pacifism and resistance that makes the islands so inspirational. I'd like to express my gratitude to Jahana Etsuko at the House of Nuchi du Takara Anti-War Peace Museum, Uchimura Chihiro at Fukutsu-kan, the staff at Okinawa Prefectural Archives, Okinawa Prefectural Museum and Art Museum, Himeyuri Peace Museum, Okinawa Prefectural Peace Memorial Museum, Haebaru Town Museum, Okinawa Karate Kaikan, Sakima Art Museum, and Okinawa City Museum of Postwar Culture and History (a.k.a. Histreet). Among the members of the citizens' groups I'd like to thank are Hideki Yoshikawa (Okinawa Environmental Justice Project), Masami Kawamura (Informed-Public Project), Sunagawa Kaori, Sakurai Kunitoshi, Iha Yoshiyasu, members of the Ginowan Chura Mizu-kai and PFAS Osen kara Shimin no Seimei o Mamoru Renraku-kai, Ohata Yutaka, Nakasone Yumi, and Kudaka Masaharu and Iha Hiromasa of the Ishikawa Miyamori 630 Kai. I would also like to express my immense appreciation to Ginoza Eiko, founder of the Allen Scholarship Association Okinawa, who ensured the pacifist spirit of the late marine Allen Nelson persisted through providing funds to children in Vietnam.

Based on the bitter lessons of how militarized propaganda can fuel wartime atrocities, today's media in Okinawa embodies all that journalism should be: committed to public service and fearless questioning of the authorities. *Okinawa Times*, where I work, was founded in 1948 in the rubble of the war, and it has never forgotten its origins. My colleagues are a constant source of strength and inspiration, including Abe Takashi, Akamine Yukiko, Gibu Katsuki, Chinen Kiyoharu, and Miyagi Eisaku. Elsewhere in the Okinawa media, I would like to thank Kuniyoshi Nagahiro, Matayoshi Ken, Nojima Hajime, Shimabukuro Natsuko, and Taira Izumi. Among the journalists in mainland Japan whom I'd like to thank are Fuse Yujin, Kusakabe Satoshi, Ota Masakatsu, Otake Tomoko, Sawa Yasuomi, and Taketani Naoko, as well as the editors of my Japanese-language books, Nakamoto Naoko at Iwanami Shoten and Yamamoto Kunihiko at Kōbunken.

My research has been supported by US veterans and whistleblowers who risked retaliation for revealing how their military's presence in Okinawa harms service members and dependents. Particularly, I'd like to thank Bill Horn, Bruce Lieber, and Daniel Plemons. (For those whose names I cannot print, you know who you are, and I am grateful for your trust.) Although, the US military in Okinawa does not need to follow Japanese laws, it does need to obey (some) American ones, including the Freedom of Information Act (FOIA). I owe a large thank-you to these overworked/underappreciated FOIA officers for their diligence in processing my deluges of requests. As journalists, we demand transparency from the authorities; likewise, I believe our own work should be open to scrutiny, so in this spirit, I have donated the bulk of my FOIA-obtained documents to Okinawa Prefectural Archives and libraries at George Washington University, University of Hawai'i at Mānoa, and Okinawa International University which, in 2019, opened the Jon Mitchell Collection to the public.

While writing this book, I have bounced chunks and chapters in varying states of disrepair to readers, including Abe Kosuzu; Tokuyama-Maedomari Kiyomi; Sato Manabu; Mori Keisuke; and Mark Selden, the editor of this book's series and founder of *Asia-Pacific Journal: Japan Focus*, the most comprehensive English-language resource about Okinawa. Feedback from these readers was invaluable; any errors that remain are entirely my own fault. At Rowman & Littlefield/Bloomsbury Academic, the editorial team of Ashley Dodge, Laney Ackley, Della Vaché, and Niki Guinan have thrown their dedication 110 percent behind this project; the publishing world is fortunate to have them. Meanwhile, I am supremely grateful for Yuken Teruya for creating the original *obi* that encircles this book—*The Ryukyu Beltway*—and Chloe Batch for her powerful cover design.

ACKNOWLEDGMENTS

Due to ongoing opacity from the US and Japanese governments over their unjust policies toward Okinawa, any history of the islands is ultimately a work in progress. Accordingly, I would be remiss not to end this book without an appeal for any information that can further our understanding. Please feel free to contact me in confidence at jon.w.mitchell@gmail.com.

INDEX

5/15 memo 137

ABCD powers 46–7
Abe, Shinzo 164–5, 176, 181–2, 197, 200, 211. *See also* Liberal Democratic Party (LDP)
accidents 116–19
   aircraft 97–9, 143, 164, 188
   military traffic 117, 130
   Miyamori Elementary School jet crash 97–9
   nerve agent 120–1
   weapons testing 97
Agent Orange 119–20, 194
Ahagon, Shōkō 82, 87, 90, 121, 192–3
Ainu 28, 39, 168
Air America, Inc. 95, 98
aircraft accidents 97–9, 143, 164, 188
Akamine, Mamoru 7, 15
Akutagawa Prize 170
All Okinawa movement 179–80
All-Island Struggle (Shimagurumi Tōsō) 1, 91–3
American Civil Liberties Union (ACLU) 89–90
American Village 194–5
Amnesty International 188
antibase movements 99–101, 154
anti-Okinawan hate 181–2, 212
Arasaki, Moriteru 91, 154, 210
Arirang Memorial 198
aristocracy (*yukatchu*) 34–5
Armitage, Richard 165, 176–7
art as resistance 214–15
artillery training 143–4, 156
assimilation 39–42, 47, 217
Atlantic Charter 69

atomic weapons testing 78–9, 96. *See also* nuclear weapons
atrocities 103–4
   whitewashing 166
   World War II 56–8

Bankoku Shinryō Council on US Military Base Issues 218
Battle of Dien Bien Phu 113
Battle of Guadalcanal 48–9
Battle of Midway 48
Battle of Okinawa
   fatalities 66
   female nursing units 58
   film screenings 149
   group suicides 53–4, 56
   kamikaze attacks 54–5
   land battle 55–8
   memorials 152, 197
   textbook revision 4, 148–9, 164–5
Battle of Saipan 49
Battle of Tsushima 37
Bettelheim, Bernard Jean 15, 19
biological weapons 46, 96
Black Panther Party 122
Black Ships 26, 65
Board, William 23–4, 196
bombing of Hiroshima and Nagasaki 63–4
Buckner, Simon Bolivar, Jr. 53, 60, 70
bunto kaiyaku (divided-islands proposal) 33, 77
Butler, Smedley, *War is a Racket* 208

Cairo Declaration 69–70
Camp Chinen 95, 196–7
Camp Foster 195
Camp Gonsalves 191–2

INDEX

Camp Kinser 195–6. *See also* Makiminato Service Area.
Camp Schwab 162, 179–80
Camp Zukeran 83
Caraway, Paul 109–10, 112, 114
censorship 50, 94, 165, 196. *See also* textbook revisionism
Central Intelligence Agency (CIA) 77, 101, 125–6
  Camp Chinen 95, 196–7
  LDP funding 127–8
  A Master Narratives Approach to Understanding Base Politics in Okinawa 203–4, 211
  propaganda 94
chemical weapons 46, 62, 96, 119, 130
  removal from Okinawa 131
  sarin 120
Chiang, Kai-Shek 69, 199
Chibana Army Ammunition Depot 96–7, 115, 120–1
Chibana, Shōichi 147–9, 159
Chibichiri Gama 53–4, 149
Chicago Tribune 97
children, military mobilization of 58
China 5, 7, 51–2
  Confucianism 8
  gray-zone operations 184, 198
  maritime trade 9–10
  sovereignty claim over Okinawa 182–5
  Tiananmen Square 157–8
  tribute 8, 10, 14–15
Chō, Isamu 49, 52
Christianity
  Japan's ban on 13
  missions 15
Churasan 169–70
Civil Affairs Handbook: Ryukyu (Loochoo) Islands 52
civil rights movement
  Okinawa 5
  United States 1

closed-port policy, Japan 17
Cold War 4, 79, 157
colonialism 11, 15, 17, 28, 36–8, 47–8, 65, 70, 112–13, 164. *See also* occupation
comfort women 37, 50, 150, 198
communism, "falling-domino principle" 113
"Compact between the United States and the Kingdom of Lew-Chew" 24–5
Confucianism 8
conscription 28, 40–1
Constitution of Japan (*kenpo*) 34–5
  Article 9 76, 100, 104, 110, 177, 217
  Article 20 166
  Article 95 137–8
Convention entre la France et les Iles Liou-Tchou 30
Cornerstone of Peace (*Heiwa no Ishiji*) 152, 197
crime 130. *See also* sexual assault
  homicide 85–6, 117, 130, 155, 184, 186
  Okinawa System 117–18
  postreversion 143
Crown Prince Akihito 146–7

Day of Disgrace 81
Declaration on the Granting of Independence to Colonial Countries and Peoples 104–5
democracy 72, 109
  "showcase of" 90–1
  USCAR-GRI system 89–90
Democratic Party of Japan (DPJ) 184
  capitulation to the US 175–6
  investigation of the secret agreements 174–5
  US opposition to the 175
deterrence 4, 204
  Kadena Air Base 204–5
  US Marine Corps 205–6
  US military presence as 175

development 139–40, 161
dialect plaques (*hogen fuda*) 41, 47, 93
diaspora 3, 42–3, 71, 213–14
dioxin 119, 163, 196
diplomacy
    gunboat 25, 65
    hostage 22
discrimination 3, 122
    anti-Korean 42, 57–8, 181, 212
    anti-Okinawan 4, 39, 52, 160, 203, 213
    racial 1, 57–8, 167–8
    structural 86–7, 181–2, 210
"disposition" 32
dojin ("dirt people") 39, 42, 187
Dower, John W. 18, 76
drinking water contamination 74, 185, 194
dugong 162
Dulles, John Foster 101

ecocide 118
education
    hogen fuda (dialect plaques) 41, 47, 93, 167–8
    peace 149
    protest against Hinomaru and "*Kimi ga Yo*" 146–8
    textbook revisionism 148–9, 164–5
Eisenhower, Dwight 86
    Executive Order 10713 92–3
    "falling-domino principle" 113
    State of the Union address 90–1
    Visit to Okinawa 102–3
elections 89, 150
    chief executive 126–7
    gubernatorial 161, 178–9
    Japan's lower-house 174
    local government 71–2
    national parliament 132–3
Elephant's Cage 159
Emperor Hirohito 3, 46, 48, 51, 55
    post-war role 76–7
    surrender of Japan 64–5, 70–1

Emperor Hongwu 9
Emperor's Blood and Iron Corps 58, 66, 151
Emperor's Message 75–9, 146
endangered languages 168, 214
environmental contamination 3, 143, 162–3, 185–6, 195–6. *See also* ecocide
Executive Order 10713 92–3
Expo 75 140, 146

"falling-domino principle" 113
feng shui 14
Field Service Code (*senjinkun*) 46, 48
Fifth National Industrial Exhibition 39
Fija, Byron 214
First Opium War 15
First Sino-Japan War 36, 40, 182–3
forced labor 57–8
Foreign Broadcast Information Service 95
"forever chemicals" 185, 194
Free the Army tour 123
French Indochina 112–13
Fukuchi, Hiroaki 104
Futenma Air Station 173–4, 178, 205

G8 summit 169
"Gandhi of Okinawa" 82
General Mobilization of the National Spirit 46
Ginowan City 62, 83–5, 156, 194
Global Times 184, 217
Gokokuji bell 25, 64
Gorbachev, Mikhail 157
Government of the Ryukyu Islands (GRI) 89–90, 104, 109
Grant, Ulysses 31–3
gray-zone operations 198
Great Britain, First Opium War 15–16
Great Eastern Co-Prosperity Sphere 46–8
group suicides 53–4, 56, 149
Guam 4, 173

Guam International Agreement 174–5, 208–9
Gulf War, Japan's financial support 151
gunboat diplomacy 25, 65
gunshin (War Deity) 48–9
Gushikawa Village incident (1968) 118–19

Hague Convention, Article 46 72
hajichi (tattoo) 40
Hara, Kimie 183, 198
hara-kiri 60–1
Harris Treaty 27
Hatoyama, Yukio 174–6
Henoko protests 162–3, 192
Heroin. *See* narcotics
Higa, Shūhei 90
Himeyuri Peace Museum 197
Himeyuri Student Corps 58, 60
Hinomaru 104, 146–8
Hitotsutsubo Anti-War Landlord Association, 145
hogen fuda (dialect plaques) 41, 47, 93, 167–8
homicide 85–6, 117, 130, 184, 186
homogeneity. *See* myth of homogeneity
hondo nami 129, 141
Hope, Bob 122–3, 193
Hosokawa, Morisada 51
hostage diplomacy 22
House of Nuchi du Takara Anti-War Peace Museum 192
Human Pavilion (Jinruikan) 39–40, 168
human rights 73, 104, 167. *See also* discrimination
Hurt, Isaac Jackson 86

identity, Okinawan 211, 213–14
Iejima 192–3
 land seizures 82–5
 LCT explosion 74–5
Immigration Act (US, 1924) 43, 48
Imperial Precepts to Soldiers and Sailors 35–6

Imperial Rescript on Education 36
Inamine, Keiichi 161
independence movements 112–13
 Okinawa 127, 216–17
 Taiwan 200
indigeneity, Okinawan 4, 39–40, 168–9, 211
infrastructure, Okinawa 107, 139
internment camps 151
 Okinawa 64, 71, 74, 82, 162
 US 48
invasion of Taiwan 28–9
Irei no Hi 197
Isahama land seizures 83–5
Ishihara, Shintarō 184
Ishikawa, Mao 131, 216
Ishikawa Tragedy 97–9

Japan. *See also* Constitution of Japan; Meiji government; reversion
 annexation of Ezo 28
 annexation of Korea 37
 antibase movements 99–101
 anti-Korean discrimination 42, 57–8, 181, 212
 anti-Okinawan hate 181–2
 attack on Pearl Harbor 47–8
 ban on Christianity 13
 ban on Okinawan languages 47. *See also hogen fuda* (dialect plaques)
 closed-port policy 17
 collective self-defense 177
 colonialism 36
 constitution 34–5, 76
 end of the feudal system 41
 Field Service Code (*senjinkun*) 46, 48
 General Mobilization of the National Spirit 46
 Imperial Precepts to Soldiers and Sailors 35–6
 Imperial Rescript on Education 36
 invasion of Taiwan 28–9
 kamikaze tactics 54–5

Law on the Provisional Public Use of Land in Okinawa (1972) 137–8, 142
Legislation for Peace and Security 177
Meiji revolution 27–8
militarism 45–6, 49, 76
military mobilization of children 58
National Mobilization Law (1937) 46
NIMBY-ism 160, 209–10
occupation of Manchuria 45
occupation of Shuri Castle 31–2
Perry's arrival 20–3
position on reversion 125–6
sakoku 13
Self-Defense Force (SDF) 144, 151, 158–9, 169, 191, 198
Sengoku Jidai (Warring-States Period) 11
sovereignty 5
special procurement of American forces 79
State Secrecy Law (2013) 176–7
sympathy budgets (*omoiyari*) 142
Taiwan contingency 200–1
Tokugawa shogunate 11–12
trade with the US 17–18
US military presence in 158–9
US occupation 75–8
Yasukuni Shrine 36, 166
Japan Times 5
Japanese Self-Defense Forces (SDF) 144, 151, 158–9, 169, 191, 198, 206
Jinmin 92
Johnson, Lyndon B. 110–11
Junk Heap of the Pacific 72–3

Kadena Air Base 115, 156, 193–4, 200, 204–5
  court ruling on noise pollution 145
  PFAS contamination 185–6, 194
  rioting 131
  vulnerability to enemy attack 206
kamikaze 54–5

Kansai Okinawa Kenjin Kai 43
Kanto Plan 140
karate 14, 39
Katsuyama incident (1945) 73–4
Kaysen Report 108–10
kenjin kai (prefectural associations) 43, 214
kenmin taikai 116–17, 120, 130–2, 154–5, 159, 165, 218. *See also* protest; resistance
Kennedy, John F. 108
Kerama Islands 53, 197
"*Kimi ga Yo*" 145–8
Kina, Shōkichi 170, 215
King, Martin Luther, Jr. 1, 157
King Shō Hashi 9
King Shō Nei 12–13
King Shō Tai 31
Kinjo, Minoru 149, 193
Kishi, Nobusuke 101–2
Kissinger, Henry A. 127–8, 135
Koizumi, Junichirō 162–3
Konan Maru 50
Konbu Association to Protect the Land 121
Konoe, Fumimaro 51
Korea 36–7
Korean laborers 51, 57–8, 63, 193
Korean War 79
Koza Riot (1970) 130–1
Kunigami Village 122, 192
kyūkan onzon 34, 38–9

land seizures
  compensation 93
  Iejima 82–3
  Isahama 83–5
  Okinawa 81–2, 89–90
  protest 121
language/s
  dialect plaques (*hogen fuda*) 41, 47, 93, 167–8
  endangered 168, 214
  Okinawan, ban on 47, 57

INDEX

Ryukyuan 41
Uchinaaguchi 168, 214
Law on the Provisional Public Use of Land in Okinawa (Japan, 1972) 137–8, 142
Lawless, Richard 175
LCT explosion 74–5
Liberal Democratic Party (LDP) 101, 109–10, 121, 133, 165, 173, 218
    1998 gubernatorial election 161
    CIA funding 126–7
local government, elections 71–2
Luo, Yuan 182, 184

MacArthur, Douglas 65, 75–6, 199
McCormack, Gavan 174, 208–9
Makiminato Service Area 114, 142–3, 195–6. *See also* Camp Kinser
Manchukuo 45
Manchuria 37, 46
Mao, Zedong 79, 95, 113
March of Beggars (Kojiki Kōshin) 83
Marco Polo Bridge Incident 46
maritime trade 7–10, 13–14, 24–5. *See also* trade
Marshall Islands, atomic weapons testing 78, 96
Master Narratives 203–4
Matsuda, Michiyuki 30–1, 41
Matsushima, Yasukatsu 185, 210
Medoruma, Shun 170, 214
Meiji government
    ban on tattooing 40
    kyūkan onzon 34–5
    Ryukyu shobun 29–32
Meiji revolution 27–8
Memorial to Fallen Journalists 196
metsuke 14
migration 42, 91–2. *See also* diaspora
militarism 45, 47, 76
military training 208
mitsuyaku (secret agreements) 125, 134–6, 174
Miyako Island 14, 30, 33–5, 111, 197
Miyamori Elementary School 97–9

Monument to World Peace 193
murder of Nagayama Yumiko 85–6
MV-22 Osprey 177, 194–5, 208–9
    accidents 188
    protests against deployment at Futenma 178
    protests against helipad construction in Takae 186–7
myth of homogeneity 41, 168, 214

Nagayama, Yumiko 85–6, 91
Naha Military Port 114
Nakamura, Fumiko 149
narcotics, Okinawa System 117–18. *See also* crime
National Mobilization Law (Japan, 1937) 46
national parliament, elections 132–3
National Security Decision Memorandum 13 128
National Security Decision Memorandum 230 141
negligence 74–5, 98, 117, 163
nerve agent 120–1, 130, 135
New York Times 164, 182
NHK poll (2022) 190, 197–8
nihonjin ron 167, 213
NIMBY-ism 108–9, 160, 209–10
Nimitz Proclamation 52–3, 89
Nippon Hōsō Kyōkai (NHK) 63–4, 164, 169–70
Nishime, Junji 127, 150
Nishiyama, Takichi 136, 174
Nixon, Richard M. 127–9, 133, 135, 140
North Korea, missile tests 198–9
NSC 13/3 77–8, 81
nuclear weapons 96
    accidents 119
    mitsuyaku (secret agreements) 134–6, 174
    North Korea 198–9
    removal from Okinawa 128–9
Nye, Joseph 159, 165, 176, 208
Nye Report 158–9

Obama administration
  expansionism 199
  opposition to the DPJ 175
occupation 1, 4, 48
  Japan 75–6
  Manchuria 45
  Nanking City 46
  Okinawa 69–74
Okinawa
  assimilation 39–42, 47
  biological weapons testing 96
  Camp Chinen 95
  Camp Zukeran 83
  Chibana Army Ammunition Depot 96–7
  China's sovereignty claim over 182–5
  civil rights movement 5
  comfort women 37, 50, 150, 198
  conscription 40–1
  Crown Prince Akihito's visit to 145–6
  diaspora 42–3
  drinking water contamination 74, 185–6, 194
  elections 71–2, 89, 126–7, 132–3, 178–9
  environmental contamination 3, 143, 162–3, 185–6, 195–6
  expansion of US military bases 81
  high commissioner 92–3
  infrastructure 107
  internment camps 64, 71, 74, 151, 162
  Kadena Air Base 115
  Katsuyama incident (1945) 73–4
  kenjin kai (prefectural associations) 43
  kyūkan onzon 38–9
  land seizures 81–2, 89–90
  LCT explosion 74–5
  military importance 113
  military mobilization of civilians 51–2
  Naha Military Port 114
  Ordinance to Regulate Dialects 41
  overconcentration of bases 140, 205–6, 210
  reversion 103–4, 108, 110–12
  role supporting US military operations in Vietnam 114–15
  Sato's visit to 111–12
  sotetsu jigoku (cycad hell) 42
  sovereignty 80–1
  strategic trust arrangement 78
  Thirty-Second Army 49–51, 57, 59
  tourism 140, 195, 211
  UNESCO World Heritage sites 170–1
  US invasion 50, 52–4
  US Marine Corps presence 99, 141, 205–6
  USCAR-GRI system 90–2
  war memorials 152, 197–8
  Yaejima Approved Prostitution Zone 115–16
  zaru keizai (sieve economy) 107–8
Okinawa boom 169–71, 215
Okinawa Culture Awareness Training (OCAT) 163–4
Okinawa Human Rights Association 104, 123, 210
Okinawa International Ocean Exposition 140
Okinawa International University helicopter crash (2004) 164, 215
Okinawa Liberal Democratic Party (LDP) 96
Okinawa Morning Star 94
Okinawa Peace Memorial Park 197
Okinawa People's Party 92
Okinawa Prefectural Archives 151–2
Okinawa Promotion and Development Plan 139–40
Okinawa Shimpo 47
Okinawa System 3, 117
Okinawa Times 5, 203, 217
Okinawan indigeneity 4, 39–40, 168–9
Okinawan Women's Research Group 150

INDEX

Ōmasu, Matsuichi 48–9
omoiyari (sympathy payments) 136
Onaga, Takeshi 178–80, 189, 209
One Foot Association 149
Operation Iceberg 52–4. *See also* Battle of Okinawa
Operation Red Hat 131
opium 45, 117
Ordinance 109 81
O'Shea, Paul 205–6
Ōshiro, Shōko 216–17
Osprey. *See* MV-22 Osprey
Ota, Masahide 151–2, 154, 159–61
Oura Bay 136, 162–3, 174, 179–81
Owarai Beigun Kichi 215

Pacific War Council 69
pacifism/non-violence 1, 5, 100, 150, 159–60
    Konbu Association to Protect the Land 121
    Ota administration 151–2
Paiwan 29
peace education 149
Pearl Harbor 47–8
People's Republic of China 79, 140
per- and polyfluoroalkyl substances (PFAS) 185–6, 194–5
Perry, Matthew Calbraith 18, 22–6, 65, 196
    arrival in Japan 20–1
    arrival in the Ryukyu Kingdom 19–20
police violence 180–1
policy/ies
    closed-port (*sakoku*) 13, 17
    kyūkan onzon 34
    language 47, 57
    "One China" 199
    Reverse Course 78
    rinichi (separation from Japan) 93–4, 109–10
    "strategic ambiguity" 200
politics, reform 35, 72

poll tax. *See also kyūkan onzon*
    protest 34–5
    Shuri government 30
pollution, radioactive 118. *See also* environmental contamination
postreversion
    aircraft accidents 143, 188
    crime 143, 152–6
    Crown Prince Akihito's visit to Okinawa 145–6
    demilitarization 190–1
    environmental contamination 3, 143, 162–3, 185–6, 195–6
    Expo 75 140
    Okinawa Promotion and Development Plan 139–40
    protest against Hinomaru and "*Kimi ga Yo*" 146–8
    sympathy budgets (*omoiyari*) 142
    textbook revisionism 4, 148–9, 164–5
post-traumatic stress disorder (PTSD) 66
Potsdam Declaration 63–4, 70
power projection 207–8
Prefectural Route 104, artillery training 143, 156
preserving the old customs (*kyūkan onzon*) 34–5
Price Report 90–2, 96–7
propaganda 46–8, 56–8, 63, 78, 91, 114. *See also* Central Intelligence Agency (CIA)
    kamikaze 54–5
    rinichi (separation from Japan) 93–4
    Shurei no Hikari (The Light of Courtesy) 94
prostitution 3, 115–16, 210
protest 90
    antibase movements 99–101, 154, 163
    anticolonial 112–13
    artillery training 144
    conscription 40–1
    Crown Prince Akihito 146

environmental   122
helipad construction in Takae   186–7
Henoko   162–3, 192
Hinomaru and "*Kimi ga Yo*"   146–8
land leases   145, 159–61
land seizures   121
missile deployment   121–2
Osprey deployment at Futenma Air Station   178
Oura Bay   179–81
poll tax   34–5
Shimagurumi Tōsō (All-Island Struggle)   91–3
sit-in (*suwarikomi*)   83–4, 99, 121, 186
student   122
US occupation   1, 111
US-Japan Security Treaty (Anpo)   102
Vietnam War   114, 123
violence   131–2
psychological warfare   52, 132. *See also* propaganda

quasi-colony   38, 41

racial discrimination   1, 39, 52, 57–8
   internment camps   48
   UN report on   167
radioactive pollution   118
reform   109
   education   75
   Meiji government   28, 31
   political   35, 72
   USCAR   123
Reischauer, Edwin O.   126
resistance   3–5, 14, 43, 73–4, 91, 147–8, 218. *See also* protest
Reverse Course policies   78
reversion   103–4, 108, 110–12
   commemorations   189–90
   compensation payments to the US   136
   hondo nami   129
   mitsuyaku (secret agreements)   134–8

NHK poll   190
nuclear question   134–6
terms   128–9, 133–4
use of bases   137–8
US-Japan negotiations   125–6
Reversion Council (Fukkikyō)   103–4, 111, 133
rinichi (separation from Japan)   93–4, 109–10
rioting   130–1. *See also* protest; resistance
Roosevelt, Franklin D.   69–70
Russia   37. *See also* Soviet Union
Ryukyu Archipelago   7, 41
Ryukyu Disposal   29–34, 40
Ryukyu Kingdom   3, 5, 40
   aristocracy (*yukatchu*)   34–5
   bunto kaiyaku (divided-islands proposal)   33
   golden age   10
   Japan's annexation of the   31–2
   Japan's claims of ownership   29
   merchants   9–10
   orientation toward China   14–15
   Perry's arrival   19–20
   Perry's plan for annexation   21–2
   poll tax   30
   Samurai invasion (1609)   12–15
   Shuri Castle   10–11
   trade with China   7–8, 10, 13–14
   trade with Japan   9
   trade with the US   24–5
   tribute missions   8–10, 14–15
Ryukyu Shimpo   39–40, 133, 178

Saipan   49, 71, 78–9
sakoku   13
Samurai invasion (1609)   12–15. *See also* Meiji revolution; Satsuma domain; Shimazu clan
sarin   120
Sato, Eisaku   114, 128
   meeting with LBJ   110–11
   meeting with Nixon   128–9, 133, 135
   visit to Okinawa   111–12

Satsuma domain   11–15, 30–1
Sebald, William   76–7
Sekai   146
Senaga, Kamejiro   92–3, 132
Sengoku Jidai (Warring-States
    Period)   11
Senkaku Islands   183
    gray-zone operations   184
    sovereignty dispute   182–4, 198–9
Seventh Psychological Operations
    Group   94, 114, 132
sexual assault   56, 73–4, 85, 117, 152–6,
    186
Shikiya, Kōshin   72
Shimagurumi Tōsō (All-Island
    Struggle)   91–3
Shimazu clan   11, 33. *See also* Meiji
    revolution
Shindō, Eiichi   146
Shinto   35–6, 40, 47
Shurei no Hikari (The Light of
    Courtesy)   94, 114
Shuri Castle   10–13, 31–2, 51, 59, 91, 170
soft power   93, 184
sovereignty
    Japan   5
    Okinawa   80–1
    Senkaku Islands   182–5, 198–9
Soviet Union   64, 70
    atomic weapons testing   79
    dissolution   157
Special Action Committee on Okinawa
    (SACO)   155, 160, 186
State Secrecy Law (Japan, 2013)   176–7
Statue of Peace Through Generations   149
Status of Forces Agreement (SOFA)   102,
    137, 141–2, 186, 196, 208
Stimson, Henry   63–4
Storm of Iron   59–60. *See also* Battle of
    Okinawa
strategic trust system   78
structural discrimination   86–7, 181–2,
    210
student protest   91, 122, 131, 177

suicide
    forced   144, 165
    group   53–4, 149
    hara-kiri   60–1
    kamikaze   54–5
Sunagawa court case (1959)   99–100
surrender   46, 48, 56–7, 59–60, 63–5,
    70–1
sute ishi   59, 77
suwarikomi (sit-in)   83–4
sympathy budgets (*omoiyari*)   136, 142,
    158

Taft-Katsura Agreement   37
Taiwan   36. *See also* China
    China's sovereignty claim over   183,
    199
    independence movement   200
    invasion of   28–9
Taiwan contingency   200
Takae helipads   186–7
Takazato, Suzuyo   115, 153, 210
Tamaki, Denny   189–90
tarifs   27, 36
tattoo (*hajichi*)   40
tennoism (emperor worship)   148–50
Teruya, Yuken
    My Father's Favorite Game   215
    You–I, You–I 215
textbook revisionism   4, 148–9, 164–5
Thirty-Second Army   49–51, 57–9
tokkōtai. *See* kamikaze
Tokugawa shogunate   11–12, 17, 19, 33
Tokyo War Crimes Trials   75, 77
tourism   3, 140, 195, 211
Toyama, Kyuzo   42
Toyama Maru   50
Toyotomi, Hideyoshi   11
trade
    opium   117
    tarifs   27, 36
Traktaat tusschen Nederlanden en
    Lioe-Kioe   30. *See also* Ryukyu
    Kingdom

Treaty of Nanking   15–16. *See also* China; Great Britain
Treaty of Peace and Amity   22–3, 25. *See also* Japan; United States
Treaty of Portsmouth   37
Treaty of San Francisco   79–81, 93, 133, 182
Treaty of Shimonoseki   36–7. *See also* China; Japan
tribute   8–10, 14–15, 30
Tripartite Pact   47
Truman, Harry S.   63, 70
Trust Territory of the Pacific Islands   78
Tsushima Maru   50

Uehara, Kōsuke   104, 132
UN Economic Commission for Asia and the Far East   182
unexploded ordnance (UXO)   144, 163
unionization   78, 104, 115, 130
United Nations   78, 179
   Declaration on the Granting of Independence to Colonial Countries and Peoples   104–5
   Human Rights Committee recommendations   167
   report on discrimination against Okinawans   167
United States
   administrative control of Okinawa   3–4
   civil rights movement   1, 87
   Immigration Act (1924)   43, 48
   internment camps   48
   invasion of Okinawa   1, 53
   military importance of Okinawa   113
   National Security Decision Memorandum 13   128
   occupation of Okinawa   69–74
   position on reversion   125–6, 128
   power projection   207–8
   "strategic ambiguity"   200
   strategic trust system   78

Taiwan contingency   200
trade with Japan   17–18
trade with the Ryukyu Kingdom   24–5
University of the Ryukyus   91, 151
US Civil Administration of the Ryukyu Islands (USCAR)   89–90, 111, 126, 128, 133
   high commissioner   92–3, 109–10, 150
   media censorship   94
   Price Report   91–2
   reform   123
   rinichi (separation from Japan)   93–4
US Department of Defense, Nye Report   158–9
US Forces Japan (USFJ)   204
US Freedom of Information Act   203
US Marine Corps   141
   OCAT   163–4
   response to the Okinawa International University helicopter crash   164
   role in deterrence   205–6
Ushijima, Mitsuru   49, 59
USINDOPACOM   199
U.S.-Japan Alliance: Anchoring Stability in Asia   176–7
US-Japan Roadmap for Realignment Implementation   173–5
US-Japan Security Treaty (Anpo)   101–2, 126, 190, 199, 207–9
USS *Bowfin*   50
USS *Missouri*   65
USS *Ticonderoga*   119

Versailles Peace Conference   37–8
Vietnam War   3, 113–16
   Agent Orange   119–20
   protest   114, 123
violence   117
   homicide   73, 85–86, 117, 143
   Koza Riot (1970)   131
   military   56, 73–4, 163
   police   180–1
   protest   131–2

sexual assault   56, 73–4, 85, 152–6
   Uruma City murder (2016)   185–6
Voice of America   95, 132
voting rights, women   72. *See also*
   elections

Wall Street crash   45
Wall Street Journal   120
war crimes   56–7, 76–9
war memorials   197–8
Washington Post   109, 175
weapons of mass destruction. *See*
   biological weapons; chemical
   weapons; nerve agent; nuclear
   weapons
Weiner, Tim, *Legacy of Ashes: The History of the CIA*   101
whistleblowers   177
"Why We Are Here"   4, 113
WikiLeaks   175
Williams, Samuel Wells   19–20
women   40. *See also* comfort women
   Himeyuri Student Corps   58, 60
   as leaders in peace movement   83, 121, 149, 153–4
   sexual assault   56, 73–4, 85–6, 152–6
   suffrage   72
World War I   37–8
World War II   1, 46. *See also* Battle of Okinawa
   atrocities   56–8
   Battle of Guadalcanal   48–9
   Battle of Midway   48
   Battle of Saipan   49
   bombing of Hiroshima and Nagasaki   63–4
   kamikaze attacks   54–5
   official surrender of Japan   64–5
   Operation Iceberg   52–4
   Pearl Harbor   47–8
   US attack on Okinawa   50

Xi, Jinping   200

Yaejima Approved Prostitution Zone   115–16
Yamashiro, Chikako   215
Yamashiro, Hiroji   179–80, 187
Yamato   55
Yara, Chōbyō   127, 133–4
Yasukuni Shrine   36, 166
Yomitan Village   53, 143, 193
   Hinomaru and "*Kimi ga Yo*" protests   147–8
yukatchu (aristocracy)   34–5, 38, 41

zaru keizai (sieve economy)   107–8, 115–16
Zengunrō   115, 129–30
Zō no Ori. *See* Elephant's Cage